Analysing the Screenplay

Most producers and directors acknowledge the crucial role of the screenplay, yet the film script has received little academic attention until recently, even though the screenplay has been in existence since the early twentieth century.

Analysing the Screenplay highlights the screenplay as an important form in itself, as opposed to merely being the first stage of the production process. It explores a number of possible approaches to studying the screenplay, which suggest the depth and breadth of the subject area, including:

- the history and early development of the screenplay in the United States, France and Britain
- the process of screenplay writing and its peculiar relationship to film production
- the assumption that the screenplay is standardised in form and certain stories or styles are universal
- the range of writing outside the mainstream, from independent film to story ideas in Bhutanese film production to animation
- possible critical approaches to analysing the screenplay.

Analysing the Screenplay is a comprehensive anthology, offering a global selection of contributions from internationally renowned, specialist authors. Together they provide readers with an insight into this fascinating yet complex written form.

This anthology will be of interest to undergraduate and postgraduate students on a range of Film Studies courses, particularly those on scriptwriting, film production, creative writing and screen narrative.

Jill Nelmes is a senior lecturer at the University of East London, UK. Her research interests include gender and film, and screenwriting. She studied screenwriting at UCLA, has had a number of screenplays in development and was a script reader in Hollywood for over two years. Jill Nelmes is editor of *The Journal of Scriptwriting* and *Introduction to Film Studies*, currently in its fourth edition.

Analysing the Screenplay

Edited by Jill Nelmes

Routledge
Taylor & Francis Group

LONDON AND NEW YORK

First published 2011
by Routledge
2 Park Square, Milton Park, Abingdon, Oxon OX14 4RN

Simultaneously published in the USA and Canada
by Routledge
270 Madison Ave, New York, NY 10016

*Routledge is an imprint of the Taylor & Francis Group, an informa
business*

Typeset in Baskerville by
HWA Text and Data Management, London
Printed and bound in Great Britain by
TJ International Ltd, Padstow, Cornwall

British Library Cataloguing in Publication Data
A catalogue record for this book is available from the British
Library

Library of Congress Cataloging-in-Publication Data
Analysing the screenplay / edited by Jill Nelmes. -- 1st ed.
      p. cm.
   Includes bibliographical references and index.
   1. Motion picture authorship. 2. Motion picture plays–
Technique. I. Nelmes, Jill, 1954-
PN1996.A64 2010
809.2'3--dc22   2010010378

ISBN 10: 0-415-55633-3 (hbk)
ISBN 10: 0-415-55634-1 (pbk)
ISBN 10: 0-203-84338-X (ebk)

ISBN 13: 978-0-415-55633-0 (hbk)
ISBN 13: 978-0-415-55634-7 (pbk)
ISBN 13: 978-0-203-84338-3 (ebk)

To my family

Contents

Figures

Contributors

Sue Clayton is a UK independent feature film writer and director. She is currently directing *Asylum: The Road Home* for the BBC. Current screenwriting/directing projects include *Jumolhari*, a feature film to be made in Bhutan, and an adaptation of D. H. Lawrence's *The Lost Girl*. She is Director of the MA in Screenwriting for Film and Television (Retreat Programme) at Royal Holloway University of London. Recent publications include 'Film-Making in Bhutan: The View from Shangri-La', *New Cinemas* 5(1) (May 2007); 'Visual and Performative Elements in Screen Adaptation', *Journal of Media Practice* 8(1) (Oct. 2007).

Ken Dancyger is a Professor of Film and Television in the Tisch School of Arts at New York University. He has been writer director, producer and script consultant on various films and published extensively. His books include *Broadcast Writing, Alternative Scriptwriting, The Technique of Film and Video Editing* and *Writing the Short Film*. Ken has completed a 5th edition of his history of editing book, *The Technique of Film and Video Editing*, and is currently working on a memoir, *The War That Never Ended*.

Adam Ganz is a lecturer in media arts at Royal Holloway University of London. He studied at Cambridge and Bristol Universities and the National Film and Television School. He has written extensively for radio, film and television and has research interests in screenwriting, digital cinema and narrative. He has directed several short films, shown at festivals around the world and on television and has worked as a script consultant for the BBC, Complicité and Working Title, and on several large multimedia projects.

Barry Langford is Senior Lecturer in Film Studies at Royal Holloway, University of London. An academic and screenwriter, his areas of research interest and publication include the representation of the Holocaust in film and television. He is the author of numerous academic articles and essays and two books, *Film Genre: Hollywood and Beyond* (2005) and *Teaching Holocaust Literature and Film* (with Robert Eaglestone, 2007). His Holocaust-themed short screenplay *Torte Bluma* was filmed by Benjamin Ross in 2004–5 and premiered at the 2005 Edinburgh Film Festival, going on to win awards at festivals in Los Angeles and Palm Springs. He has several other screenplays for film and television in various stages of development.

Torey Liepa teaches in the department of American Culture and Literature at Bilkent University in Ankara, Turkey. He has published articles on speech in *The Birth of a Nation* and on the development of inter-title writing in the films produced by Thomas Ince, and is currently working on a manuscript on the emergence of dialogue in the silent cinema.

Ian W. Macdonald is Director, Louis Le Prince Centre for Cinema, Photography and Television, at the Institute of Communication Studies, University of Leeds, where he researches and teaches screenwriting and media practice. He has worked for the BBC, London Weekend Television, the British Film Institute and as Head of the Northern Film School at Leeds Metropolitan University. A co-editor of the *Journal of Screenwriting*, he has published several articles on screenwriting during the silent era, and has managed a British Academy-funded research project on early British screenplays.

Kathryn Millard is a writer and filmmaker and is Associate Professor at Macquarie University, Sydney. Her credits as writer, producer and director include award-winning features, documentaries and essay films. Kathryn publishes on topics including screenwriting, screen history, colour, photography and social psychology and film.

J. J. Murphy is a filmmaker. He has written articles that have appeared in *Film Quarterly*, *Film Culture*, *Millennium Film Journal*, *Field of Vision*, *Film Studies: An International Review*, and the *Journal of Screenwriting*. He is the author of *Me and You and Memento and Fargo: How Independent Screenplays Work* (Continuum, 2007). He teaches film production, screenwriting and cinema studies in the Department of Communication Arts at the University of Wisconsin-Madison, USA.

Mark O'Thomas is a senior lecturer at the University of East London and director of Theatre and Performing Arts. He has directed and produced a number of stage plays and has also adapted novels for the stage and screen.

Steven Price lectures in English and Film at Bangor University, Wales. He is the author of *The Screenplay: Authorship, Ideology and Criticism* (2009) and *The Plays, Screenplays and Films of David Mamet* (2008). He has previously published extensively on the work of David Mamet and other contemporary American and British dramatists, including Harold Pinter, Samuel Beckett, Edward Albee, and Martin McDonagh, and is co-author of a book on Oscar Wilde's *Salome*.

Jule Selbo is an Assistant Professor at California State University, Fullerton, where she leads the screenwriting area. Her academic research focuses on genre, early screenwriters and the craft of screenwriting. She continues to work professionally in the film and television industry. Her feature film credits include *Hard Promises* and the award-winning scripts for Disney: *Hunchback of Notre Dame, Part Deux* and *Cinderella II*. She has written and produced over 200 hours of television, including George Lucas's *Young Indiana Jones Chronicles* as well as *Hercules, Melrose Place* and *HBO'S Prison Stories: Women on the Inside* and several PBS series. Her textbooks *SCREENPLAY, Idea to Successful Script* (2007) and *THE REWRITE; First Draft to Marketplace* (2008) are published by Garth Gardner Inc. She is currently at work on a book *Genre for Screenwriters*.

Andrew Spicer is Reader in Cultural History in the Faculty of Creative Arts, University of the West of England. He has published widely on British cinema, including *Typical Men: The Representation of Masculinity in Popular British Cinema* (2001), *Sydney Box* for the British Film Makers series (2006) and numerous chapters and articles notably 'The Author as Author: Restoring the Screenwriter to British Film History', in *The New Film History* (2007). He is a member of the editorial board of the *Journal of British Cinema and Television* and in December 2008 co-edited special issue 5(2), on Screenwriting. He is currently working on a critical study of the producer Michael Klinger.

Paul Wells is Director of the Animation Academy in the School of Art and Design, Loughborough University. His publications include *Understanding Animation, Animation: Genre and Authorship, Fundamentals of Animation, Re-Imagining Animation* (with Johnny Hardstaff), and his most recent book, *The Animated Bestiary*. Wells is also a writer, director and broadcaster, touring globally conducting workshops based on his book *Scriptwriting*. He recently wrote and directed a documentary on John Coates, producer of *The Yellow Submarine*, and was series consultant for the BBC's 'Animation Nation'. He has curated animation programmes and exhibitions, and lectured at festivals, conferences and arts events worldwide.

Acknowledgements

To Natalie Foster at Routledge for commissioning *Analysing the Screenplay*, of course the contributors without whom would the anthology would have been impossible, Professor Haim Bresheeth, my mentor at UEL, who planted the idea in the first place, Robert Murphy for his support and good humour and my daughter Corrina for her understanding.

Permissions

Figure 5.1: The strapline for *Klinger News* with a typical headline; Figure 5.2: Michael Klinger in his pomp: on the set of *Gold* (1974); Figure 5.3: A still from the animated titles that had been produced for *The Chilian Club*; Figure 5.4: Rank's advert in *Klinger News*. Images reproduced with kind permission from Tony Klinger.

Figure 6.1: A Story Meeting for Halas and Batchelor's production of *Animal Farm* in 1953, © Halas & Batchelor Collection

Figure 9.1: Dr Aswani and the Charlie Circle, with the boot cake from the film *The Boot Cake* (2008); Figure 9.4: Dr Aswani and the Charlie Circle, with a life-sized cut-out of Charlie Chaplin from the film *The Boot Cake* (2008). Photographs taken by Himman Dhamija, reproduced with kind permission from Kathryn Millard. *The Boot Cake* © 2008 Film Finance Corporation Australia Ltd, New South Wales Film and Television Office and Charlie Productions Pty Ltd.

Figure 9.2: *Grain Barge* (2007) from the exhibition series: *The Long Walk* (2007), Liverpool Museum.; Figure 9.3: *The Long Walk* (2007) from the exhibition series: *The Long Walk* (2007), Liverpool Museum. Photographs reproduced with kind permission from the artist © 2007, Bernard Fallon.

Chapter 1

Introduction

Jill Nelmes

Even though the screenplay has been in existence since the first scenarios of the early twentieth century the form has received little academic attention. This is mostly because film has been seen as part of an industrial and technological process, in which the screenplay is considered merely the first stage towards the final product, the feature film, and therefore not on a creative par with the stage play, prose or poetry, which are more immediate creative forms with a less complex production process. Yet most producers and directors acknowledge the crucial role of the screenplay hence Hitchcock's often quoted mantra was 'the script, the script, the script' (Truffaut 1986: 56). Despite this fact academic attention has been diverted towards the director and the final stages of film production rather than the study of the screenplay. Somewhat ironically, because of the general interest in writing in this form, there are a plethora of publications on the subject of how to write a screenplay but there has been a meagre amount of published academic work which analyses the screenplay itself. There is though a growing recognition of the paucity of research on the subject and an acknowledgement of the importance of the screenplay as a form in itself which exists independently from the film. Academic periodicals such as the *Journal of Media Practice* have described the area as under-researched and the *Journal of British Cinema and Television* published a special issue devoted to aspects of screenwriting, pointing out that, 'discussion of screenwriting is a notable blind spot in both British cinema and television studies' (Cook and Spicer 2008: 213). Indeed it would appear this imbalance is now beginning to be redressed and in the last year two important books on the subject have been published: Steven Maras's *Screenwriting: History, Theory and Practice* (2009), which gives an overview of the subject area, and Steven Price's *The Screenplay: Authorship, Theory and Criticism* (2010), which, as well as discussing theory and authorship, applies textual analysis as a method of studying the screenplay; in addition the *Journal of Screenwriting* was founded with the aim of encouraging research in the area. These new publications indicate a surge of interest in the subject and it would therefore seem an opportune time to publish an anthology whose aim is to highlight the screenplay as an area of academic study, clearly connected to the study of film but also with a separate existence. The book explores a range of approaches to studying the screenplay, often from very different perspectives, giving a sense of the depth and breadth of the subject area. The contributors are widely recognized experts in their field and the anthology is divided into four sections; first, the history and development of the screenplay; second, craft and process in the screenplay; third, alternatives to the mainstream screenplay; and fourth, theoretical and critical approaches. It is hoped the reader will find the anthology a stimulating mix of historical perspective and theoretical analysis of this fascinating and complex form.

History and early development of the screenplay

The three articles in this section consider the early screenplay in the United States and Britain, a period in which the screenplay was very much in its infancy and still developing as a form. The first two chapters focus on early film in the United States; Torey Liepa's chapter 'The Popular Film Writing Movement and the Emergence of Writing in American Silent Cinema', discusses how and why writing became a public activity for a short period from 1910 to 1920, by which time the studios had developed their own writing practices and film writing was largely regulated; Jule Selbo's chapter 'Screenwriters Who Shaped the Pre-Code Woman and their Struggle with Censorship', outlines the role of women screenwriters and the portrayal of independent women in American films produced during the Pre-Code era, before the Hay's code was implemented, arguing that by the mid-1930s the effect of the Code was being felt and had tremendous impact on film content, particularly in the depiction of strong-minded women in favour of the home-loving, passive female.

Ian Macdonald's chapter 'Screenwriting in Britain 1895–1929' looks at the development of the screenplay in the UK before sound, dividing this into three periods, the early 1900s to 1910, in which the screenplay was beginning to emerge as a form; 1911 to 1924, when the screenwriter as professional had emerged, although trusted scenario writers were still scarce; and 1924 to the coming of sound in 1929, which saw a significant rise in the number of new screenwriters. The chapter points out that screenwriting developed as a form by appropriating many of the terms and concepts used in theatre and that film had changed from being a writer-led to director-led medium by the arrival of sound in 1929.

Development, craft and process in the screenplay

This section analyses the process of screenplay writing and its peculiar relationship to film production, being separate from, yet part of this process. The screenplay commences with the development of an idea, progressing step by step to the shooting-script stage, a process which may take many years. The screenwriter will often complete many rewrites, working with both the director and producer, in what is very much a collaborative process. A screenplay may be developed and then for various reasons not go into production, even after many attempts, as was the case in Andrew Spicer's chapter 'An Impossible Task? Scripting *The Chilian Club*'. The chapter discusses how the screenplay went through many years of development, from a first draft in 1972 and then being rewritten by a number of writers including director Mike Hodges. The producer, Michael Klinger, made one last attempt to resurrect the project by submitting it to Handmade Films where it was rejected and finally laid to rest in 1985. Paul Wells's chapter 'Boards, Beats, Binaries and Bricolage' explains the process of developing an animation film, a process which is very different to writing for conventional film where, he argues, it is not helpful to think of animation in terms of the screenplay but one in which visualization is central to development of an animation film and the storyboard is a vital part of this process.

Ken Dancyger's chapter 'The Flexibility of Genre: The Action-Adventure film in 1939', argues that all films make use of genre, pointing out not only how flexible genre can be but what a useful tool it is for the screenwriter. Referring to four examples of action-adventure films filmed in 1939, one of the greatest years in Hollywood production, the chapter examines their content suggesting they have much commonality in terms of genre but also each film, in very different ways, pushes the boundaries of the genre to create a unique and powerful story.

Alternatives to the mainstream screenplay

The third section challenges the assumption that the screenplay is internationally standardized in form and suggests there are many ways of outlining a film story, questioning the concept that certain stories or styles are universal, exploring writing in independent cinema and film outside Western notions of narrative. Adam Ganz, in Chapter 8, suggests how interaction design can be usefully applied to building the film story and how the concept of the 'self-teaching system' may help in developing a film. Kathryn Millard pushes this point further in 'The Screenplay as Prototype', arguing the screenplay may be unnecessary or even a hindrance to the film development process and suggests alternative ways of creating a template for a film, in which a screenplay could usefully be conceived as a design prototype, rather than a literary document. Millard suggests that the screenplay is limiting and inflexible, and that excluding image and sound from the traditional screenplay is an impediment to creativity. J. J. Murphy's discussion of the collaboration between writer Jon Raymond and director Kelly Reichardt is a fascinating case study of their working relationship in American independent film, a style of film which is usually auteur-based and director-controlled. Murphy explains how the writer and director have developed a unique way of working together and are a highly successful and intuitive partnership, in which Raymond brings an internal vision while Reichardt focuses on the visuals.

Sue Clayton's chapter 'On Screenwriting Outside the West', points out how little has been written about screenwriting in world cinema and discusses the work of writers and directors from four very different countries; Iranian filmmaker Mohsen Makhmalbaf, Brazilian Braulio Montavani who wrote the screenplay for *City of God* and *The Elite Squad*, Vietnamese filmmaker Tran Anh Hong and finally Khyentse Norbu, the writer/director from Bhutan where Clayton was invited to work on a collaborative film project and teach screenwriting.

Theoretical and critical approaches

The fourth section of the anthology proposes possible critical approaches to analysing the screenplay in which the chapters offer a very different range of methodologies. Steven Price's chapter 'Character in the Screenplay Text' explores the notion of character in the screenplay, discussing how characters in the novel can be expressed through their inner world while the screenplay, out of necessity, must take a very different approach. The chapter, by close analysis, compares the depiction of character in two very different screenplays, David Mamet's *House of Cards* and Graham Greene's *The Third Man*. My own chapter 'Realism and Screenplay Dialogue' offers an analysis of the function of dialogue as a means of increasing the realism of the film world, arguing that the use of what appears to be realistic dialogue is actually a contrivance which draws the audience more deeply into the film. Mark O'Thomas's chapter provides a comparative approach between the play and the screenplay form, using *The Talented Mr Ripley* as a case study, while Barry Langford examines the tension between screenwriting practice and film theory and suggests methodologies which could be applied to the screenplay such as those of Frederic Jameson. The chapter then, by means of a case study, looks at how two different screenplays engage with narration and trauma with regard to the Holocaust.

References

Cook, J. and Spicer, A. (2008) 'Introduction', *Journal of British Cinema and Television*, 5(2): 213.
Maras, S. (2009) *Screenwriting: History, Theory and Practice*, London: Wallflower.
Price, S. (2010) *The Screenplay: Authorship, Theory and Criticism*, London: Palgrave.
Truffaut, F. (1986) *Hitchcock*, New York: Simon and Schuster.

Part I

History of the form

Chapter 2

Entertaining the public option

The popular film writing movement and the emergence of writing for the American silent cinema

Torey Liepa

> ... every man imagines himself a heart-breaker, horse-trainer and an ad writer. It would be wholly true to add that every other man and many women believe they could write photoplays, – if somebody would only tell them how!
>
> (Bagg 1913: 8)

American film production was torn between conflicting tendencies in the 1910s, and writing was the troublesome cause. Fortune and fame in the booming industry seemed within grasp of the amateur writer simply by putting ideas to paper, leading to the submission of hundreds of thousands of story ideas, synopses, scenarios and scripts to film companies. Encouraged through promotion in the trade press, screenwriting manuals, and elsewhere, writing for film was initially advertised as a task for which the industry not only desired, but needed creative input from the public. By the end of the decade, however, film writing had become a largely regulated and institutionalized function within the industry's own production apparatus. As the industry took shape throughout the decade, consolidating into several dominant studios and streamlining and rationalizing production, writing was increasingly assigned to an ascendant class of professionals. By 1917 prospects were bleak for the amateur as the distinction between novice and professional gained definition; the trade journal *Motography* asserted, 'There are only two classes of motion picture scenario writers – a few whose work is in real demand, who collaborate with the producers and get good prices; and a great many whose work is of little or no value and most of whom never will succeed' (*Motography* 1917: 651–2). The diminishing prospects of success for amateur writers reflects the manner in which the newly consolidated American culture industry quickly defined and regulated its boundaries and its interests.

By 1917 script and intertitle writing had become thoroughly institutionalized elements of film production, situating writing at (or at least near) the centre of the creative process. That same year, *Moving Picture World* columnist Epes Winthrop Sargent reflected on the past decade of film writing pointing out that, in the decade from 1907 to 1917, American filmmaking had changed dramatically. The result of that decade of development, Sargent argued, was that film writing had come full circle. 'Ten years ago,' Sargent wrote, 'we stood just where we stand today in the writing of photoplays' (1917: 1491–2). What Sargent described, however, was not the relative role of writing in film production, which had unquestionably changed, but rather the way writing had mediated the relationship between the public and the industry. For in some ways, 1917 resembled 1907, when the film industry had been a closed shop, in which filmmakers either wrote their own material or, perhaps more often, did not bother with writing at all. In 1917, though writing had become an important aspect of film production and film form, film production was again largely closed to the general public and the amateur writer in particular.

Yet much like the cinema itself, which gained immense popularity through the proliferation of the Nickelodeon, film writing was born, if not conceived, in the public sphere. Through the widespread solicitation of first story synopses, from 1909 to 1911, and later more complete continuity scripts, the industry exploited newfound channels of creative production not only for story material, but also often for the specificities of film style and form, suggesting a greater degree of permeability with regard to the film production process. Writing would become a central component of film production, however, only after it had been extracted from this dispersed field of cultural production and resituated within the professionalized realm of the industry. The question then remains: to what extent did professional film writing, having emerged through a rite of passage in the public sphere, retain traces of that lineage? What, if anything, can the popular character of early film writing tell us about film writing in general?

While public engagement with film writing was a nationwide phenomenon involving a massive number of participants, it was also relatively short-lived. Those who have previously addressed this movement have tended to highlight this brevity. Janet Staiger and Kristin Thompson argue that the freelance film writing movement was more or less finished with the popularization of the feature film (Staiger 1985: 132; Thompson 1985: 166). Likewise, Anne Morey emphasizes that, while the 'screenwriting craze' lasted throughout the decade (the 1910s), by 1916 studios were no longer 'genuinely interested in buying products on the freelance market' (Morey 2003: 1). Kathryn Fuller maintains that during the 1910s the film industry had successfully 'truncated most avenues of amateur participation in script production' (Fuller 2001: 116). By emphasizing the movement's closure, these accounts characterize amateur writing as a frail and terminal mode of production, destined to be displaced by industrial-scale mass production. This perspective obscures the possibility that, emerging as it did in such an open, participatory context, film writing, though institutionalized in the industry for ostensibly pragmatic, functionalist reasons, retained traces of a popular sensibility. The participatory reputation of film writing would help the industry retain a connection to its popular base even as production became closed to the general public, and moreover granted early film writing considerable cultural influence beyond its impact on studio production.

Though the direct transmission of script material from amateur writers to film screens may have been minimal, the indirect influence of this movement on the development of film writing and American cinema more generally was large. Steven Maras emphasizes that the movement, 'Even if viewed conservatively as a promotional campaign largely conducted by production companies ... still forms a context for various kinds of statements ... about who can write, and what writing is like for the public' (Maras 2009: 137). For Maras, the early film writing movement is primarily important for the way it established terminology and ways of addressing film writing in general. Yet the movement's impact was not limited to discourse alone. For an industry attempting to expand by catering to as large an audience as possible, the encouraging of productive participation from the public not only helped augment interest in the cinema, but furthermore played a significant role in naturalizing a rationalized mode of production that had not developed organically, but rather was imposed 'from above' by an emerging oligarchically structured industry. The legacy of these amateur writers played an important role in the negotiation of the productive possibilities of film writing for the coming decades, and such a relationship had a resolute impact on film production and film form.

During its formative years, American film writing was held in a tension between the sometimes-similar yet often-divergent interests and desires of film producers within the consolidating industry, amateurs outside of the industry, and professional writers somewhere in between. These parties each had different uses and goals for film writing, and writing accordingly developed in response to the tensions between them. However, writing for film did not respond equally to the interests of those inside and outside the industry. Rather, throughout the 1910s the film industry gradually learned how to best take advantage of popular film writing, without granting outsiders significant access to the industry. While the popular film writing movement framed film consumers as central to film production, and while this framing of the film industry as a semi-public institution would remain, commercial-industrial developments quickly rendered film production anything but participatory and open, and film writing as exploitable labour.

* * *

Despite the role that the popular film writing movement played in the early development of film writing, however, the emergence of writing in the American cinema has received little critical attention. Contemporary understandings of 'screenwriting', or 'the screenplay', moreover, tend to skew perceptions of early film writing by imposing contemporary models of production on past events and working backwards to locate the starting point of a telos. This bias elides the important fact that the social context circumscribing the emergence of film writing is quite different from that which later emerged. Early film writing accordingly should be reconsidered as a historical moment capable of leading to many potential outcomes rather than simply a precursor to the one (or several) that came to pass. The fact that particular notions of screenwriting and the screenplay tend to dominate understandings of film writing today can then be seen to reflect culturally and economically specific (rather than universal and inevitable) tendencies in the American film industry that have historically occluded the emergence of other possible systems of cultural production.

This bias extends to the fundamental understanding of the role that film writing has played in film history. Maras criticizes the automatic placement of early screenwriting within the limiting binarism of 'conception and execution', whereby screenwriting is conceptualized primarily as preparatory work for what is considered to be the more legitimate or central filmmaking process – a kind of 'blueprint' for filming (Maras 2009: 5, 121, 123). Such a view grants secondary status to film writing with a pen or typewriter, in relation to the supposedly more substantive act of filming with a camera. Accordingly, this perspective tends to consider early screenwriting significant primarily for its relationship to continuity – for the way written instructions rendered filmmaking more efficient and logical.[1] Viewing film writing schematically in terms of conception and execution therefore adopts a functionalist-productivist perspective that confers special, fundamental significance upon the means of production of the end product (the viewable film). Focused as it is on the abstract systemization of production processes, such a position limits understanding of the multiplicity of roles film writing can and has served, and furthermore takes industrial practice at face value, rather than interrogating it for deeper cultural or social meanings. The concept of film writing as a blueprint for production, moreover, fetishizes film writing as the continuity script – a form that served a specific function in the history of the production process, but which, in fact, was only one of many historical iterations of film writing. As film writing emerged from the public sphere as freely exchangeable and commodified labour, its material and discursive forms extended well beyond the development and institutionalization of the reified continuity script.

A more inclusive approach, considering film writing both discursively and dialectically as the product of a labour struggle (however concealed), can modify functionalist-productivist historical understandings by re-evaluating how writing for the early cinema operated as more than simply 'screen' or 'script' writing but rather involved a combination of numerous activities, including story conceptualization, continuity scripting (the breakdown of story material into scenes and shots), and intertitle writing (in myriad forms). Though silent film story, script and intertitle writing are often discussed as separate and distinct categories, such a distinction in many ways compartmentalizes film writing in accordance with the rationalization and division of labour which occurred in Hollywood during the late 1910s, but in fact was previously less well-defined. A reconsideration of the script in the broader context of 'film writing' re-establishes the value of the labour involved both in story creation (or selection) and in the writing of intertitles. Film writing, in the shape of the continuity script, as a fully commodified form (standardized, exchangeable and reproducible) in many ways harmonizes with the demands of later modes of studio film production. However, much of what writing contributed to the cinema extended beyond the formal breakdown of story material into scenes, and scenes into shots connected through a system of continuity. Writing contributed to films not only structure and efficiency through the continuity, but just as importantly broader conceptual framing in the raw story material of synopses and scenarios, and specific filmic detail in the form of both a mise-en-scène intensified through film writing that had adopted naturalist-style literary description, as well as more complex levels of characterization and vernacularity presented through intertitles. For film writing, then, an understanding of the multiple forms (or genres) of writing that circumscribed its emergence can help illuminate the broader power that film writing wielded within the industry as a whole. An understanding of the social relationship that generated this writing, moreover, can shed light upon the mysterious place from where that power derived.

The beginnings of American film writing

With demand for films growing exponentially at the outset of the 1910s, American film producers struggled to produce original story material quickly enough to meet the demands of an audience eager for novelty. The intense growth realized during the Nickelodeon Boom caused film consumption to increase to such a degree that, in early 1911, trade commentator Robert Saunders Dowst explained, 'Within the last few years there has occurred so enormous an expansion in the motion picture business that the leading companies are searching high and low to unearth clever and original ideas' (Dowst 1911). Sargent described the crisis somewhat differently, suggesting that by 1909 filmmakers 'had stolen about all they dared to steal', and required new material (Sargent 1917: 1491). To augment productive capacity, filmmakers solicited story material from the growing fan base increasingly enamoured of the new amusement. Unlike other areas of film production such as directing, editing or working the camera, writing was early on framed as a type of creative labour open to the public, with little specialized knowledge required. This solicitation initiated a massive amateur film writing movement and possibly the largest movement of public creative production in the history of the American film industry.

Film writing, as late as 1909, was still an ill-defined practice, accomplished (if at all) through a patchwork of freelance work, improvisation and, often, borrowed ideas, operating as a cottage industry, with diverse and irregular production practices.[2] Though by 1911 some film companies had established fledgling scenario reading and writing departments, this general disorganization would persist throughout the early 1910s, leading unprepared film producers facing a crisis of supply to look outside of the industry and into the mass public for creative assistance, rather than inward, or to related 'disciplines' like drama and literature. Film companies had not yet developed self-sufficient means of producing their own story material, and similarly, drama and literature writers were on one hand ill-equipped to write for the specific demands of the cinema, and on the other insufficient in number. The Motion Picture Patents Company, beginning its regulation of the industry in January 1909, helped establish regular production methods, but ultimately failed to transform film writing into a fully institutionalized practice, such that even by 1911 those newly formed departments had yet to develop a reliable system of self-sufficient production.

In the early 1910s films began expanding from short one- or two-reel subjects to longer running times. With the widespread emergence of the multiple-reel film in 1913, filmmakers began to realize the value of maintaining written instructions on the material to be filmed, as the feature demanded greater clarity within increasingly complex narratives. The increased technical and creative needs of the feature film, combined with a lack of fresh ideas in general, created the perfect storm within the industry for the initiation of a widespread solicitation of the public for assistance. Upon doing so, the industry immediately recognized a valuable yet inexpensive source of creative material in this untapped reservoir of production of scenarios and scripts. Studios responded by engaging and stimulating the public interest in film writing through advertising, contests, screenwriting schools and other enticements. As public film writing expanded, intermediary entities like trade journals, 'photoplay' writing manuals, writing clubs and scenario-reading departments attempted to organize the unruly and undisciplined mass of amateur writers. These intermediary institutions played fundamental roles in the development of film writing, and can provide insight into what film writing meant for the various parties involved and how film writing would be negotiated over the course of the decade.

A call for papers: soliciting the public

Sargent credited the Essanay and Pathé companies with the first public solicitations for material, both companies running magazine ads in 1909 encouraging writers to submit plot ideas. Vitagraph and Lubin were not far behind, and, as Sargent put it, 'after that came the deluge'. These ads instigated such a substantial production of amateur writing that trade journal editors 'had to turn schoolmasters', offering writing suggestions to the newly interested (Sargent 1917: 1491). Studios soon began hiring scenario editors to review the massive amount of manuscript material and continue to solicit new ideas.

To further nurture this public participation, numerous writing contests offered cash prizes and the possibility of having winning scenarios produced. In March 1912, for example, the Photoplay Enterprise Association, of Boonville, Indiana, promised 'Two hundred dollars in cash prizes ... for the three best pictureplay scenarios submitted' (Sargent 1912c: 766). Essanay matched the $200 offer in a contest run in a Chicago newspaper, while the Powers Company offered $100 (*Motography* 1913: 450; *Bioscope* 1912b: 407). Throughout the 1910s, prize values increased, such that by 1914, the Chartered Theaters Corporation and 'a New York paper' offered $1,750 for the best two- to three-reel American comedy (*Motography* 1914: 6). The following year, American Film of Chicago promised the winner of its contest $20,000 (*Motography* 1915: 5).[3] While the riches promised, in all likelihood, rarely found their way to the rightful victors and many began to claim these contests were purely advertising stunts, the proliferation of such contests attests to the expansiveness of the movement.

While some interest in film writing was certainly generated by contests, broader interest was generated by the promise of direct compensation – payment (usually by mailed check) from film companies to writers for submitted material. In 1912, Universal offered 'from $5 to $1,500' for accepted photoplays (*Bioscope* 1912e: 879). The following year, film writing manual author William Lewis Gordon described payments from $5.00 to $100.00, with the possibility of up to $300 for three-reel films (Gordon 1913: section 5). The promise of these profits combined with the fascination of telling one's story to the public through the new medium further fuelled a wildfire of public participation. In July 1911 writer Emmett Campbell Hall revealed annual writing profits of $1,485, earned by spending 'one-half of [his] working time' writing, and having been compensated between $5 and $90 for scenarios (Hall 1911: 109). Such early revelations of large profits gained by leisurely writing for the screen did much to attract amateurs to the field.

To further focus this interest, as early as 1912 trade journals and film writing manuals began listing companies buying scenarios and the kinds of scenarios they desired. A typical ad described the preferred features:

> **REPUBLIC**. (I. Bernstein, Editor) 145 West 45 Street, New York City. Wants light comedies, short farces and full reel farces. Particularly interested in full reel farces. Can use southern dramas of the Civil War in which bodies of troops are not required. Independent.
>
> (Sargent 1912e: 726)

As a corollary to these solicitations, and to satiate public curiosity about what happened to their submitted writing, trade journals began describing the physical passage of submitted story material through the acquisition, development, and production process, detailing how submitted material was received, reviewed and evaluated.[4] These descriptions, designed to simulate and sensationalize public access to private industry, engaged and solicited amateur writers as consumer-producers who, with minimal training, could master the intricate channels of industrial production.

Given these various strategies of conscription, writing for the screen quickly resembled what Edward Azlant has described as a 'swollen public fantasy' – but the movement was more than just fantasy. By early 1912, screenwriting manual author and *Photoplay Magazine* editor Arthur W. Thomas estimated that there were around 6,000 photoplay writers in the country, averaging 30 photoplays each, for a total of 180,000 manuscripts submitted per year, to around 30 companies. Thomas reiterated the belief that 'there are more photoplay writers and would-be authors from the various vocations of life trying to "make good" in that particular field than in any other line' (Thomas 1912: 85). This engagement gripped the country to such a degree that *Photoplay* magazine estimated the industry was receiving around 1,000 unsolicited manuscripts per day in 1914, and by the end of 1915, Mack Sennett suggested that, 'A large percentage of the population of the country seem [sic] to be writing or attempting to write screen plays' (Azlant 1980: 138; Sennett 1915: 2007).

The trade press, writing manuals and the emergent discourse on film writing

In order for the film industry to successfully nurture and harvest the growing field of freelance production, amateur writers needed instruction on how and what to write. Pamphlets distributed by filmmaking companies, available by mail upon request beginning in 1909, were among the first written materials offering advice. Vitagraph was reportedly the first such company to provide this assistance, and soon thereafter several companies, including Essanay, Kalem and Lubin were offering to send film writing 'instruction sheets' to those who desired guidance (*Moving Picture World* 1911: 541; *Bioscope* 1912c: 559).

Supplementing studio pamphlets, numerous film writing correspondence schools quickly sprang up throughout the country. The schools advertised heavily in the trades:

Plots Wanted for Motion Picture Plays
You can write them. We teach you by mail in ten easy lessons. This is the only **correspondence course** in this line. We have many successful graduates ...
They are selling their plays.
No experience and only common school education necessary. Writers can earn $50 a week. Demand increasing. Particulars Free.
ASSOCIATED MOTION PICTURE SCHOOLS
634 Sheridan Road, Chicago
(*Photoplay Magazine* 1912: 2)

Initial opinion of correspondence schools was optimistic. As early as 1910, one trade commentator suggested that while 'there are many fakirs', some were legitimate (J.M.B. 1910: 1180). Attitudes towards the schools quickly turned sour, however, and by 1913 trade press writers regularly campaigned against them.[5]

To supplement the advice provided (or not provided) through schools, more intimate forums for discussions of film writing emerged, in the shape of film writing clubs established in major cities around the country. Epes Sargent relished his role, and the corollary local and national notoriety, managing not only a prominent film writing column, but also marshalling film writing groups in New York. Meeting on a nearly monthly basis from late 1912 through 1914, and later more sporadically, these clubs provided intimate forums for aspiring and successful writers to talk shop.[6] The clubs counted amongst their ranks many of the best-known film writers of the early- to mid-1910s, rendering them important forums for the discussion and debate of film form. Sargent himself often transferred these discussions to his columns, bringing the discourse both to the industry and the wider public. A tendency towards increasing exclusivity, symptomatic of the larger forces affecting film writing at the time, however, tended to mar the reputation of accessibility of these clubs, and, like film writing itself, major film writing clubs increasingly became the domain of industry insiders.

Perhaps to compensate for the lack of reliable advice to be gained from correspondence schools and the difficulty of accessing film writing clubs, throughout the early to mid-1910s the trade press developed a significant discourse on film writing, providing ample advice on matters of story, scenario, script and intertitle composition to budding writers. *Moving Picture World* contained an unrivalled discussion on the topic, and touted itself as an invaluable resource for writers.[7] At the end of 1911, trade press contributor William Kitchell commented that, even within the past year, compensation for the amateur writer had improved significantly, in part due to the constant advocacy from *MPW* (Kitchell 1911: 811).

Sargent's columns in *MPW* were the central locus for this discourse. A former vaudeville reviewer, film writer and scenario editor, Sargent in many ways served as a barometer for changes occurring with film writing. Though his articles appeared in *MPW* as early as October 1910, Sargent launched his first regular column, 'Technique of the Photoplay', in July the following year, covering writing technique and the general culture surrounding 'photoplay' writing (Sargent 1910: 921).[8] 'Technique,' lasted only until September 1911, but was soon followed by the column 'The Scenario Writer', and then, in April 1912 the more prestigiously named 'The Photoplaywright', which ran until 1918 (Sargent 1911a: 895; Sargent 1914a: 199–200, 238). By September that year Sargent was cited by the British trade journal *Bioscope* as 'the leading authority' on 'photoplaywriting' (*Bioscope* 1912d: 743). Following Sargent, *Scenario Magazine* (later renamed *The Photoplay Author*) provided a more focused format, exclusively dealing with film writing.[9]

The Photoplay Scenario, established in 1914 by A. W. Thomas, was similarly devoted entirely to scenario writing, as was a series of columns run under the same title in *Motography* beginning in May 1916. Sargent's column was something of an ambiguous advocate for film writing, both popular and professional, simply for the breadth and depth of its discourse. Though the degree of Sargent's actual influence is debatable, his column certainly functioned as a crucial discursive site for the emerging field, where tensions underpinning film writing could be aired. While an industry 'insider' himself (if somewhat peripheral), Sargent's columns typically advocated for the interests of the amateur and helped promote writing as a legitimate aspect of film production and film form.

The trades in general offered substantial advice – both general and detailed – on film writing. For Maras, this advice reflects what he describes as 'particularism', or the fashioning of writing technique as a specialized field of knowledge, and therefore a contested sphere of production in which one could only participate with knowledge of the specialized techniques determined by gatekeepers and authorities in the field. As he argues, with the emergence of particularist advice on

Figure 2.1 Epes Winthrop Sargent on the cover of the June–July 1913 issue of *The Photoplay Author*

film writing, knowledge of proper technique begins to function as 'a key marker of the difference between the aspirant or amateur writer, and the successful scenario writer' (Maras 2009: 162). 'Technique', then, began to serve as a stamp of authentication on particular examples of otherwise similar commodities.

Recommendations for the ideal submission format were one prominent example of this type of particularist advice. Amateur film writing inhabited various forms throughout the 1910s, ranging from brief story synopses to fully developed scripts listing scenes, describing mise-en-scène, and including intertitles and other directions. While some initially felt that (given the relatively improvised production methods of the major studios) a legitimate scenario could be as short as a half sheet of paper, such positions quickly gave way to a preference for the more fully developed script. By the end of 1911, *MPW* noted, 'Most directors prefer the well-developed scenario' (*Moving Picture World* 1911: 541). In 1912, Sargent credited prolific screenwriter Bannister Merwin with developing 'the permanent form of photoplay'. Merwin's scripts included lengthy descriptions of motivation and detail, which, Sargent argued, 'makes for absolute clearness', and promoted standardized production (Sargent 1912f: 926). Such a style not only provided a more complex form with which film writers could busy themselves, but also added a further degree of specialization which those writers with some access to the industry could wield over those on the outside. Amateurs, accordingly, were led to believe that if they did not learn and follow the proper writing and increasingly byzantine submission procedures, their writing would be rejected outright.

One should be wary, however, of considering trade press discourse as indexically related to the film industry or film culture more generally. The film trade press addressed exhibitors, distributors and suppliers of exhibition materials and hardware, and tended to cater to their needs and interests more than to those of the general public. Sargent's advice, moreover, should be taken with a grain of salt. As a lesser film writer (generally with Lubin) and film writing manual author himself, his advice often served his own needs, desires and tastes, and occasionally contradicted itself, at times bordering on the arbitrary whims of journalistic dilettantism. At the very least, however, the substantial discourse on film writing in the trade press reflects a growing crisis in film production and the appeal to both industry and public to address it. Debates and contradictions in that discourse can likewise reveal tensions regarding how the crisis could and should be resolved. Trade press writers might not have been disinterested parties or objective commentators, but their discourse nevertheless reveals the important roles being negotiated in the film industry at the time.

While journals such as *MPW* and *Motography* tended to speak to industry insiders, to meet the growing demands of eager amateur writers, a substantial volume of manuals instructed novices on proper film writing technique. Frederick A. Talbot's 1912 *Moving Pictures: How They are Made and Worked,* for example, was lauded in the trades as 'a work for the general public, more than for the man behind the scenes' (*Bioscope* 1912a: 183). By offering advice on everything from format and presentation to generic and moral constraints, these film writing or 'photoplay' manuals helped promote, orchestrate and regulate the massive movement of independent writing, negotiating proper and ideal writing protocol and form for roughly 11 years, from 1911 until around 1922. During this period over 90 film writing books were published in English – a collection that Azlant speculates to be 'the largest body of instruction in an aspect of film production within the materials of film history' (Azlant 1980: 134). The bulk of these manuals were issued from 1913 to 1916, reflecting both the emergence of and a sustained public engagement with writing as a viable and important aspect of film culture.[10]

Like trade journals, manuals dealt with myriad aspects of film writing. Both journals and manuals, for example, devoted considerable space to negotiating the ideal use of intertitles, with many manuals devoting a chapter to the writing of 'leaders' (as they were called). Discourse on the topic ranged from discussions on the basic nomenclature for these devices to their specific usage, as well as the broader theoretical and phenomenological questions they introduced to the medium. For some, the absence of intertitles represented the vanguard form, while an abundance of titles was archaic. For others, a minimal use of titles was preferable, yet the absence of titles was impossible. For yet others, dialogue titles were more cinematic than expository titles, despite the theatrical heritage of speaking characters, and for others still exposition had become a cornerstone of film narration.

Again, Maras's application of particularism is valuable here, as screenwriting manuals helped to establish a kind of hierarchy amongst writers, whereby manual authors spoke with the authority of the industry, and were able to define what was considered legitimate and modify those definitions to control access to production (Maras 2009: 25). Given the diverse authorship of these volumes, taken collectively they often produced vague, contradictory and at times superficial suggestions, and one should be cautious of simple confusion and charlatanism. Despite this caveat, however, the synthesis of the diverse advice found in manuals and trade journals presents a complex discourse that offers more than simply an example of journalistic opportunism, but rather a window into a chaotic moment in American cultural production. The disorder that this discourse reveals eventually required forces of authority to impose shape and definition, enabling film writing to develop the consistency of commodifiable labour, in turn allowing writing to function desirably as a useful and exploitable endeavour.

* * *

Yet while the popular screenwriting movement had such a dominant role in American culture that, as Sargent suggested, 'From 1910 to 1914 it seemed as though every American above the age of ten was writing for the pictures', this creative energy was extinguished as film writing was gradually absorbed into an industry rapidly expanding and institutionalizing its production apparatus (1917: 1491). The reification of film writing practices during the 1910s was part and parcel of the broader institutionalization occurring in the industry, and the increasing dominance of the script in film production and intertitles in film form. Trade journals had hinted at this future as early as 1910:

> The producers of moving pictures will welcome the time when only bright and accomplished writers will contribute to their repertories. In none of the arts are there so many amateurs and poorly equipped aspirants for distinction than in play writing, persons who are depending upon natural ability, chance or accident to make a hit and be recognized, mere junk producing ink slingers.
> (*Moving Picture World* 1910: 335)

In many ways, the insufficiencies and impracticalities of the movement that prevented the industry from fully realizing the potential of amateur film writing provided the industry with clues as to how best to regulate its own practices, initially compensating for the deficiencies of amateur production, and later supplanting it altogether. Some companies, as early as 1912, attempted to curtail the submissions of the scenarios they had quite recently sought. Essanay reportedly mailed the following notice to its contributors in 1912:

> We thank you for submitting enclosed scenario for our consideration, but at present time we have a very large stock of same on hand, yet to be produced, and, as we receive about five hundred scenarios a week, we feel that we cannot bestow upon each one the careful thought that we would care to, and is due to the author. Therefore, we will not solicit any more scenarios for several months, at which time we shall be glad to hear from you again.
>
> (Sargent 1912d: 1163)[11]

By the end of the decade, the industry had turned its back on the massive body of amateur writers in favour of professional writers, inciting Sargent to proclaim, 'Photoplay writing is no longer the toy of the multitude. It is a profession' (Sargent 1918: 1136). As writing became increasingly central to the cinema, studios began developing in-house writing departments for story ideas, continuity scripts and intertitles, and accordingly pulled back on the reins of public involvement in these aspects of film production. Writing departments allowed studios to maintain stables of writers able to write proprietary material in-house and likewise rework purchased material to meet studio desires. With these developments, amateurs were increasingly edged out of the picture. Vitagraph, in 1912, was one of the first studios to create specially defined positions of 'title and sub-title draughtsmen' as adjuncts to scenario writers, and by 1915 the need for such specialists increased dramatically (Staiger 1985: 146). At the same time, studios culled talent from the ranks of the literary establishment, including the theatre and the press, as well as those few amateurs who had succeeded. Sargent described the process as a 'gradual absorption of real writers by the studios', whereby many amateur contributions were ignored and many writers simply gave up (Sargent 1917: 1491–2). By 1917, outsiders were effectively blocked from participating in production.

Conclusion

Though the popular film writing movement was a relatively short-lived phenomenon, while it endured, it burned brightly – brightly enough that, despite the increasingly rigid borders of the industry, even a relative insider like Sargent was sceptical of film writing becoming entirely closed to the public. Predicting future writing possibilities in September 1912, Sargent wrote:

> We do not believe that any company will ever succeed in writing all its own plays, and making good, no matter how clever may be the staff members. It was because of the inability of the directors to supply fresh ideas that the first call for outside scripts was made, and the only companies that we know of

that make all their scripts in the studio are doing poor work because of the sameness of the idea. There is not more than one writer in a thousand who can write two good photoplays a week for a year and repeat his performance.
(Sargent 1912h: 1073)

While industry concerns would certainly dominate the later development of film writing, they would always be tempered and in many ways underwritten by popular influence. The legacy of amateur film writing, in fact, continues to loom large today with the profusion of screenplay manuals, romantic success stories of screenwriters who 'made it', and screenwriting courses offered in colleges around the country, still promising to divine market demands and convey them to eager novices.

Though the number of complete scripts written by amateur authors during the movement and directly transformed into films is ultimately undeterminable, it is likely that without copyright protections for amateur writers film companies were often able to incorporate material from submitted writings more or less as they wished, with or without compensation or credit given. Contempory accounts nevertheless suggest a minimal direct influence; in 1910 *MPW* noted that Vitagraph accepted only 2 per cent of submitted manuscripts (*Moving Picture World* 1910: 335).[12] Similarly, Giles R. Warren, scenario editor at Lubin in December 1910 complained that only two-thirds of 1 per cent of the total script submissions over the past six months (33 of 5000) was found to be suitable for production (Warren 1910: 1424–5). By 1916, Sargent asserted, 'probably eighty per cent of the [submitted] scripts do not pass the first reader'. However, considering the sheer magnitude of the body of writing being submitted, even this remaining 20 per cent could have a profound impact (Sargent 1916: 7). Moreover, if one considers the 33 suitable scripts Lubin procured over a six-month period, one can estimate that an amateur writer directly influenced up to one Lubin production per week. And such figures would not include those scripts inspired by amateur submissions, but rejected by the studio, and later transformed by studio ghostwriters. Hinting at this practice, June Mathis, then script editor at Metro, explained away plagiarism suspicions by claiming that similar ideas derived from 'an unconscious, "wireless" network of inspiration that vibrated throughout the land' (Palmer 1922: 190). Whether amateur film writings generally made it directly to the screen or not, it is certain that the great bulk of amateur-submitted photoplays provided the film industry with ample 'inspiration'.

Thus, amateur film writing can and should be evaluated for its role in production, where it had direct and indirect influences on film form and content, rather than simply as a popular hobby or pastime that served only as a corollary amusement for film fans. These writers and their work furthermore played symbolic roles in industry discourse, often as a counterweight to the demands of potentially unruly productive labour. Amateur writing functioned importantly as a contested terrain within the strategies of industry elites, as a site where popular access to film production could be limited by making the procedures necessary for participation more difficult. But the amateur film writing movement retained significance even for those more professional writers who mastered the increasingly complex demands of film writing. As professional writers began to realize their value within the industry, making demands for screen credit or pay increases, studios could check such demands by raising the possibility of flooding the industry with unskilled amateurs. Film companies could thus wield popular participation in the industry as a menacing spectre threatening to overwhelm the already reduced position of writers in the industry ('there are thousands who would kill for your job'). In this respect, public screenwriting, as a reservoir of surplus labour, could be reserved as an antidote for the potentially destabilizing threat to management posed by the prospect of skilled writers gaining the weight and influence of organization.

This movement, moreover, represents a highly participatory moment in the history of popular film culture. While many point out the limited tenure of the screenwriting craze as an indication of its inefficacy, in another respect, the movement dominated film culture during one of its most formative eras. Amateur screenwriting had limited influence only when viewed from the standpoint of the industry, measured in terms of amateurs credited for actual films produced, and according to the end needs and not the creative acts of labour involved. Viewed from within the discourse of its own time period, this movement reflects an industry whose identity was in turmoil, discovering how its boundaries could or should be exploited and regulated. The instability of the amateur writing movement not only allowed the industry to test those boundaries, but also naturalized film writing as the product of popular, free labour in the process. The movement, therefore, is perhaps more significant to film history for what it can tell historians about the relationship between film producers and consumers 'before the industry' and labour relations in the emerging industry, than it is to functionalist questions of film production. Whether or not the amateur public ever actually contributed significant intellectual material to film production is less important, therefore, than the fact that film writing initially emerged from within the province of the public sphere as part of a massive popular movement of writing. As film writing became increasingly important, to the extent that by 1915 William Fox argued, 'The scenario is the basis of all good pictures', its legacy of public engagement would persist, and while the amateur status of film writing would gradually disappear, traces of the popular influence on film production would remain (Fox 1916: 1155).

Notes

1 See e.g. Staiger 1985: 125, 137–9.
2 One prominent exception was Roy L. McCardell, hired in 1897 by the Biograph Company as a staff author, editor, producer and 'press man', to write material for its mutoscope films. See Hamilton 1990: 3; Azlant 1997: 230–4. For more on pre-1909 instances of film writing, see Loughney 1997: 278–80.
3 This was truly a substantial sum, equivalent to the buying power of over $400,000 in 2010. $100 in 1912 had the buying power of approximately $2200 in 2010.

4 See e.g. Sargent 1912a: 32; 1913a: 44; Condon 1913: 147–52.
5 See e.g. Sargent 1913b: 458 or Ball 1913: 33–4.
6 Two of the most prominent New York clubs were the Inquest Club and the Ed-Au (Editors-Authors) club. Alongside the New York clubs, other branches were founded throughout the country, in places like Chicago, Boston, Pittsburgh and Ohio.
7 Sargent encouraged his readers to keep abreast of current production trends by reading the 'Stories of the Films' column, suggesting that his advice provided the key to their success (Sargent 1911b: 981).
8 Listed as 'Epes Winthrop Sargent (Chicot)'. Sargent was writing as 'Chicot' for Film Index at the time (Azlant 1997: 246–8).
9 Established by Thadee Letendre, the journal ran from 1912 to at least 1914 (Sargent 1912g: 650).
10 Thadee Letendre, who would later work for Universal and edit *The Photoplay Author,* reportedly issued the first book-length work on photoplay writing. Letendre's book was likely published in 1910 or 1911. See Sargent 1912g: 650; 1914b: 425.
11 *Biograph* issued a similar statement, and by 1912 many others would soon follow suit. See e.g. Sargent 1912b: 200.
12 An account from the following year listed the acceptance rate at 1 percent (R.V.S. 1911: 294).

References

Azlant, E. (1980) 'The Theory, History, and Practice of Screenwriting, 1897–1920', unpublished dissertation, University of Wisconsin-Madison.
— (1997) 'Screenwriting for the Early Silent Film: Forgotten Pioneers, 1897–1911', *Film History* 9: 228–56.
Bagg, E. N. (1913) 'Arthur Leeds – Ideal Preparator', *Photoplay Author* 1(12): 8.
Ball, E. H. (1913) *The Art of the Photoplay,* New York: Veritas Publishing Co.
Bioscope (1912a) 'Reviews of Recent Publications', 18 Jan.: 183.
— (1912b) 'The Picture Playwright', 8 Aug.: 407.
— (1912c) 'The Picture Playwright', 22 Aug.: 559.
— (1912d) 'The Picture Playwright', 5 Sept.: 743.
— (1912e) 'The Picture Playwright', 19 Sept.: 879.
Condon, M. (1913) 'What Happens to the Scenario', *Motography* 9(5): 147–52.
Dowst, R. S. (1911) 'Photoplay Scenario Writing', *Nickelodeon* 5(5): 137.
Fox, W. (1916) 'The Scenario Makes the Picture', *Motography* 15(21): 1155.
Fuller, K. (2001) *At the Picture Show: Small-Town Audiences and the Creation of Movie Fan Culture,* Charlottesville, VA: University Press of Virginia.
Gordon, W. L. (1913) *How to Write Moving Picture Plays,* Cincinnati, OH: Atlas Publishing Co.
Hall, E. C. (1911) 'Some Scenarios – and Others', *Moving Picture World* 9(2): 109.
Hamilton, I. (1990) *Writers in Hollywood, 1915–1951,* New York: Carroll & Graf Publishers.
J. M. B. (1910) 'Books and Correspondence Schools', *Moving Picture World* 7(21): 1180.
Kitchell, W. H. (1911) 'The Films of the Future', *Moving Picture World* 10(10): 811.
Loughney, P. (1997) 'From Rip Van Winkle to Jesus of Nazareth: Thoughts on the Origins of the American Screenplay', *Film History* 9(3): 277–89.
Maras, S. (2009) *Screenwriting: History, Theory and Practice,* London: Wallflower Press.
Morey, A. (2003) *Hollywood Outsiders: The Adaptation of the Film Industry, 1913–1934,* Minneapolis, MN: University of Minnesota Press.

Motography (1913) 'Prizes for Scenario Writers', 9(12): 450.

— (1914) 'Prize Scenario Competition', 12(1): 6.

— (1915) 'This is the *Result!*', 13(11): 5.

— (1917) 'Better Treatment for the Story Writer', 18(13): 651–2.

Moving Picture World (1910) 'Scenario Writing for Moving Pictures', 6(9): 335.

— (1911) 'Technique and the Tale', 10(7): 541.

Palmer, F. (1922) *Palmer Plan Handbook*, vol. 1, 2nd rev. edn, Hollywood: Palmer Photoplay Corporation.

Photoplay Magazine (1912) 'Plots Wanted for Motion Picture Plays', Feb.: 2.

R.V. S. (1911) 'Scenario Construction', *Moving Picture World* 8(6): 294.

Sargent, E. W. (1910) 'Motion Picture Economies', *Moving Picture World* 7(17): 921.

— (1911a) 'The Scenario Writer', *Moving Picture World* 10(11): 895.

— (1911b) 'The Scenario Writer', *Moving Picture World* 10(12): 981.

— (1912a) 'One Place at a Time', *Moving Picture World* 11(1): 32.

— (1912b) 'Thanhouser Not Buying', *Moving Picture World* 11(3): 200.

— (1912c) 'A Prize Contest', *Moving Picture World* 11(9): 766.

— (1912d) 'Save Postage Stamps on Essanay', *Moving Picture World* 11(13): 1163.

— (1912e) 'The Photoplay Market', *Moving Picture World* 12(8): 726.

— (1912f) 'The Future Script', *Moving Picture World* 12(10): 926.

— (1912g) 'Late But Out Now', *Moving Picture World* 13(7): 650.

— (1912h) 'The Staff Authors', *Moving Picture World* 13(11): 1073.

— (1913a) 'Producing Photoplays', *Moving Picture World* 15(1): 44.

— (1913b) 'Those Schools', *Moving Picture World* 15(5): 458.

— (1914a) 'The Literary Side of Pictures', *Moving Picture World* 21(2): 199–200, 238.

— (1914b) 'Wright's Second', *Moving Picture World* 21(3): 425.

— (1916) *Technique of the Photoplay*, 3rd edn, New York: Moving Picture World.

— (1917) 'Photoplay Writing Then and Now', *Moving Picture World* 31(10): 1491–2.

— (1918) 'It's a Profession', *Moving Picture World* 36(8): 1136.

Sennett, M. (1915) 'The Modern Scenario Department', *Moving Picture World* 26(12): 2007.

Staiger, J. (1985) 'The Hollywood Mode of Production to 1930', in D. Bordwell, J. Staiger and K. Thompson (eds), *The Classical Hollywood Cinema: Film Style and Mode of Production to 1960*, New York: Columbia University Press, 85–153.

Thomas, A. W. (1912) 'With the Photoplay Writer', *Photoplay* 2(6): 85.

Thompson, K. (1985) 'The Formulation of the Classical Style, 1909–1928', in D. Bordwell, J. Staiger and K. Thompson (eds), *The Classical Hollywood Cinema: Film Style and Mode of Production to 1960*, New York: Columbia University Press, 155–230.

Warren, G. R. (1910) 'Scenarios', *Moving Picture World* 7(25): 1424–5.

Chapter 3

Screenwriters who shaped the Pre-Code woman and their struggle with censorship

Jule Selbo

The years of American filmmaking from the introduction of sound to the resolute enforcement of 'The Code to Govern the Making of Talking, Synchronized and Silent Motion Pictures' are often referred to as the Pre-Code Era. These years (1929–34) have been laudably explored in the economic, social and political arenas by film historians.[1] There have also been examinations of performances and popularity of particular actors and actresses in Pre-Code films.[2] However, to date, there has been little examination of the screenwriter's contributions in ideation and scripting of the film narratives that explored the topics and themes of relevance to an American populace of the time. The screenwriters of the early 1930s reflected – as well as helped fashion – the contemporary goals and dreams of many Americans and especially those of an American female no longer content in her pre-war role whom Kenneth Turan points out were: 'fearless women who did what they wanted to or had to no matter what the consequences (and were there ever consequences) were a pre-Code staple' (2003: E-9).

The advent of sound in American film in the late 1920s made possible a new type of film narrative, one that could, due to the addition of on-screen dialogue, more efficaciously and realistically explore points of view and concepts concerning social and political mores. This technological addition to film arrived at a time when American society was in flux, its attitudes having been shaped by a post-First World War disillusionment, caused by the greed and lack of judgement that led to the 1929 stock market crash and Great Depression. There was a disdain of Prohibition as well as a global sense of the world through the popularity of radio broadcasting. Rural (and often naïve and poor) Americans were moving to the cities in hope of securing jobs to support themselves in a rapidly changing and sometimes-unethical urban society. This opportunity to realistically explore the lifestyles, insecurities, dreams and possibilities of the 'new American' and especially the 'new American female' in film narrative was short-lived, mostly because of a censorship document referred to as the Hays Code that found its stronghold in the mid-1930s. The Code altered not only the screenwriter's ability to credibly present an American reality, but forced the screenwriters' portrayal of a strong and independent female underground for nearly two decades.

The role of the screenwriter in the early 1930s was diametrically different from the freelance writer-for-hire today. In 1929, 122 million people bought over two billion movie tickets;[3] MGM, Warner Bros., Columbia, Paramount, RKO and United Artists churned out films at such a staggering pace (a typical feature was shot in ten days and found its way into the theatres four to six weeks later) that studios found it necessary to have actors, directors – and most importantly – screenwriters under contract. Screenwriters were needed to write constantly to feed the appetite for films. In 1930, studios had nearly 800 screenwriters under contract (Buhle and Wagner 2002: 4). Screenwriters worked long hours, wrote numerous scenarios, pitched them to their production heads and – when given the green light on a project – wrote the scripts, and in many instances, were asked by studio heads to be on the set during production so as to ensure adherence to the approved script's story, attitude and point of view. Screenwriters had direct access to the boss, they had offices on the lot, had lunch at the commissary, knew the players. Directors, in many cases, were hired to shoot the script, to simply bring the writers' work to celluloid. The fast-paced production style, so dissimilar to the production schedules of major motion pictures today (in actuality closer to the current production pace of weekly American television series today) created an atmosphere where the screenwriter's story, words, characters and intent had a greater opportunity to make it, without much alteration, to the screen. Female writers such as Frances Marion, Dorothy Davenport, Anita Loos, Zoe Akins, Dorothy Howell, Becky Gardiner – and of course, Mae West – were among the top screenwriters focusing on female roles. Their male counterparts included Ben Hecht, John Lee Mahin, David Boehm, Robert Riskin, John Meehan, Kubec Glasmon and John Bright. All these writers explored female characters that were gutsy, socially discontent and daring – women who were sweethearts, wives and mothers, but also breadwinners.

The screenwriter with purpose

Screenwriter and director Billy Wilder[4] may have hit on a certain truth regarding the perception of the screenwriter's task in film production, 'Audiences don't know somebody sits down and writes a picture. They think the actors make it up as they go along' (McBride 2002: 18). Despite this general confusion of the writer's position by the ordinary populace, the film industry (albeit at times reluctantly) has always nodded towards the importance of the writer, acknowledging that, without a good script, a project can flail at all points of production and that 'a writer is essential to the survival of the industry' (Iglesias 2001: 149). The accomplished screenwriter is more than likely a writer whose purpose is, from conception of story to construction of themes and plots, to reflect the world as he or she sees it, to communicate ideas, present questions and perhaps suggest answers to societal problems as well as construct characters within the narrative which express the pros and cons of the chosen subject. Over the last one hundred years screenwriters have explored social inequities such as racism and rights of the underprivileged, the pros and cons of war, government corruption, industrial cover-ups, family dramas and more, using various genres so as to retain a sense of 'entertainment' while presenting strong points of view. Many early screenwriters were motivated to honestly reflect their times: Lois Weber, director and screenwriter of silent films in the 1920s, explored story elements like abortion, birth control, alcoholism and drug addiction in films such as *Where Are My Children?*, *The People Vs. John Doe and Hop*). The 1933 adaptation of *42nd Street* by screenwriters Rian James and James Seymour was lauded for its nod to an honest reality: 'Depression, chorus girls fainting from lack of food, unusual suggestion of easy morals, the idea that people do occasionally get drunk and sometimes drop dead. It's (got) a serious social conscious and (is) bitter in its desperate optimism … (a) message picture with a soft-shoe shuffle … its success comes, perhaps from its authenticity. (Fox 1972: 36–7)

Screenwriter and novelist W. R. Burnett, author of the novel *Little Caesar* (1931) as well as a screenwriter on *Scarface* (1932) and *High Sierra* (1941) expounded: 'My primary purpose was always the same as Balzac's: to give the most realistic picture of the world around me that I could possibly do' (McGilligan 1986: 81–2). Preston Sturges's impetus in writing the 1944 film *The Miracle at Morgan's Creek*: 'I wanted to show what happens to young girls who disregard their parents' advice and who confuse patriotism with promiscuity. As I do not work in a church, I tried to adorn my sermon with laughter so that people would go to see the picture instead of staying away from it' (Buening 2005). Two of the top female screenwriters in the late 1920s and early 1930s, Frances Marion and Adela St John, bemoaned the fact that, despite women getting the right to vote, the role of women in American society was still far from equal. 'They knew it was their own movies that provided the fodder for a revolution in mores, attitudes, and dreams' (Beauchamp 1998: 193).

The freedom to honestly explore a variety of topics concerning the American female, both politically and non-politically correct, that a screenwriter enjoyed in the early 1930s was seriously hindered when certain elements, social and political and economic, provided the opportunity for an escalated enforcement of the Production Code in 1934.

The road to American film censorship

In the early 1920s, religious and moral watchdog groups such as the Catholic Legion of Decency and the Women's Christian Temperance Union, fearing the influence of the growing popularity of motion pictures on American souls, minds and libidos, lobbied for a nationally recognized censorship document designed to exert control over the narrative and visual content of American films. Their voices were loud and vociferous. Journalist and satirist H. L. Mencken was among those who thought the reforms suggested at the 1926 Eucharist Congress in Chicago were detrimental to America: 'Heave an egg out of a Pullman window and you will hit a Fundamentalist almost anywhere in the United States today. They are everywhere that learning is too heavy a burden for mortal minds' (Doherty 1999: 31). State censorship boards focusing on moving pictures had been in place for years, however there was no uniformity in their demands and each state took it upon itself to literally excise from the film print any scenes they found objectionable – states averse to the consumption of alcohol edited out specific scenes, states averse to nudity or various levels of sexuality or certain political statements removed scenes (as well as title and dialogue cards at will, etc.), often causing narrative disarray and making thematic threads unrecognizable. This destructive cutting of films was not only costing the studios money (prints of films were rarely reassembled) but was obviously frustrating to the filmmaker who desired his or her film to be seen as it was intended it to be seen. In 1922, Will H. Hays, the former presidential campaign manager for Warren G. Harding who had subsequently been rewarded with the post of Postmaster General, and then made a name for himself as an outspoken opponent of sending obscene materials through the mail, was recruited by the Hollywood film studio chiefs. Hays understood politics, therefore he seemed to be a perfect candidate to head the Motion Pictures Producers and Distributors of America (MPPDA) and address (or appease and avert) the call for a national code of film censorship. By 1924 Hays had established 'The Formula' which broadly vetted narrative material for its suitability for general film audiences (Jacobs 1995: 10). Studio heads paid little attention to the Formula's advisements, mostly due to the fact that attendance at theatres was booming and the studios were making profits. Molly Haskell points out,

> The Hays Office (was) only window dressing, a self-protective move set up in 1922 by the industry to forestall intervention by government or civic groups outraged by the evils of Hollywood. Will Hays (got) his orders from the head office like everybody else, and the famous scissors were largely a ploy of studio propaganda to keep the real censors at bay.

Haskell notes that the studios really wanted Hays to concentrate on keeping reports of orgies (such as another Fatty Arbuckle debacle) and scandals (such as another William Desmond Taylor exposé) out of the media spotlight (Haskell 1987: 117–19).

The pro-censorship reformers, outraged by film narratives depicting sexual equality, the humanization of gangsters or kept women, consumption of alcohol, disobedient and wild teens, illegitimate pregnancies, interracial relationships and other subjects that did not uphold what they considered to be the American ideal of hearth, home and righteousness, kept up constant streams of invectives in the press and from the pulpits in favour of strong and enforceable censorship. In 1927, Hays introduced a new document that was created in part by MGM's studio chief, Irving Thalberg: The 'Don'ts and Be Carefuls'. The studios, again, paid only lip service to its advisements. Jacobs and Maltby have noted that a form of 'self-regulation' was practised by the studios prior to 1930 (this self-regulation was not meant to take a stand on any particular moral ground but to ensure the widest audience appeal), however, this self-regulation was not a standard practice and each studio acted as was most convenient or most profitable (Jacobs 1995: 19). Frustrated, the reformers accelerated their efforts. By 1930, 'The Code to Govern the Making of Talking, Synchronized and Silent Motion Pictures' was written by Father Daniel Lord at the behest of the devout Catholic publisher of the *Motion Picture Herald*, Martin Quigley. This was a censorship guide designed to curb the presentation of narratives and characters that could 'lower the moral standards' of the audience (Motion Picture Code 1930). Hays adopted this code and he asserted that no film was to be released without the approval of his Studio Relations Committee (SRC). Much of the code is focused on sexual and gender relations and directly affected the portrayal of the American female.[5] The enforcement of this Code was, for a short period of time, also unsuccessful due to formation of the Hollywood Jury, a group made up of studio heads that could vote to put aside any SRC recommendation. A ternary of circumstances enabled the Production Code to gain its stronghold:

1 The economics of the Depression, which included some studios facing bankruptcy, thus making the consequences of reduced audience attendance due to pulpit preaching and the picketing of watchdog groups a real concern.
2 The threat of Franklin Delano Roosevelt's administration to create a Federal Regulation Board of film censorship as part of the National Recovery Act, thus taking power away from the studios.[6]
3 The ascendancy of Irish Catholic Joseph Breen to a powerful position in the PCA in 1934, a man with a messianic will, enormous organizational skills and a bulldog mentality.

The female character in Pre-Code Hollywood

Because Pre-Code films did not live for titillation alone, they at times were simply dramatic films that used the era's freedoms to tell different kinds of stories. That enabled them to provide terrific roles for actresses who relished the chance to play richer, more complex parts than they otherwise would have had.

(Turan 2005)

'Goodness has nothing to do with it.' Mae West's famous line from her 1933 screenplay, *I'm No Angel*, was said in response to a query about the heroine's ability to strive for and achieve success. The line also reflects the work of some of the most interesting screenwriters in Pre-Code Hollywood. Goodness had nothing to do with the stories these screenwriters were interested in telling – stories that explored the changing values and expectations of the American woman who emerged from the First World War. Many of these American women, who had been accustomed to living under male dominance, could now seek financial and social independence with a sense of gender power. The 1920s had brought suffrage and, for many, the Depression ushered in a necessity for women to create their own destinies. Women were graduating from high schools and colleges in growing numbers. According to the 1900 Beverly LaHaye Institute figures, 56,800 women graduated from American high schools. By 1930, that figure had grown to over 360,000. Female college graduates exceeded 50,000 in 1930; up from only 5,000 in 1900 (Carter and Prus 1982: 163–71). Educated women forged into the business world and were primed to desire a new life. The Pre-Code screenwriters created for audiences new role models: female characters who were celebrated, not punished, for being intelligent, forward-thinking, rule-breaking, soul-searching and complex human beings.

A Pre-Code Era female character could be upfront about her sexual desires, as seen in films such as *Trouble in Paradise* (1932), *A Free Soul* (1931), *Illicit* (1931), *Red Dust* (1932) and *Red-Headed Woman* (1932). The Pre-Code female character did not have to be a virgin to attract the desired man. She could demand the right to 'try out sexual partners' before committing to marriage – as seen in films such as *Design for Living* (1933), *Indiscreet* (1931), *Back Pay* (1930), *When Ladies Meet* (1933) and *Morocco* (1930). A Pre-Code female character could choose lust over love and security, as seen in *Red Dust* and *Three on a Match* (1932). She did not have to suffer in silence when confronted with a cheating husband; she could take action and, as in *The Divorcee* (1930), be comforted by the knowledge that a divorced woman was not destined to be a social outcast. Female characters in the Pre-Code era could decide to get an illegal abortion and be socially understood as in *Mary Stevens, MD* (1933) and *Road to Ruin* (1934). She could point to sexual harassment in the workplace, she could flirt with lesbian desires as well as defend herself in court in a male-dominated system and gain respect. Popular female characters in Pre-Code films were not passive, they provided role models for American women who wished to identify and pursue their ambitions in the man's world.

'Anyone looking for a pocket of film history in which male–female relationships were presented as healthy, sane, and lively should look no further than 1929 to 1934', writes Mick LaSalle in *Dangerous Men*, 'That men and women were equal partners in the adventure of life was not something asserted by the movies (of the PreCode Era), but something so understood as to need no asserting' (LaSalle 2001: 130). Screenwriters were creating situations where men and women were on an equal footing, both responsible for thinking, doing and taking an active part in their journeys for survival and quests of personal goals.

Sampling of the screenwriters in the Pre-Code era

Metro-Goldwyn-Mayer was the richest, most powerful studio in the Pre-Code era and home to many top screenwriters. Production head Irving Thalberg produced almost a film a week (Beauchamp 2003: 125). He is often cited as the most innovative studio boss in the film industry, and he believed in the writer.

Screenwriter Frances Marion, one of the most highly regarded writers in the MGM stable, wrote in her autobiography, 'Thalberg withheld any criticism that might destroy our creative forces, saying "A picture is only as good as its writer. A writer is only as good as his inspiration." Thalberg did not want to dictate or impose too many ideas on the screenwriter. He said, "You're the creators, not I."' (Marion 1972: 145)

Marion, given the freedom to submit scenarios that reflected her own interests, explored the rights of a single father (who battles alcoholism) to raise his son in *The Champ* (1931). The story also features a woman who left her first marriage to find satisfaction and sense of self. Marion took on the examination of the prison system in *The Big House* (1930) inspired by the 1929 prison riots over violent and substandard living conditions. Marion and George Hill penned *The Big House*, a narrative that centred on a first time lawbreaker, a young and naïve man who is put in with hardened criminals and, for his self-preservation, begins to adopt criminal codes of behaviour – and then is killed in a prison riot just as it becomes clear that he was innocent all along. 'When we finish the picture, we want to feel that the story of John Morris is the story of only one of thousands of boys whose lives are thrown away on a criminal and ineffectual system which can be righted and will be if the eyes of the world are turned upon present day conditions' (Beauchamp, 1998: 255). Marion explored the vagaries of divorce in *Their Own Desire* (1929). *Cynara* (1932) is built on a fatal-attraction scenario; the betrayed wife holds the strength and power to decide if she wishes to continue with the marriage. *Dinner at Eight* (1933) examines a lower class female's breaking into a strict social class structure as well as using sexual relations to gain power in her relationship. These films connected with audiences, were box office hits and Marion won Academy Awards for *The Champ* and *The Big House*.

Marion referred to the reformers intent on film censorship as 'constipated citizens' and did not relish the idea of morality-pushers gaining a strong foothold in Hollywood. She called the Hays Office 'the neatest double-cross the Moguls ever met' and a 'poison which they themselves have brewed' (Beauchamp 1998: 138–41). In her biography *Off with their Heads*, Marion wrote,

> Every time the good ship Respectability threatened to sink, Will Hays stepped forward to man the lifeboats. Our work at the studio became more and more complicated. The scenarists resented having their wings clipped; they dared not write frankly on any vital issue. Whenever stories were attacked by New York critics as imbecilic and fit only for the consumption of ten-year-olds, we mailed these critics a sheaf or two of 'cuts' (that were) demanded by the Censors.
>
> (Marion 1972: 94)

From 1929 to 1934, Marion wrote 21 films (some in collaboration with others) but after the Hays Code took full effect in 1934, she is credited with only six produced screenplays before 1946, again some in collaboration. Frances Marion lamented the role of the screenwriter after the PCA took firm control of film content and narrative and said '(screen)writing became like writing on the sand with the wind blowing' (1972: 94).

Anita Loos, one of MGM's contract writers, was often assigned to be on the set during production to ensure that the director properly brought out the comedy and content of her scripts. Loos observed, 'The directors were dunces, you know. That they ever made anything good was due to Irving Thalberg. He handed them (our) scripts that were practically foolproof' (Beauchamp 2003: 125). Loos began her career as a silent film scenarist, writing *The New York Hat* in 1912 for D. W. Griffith and by 1916 her silent film title cards took aim at those who wanted to censor, 'Women who cease to attract men often turn to reform as a second choice' (Beauchamp, 2003: 41). Loos was an early proponent of women's liberation; in 1921, she was among the first to join the Lucy Stone League – an organization that fought for the right of women to retain their maiden names (Loos 1974). In 1926, she wrote a novel about two gold-digging blondes who, with great glee and determination, use their female attributes to snare wealthy men and, without any guilt, happily flourish as a result. The novel was *Gentlemen Prefer Blondes* and Loos became one of the most appreciated wits of the decade. Loos is often credited with perfecting the so-called 'bad girls' in film. In Pre-Code films, the 'bad girl' is a woman who understands the joys and power of sexuality and does not require the blessing of matrimony to embrace it. The 'bad' girl rejects domesticity and motherhood and seeks financial independence and, sometimes ruthlessly, sexual and class-defying thrills. And, most importantly, the 'bad girl' is not forced to pay for her ambition, aspirations or sense of morality.

When Thalberg invited Loos to write for MGM she penned the screenplay *Red-Headed Woman*. This film comedy generated enormous publicity, much of it hostile, because it dared to depict a lower-class secretary, Lili (Jean Harlow), who seduces her wealthy, happily married boss so as to climb the social ladder. Audiences were enthralled to see soulless, ambitious Lili breaking down class barriers by promising – and living up to – promises of sex. This film was instrumental in increasing the pressure from the moral watchdog groups that believed that the Hays Office was failing the public by allowing this film to be released. However, that same public, clearly not sensing the narrative 'failure' of Lili not being punished for her ambitions, made *Red-Headed Woman* a box office hit (Beauchamp 2003: 127). Once the Hays Code was in full enforcement in 1934, a frustrated Loos headed back to New York to pursue writing books and plays. Hollywood did tempt her back with lucrative paychecks, however her Post-Code scripts lacked the Loos view of the world. In late 1934, she wrote *The Girl from Missouri*, a story that was the exact opposite of the *Red-Headed Woman*. In this latter film, Eadie (Harlow) wants to marry a millionaire but refuses to give up her virtue until the wedding ring is on her finger. After 1934, most of Loos's screenplays featured married woman supporting their husband's desires. Chafing under the Code, Loos managed to slip a dig in with this sarcastic line spoken by Princess Tamara, one of 1939 characters Loos highlighted in her adaptation of *The Women*: 'We're off for Hollywood, where dear Mr. Hays will protect me.'

Screenwriter John Meehan created one of the most talked-about screenplays, *The Divorcee*, a story of a woman who works in advertising who agrees to marriage only with the promise of equality in all areas of their lives. When she discovers her husband's infidelities and decides to settle the score by seducing various partners herself, she demands respect and presents a fresh look at the roles of men and women in marriage. This film, starring one of the top stars of the era Norma Shearer (she won an Academy Award for her role), clearly rests in the Pre-Code style of narrative for the wife challenges conventional morality yet remains both respectable and unpunished. This film uses sexual play to make its point, but it is not about sex – it is about gender equality and respect. In 1931, Shearer starred in *A Free Soul*, penned by Becky Gardiner and John Meehan, a film story of a socialite who demands the right to pursue free love. Shearer embodied the character with such ferocity that she became a public spokesperson for the rights of women to have 'a past' before considering marriage: 'I feel that the morals of yesterday are no more. Economic independence has put woman on the same footing as man. A woman of today is good or she is bad according to the *way* she does a thing – and not because of the thing itself' (LaSalle 2001: 106).

> Although in terms of nudity, profanity and bloodshed considerably more is allowed on today's screens than in pre-code films could have imagined, the freshness of these Warner Bros. movies, their casual and unfettered sophistication, enables them to feel surprisingly more adult than Hollywood's current predilection for lead-footed sex and violence.
>
> (Turan 1994)

Warner Bros. was known as the purveyor of brash, cynical, modern films – mostly driven by a male protagonist involved in the crime world. However, there are a few memorable female-driven Pre-Code films in the Warner Bros. vaults that stand out – such as *Fog Over Frisco* (1934), penned by Robert N. Lee; Bette Davis, in her role as spoiled rich Arlene, says to her lover, 'I hate the word right. No one has any rights about me but me.' Kubec Glasmon's script for *Three on a Match* centres on three female high school classmates who meet by chance years after graduation. The perfect, privileged classmate who is now a rich society woman has become restless in her role as wife and mother and descends into a sordid affair with a criminal. She becomes a victim of alcohol and drugs and gives up her child. She is not redeemed at the end of the film; she remains a lost soul – although this is not due to social ostracizing, but due to her decision to adhere to her own sense of self. Screenwriters David Boehm and Robert Presnell Sr. penned *Employee's Entrance* (1933), a story that takes place in the depths of the Depression and centres on sexual harassment in a failing department store. To boost sales, the bosses force the female employees to date the customers. Another film story dealing with sexual harassment is *Female* (1933) written by Kathryn Scola and Gene Markey – however here, the female Alison Drake (Ruth Chatterton) perpetrates the harassment. This is a story of a woman who is president of an automobile company; she invites home male employees to satisfy her sexual urges and discards them the next morning. If they complain, she transfers them to the 'Montreal office'. She tells a friend, 'To me a woman in love is a pathetic spectacle, I treat men exactly the same way they treat women' (Turan 1994). Drake finally does fall in love and this causes an internal struggle. She faces three difficult questions. What should be dominant: career or love? Is it possible to continue her career while making a commitment to marriage? Does she lose a sense of self if she commits to loving someone else? Ultimately, Drake chooses love and turns over the reins of the company to her future husband, a story turn that in all probability pleased the censorship groups but is disappointing to an audience today (and perhaps to the female audiences of 1933).

Perhaps the Warner Bros. Pre-Code film that created the largest stir was *Mary Stevens, MD* written by Robert Lord and Rian James, based on a story by Virginia Kellogg. The film centres on an intelligent, respected, accomplished female doctor who has a sexual affair and becomes pregnant. She keeps her abortion secret from her friends and lover. The female protagonist is not only succeeding in a man's world but takes complete charge of her body and decisions for her future.

Paramount employed screenwriter Ben Hecht to adapt Noel Coward's play *Design for Living*, the story of a woman who refuses to choose between two suitors and finally, happily, settles for a ménage-à-trois. Other Paramount screenwriters exploring social constraints and freedoms of women were Jules Furthman, Grover Jones and Sam Raphaelson, but perhaps the most famous screenwriter who worked exclusively for Paramount was Mae West.

Screenwriter and actress Mae West created a new woman for the films of the early 1930s. The characters she wrote were strong, sexual and ambitious. West believed in 'a single standard for men and women' (Weintraub 1967: 16). English writer Hugh Walpole wrote, 'Only Charlie Chaplin and Mae West in Hollywood dare to directly attack with their mockery the fraying morals and manners of a dreary world' (West 1959).

Mae West created female characters that called the shots in business – as well as in relationships. Her leading female characters were not passive, they were, in West's words, 'the kind of dame that always asks for more than she expects to get – and then gets more than she asked for' (Weintraub 1967: 16) Middle-aged and lustful, her female characters were embraced by the audience but considered 'filthy' and 'dangerous' by the censors. Father Daniel Lord, one of the writers of the Code, cautioned Paramount, stating they would face a 'day of reckoning' if they continued to produce Mae West films (Leff and Simmons 1990: 30),

West's background was vaudeville and Broadway. Her 1926 play, *SEX*, caused her to be thrown into a New York jail as the creator of an indecent public performance. The subsequent trial was covered by the newspapers and made Mae West a star. The plot centred on a young prostitute and a society matron; both women pick up sailors for love and excitement. West's character, the prostitute, points out the only difference between the two of them 'is you can afford to give it away' (West 1925). Paramount, nearly bankrupt, wooed West to Hollywood. West knew her worth and, true to the characters she created on screen, demanded her pay cheque reflect her talent. Her script fee was $100,000 and when audiences packed the theatres to see her films, she was soon making $500,000 a year. Mae West, along with William Randolph Hearst, had one of the highest incomes in America in the early 1930s (West 1959).

Mae West stated her purpose for writing for an audience:

> The very best thing that I have done for the public during this Depression has been the humorous manner – even ribald sometimes – in which I have treated sex. My fight has been against depression, repression and suppression. You know *A Farewell to Arms*, a great picture, was a story of sex, but it was tragic and depressing. Men saw it and were afraid ever to fall in love again. They didn't even want to take a pretty girl around the corner and give her a kiss. I don't want to leave that sort of feeling with them. I want to treat sex and love lightly – enough to make both men and women feel that life is worth living; that is still holds heaps of fun, no matter what the conditions.
>
> (McCreadie 1995: 78–9)

West's first two films, both released in 1933, *She Done Him Wrong* and *I'm No Angel*, topped the list of box office hits for the year. *She Done Him Wrong* was nominated in the Academy Awards' Best Picture category. Dialogue such as 'When a girl goes bad, men go right after her' infuriated those in the censorship office, but West retorted. 'Theft and unmarried love are put on the same evil level. To me, a state of love is beyond that moral fence. A man and a woman in love commit no sin if their codes are decent and they are honest only to two people: each other' (Leff and Simmons 1990).

In *I'm No Angel* West created a lead character, carnival performer Tira (portrayed by West). Tira aggressively chooses and pursues Jack (Cary Grant), the man she desires. She also uses intelligence and street-smarts to rise to the top of her profession as a lion tamer and becomes a financial success. Jack loves Tira, proposes to her and she says yes. When he breaks the engagement because he (wrongly) thinks she's cheated on him, Tira takes Jack to court for breach of promise. She defends herself and exposes the double standard; a man can have affairs without risking social ostracism, a woman cannot. A man can engage in pre-marital sex, a woman who does risks public condemnation. A man can defend his honour, a woman who does is considered a bully. Tira defends her honour with guts and humour (echoing West's real-life experience in the New York courts) and not only wins over the judge and jury – she also restores the love of her man.

Mae West and the PCA

Unfortunately for Mae West, her rise to Hollywood stardom coincided with the ascent of a man named Joseph Breen to the top job in the Production Code Administration (PCA), the new nomenclature for the SRC. Breen, a Catholic and an Irishman, was a man determined to get his way. He said to Will Hays, then president of the MPPDA, 'I am so enthusiastic about this whole (censorship) business and so willing to work that I'd be tempted to *bite the legs off* of anybody who might dare to cross me' (Leff and Simmons 1990: p. xii). The deepening effects of the Depression, the advancements in radio and FDR's interest in creating a Federal censorship board aided Breen in his quest to bring the studios to heel. By 1933 Hollywood film revenues and attendance had fallen 40 per cent. (Mintz, 2003) Therefore the increase of pressure in 1934 caused by the Catholic Legion of Decency's plan to stage a Protest Week and the Episcopalians joining a boycott of certain films, further eroded the studios' power.

West reacted to the new aggressive enforcement of the Hays Code with characteristic determination:

> When I knew that the censors were after my films and they had come to okay everything, I wrote scenes for them to cut. These scenes were so rough that I'd never have used them. But they worked as a decoy. The PCA cut them and left the stuff I wanted. I had these scenes in there about a man's fly and all that, and the censors would be sittin' in the projection room laughing themselves silly. Then they'd say 'cut it' and not notice the rest. Then when the film came out and the bluenoses were outraged, the censors came and said, 'Mae, you didn't show us that.' But I'd show them the scripts they had okayed themselves.
>
> (Leff and Simmons 1990: 46)

The PCA increased efforts to curb West, they would not only delete lines such as 'Tira is a girl who has satisfied more patrons than Chesterfields', but insist on changes in character motivations and final outcomes of West's stories. The production of West's film, *Belle of the Nineties* (1934) became a nightmare. The initial Production Code letter ran to four and a half pages of required deletions. West lamented the final outcome of the film, saying it was disappointing because it was no longer 'a good story because they [the PCA] made me make it three times before I found out what they wanted' (West 1959). When the film was released, *Variety* critics skewered it for its 'benefit-of-the-clergy finale, an obvious curtsey to Joe Breen' (Abel 1934) and West herself suffered the consequences of the bad reviews and the poor box office.

Paramount soon found that subsequent Mae West films, without her strong point of view of the female's place in society, were not box office draws. West issued a statement on the Code:

> Strict censorship has a reverse effect. It creates resentment on the part of the public. They feel their freedom of choice is being dictated. They don't want their morals legislated by other than criminal law ... Every person who is not a moron or a mental defective of some sort carries a very effective censor and super critic of his action in his cerebral cortex – and in his heart. If that

Figure 3.1 The Production Code's 'Seal of Approval' was designed to be shown full-screen along with the major film credits. Due to audience's negative response, the seal was soon diminished in size and placed among the production crew credits.

doesn't work, no amount of censorship from the outside will do anybody any good.

(Weintraub 1967)

Mae West left Paramount by 1940, leaving with a final jab at the Production Code: 'I believe in censorship. After all, I made a fortune out of it' (Weintraub 1967). West went on to do radio, television and entertain in Las Vegas, working for 40 more years, but she was never again in a position to write or produce films. West's voice was original, her point of view both challenging and entertaining. One can only imagine, if she had been given the chance to mature as a screenwriter, the body of work she might have left for today's film audiences.

Post-Code and the screenwriter

As enforcer of the puritanical Production Code, Breen dictated 'final cut' over more movies than anyone in the history of American cinema. His editorial decisions profoundly influenced the images and values projected by Hollywood during the Great Depression, World War II and the Cold War.

(Doherty 1999)

With Joseph Breen now enforcing the Hays Code, the characterization of the American female changed dramatically. Breen's mandates were varied – for instance, films could not be offensive to foreign governments due to the risk of affecting foreign markets, they could not denigrate specific industries or lobbies such as the coal industry or newspapers or religious groups – but it could be argued that among the narratives that came under the closest scrutiny were those concerning the role of the female and her desires. 'Under the pressure of Breen's notion of compensating moral values, representations of upward mobility became much more guarded and circumspect. In the most extreme cases, one finds an insistence upon the defeat of the heroine's social aspirations' (Jacobs 1995: 133). Stories with female characters pursuing aspirations of gender and workplace equality as well as desires to explore uncharted social territories, were now in danger of being randomly rewritten – by producers, censors, anyone available, to fulfil the censors' mandates. Breen and the PCA office caused films to be held from release, and other films to be rewritten, recut or reshaped to fit the edicts of the Code. In fairness, Breen, who 'felt a sacred duty to protect the spiritual well-being of the innocent souls who fluttered too close to the unholy attractions of the motion picture screen' (Doherty 1999: 9), was willing to listen to producers defending a story's needs for certain character traits, plot devices and themes. At times he could be persuaded to allow an 'edge' to characters if, ultimately, the 'proper' conclusion (punishment) was meted out for unapproved (thus unacceptable) actions. Doherty gives Breen credit for being 'a hard worker' for seeing possible cuts and trims to refocus 'dicey' material – noting that Breen saved the studios' investments by making screenplays acceptable. (Doherty 1999: 83).

Unfortunately, Doherty does not address the fact that the PCA was, in many cases, changing not only content but also the intent of the screenwriter/filmmaker and that 'acceptable' was in the narrow purview of the PCA. Eviscerations of material were numerous. An often-used example of the PCA's blatant manipulation of narrative is *Baby Face* (1933) penned by Gene Markey and Kathryn Scola. Its original Pre-Code release featured a young woman, Lily (Barbara Stanwyck), who has been pimped by her father from the age of 14. After her father's death, she is counselled by an elderly male friend (using the words of Nietzsche) to 'crush all sentiment'; to embrace and use her female attributes, to use men so as to turn her poor, unfortunate and less-than-promising life around. Lily takes his advice, goes to New York, takes advantage of men (by promising and living up to her promises of sexual relations) and becomes rich and satisfied. *Baby Face* was recut and redialogued and rereleased in a Post-Code version. At the PCA's insistence, the young woman's early abuse and forced prostitution are never clearly referred to, the elderly man (by recutting and putting new words in his mouth while using an over-his-shoulder shot to focus on Lily's face) now advises Lily to focus on morality and sexual abstinence until finding the love of a good man. Lily's subsequent rise in New York comes as the result of flirtations, not from follow-through of sexual promises – and in the end, she realizes that 'true love' is a woman's greatest satisfaction.[7] Michael Asimov points out in his article 'Divorce in the Movies: From the Hays Code to *Kramer vs. Kramer*' that in the Pre-Code era divorce themes were candidly portrayed and explored, as in *When Ladies Meet*, *Three on a Match* and *The Divorcee*. However, under Breen's Production Code Administration, serious divorce stories were nearly blotted off the screen (Asimov 2000: 7). Post-Code films tended to deal with divorce in a comedic manner, with husband and wife reuniting again at the end of the film: films such as *His Girl Friday* (1940), *Philadelphia Story* (1940), *My Favorite Wife* (1940) and *Palm Beach Story* (1942). Screenwriter Herman Mankiewicz commented on the strictures put on the writers: 'The hero and the heroine must be virgins. The villain can lay anybody he wants, have as much fun as he wants cheating and stealing, getting rich and whipping servants. But you have to shoot him in the end' (Leff and Simmons 1990: 46). When MGM was planning a production of *Anna Karenina*, Breen sent a letter insisting that Anna's pregnancy by Vronsky be eliminated and that Anna and Vronsky never cohabit, that there be no evidence of physical contact between the two. Screenwriters S. N. Behrman and Clemence Dane, while working on their adaptation, lobbied for and received permission for the two to live together but were told to make sure that Anna and Vronsky never, for one moment, enjoyed their relationship (Leff and Simmons 1990: 63). The film adaptation of Lillian Hellman's *The Children's Hour* also suffered; this story, based on an intimate relationship between two women, was only approved for release when all lesbian elements and references to their emotional feelings for each other were erased.[8] It wasn't until the 1982 *Personal Best*, penned by Robert Towne, that the subject of a love affair between two women was explored in a mainstream Hollywood film. Inter-racial sexual relationships were also forbidden; this edict was added in the third draft of the Production Code to placate Southerners (Doherty 1999: 234). Doherty reports that this was more a political move than a moral assertion and that Breen and others on the PCA committee chafed under its addition. However, once adopted as an element of the Code, the Breen office followed the directive. Stories exploring inter-racial relationships could not be approved by the PCA, thus almost certainly blocking distribution possibilities, therefore it can be assumed that screenwriters, with an eye on getting their work produced, avoided construction of narratives exploring this topic that would not be cleared for production. It wasn't until a *Patch of Blue* (1965) and *Guess Who's Coming to Dinner* (1967) that inter-racial relationships were given serious consideration in Hollywood's studio-financed films.

> A Hollywood filmmaker, under the Breen Office might be likened to a poet struggling with the rules of a Shakespearean sonnet. The formal restrictions are preconditions for the creative act: fourteen lines, iambic pentameter, three quatrains capped by a rhyming couplet pithily wrapping up the package. Within the constraints the poet is free to pick words and hone the phrasing … The virtues of sonnet poetics are discipline, suspense, precision and grace under expressive pressure. The flaws are stilted conventions, formulaic predictability, stale tropes and suffocating rigidity.
>
> (Doherty 1999: 98)

Under the strict Breen reign, screenwriters were expected by producers to create 'approved' screen worlds that supported a morality and expectation of conduct that was both instructive and destructive to the ambitions and world-view of American women. As self-regulation became more entrenched after 1934, it reinforced patterns of narrative development, of formal unity and closure, typical of the classical Hollywood cinema as a whole. These formal systems unobtrusively circumscribed the representation of female aggressivity, ambition and illicit sexuality' (Jacobs 1995: 149).

The newly formed Screen Writers Guild, gaining strength in the 1930s, blamed the Hays Code for the failure of screen stories 'to deal with the everyday scene of life around us' (Ward 2002). The sign of the new order was a title card superimposed over the oval seal of the MPPDA before the credits: 'This Picture Has Been Approved by the Production Code Administration of the Motion Picture Producers and Distributors of America'. Industry magazine *Variety* weighed in against the censors who were trying to control Hollywood output, applauding Mae West's *Diamond Lil* and a few other films that managed to slip a few things 'past the chipmunky Tsar Hays and his band'.[9] The audience also weighed in – when the Production Code Seal of Approval appeared on a separate frame before the beginning of the film, audiences greeted 'the emblem with jeering, booing and what the Hollywood Reporter called "a good community 'hiss'"' (Doherty 1999: 75) After these initial receptions, the size of the seal was diminished and placed innocuously (one could suggest the term 'hidden') in the title credits.

Unfortunately many female-driven Pre-Code films did not, retroactively, receive the seal of approval and were banned or (perhaps a worse fate) reissued in re-edited, redialogued 'acceptable' versions. Many box office hits such as *Trouble in Paradise, Design for Living* and *Red-Headed Woman* could not enter the normal rerelease calendar given to most films of the time, a practice that studios engaged in to recoup their investments. Other films that did not meet the PCA criteria for rerelease included *The Story of Temple Drake, George White's Scandals, She Done Him Wrong* and *I'm No Angel*. Some Pre-Code classics such as *Ecstasy, Children of Loneliness, Love Life of a Gorilla, Tabu* were only shown in art houses because they did not receive the Production Code Seal of Approval. Other films, failing to meet the standards of the Code, were never released. Many Pre-Code films, shoved aside because they were no longer marketable, have been lost, films such as *Convention City* (1933) and *White Heat* (1934). Mark Vieira writes 'The Hays Code endured until 1968, depriving generations of moviegoers of a wide range of ideas and images and in some cases, coherent works of art' (1999).

In conclusion

> Our (women's) instincts were substantiated by the movies: the 'virgin' was a primal, positive figure, honored and exalted beyond any merits she possessed as a woman (and eventually made to pay for her 'superiority' in the professional virgins and teases of the fifties), while the 'whore', Americanized into the good-bad girl, was publicly castigated and cautioned against – and privately sought by men.
>
> (Haskell 1987: p. xvi)

For a brief five years in the early 1930s, Hollywood screenwriters enjoyed the opportunity to write, and see produced, stories that explored the role of the American female as they saw it – or wished it to be. These screenwriters created, for American women, role models that inspired independent thinking and a demand for gender equality. When the Production Code Office began to resolutely harness control of screen narratives in 1934, screenwriters became severely hampered in their quest to truthfully explore the human condition of the evolving post World War I American woman. Margaret Thorp's 1939 research, *America at the Movies* states approximately 40 million people out of America's 130 million were regular and repeating patrons at the 1700 movie theatres located in 9000 cities and towns. The audience was primarily middle-class whites between the ages of 14 and 45, 'and the most important segment of which was the adult female – "the average citizen's wife"' (Balio 1993: 2). Those females in the audience seeking realistic or inspirational narratives that reflected their ambitions, dreams or world-views were provided with a circumspect morality and instructional viewpoint that communicated a narrow view of possibilities and appropriate desires.

Professional screenwriters working under the restrictions of the PCA in the late 1930s and 1940s were obviously cognizant of the censorship codes and, in reaction, were forced into a form of self-censorship. Maltby and Jacobs seem to straddle a fence on their assessment of content of Pre-Code and Code film narratives, suggesting that the Code enhanced screenwriting (forcing screenwriters to be more clever, fashion entertaining analogies and innuendos to get around censors or pursue the adaptations of literature) and point to the fact that many of the American Film Institute's Top Ten Films were produced during the strictly enforced Code era and that 1939 is still considered one of Hollywood's best years of film output (Jacobs and Maltby 1995). They are assessing from the viewpoint of box office and lasting entertainment value – and have not taken into consideration the role of the female characters in those films. In *The Philadelphia Story* (1940) charismatic and strong-minded Tracy (Katharine Hepburn) learns a proper and good wife must support her husband despite his faults and weaknesses and only in learning to do so will she experience self-worth. In *Casablanca* (1942) Ilsa (Ingrid Bergman) tells Rick he must do her thinking for her. In *All About Eve* (1950) Margo Channing (Bette Davis) learns that a successful career is not enough, a woman can only sustain lifelong happiness with a loving husband by her side. These highly regarded films (and deservedly so from many standpoints) were approved by the PCA because of the portrayal of the female and lessons she learns in the film.

The woman of 'dangerous' or unapproved ambition was often relegated to film noir roles in the 1940s. The 1950s female was taught in home economics classes across America that the care of children and husband was expected woman's work: 'have dinner ready. Prepare the children. Touch up your makeup. Never complain. Try to make your home a place of peace and order where your husband can renew himself in body and spirit.'[10] This idea of a woman's role was supported on screen in films as well as on television in series such as *Leave it to Beaver* and *Ozzie and Harriet*. An examination of the late 1950s and early 1960s 'women's films' featuring repressed and depressed women in relation to edicts of the Code would be an interesting study in relation to the image set by the PCA of the 'proper female'. It wasn't until the early 1960s with John F. Kennedy's

Commission on the Status of Women that female characters onscreen began to regularly question the status quo.

It is important to acknowledge the aim of many screenwriters: to hold up a mirror to their worlds and to affect and inspire audiences. In the Pre-Code era, a five-year span of time in America's film history, a realistic portrayal of the evolving American female was aspired to and embraced in film narratives. In 1934, a particular view of the American female perpetrated by a Production Code written largely by religious reformers was fashioned and mandated and greatly influenced the portrayal of the American female. No one will ever know what certain effect the Code had on the self-esteem and aspirations of the American female or what retardation of struggle for gender equality this caused. Its effect on the American screenwriter of the era is, however, apparent. One has only to look at the shift in ideation of story, execution of film narrative – and listen to the words of the screenwriters themselves: 'writing became like writing on the sand with the wind blowing' (Marion 1972).

Notes

1 Among them Thomas Doherty, Lea Jacobs, Richard Maltby, Leonard J. Leff and Jerold Simmons.
2 Among them Molly Haskell, Mick LaSalle, David Stenn.
3 http://www.fakes.net/boxofficestats.htm (accessed March 2007).
4 *Some Like it Hot* (1959), *The Apartment* (1960), *The Private Life of Sherlock Holmes* (1970) and more.
5 http://www.artsreformation.com/1001/hays-code.html
6 In 1915, the Supreme Court of the United States ruled that motion pictures were not entitled to First Amendment protection because they were deemed to be solely a business enterprise. This was not reversed until 1952.
7 Both versions, Pre-Code and Post-Code, are now available on DVD.
8 http://www.brightlightsfilms.com/28/thesethree1.html (accessed March 2007).
9 http:/www.mae-west.org/old/Variety (accessed March 2007).
10 http://jade.ccccd.edu/grooms/goodwife.htm

References

Abel (1934) *Variety Reviews, Belle of the Nineties.* URL: http://www.mae-west.org/old/Variety/BOT90.html (accessed March 2007).
Asimov, Michael (2000) 'Divorce in the Movies: From the Hays Code to Kramer vs. Kramer', *Legal Studies Forum* 24(2): 1–62. http://papers.ssrn.com/sol3/papers.cfm?abstract_id=214869.
Baer, W. (2008), *Classic American Films: Conversations with the Screenwriters*, Westport, CT: Praeger.
Balio, Tino (1993) *Grand Design*, History of American Cinema, 5, Berkeley and Los Angeles, CA: University of California Press.
Beauchamp, Cari (1998) *Without Lying Down*, Berkeley, CA: University of California Press
— (2003) *Anita Loos Rediscovered*, Berkeley and Los Angeles, CA: University of California Press.

Buening, Michael (2005) *PopMatters* film review, 6 Sept. URL: http://www.opmatters.com/fil/revews/m/miracle-of-morgans-creek-dvd.shtml (accessed Sept. 2009).

Buhle, Paul and Wagner, David (2002) *Radical Hollywood*, New York: New Press.

Carter, Susan B. and Prus, Mark (1982) 'The Labor Market and the American High School Girl 1890–1928', *Journal of Economic History* 42(1) (March): 163–71.

Doherty, Thomas (1999) *PreCode Hollywood: Sex, Immorality and Insurrection in American Cinema, 1930–1934*, New York: Columbia University Press.

Donohue, Chris (2003) 'Written By', *Writers Guild of America Magazine*, 7(5).

Ehins, Marjorie (2001) *Culture on Trial*. URL: www.fepproject.org/archives/sexandscens2001-02.html

Fox, Julian (1972) 'A Crack in the Dream: An Aspect of Hollywood in the Hungry 30s, Part 1', *Films and Filming* (August); 'A Crack in the Dream: An Aspect of Hollywood in the Hungry 30s, Part 2: The Sun still Shines Behind the Clouds', *Films and Filming* (September);

Haskell, Molly (1987) *Reverence to Rape*, 2nd edn, Chicago: University of Chicago Press.

Howell, Dorothy and Swerling, Joseph (1931) *Ten Cents a Dance*, Columbia Pictures.

Iglesias, Karl (2001) *The 101 Habits of Highly Successful Screenwriters*, Avon, MA: Adams Media Corporation.

Jacobs, Lea (1995) *Wages of Sin*, Berkeley and Los Angeles, CA: University of California Press.

— (1999) 'Industry Self-Regulation and the Problem of Textual Determination', in *Controlling Hollywood, Censorship and Regulation in the Studio Era*, New Brunswick, NJ: Rutgers Press.

— and Maltby, Richard (1995) 'Rethinking the Production', *Quarterly Review of Film and Video* 15.

Kramer vs. Kramer (Written Robert Benton, from novel by Avery Corman, dir. Robert Benton, Columbia Pictures USA, 1979; 105 mins).

LaSalle, Mick (2001) *Complicated Women: Sex and Power in Pre-Code Hollywood*, New York: St Martin's Griffin Press.

— (2002) *Dangerous Men: PreCode Hollywood and the Birth of the Modern Man*, Thomas Dunne Books.

Leff, Leonard J. and Simmons, Jerold L. (1990) *Dame in the Kimono*, New York: Grove Weidenfeld.

Loos Anita (1974) *Kiss Hollywood Goodbye*, New York: Viking Press.

— and Katherine Brush, *Red-Headed Woman* (1932) MGM Pictures.

Luce, Clare Booth and Anita Loos, *The Women* (1939) MGM Pictures.

Maltby, Richard (1999) '*The King of Kings* and the Czar of All the Rushes: The Propriety of the Christ Story', in *Controlling Hollywood, Censorship and Regulation in the Studio Era*, New Brunswick, NJ: Rutgers Press.

Marion, Frances (1972) *Off with their Heads*, New York: Macmillan Co.

McBride, Joseph (2002) 'Written By', *Writers Guild of America Magazine*, (May, issue 5).

McCreadie, Marsha (1995) *The Women Who Write the Movies: From Frances Marion to Nora Ephron*, New York: Carol Publishing Corporation.

McGilligan, Pat (1986) *Backstory, Interviews with Screenwriters of Hollywood's Golden Age*, Berkeley and Los Angeles, CA: University of California Press

Mintz, S. (2003) 'Back to the History of American Film'. URL: http://www.digitalhistory.uh.edu/historyonline/hollywood.cfm (accessed March 2007).

Motion Picture Code (1930) http://www.artsreformation.com/a0001/hays-code.html (accessed Feb. 2007).

Smith, Imogen Sara (2009) 'Sinner's Holiday', *Bright Lights Film Journal* 63. http://www.brightlightsfilm.com/63/63precodesmith.php

Thorp, Margaret (1939) *America At The Movies*, New Haven, CT: Yale University Press.

Turan, Kenneth (1994) *Los Angeles Times*, Calendar Section, 31 July.

— (2003) *Los Angeles Times*, Calendar Section, 17 May: E9.

— (2005) *Los Angeles Times*, 20 May.

Uncle Scoopy's Movie House, URL: http://www.fakes.net/boxofficestats.htm (accessed March 2007)

Variety Reviews, Diamond Lil, 1934, URL: http://www.mae-west.org/old/Variety (accessed March 2007).

Vieira, Mark (1999) *Sin in Soft Focus: PreCode Hollywood* (1999) New York: Harry N. Abrams.

Ward, Richard (2002) 'Golden Age, Blue Pencils; The Hal Roach Studios and Three Cases of Censorship during Hollywood's Studio Era', *Media History Journal* 8(1) (June): 103–19.

Weintraub, Joseph, ed. (1967) *The Wit and Wisdom of Mae West*, New York: G. P. Putnam & Sons.

West, Mae (1925) *SEX*, Daly's 63rd Street Theatre, produced by Main Stem Boys and Mae West, New York.

— *'I'm No Angel'*, 1933, Paramount Pictures.

— (1959) *Goodness has Nothing to Do with it*, Prentice Hall.

Chapter 4

Screenwriting in Britain 1895–1929

Ian W. Macdonald

The story of the development of screenwriting as a discrete practice is one of *habitus*, labour relations, cultural assumptions and inter-medial borrowings. It is a narrative lying within the larger one of cinema, following the same contours of growth and retrenchment and with the same concerns about how to match production technology with audience comprehension. But it also has its own history of creating and rationalizing specific ways of working, and of negotiating spaces for these within broader industry practice. This chapter introduces that history, during the silent era of the British film industry.

The earliest 'screenwriters'

Screenwriting has never been a heavily populated profession. During the whole silent film period only around 360 people (including around 60 women) can be identified as specialist screenwriters, almost all from 1912 onwards.[1] However, even identifying 'the screenwriter' as a meaningful role remains problematic until the later 1900s, mainly because the early 'cameraman' system of production did not demarcate a specific role of writer; 'the operator would select the subject matter and stage it as necessary' (Staiger 1985: 116).[2] From around then, and particularly from the early 1910s, a new 'wave' of specialist writers established their role as a professional one, developing and rationalizing normative practice throughout the 1910s and attempting to secure their status as the 'author' of a film, similar to that of a playwright. By the mid-1920s, they had already lost ground to the director, and by the time the industry began to pick up after the mid-decade slump, a new set of practices were forming around a third 'wave' of screenwriting activity. Charles Barr describes pre-1930 film industry development as occurring in stages (Barr 2009: 145); the waves of screenwriting activity are responses to these.

In the earlier 1900s, the role of writing was not demarcated from other roles: everyone did what they felt they could do; for example, film company owner Cecil Hepworth paid tribute to Percy Stow both for his direction of 'trick' films and his ability and willingness to 'take ... turns at the developing and printing machine' (1951: 53). At Hepworth's, whoever was responsible for the screen idea merely offered the story, which was written up to be approved by Hepworth. The earliest noted credit as scriptwriter in Denis Gifford's *British Film Catalogue*, vol. 1 (2000) is Hepworth himself for his *Alice in Wonderland* (1903).[3] This 16-scene 800 ft (or around 13-minute) film, which links key scenes as a narrative framework, has been recognized as significant (Low and Manvell 1948: 83–5; Higson 2002: 42–64). It was ambitious, and based around scenes as pictures.

> We did the whole story in 800 feet – the longest ever at the time. Every situation [i.e. scene] was dealt with, with all the accuracy at our command and with reverent fidelity, so far as we could manage it, to Tenniel's famous drawings.
>
> (Hepworth, 1951: 63)

In 1904, with British industrial production having doubled in a year, and with this increase made up of longer films lasting anything from two to sixteen minutes, Hepworth found it necessary to employ actor Lewin Fitzhamon as 'stage manager', the early term for director. This meant Fitzhamon 'wrote, stage-managed, directed and acted in around two films a week for eight years' (Gifford 1986: 315). Despite the speed of this turnover, there were still formal written scripts for this; 'Fitz' later recalled that there were 'scenarios' at Hepworths in 1904, typed by Ethel Christian who ran a theatrical typing agency;[4] 'The game at first was to submit a scenario', to be approved by Hepworth (Gifford 1986: 315–16). Significantly Fitzhamon claims that by the end of 1904 the public was also sending in story ideas, which Hepworth would pay for, and which Fitz would adapt himself on Sunday mornings (S. Brown 2008: 2). Fitz carried a notebook in which he also wrote ideas for scripts in the evenings, but scripts were not given to the actors; instead they followed verbal instructions during rehearsals, and presumably also during shooting itself (S. Brown 2008: 2). It seems, therefore, that at least one major British film production company ran a 'quasi-director' system from around 1904, where responsibility for constructing the narrative lay with the 'stage-manager', based on screen ideas proposed by himself or others. The formality of a 'film-script' seems important only to this stage-trained director and to Hepworth himself.

By 1907 the provenance and suitability of film story ideas were issues that began to surface in the trade press. An American article on 'The Requirements of the Film Plot' appeared in the newly revamped *Kine Weekly* (1907a), though the following week the journal pointed out that 'a well known manager' had shown them a cupboard full of 'new subjects', not all of them practicable, 'for it is an unhappy fact that some of the most original ideas are most difficult to put into practical form', although there were sufficient to 'ensure a steady stream of good class subjects' (*Kine Weekly* 1907b). The linked issues of suitability and the need for an endless surplus of story material were already present in the industry.

Screenwriters themselves are generally uncredited in trade literature until 1912 (Gifford 2000: p. ix), though they were clearly employed before then. Clarendon Films' founder-partner Percy Stow employed Langford Reed from 1907 to 1909 as a story writer, and he is credited as writing a script of Shakespeare's *The Tempest* – lasting around 12 minutes – in November 1908. For the moment at least, Reed is the first clearly identifiable specialist screenwriter in British film production, though there are several earlier filmmakers who might now be termed writer-directors. Reed continued screenwriting until 1922, being well enough known as a 'photo-playwright' in 1915 to be selected as the first to be featured in a series of biographical articles for the *Bioscope* (Elliott 1915b).

The second 'wave'

Until the early 1910s, almost all films were shorter than 15 minutes long. From 1911, in line with the European trend towards longer 'feature' films, multiple reel films grew in number, becoming the norm from 1916.[5] Production during the silent period reached a peak of 832 fiction titles in 1914 (Figure 4.1), after which the number of titles falls to just 109 in 1918, but this is mitigated by an increase in the length of individual films. By 1919 most productions were five-reelers or longer, and by 1923 most were six-reelers or more, lasting perhaps 75–90 minutes plus.[6] There was a post-Great War 'bounce-back' to 210 fiction titles in 1920, but production slumped again to a mere 52 in 1925, before the Cinematograph Films Act 1927 (the 'quota' Act) and other changes began to increase British production once again. By the start of the 1930s (and the phasing out of silent film production) the British film industry was producing just over 100 titles per annum.[7]

The changeover from numerous small titles to fewer larger ones reduced the demand for many different, short and simple screen ideas to a much smaller number of longer, more complex (and more financially risky) productions, including film series and serials. The demand for screenwriters was therefore reduced overall, but those who were required needed to be craftsmen and women of some skill and experience. By 1918, the skills required for such screenwriting

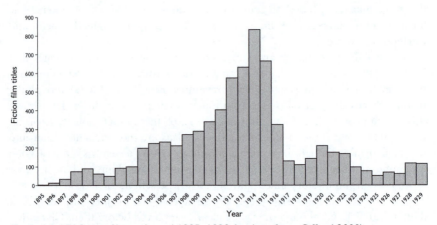

Figure 4.1 UK fiction films released 1895–1929 (analysis from Gifford 2000)

were significantly more specialized than they had been in 1908, when craft skills and norms began to be formalized.

The new division of labour provided a route for promising aspirants to enter the film industry. Writers could be taken on as Scenario Editor, where they read submissions, and formatted stories into scripts as well as writing screenplays themselves, as did Victor Montefiore at Hepworths (S. Brown 2008: 4). Montefiore also wrote articles and a pamphlet on best screenwriting practice (1915) contributing, with others like Eliot Stannard at B & C and later Adrian Brunel at the British Actors Film Company, to the establishment of the 'doxa' of screenwriting based on a range of beliefs about art and good practice, and focused on notions of dramatic construction including that of the 'well-made play'. Such gatekeepers and opinion-formers were in a position to establish norms, but as they did so they raised the bar for amateurs. In the mid-teens screenwriters like the determined (but not himself hugely experienced at that point) William J. Elliott was telling the 'Incompetent Amateur' to go, 'and it's up to us to see him off' (1915c). By 1919, director Maurice Elvey explained the extent of skills necessary for the professional screenwriter who was, as a consequence, a scarce commodity.

> The number of people in London who can be trusted to turn out a scenario on which a [director] can really get to work without fear of being stopped by some technical error can be numbered on one's fingers. A scenario writer must know something of photography, scene setting as applied to studio work, the possibility of lighting effects from searchlights to candles, psychology, costumes and the artistic temperament.
>
> (Elvey 1919: 1)

One result of increasing the level of craft skills was that the general trawl for ideas, through advertisements and the occasional competition, became more dispiriting. It resulted in 'stacks and stacks of "synopses" and "scenarios" from servant-girls and office-boys. If the disappointment doesn't sour you then this daily avalanche of puerile piffle will unbalance you', said the former scenario editor Adrian Brunel (c.1922).

Stage and literary sources, as fully constructed fiction, became popular targets for adaptation, with publishers sending off their latest works to scenario editors 'tied together like firewood' (Stannard 1921a: 140). Film companies leapt on almost anything, to the chagrin of the freelance writer.

> At best it is a cut-and-slash trade … [The] work must be translated from rhetoric into continuous action; it is this terrible screen need for perpetual motion that has caused so many indifferent and oft-time lamentably bad books and plays to be eagerly sought after by film manufacturers.
>
> (Stannard 1917: 108)

Screenwriters themselves found the profession a struggle, with the need for oversupply creating a buyers' market. Adrian Brunel suffered rejection at the hands of Clarendon in 1912 and 1913, and William J. Elliott, who may have worked for Hepworth (S. Brown 2008: 3) but was first credited in 1914 as a screenwriter for London Films,[8] disarmingly claimed to have received 275 refusals and 10 acceptances during his first year as a screenwriter (1915a). 'I suppose', he said, 'I must now be regarded as a successful photoplay writer' (1915a). Adrian Brunel was provoked into writing to *The Cinema* in 1921 pleading for more film finance, particularly payment for screenwriters' time to work on scripts.

> Two or three [British screenwriters] are over-worked and are over-producing – while the others chase about for commissions. It is a hard job and some of the more fortunate ones will occasionally obtain a commission to do, say, a five reel adaptation for £100. A conscientious writer will take a month at least to do this ... but the poor devil is driven and must live; he cannot afford more time and must chase round for another commission.
>
> (Brunel 1921: 1)

As always, the less well-known writers got work providing uncredited material, or scenarios which were not produced. Former actor Gerald de Beaurepaire adapted a novel *Barnaby* for Barkers in 1919, and stayed with them as 'scenarist'. His account describes his industrial function.

> Much of what my fellow-scenarists and I wrote, down at Ealing Film Studios, between 1918 and 1925 did not get to the point of being 'shot'. In those days we just had to write SOMETHING in case an IDEA was needed ... Harry Engholm and I did a bit of freelancing together – I think it was for Stolls – and the outstanding script I can remember was an adaptation of Conan Doyle's great boxing story, 'The Croxley Master'.
>
> (De Beaurepaire 1961: 2)

The potential for female employment was thought to be good, particularly because of the perception that cinema was attractive to women; 'women's stories' were considered an important genre (Newey 2000: 151). Despite that, only around 17 per cent of credited screenwriters during the whole silent period were women, some of whose activity may also have been mediated or negotiated through familial or domestic structure (Newey 2000: 160–1); there were certainly family relationships in the professional lives of Ethyle and Ernest Batley, Lisle and Nellie Lucoque, the Hepworths, the Merwins and the Morgans. Women did become noticed; while Hepworth later credited his wife Margaret with the story for *Rescued by Rover* in 1905 (1951: 66), it was not until the start of the 'second wave' that professional writers became visible, among them women like Hepworth's Muriel Alleyne (whose first credit was in 1912), Alice de Winton (1913) and Blanche MacIntosh (1913). Others include Ethyle Batley (1913); and the Marchioness of

Townshend (1913), who wrote for Clarendon Films. By the 1920s some women had made significant names as screenwriters, from Eve Unsell (from 1919 in Britain), Alma Reville (who started in London Films' editing department around 1915,[9] but whose first screenwriting credit was in 1928) to Irene Miller (from 1915) who worked for Barker and Samuelsons, and Lydia Hayward (from 1920), who was very active in the 1920s and continued more sporadically to the 1940s.

The most successful screenwriters, such as Kenelm Foss, Benedict James (a.k.a. Bertram Jacobs) and Reuben Gillmer, were indeed in demand, and the one most seriously overproducing was Eliot Stannard. He started by adapting his mother's novel *Beautiful Jim* for B & C in 1914, following up before the year was out with several other scripts for the same director Maurice Elvey, and his habitual star Elizabeth Risdon. Stannard proved himself reliable and quick, to the point that by 1920 he was regarded highly by the industry.[10] By the mid-1920s he was the *éminence grise*, writing for the upcoming new director Alfred Hitchcock, with seven of Hitch's nine silent scripts attributed to Stannard (Barr 1999: 16). His last script (of around 150 in his career) was produced in 1933. A man with an intellectual grasp of his work, he concentrated on screenwriting with few forays into other media, despite collaborating on a stage play in 1924.[11] Stannard probably contributed more than any other writer in Britain to the perception of screenwriting as a distinct art, a contribution only now being recognized (see Barr 2009: 153; Macdonald 2009).

The third wave

The 'British Film Slump' of 1924, based around a supposed crisis in November in which *Kine Weekly* pointed out 'in alarmist rhetoric that every British studio had ground to a complete halt' (Burrows 2009: 160), may not have been quite the problem it was touted as, but the general reduction in individual titles in the mid-1920s clearly reduced the produced output of working screenwriters. Fewer new entrants found a way in to the profession; Figure 4.2 shows a significant drop in new names credited as screenwriters in the mid-1920s, with just five new screenwriters credited in 1925, down from 34 in 1921. Significantly, the increase in production from 1926 was not always taken up by previously active screenwriters like the plucky William Elliott, whose last credit was as writer-director of a series of three 30-minute films in 1926, produced (perhaps in a last-ditch attempt to direct his own destiny) by a company called Raymond-Elliott.[12] Other experienced professionals who ceased writing during this period were Blanche MacIntosh, Hepworth's chief writer whose last credit was in 1923, J. Bertram Brown (1924, apart from one co-credit in 1930), Kenelm Foss (1924, also with one co-credit in 1932) and W. Courtney Rowden (1923).

Whether or not this slowdown was 'an economic caesura which knocked out the old-fashioned and allowed the modern to appear' (Gledhill 2009: 163),[13] there was still some work for the core experienced writers; the estimable Eliot Stannard continued on his prolific way, along with Lydia Hayward (whose first credit was

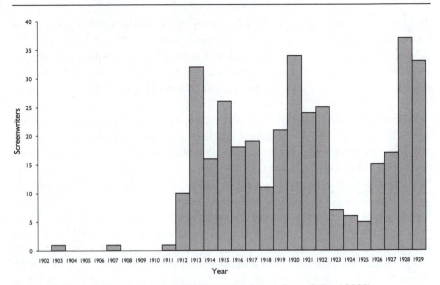

Year

Figure 4.2 First credit screenwriters 1902–1929 (analysis from Gifford 2000)

in 1920), Roland Pertwee (1919), Patrick Mannock (1920) and H. Fowler Mear (1917), but there was now room for a new generation to join some of the older guard. As Lydia Hayward explained in 1927 'there is, at the moment, a shortage … and all who are interested in seeing our industry step up from its Cinderella condition to the rank of Princess would welcome newcomers' (1927: 155). The newcomers duly showed up; there were 15 previously unknown screenwriters in 1926, 17 in 1927 and 37 in 1928 (Figure 4.2). As Geoff Brown points out (2008: 247), the writing gap was now as likely to be filled by university graduates, familiar with the intellectual interests of the Film Society and *Close-Up* magazine, as by actors or enthusiastic amateur writers working from home. New boys included Sidney Gilliat, son of the editor of the *Evening Standard*, and Cambridge graduates Roger Burford and Angus MacPhail; but also an ordinary solicitor's son, W. P. Lipscomb, whose first major credit was for the B & D talkie *Splinters* (1929), and who went on to become one of the highest paid writers in Hollywood before returning to Britain in 1943 (*The Times* 1958). These new writers were able to learn the new ropes of a changed industry quite quickly, building new contact networks in companies like Gainsborough, with the new script gatekeepers such as Angus MacPhail.

Despite the influx, Cecil Hepworth is reported as saying the rehabilitation of the British film industry was due to new methods rather than to new men (Gledhill 2003: 100), and certainly enough of the earlier cohort of screenwriters survived in sufficient numbers to support this theory. The folkloric assumption that many silent film writers 'failed' to make the transition to sound film production suggests an incompetence that may not have actually been there; those whose experience started before 1924 and who continued to write into the 1930s and beyond include

Denison Clift, George Dewhurst, Lydia Hayward, Sinclair Hill, Harry Hughes, Harry Mear and Frank Miller. They were the ones who adapted to the new ideas, and to the new practices that came with them.

The screenplay

The formalization of the written form of the screen idea became increasingly necessary for the industry before the second 'wave' of screenwriting activity, but when was a written script first used, and how did it come about? In the labour system common during the decade after 1895, formally writing down a screen idea for production planning purposes was probably unnecessary except for the more complex scenes. With many films in 1903 less than two minutes long, a written script may not normally have been more than an aide-memoire, perhaps even written simultaneously 'as shot', and useful for later sales purposes. By 1903 longer films of several scenes lasting perhaps three or four minutes were becoming more common, though still often considered as separate entities with minimal narrative linkage such as G. A. Smith's comedy *After Dark* (1902).[14] In this 15-scene film of less than four minutes, a 'policeman's lantern illumines scenes of waif, drunkard, burglar …'[15] suggesting an approach to film construction that works – as other films of the time often did – as a collection of significant moments. Similarly in Hepworth's 1906 catalogue the 1903 *Alice* is reportedly shown as – and indeed offered for sale as – separate 'scenes', (Hepworth 1951: 63). Low and Manvell quote directly from the catalogue, which refers to scenes 'preceded where necessary for the elucidation of the story, by descriptive titles' (1948: 83–4);[16] in effect creating an impression of the whole *Alice in Wonderland* narrative through linking key scenes by written text. A script may well have taken the form of a similar scene-by-scene description, without titles, though in this case Tenniel's drawings probably provided more of an inspiration for the films than any written script.[17]

   In the USA by 1905 formal scenarios were essentially descriptions of place and plot, divided into short scenes where the action was filmed, as if on a stage (Loughney 1990). As such, these outlines were very similar to those found in sales catalogues; indeed sales synopses may have been lifted almost whole from the original scenario. Scripts submitted for registration under copyright laws from 1907 in France were similar (Raynauld 1997), and there is no reason to suppose that these were very different from the scenarios presented by British screenwriters during the mid- to late 1900s. By 1909, ideas about formalizing the scenario were beginning to surface in the industry in the USA (Staiger 1985: 126), and by 1911 US-inspired screenwriting manuals were appearing in Britain. In 1912 the *Bioscope* had a regular column of news and advice for scenario writers.[18] Throughout the 1910s, manuals from successful (and indeed less successful) screenwriters were published, offering quite similar and mostly pragmatic advice, with reference to stage practice and notions of the well-made play.[19] Even the earliest manuals

CHAPTER VIII.

A SPECIMEN SCENARIO.

WE give here a sample scenario as a guide to the beginner:—

FOR LOVE OF GOLD.

Original Film Drama.

PRINCIPAL CHARACTERS.

Earl Vivian - . . . . . . - Old and Feeble.
Lieut. Vivian - . . . . - Elder Son and Heir.
Hugh Vivian - Younger Son, an Unprincipled Scapegrace.
Elsie Howard - . . . . - Niece of the Old Earl.
Hugh's Accomplice - . . . . - A Burly Ruffian.

SYNOPSIS.

Hugh pesters his cousin Elsie with offers of marriage, which are rejected, there being a mutual affection between her and the heir. Hugh tries to extort money from his father, causing a violent scene, which results in the Earl's sudden death. Elsie and Lieutenant Vivian subsequently pursue their love affairs in the presence of the dead Earl, thinking he is asleep. They only discover his death on trying to wake him to announce their engagement. Hugh is left nothing in the will, and he eventually makes an unsuccessful attempt to steal the family jewels. Becoming desperate, he bribes an accomplice to murder his brother. An attack is made at the top of a cliff, but the heir foils it, and in the scuffle Hugh falls over the cliff. Elsie succeeds in reconciling the brothers as Hugh lies dying.

Scenes 1, 3, 6, 7 - - The Library.
„ 2 - - Entrance to the Mansion.
„ 4 - - The Garden.
„ 5 - - The Terrace.
„ 8 - - A Squalid Courtyard.
„ 9 - - Interior of Dirty Attic.
„ 10, 12 - - The Drawing Room.
„ 11, 13 - - Top of Cliff.
„ 14 - - Hugh's Bedroom.

— 56 —.

Hugh struggles with her, but Elsie manages to ring the bell. As the new Earl and a footman rush into room, Hugh strikes the girl down, and makes off without the jewels.

SCENE VIII.—A Squalid Courtyard.—*The Conspiracy.*— Hugh, now very shabby, enters; looks round furtively, and knocks at a door, which is opened by an old woman. After a moment's conversation, he enters.

SCENE IX.—A Dirty Attic.—A villainous-looking man is leaning across a table asleep; on the table are bottles, glasses, clay pipes, etc. Hugh enters; they converse. (Bust view of the two plotting.) Stage view again. The bargain is concluded, and Hugh exits.

SCENE X.—The Drawing-room. Evening-time.—*Elsie pleads for Hugh's forgiveness.*—The lovers, in evening dress, are discussing Hugh; Elsie tries to make peace, but her lover is obdurate. Disappointed, she turns away, and takes up a book. A slight estrangement springs up; the new Earl saunters moodily through French window.

SCENE XI.—Top of Cliff. Blue for night effect. Bushes or other shelter at side.—*The Ambush.*—The heir is strolling along, sometimes pausing, thinking, and surveying the night. The ruffian, Hugh's accomplice, appears among the bushes, armed with iron bar; he hesitates about rushing out. The heir strolls on, stealthily shadowed by the ruffian. Hugh also appears in the bushes, urging his accomplice by signs to do his work.

SCENE XII.—The Drawing-room.—Elsie has put down her book; looks longingly at window; resolves to follow her lover and make up their little quarrel. Picks up a wrap, and exits through window.

SCENE XIII.—Top of Cliff.—*The Attack.*—Heir is leaning against a fence, smoking peacefully; in background are the two villains. The ruffian creeps up behind, and the bar is raised for the blow, when Elsie appears in distance, and utters a warning scream. The heir turns and fells the ruffian. Hugh dashes out, and

— 59 —

Figure 4.3 Scenario format in 1911; from E. J. Muddle (1911) *Picture Plays and How to Write Them*, London, The Picture Play Agency

referred to specific practice, suggesting that a format style was sufficiently common in 1910/11 to be regarded as established (though the agency of the manuals themselves in creating this practice cannot be discounted). Sample scenarios showed the title, the generic label (e.g. comedy), a list of principal characters or cast, a short synopsis (in the present tense), a list of locations attached to the relevant scene numbers, and the action, including inter-titles (see Figure 4.3). The emphasis was on plot and action.[20]

Figure 4.4 shows a page of an apparently unproduced scenario from perhaps 1913 or 1914, *The Darkest Hour* by William J. Elliott, who may have submitted it to Hepworth.[21] The 'half-quarto' style appears to have been one of the known conventions of the time,[22] but what is intriguing to the modern screenwriter is the mix of its stage conventions (the scene description, a sense of the proscenium arch in the placement of objects 'R' or 'L', and the main character 'discovered') with a clear understanding of continuity between the master scene and an inserted shot.

Shooting scripts as separate documents are not mentioned in the 1910s advice offered to would-be writers. This absence might suggest they did not exist, but a surviving script for the 14-minute *The Jewel Thieves Outwitted* (1913) suggests otherwise (see Figure 4.5). This is a handwritten foolscap page divided into scenes with basic action on the right-hand side of the page and the left-hand side left blank for notes, suggesting a more pragmatic concern with getting shots and

<u>S c e n e ... l.</u>
Room furnished as bed-sitting room. Window facing
camera, door L. A small bed and fireplace R. A
treadle sewing machine by window. A round table
in centre of room.

   Eva discovered, working at machine. Enter two
children, a boy and a girl. They run to Eva and
kiss her. She takes out a purse, gives them money,
sends them on an errand. They exit.

      Eva turns to window, as if in answer to a signal,
opens it, and leans out, talking.

   (INSERT. Flash from window of street below. Tom
standing by opposite gate, looking up, talking.)
BACK TO SCENE. Cresswell enters, sees purse, opens
it stealthily, extracts money, replaces it, exits.

    Eva shuts window, replaces purse in pocket, and
resumes her work.

Figure 4.4 Unpublished Scenario c.1913; William J. Elliott (c.1913) *The Darkest Hour.*
Nettlefold Special Collection, British Film Institute National Library

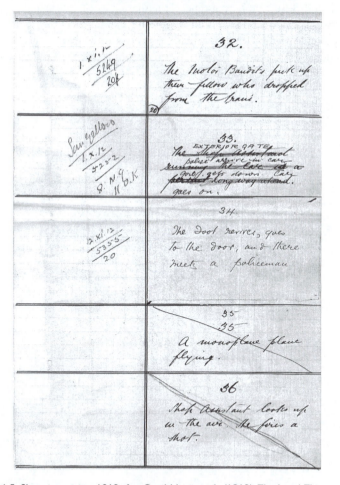

Figure 4.5 Shooting script, 1912, for Cecil Hepworth (1913) *The Jewel Thieves Outwitted.*
Fred Lake Special Collection, British Film Institute National Library.

recording takes. While it looks very different to the US-style 'continuity' in use at about the same time,[23] it has the same function of breaking up the script into shots and describing them in sufficient detail to be shot. The script appears to have been used for shooting in November 1912 by Cecil Hepworth, and includes amendments, notes of dates and footage shot (and if 'NG'; no good). Whether it was standard practice in his company to work from such a shot-list, or whether this was a personal way of working (like Lewin Fitzhamon's notebook), is not known.

The status of the main scenario (as opposed to documents used for shooting) is significant, because as writers wrote longer scripts they became more detailed and more technical. By the late 1910s the writer's version had become standardized in what has been described as 'the English style', where the construction of the script is both clearly about plot, and about specifying shots and other elements in detail (see Figure 4.6). Numbering reflects the master scene, but specific shots are included and allocated a letter within the master scene numbering system, thus privileging a sense of the scene over the shot. Scenes are sometimes also provided with sequence numbers and grouped – in this example (Figure 4.6) into episodes

```
MAIN:     "THE BACHELORS CLUB"  by I. ZANGWILL

SUB:      Scenario Adaptation by ELIOT STANNARD.

SUB:      Produced by ..

SUB:      Photography by .


                    Ep. 1.  Sc. 1.

SUB:      There is nothing half so sour in life as the awakening from
          Love's Young Dream.
          Exterior picturesque and fashionable Country Town Pub. Evening.
                Discovered coming towards camera two bachelors, one
          about 30, the other 35, and both in good spirits.  Between them
          walks Peter Parker, a man of 45.  In expression he is miserable.
          He drags his unfurled umbrella along the pavement after him.
          He has lost all pride in his personal appearance; his trousers
          are baggy, the collar of his overcoat is carelessly turned up,
          his bowler titled to the back of his head and his mood completely
          depressed.  His companions, one in smart tweeds with check
          cap and Burberry jauntily over his arm, the other in neat
          lounge with soft hat, natty bow tie and malacca cane.  They
          reach foreground, stopping at entrance to saloon and urge
          Peter Parker to come in and have one.  Peter Parker hangs back
          shaking his head.  The two bachelors step into the entrance of
          the saloon bar, still urging him to accompany them.

SUB:      But Peter Parker, in a fit of temporary insanity, has taken
          unto himself a wife, whose sole recommendation was her Bank
          Balance.
                Peter Parker, played by ..

                    Shot A.

          Close up Peter Parker from his friends' eye line.  He shakes
          his head dolefully, hesitates, takes out his watch, looks at it,
          shakes his head again and is about to turn miserably away when
          one of his friends entering past camera, steps up to him and taking
          him by arm, expostulates.  Parker, planting thirst, begins to give
          way and then with great self discipline and determination holds
          out one finger and says,

SUB:      "Righto, but only one."
```

Figure 4.6 'English style' screenplay 1921; Eliot Stannard (1921) *The Bachelors Club*. [format A] Fred Lake Special Collection, British Film Institute National Library

```
(214) EXT.COTTAGE GARDEN - SEMI LONG SHOT

          Paul and Jenny walking side by side-they
          are both happy-she tells Paul of her wonder-
          ful contentment-her pleasure in the garden-
          everything-she stretches out her arms in
          absolute abandon of happiness-Paul watches
          her with growing admiration-this action adds
          flame  to his growing like for the girl-he
          speaks to her tensely,gently,

T I T L E    "THERE IS ONLY ONE THING TO MAKE OUR
             EXPERIMENT ABSOLUTELY SUCCESSFUL"

          She looks at him-suddenly perplexed-
          he gazes down at her-makes a half movement-
          then stops,thinking-

(215) CLOSE UP PAUL

          C.U. Paul as he thinks,after half making
          a movement as though he would declare him-
          self to Jenny OVERLAPS DISSOLVE AS HE
          THINKS,TO SCENE OF HIS INAUGURATION AT
          BACHELOR'S CLUB,WHAT AWAITS HIM IF HE
          BREAKS HIS OATH

(216) EXT.GARDEN - SEMI LONG SHOT

          BACK TO: Paul pulls himself together-takes
          one of Jenny hands-talks to her-bids her
          forget what he has said-CUT

Note: This in view of Mr.Zangwill's note to hold the
          affair in suspense,and not play it too strong,which
          I think very good indeed.
```

Figure 4.7 Continuity-style script, 1921; Eliot Stannard (1921) *The Bachelors Club* [format C]. Fred Lake Special Collection, British Film Institute National Library.

– as well as into Acts, Reels or Parts synonymous with 1000 ft reels, or around 15 minutes each of screen time. Structure is therefore important on the pages of the English style script, and shots – though specified by the writer – are usually there to provide close-ups or other views of the action. They are shown as subordinate elements in the master scene. The informing poetics is not about constructing the film from shots, but about recording the action without missing out on detail. The other significant element is that the writer is here specifying all the detail, and assuming the director will follow the writer's instructions. There is evidence that scripts in this form of writer's draft, Format A,[24] were used in shooting, alongside scripts in another format, Format C (see Figure 4.7), which had shots numbered consecutively in the US continuity style and with the action written in a more prosaic style – less concerned with understanding motivation, for example.

Eliot Stannard's script for *The Bachelors' Club* (1921b) survives in both these formats, each with pencilled notes. My assumption is that the 'English style' script (format A) is what Stannard produced himself, and the continuity style (format C) is what the film company produced for the shoot. A. V. Bramble, the director, seems to have used both, though for what exact purposes is not clear.[25] The detail of format A shows that professional screenwriters were responsible for a detailed sense of the *whole* film, including specifying the shots, suggesting alternative locations and even the odd note rationalizing script suggestions. Kenelm Foss noted (1920: 23–4) that Stannard 'doped' his own scripts – that is, provided additional technical information such as a location list with scene numbers, or a list of essential props – suggesting that Stannard may have been more meticulous than most. However, it seems that until the mid-1920s the screenwriter's job was generally seen to be less 'introductory' and more central to the shooting process than might be seen today, and the script was expected to reflect both narrative construction and technical detail. In Stannard's *Mr Gilfil's Love Story* (1919) directed by Bramble, for example, a comparison of the script and the completed film shows close correlation (Macdonald, 2008). Around 10 per cent of the film comprises additional shots, such as close-ups breaking scenes up still further, but there is otherwise almost no deviation from the script, except where the director has not actually been able to achieve the drama required by the writer. This way of working may be representative – Stannard may even have been influential in establishing and maintaining this style of script – but the sense here that the writer leads and the director follows is at odds with more controlling stance of the director in the later 1920s and 1930s, during the rebalancing of the relationship between writer and director that presaged the *auteur* theory.

Screenwriting and film poetics

The inter-medial connection between theatre practices and early film production has been studied from a range of perspectives (Brewster and Jacobs 1997; Fitzsimmons and Street 2000; Burrows 2003; Gledhill 2003; Rushton 2004) including screenwriting (Salt 1992; Macdonald 2010). The screenwriting discourse of the 1910s was characterized by inter-medial borrowings and loanwords from mainly theatre practice, in the search for a vocabulary and principles applicable to fiction film narrative. An inter-medial 'bridge' was extending to the new practice, with the early manuals finding it necessary to explain differences in terms of established theatre practice. Manuals and screenplays commonly used theatrical terms such as 'business', and film terms like 'reel' were interchangeable with 'act' in some multi-reel filmscripts. Screenwriting-manual writers E. J. Muddle (1911) and C. E. Graham (1913) felt the need to explain 'enter' and 'exit' in relation to the camera's field of vision, and the term 'scene' was still sometimes used to mean 'shot' in 1917.[26] In dramatic construction the influence of the 'well-made play' was strong; the ideas of Gustav Freytag and Alfred Hennequin have been linked to film narrative construction, and there is a correlation of ideas between William Archer's 1913 textbook on writing for the stage, *Play-making*, and manuals like that of Ernest Dench (1914) (Salt 1992: 111–13; Macdonald 2010). Certainly screenwriters studied theatre practice; the screenwriter and director Adrian Brunel studied several such books in his youth including Archer's work.[27]

However, this is not simply a story of theatre practice becoming attuned to film in a 'linear march to modernity' (Gledhill 2003: 89) as one might assume from the increasing use of famous stage actors in films.[28] Nor is it a recognition of the importance of performative practices outside the narrational, as with the notion of a 'cinema of attractions' in early film.[29] Once screenwriting was established as a specialist practice, there was conscious discussion of what it should draw on for best practice, based on individual *habitus*. Gerald Turvey has noted that, while B & C's first film-makers (from around 1909) had backgrounds in music-hall, circus and popular entertainment, later employees brought experience from journalism and fiction writing as well as the legitimate theatre, and were beginning to rationalize their understanding of conceptualizing narrative fiction for the screen (2003: 85). In 1916, in his manual on film-making the director Harold Weston acknowledged a wide range of sources for film technique: painting, the theatre, the novel, poetry and still photography, as well as nodding across the Atlantic to admire films by D. W. Griffith and Thomas Ince (Weston 1916: 35). Eliot Stannard noted in 1920 that, while the scenario was 'an achievement in prose, it will rank with the Public purely as Drama [and] this being so it is the scenario-writer's business to visualize each scene he writes as "a picture"' (1920: 14).[30] Stannard was acknowledging the drama in 'artistic composition', in grouping and detail, as in painting. However, this notion of pictorial framing as a still picture – tableau-like – also suggests a view of film narration as a form of 'capture' rather than construction; of performance and presentation, rather than the creation through cutting of 'the illusion of a seamless fictional world that was fast becoming the norm' (Gledhill 2003: 93). What was in 'the picture' was what told the story, 'in the language of actions, which the heart must read', as actor-director-writer Henry Edwards put it (Gledhill 2003: 102). It was inside that picture-frame that performance and gesture conveyed, 'registered' or 'planted' the information which drove the narrative.[31]

For director Harold Weston in 1916 the basis for film narrative construction was integration, a quasi-Aristotelian unity that opposed the tendency to present 'a series of incidents insecurely linked together by a number of connecting scenes' (Turvey 2003: 87). Weston noted useful techniques like the close-up, and parallel narrative action (which he called 'dovetailing'), i.e. cross-cutting between two narrative strands in the manner of D. W. Griffith, converging at the moment of dramatic climax and thereby keeping the audience alert (Turvey 2003: 87).[32] Such unity required any adaptation to be a process of de- and reconstruction, involving analysing the original story in terms of incidents, psychology and analysis/explanation, 'in order to facilitate the elimination of superfluous characters, the possible reordering ... of events and the spacing out of film climaxes to fall at the end of a film reel' (Turvey 2003: 87). This process is no straight translation from one medium to the other, but is seen as a new piece of work; an 'adaptation proper' in Brian McFarlane's phrase (1996: 20), and the basis for any pretention to being a 'new art'.

Eliot Stannard also claimed the task of adaptation was one of reconstruction, defending his own 'modernizing' of Dickens or any other author as appropriate 'whenever I think the story will be made more vivid, clear and dramatic in picture form' (1918: 66). More generally he argued, through several articles in the late 1910s and in his 1920 manual, for the recognition of several principles not dissimilar to Weston's ideas, in a poetics of screenwriting: Theme, Simplicity, Continuity, Psychology, Atmosphere and Symbolism.[33] Everything must relate to the Theme – similar to Weston's unity – and Simplicity was for the benefit of the audience. There were therefore to be not too many characters or complications, incidents and situations, with every scene relating to the main purpose. Continuity meant narrative linearity – no flashbacks. Stannard's interest in character Psychology was in giving the character sufficient depth to interest an audience at a particular, more cultured level than seemed to be the case. Elevating the status of screenwriting to an art meant avoiding melodramatic, improbable incidents, which could be done through addressing Atmosphere; the combination of character and visual information that created the right psychological environment for the theme. In his *Mr Gilfil's Love Story* (1920), for example, Stannard counterpoints a rich but empty 'atmosphere' surrounding Wybrow's cynical seduction of Tina with the more bucolic, cheery sequences of courtship between the servants Knott and Dorcas (see Macdonald 2008).

Stannard's 'modern symbolism' included both the suggestion of general concepts such as freedom, and of elements of character, such as honest toil represented by dirty hands (Barr 1999; Macdonald 2008: 230). His way of creating symbolism is connected to his belief that the screenplay is a 'series of impressions or optical illusions' (1920: 18), and his account includes the observation (made *before* Kuleshov's 1921 experiments in the Soviet Union) that a sense of continuity is not about showing every event, but from inferring connection and causality from placing key scenes or shots together (1920: 18). Stannard's views fitted in well with the interest in montage shown later in the 1920s; Christine Gledhill's analysis of the British 'pictorial-theatrical-narrative' mode foregrounds director Cecil Hepworth's 'mosaic' style of construction (2003: 96), and Maurice Elvey's pictorialism developing into a 'collage [as a] form of construction approaching Soviet montage' in, for example, *Mademoiselle from Armentieres* (1926) (2003: 111). Gledhill notes Charles Barr traces this approach back to Eliot Stannard, but proposes that Elvey developed Stannard's symbolic approach into a 'flicker-book' style of construction which inhabited the image itself, 'cut up into various angles and points of view and recombined as in a kaleidoscope of continually shifting and differentiating perceptions' (2003: 111). She identifies this approach in 'the ultimate picture story of British cinema' (2003: 119), Hitchcock's *The Manxman* (1929), which was scripted by Stannard. Whether credited to writer or director, or both, it was this pictorial-theatrical mode that provided the roots for Hitchcock's techniques, an aesthetic allegiance later obscured by the 'very excellence' of those techniques, says Gledhill (2003: 122).

The lost art of inter-titles

In the early 1900s 'Living Pictures' tended to require some narrative explanation, especially when they were linked together as several scenes or tableaux. In the usual context of fairground exhibition live lecturers performed the same function as lantern-slide presenters, linking and interpreting the scenes on the screen. Joe Kember notes 'until at least 1907 in the United Kingdom the role of live performers seems to have been dominant', with the *Kine Weekly* noting the importance of these showmen (Kember 2006: 6). Barry Salt notes that the benefit of explanatory inter-titles was understood in 1901 with Robert Paul's *Scrooge; or Marley's Ghost*,[34] but they were not used much until multi-scene films became more common after 1903, with dialogue titles rare until after 1906 (1992: 59). How to explain the plot clearly to an audience was still an issue in 1909; while the *Bioscope* was of the opinion that a film should 'explain itself', *Kine Weekly* was announcing 'another useful novelty' in a 'special slide to accompany a film subject and bearing in easily read lettering a *préces* [sic] of the plot, so that the subject may be more easily followed by the audience' (Kember 2006: 6; *Kine Weekly* 1909). By 1908 inter-titles were common in perhaps half the films produced, mainly dramatic subjects (Fletcher 2003: 34), and 'sub-titling' was becoming one of the practices that formed a distinct specialization, an anonymous backroom operation.

Over the next two decades screenwriters continued to specify titles in their scenarios, 'but generally', said one writer in *Stoll's Editorial News* (assuring his readers that the director is largely responsible for sub-titles or, worse still, that they were the products of studio employees who had not yet developed any literary sense), 'it is found necessary to title the finished article' (1919: 3); that is, inter-titling was most usefully a post-production task. For the writer, incorporating subtitles in the script was on one level a pragmatic matter of explaining narrative or articulating speech, and on another was seen as an artistic asset with the power of poetic expression.[35] Eliot Stannard pointed out a title was useful in economically carrying forward the plot without the need for more scenes showing narrative progression (1920: 23), a style of storytelling that led to complaints in 1923 in *The Motion Picture Studio* that British films were serial incidents 'strung loosely together with a wonderful array of sub-titling to supply gaps in action' (Gledhill 2003: 160). However, Adrian Brunel was clear in 1921 about the control offered by inter-titles in assisting continuity, emphasizing changes in tone, mood and direction and helping make a character stand out (Gledhill 2003: 161). Once talkies arrived, the inter-title was not needed for dialogue and its use in explaining rapid changes or characters' inner struggles became stylistically awkward. There was overlap, with some films produced in both silent and sound versions but, as Andrew Buchanan pointed out in 1937, a comparison of the two would show that the vehicle for narrative comprehension had moved from the image to the dialogue.

> A formula has been established which … has diverted the film from its natural path and, attractive and smooth though the modern talking picture is, it quite definitely tends to retard the progress of the film which depends solely upon moving images.
>
> (Andrew Buchanan, in Gritten 2008: 272)

Buchanan, along with Paul Rotha, Adrian Brunel and others saw a schism developing between 'commercial' and aesthetic approaches, where dialogue was seen as opposing the intelligent, artistic potential of the medium – Buchanan's 'natural path'. The model was highbrow versus lowbrow; two such audiences would develop, one 'intellectual, desiring food for thought, the other, well ...' (Buchanan in Gritten 2008: 274).

'Authorship' and authority

With the professionalization of their roles, the relationship between screenwriter and director began a process of reorientation which, over some years, resulted in an increased level in the power and status of the director over the writer. In the 1910s, as specialist professionals working on scripts sometimes as long and even more technically complex than stage productions, together with the assumption drawn from theatre practice that the writer has artistic authority during rehearsal, the screenwriter – as 'author' – might claim a status equal to, and a role similar to, the playwright. In the theatre, the status of the playwright as an artist was established, but the status of the screenwriter was still under discussion in the film industry and elsewhere, mixed in with squabbles over how this 'cut and slash trade' treated the work of respectable novelists and other writers anyway. In the 1910s newly minted screenwriters attempted to form associations, lay down screenwriting principles and influence the debate over the artistic status of film narrative,[36] but it was status and power within company practice that was lacking. In 1921, novelist E. Temple Thurston complained that during a year working on scenario writing for Cecil Hepworth he 'had pleaded as an author, not for the right of decision in the matter of cast, costume, scenery but for the right ... to be allowed to have some influence of mind in the presentation of the story', like a theatre playwright (*Bioscope* 1921a: 33). He was refused, so wrote no more screenplays. Hepworth responded politely but robustly a few weeks later.

> [The screenwriter or 'author'] has an absolute and undeniable right to put as many stage directions in the scenario as he thinks fit ... [even] the exact pitch of every exterior view ... but where he stops he must let the other fellow carry on without claiming the right to vary.
>
> (*Bioscope* 1921b: 6)

Hepworth recognized the writer's pain in handing over his script-child to a foster parent, but this policy – of a major film producer – is indicative of a general realization that industrial demarcation dictated a withdrawal by the screenwriter from decision-making once the script was handed over. This was not on quasi-*auteurist* grounds that the director needed artistic control, but on the practical grounds that 'the other fellow' needed to get on with the job as outlined already, in detail, by the screenwriter.

By the end of the 1920s, this pragmatic approach, together with a stronger sense of film as a medium controlled through the camera, gave the director opportunities to take firmer control. Discussion and collaboration between writer and director was wide-ranging and ostensibly on equal terms, but the power balance had shifted further away from the writer. The 1927 exchange of comments between writer Eliot Stannard and director Adrian Brunel about the initial continuity script for *The Vortex* reveals a polite, but definite, struggle over detail that represents much more significant issues about film poetics in general. Brunel was by then a director with a firm personal sense of filmmaking in general – 'I always prefer to begin a sequence with an intriguing close-up' – and firm opinion on this particular story – 'the shop girl should smile and not have an irresistible desire to guffaw' (Brunel 1927: #1/1).[37] The writer Stannard replies with new ideas – 'open on tiny hammers hitting the wire strings of the instrument' – and his own view of film aesthetic – 'I am against trick devices which are confusing and artificial' (Brunel 1927: #2/1). Brunel then veers from the almost humble – 'what about dragging the camera back in sc.5 ...' – to the peremptory – 'no, not this' – while appealing to a shared sense of film style – 'all the 'Lubitchian [sic] possibilities of this shot need a few close-ups' (Brunel 1927: #2/1–2). Stannard, in what seems to be characteristically impatient fashion, resists Brunel for reasons of dramatic impact; 'over-use of close-ups may *kill* the real purpose of necessary close-ups which is to punch home a vital point' (Brunel 1927: #2/1; Stannard's emphasis). He continues to resist in a later exchange; 'it is *all* wrong, when establishing a new set to have endless close ups to point minor influences' (Brunel 1927: #4/1; Stannard's emphasis). Stannard believes a character's 'force and power' stems from being in the foreground of a shot, which would be lost if Brunel 'split it up with various camera angles' (Brunel 1927: #4/2). Brunel is polite but firm in his views.

By the time the exchange becomes waspish – when Brunel queries whether a doctor would do an examination in front of a house and Stannard replies curtly 'I have had my own lungs examined in the open more than once' – the differences show a fundamental disagreement over film style, though Stannard appears to know he will ultimately lose the argument (Brunel 1927: #4/3). The conclusion that might be drawn here is that Stannard is defending the older sense of how best to 'photograph' a drama, essentially capturing the action, while Brunel – a founder member of the Film Society and close associate of Ivor Montagu – sees the potential of constructing the narrative through shots. Here is a specific example of how the 're-invention, within the stabilising practices of a new international medium, of inherited pictorial, theatrical and storytelling traditions' (Gledhill 2009: 163) was negotiated on the ground; it demonstrates how the balance of power was shifting. This difference in approach may have been stressful for Stannard and similarly experienced writers in the latter part of the 1920s, who were trying to find a way past their focus on performance allied to plot selection and pace, towards an understanding of the camera as the instrument which provides power and emphasis in film narrative.

Conclusion

This story of the formation of screenwriting practice in Britain during the silent film period is a reminder that artistic, and industrial, practice is not based on a gradual and progressive discovery of a universal 'best' way of working. It is the product of labour organization and power relations, of influence and argument by certain people amongst others, of beliefs adopted from similar practice elsewhere, of commercial success or failure (and of what was perceived to be the cause), of cultural poetics and market pressures, and of technical development that can change the focus of film narrative construction from the pictorial to the conversational, with what seem to be radical consequences. As a document, the screenplay was developed from an adapted theatre-style script to a sophisticated and detailed narrative plan (while retaining many theatrical features). Once established in the 1910s, the professional screenwriter might have been accorded some of the status and influence of the stage playwright. By the end of the silent period, however, the British screenwriter was less of the lead collaborator or 'author' behind the film and more of a supplicant making suggestions, leaving more of the key decisions to others. Lower status meant more industrial constraint; screenwriters in the 1910s may have had some hopes of creating a new art of screenwriting, but by 1930 they were located rather more firmly in their industrial place as craftsmen and craftswomen.

Notes

1 There are 61 female names from 358 names credited as screenwriters in Gifford (2000) from 1895 to 1929.
2 There is also a terminological issue. The actual terms in use for 'screenwriter' were scenarist or scenario-writer, picture-playwright, photo-playwright, scriptwriter and author. The 'stage manager' of the early 1900s became 'producer' until the 1920s when the US use of the term 'director' began to be adopted more widely. In this chapter I use modern generic terms 'screenwriter' and 'director', for the avoidance of doubt.
3 Gifford (2000): item 00668.
4 Ethel Christian Ltd was still typing filmscripts in 1917, as shown by the script for The Laughing Cavalier (1917) by Eliot Stannard and A. V. Bramble. Other agencies, like the 'Rupert Typewriting and Shorthand Bureau' also included scenario work along with other 'general typewriting', including poetry, plays and author's manuscripts (advertisement in The Stage 23 Oct 1919: 32).
5 See Brewster (2004: 226–7) on the slightly later introduction of longer films in the USA.
6 Duration is problematic, as the rule of thumb of 16 frames per second (fps) for silent films is only an average. During the 1920s, projection speeds were specified individually by production companies, and could go as high as 24 fps; Gifford notes his estimations of length or duration are approximate (2000: p. xi). The standard 1000 ft reel could be oversize, and a 'standard' five-reeler of the 1920s could be anything from 4,500 to nearly 6,000 ft, and might last between 60 and 90 minutes (with thanks to Leo Enticknap, University of Leeds).
7 This total is conservative; buried within these statistics and counted as single titles are film drama series, popular since 1909/10 (Marlow-Mann 2002: 149), when the

success of characters such as Lt. Rose created a continuing demand. During the slump of the mid-1920s – as television has demonstrated again since – there was an obvious financial benefit in shooting many episodes involving the same characters in similar plots and locations.

8 This was the 20-minute His Reformation (1914). Elliott was told by London Films' Bannister Merwin that 'the play would require a lot of reconstruction' (Elliott 1915a).

9 An article 'Alma in Wonderland', Picturegoer (Dec. 1925: 48), reprinted in Morris (2008) suggests Reville was 16 when she joined London Films (Morris 2008: 36).

10 Ideal Films' Harry Rowson describes Stannard as providing a 'lay-out for a scenario' of the adaption of the life of Florence Nightingale in 1915, in one evening between 5pm and around 11pm (c.1951: 61). A few years later Stannard was being invited to give lectures, e.g. to the Stoll Picture Theatres Club on 'modernizing' in adaptation (1918).

11 Eliot Stannard and Sidney Bowkett, The Audacious Mr Squire, The Criterion, 19 Feb. 1924. Reviewed in The Stage 21 Feb. 1924: 16.

12 Gifford (2000): item 07406.

13 The quote from Gledhill refers to a belief questioned by Jon Burrows (2009: 160–1).

14 Consistent with the notion of an exhibitionist cinema of 'attractions'. See Gunning (1990).

15 Gifford (2000): item 00633.

16 The catalogue also mentions here a dissolve between each scene, a technique Hepworth remained fond of.

17 The titles mentioned here are not dialogue, but explanatory titles. Salt (1992: 107–8) refers to the American use of dialogue titles as extremely rare before 1908, but notes that this began to change towards the end of 1908, with an increasing use of them over the next few years. Salt suggests 'even' European films came to use such titles from 1909, but that by 1913 only 63 out of 171 American titles he has sampled used dialogue titles.

18 E. J. Muddle, an unknown film trade worker in Cecil Court, may have been the first screenwriting manual writer to be published in Britain in 1911. Colin Bennett of the Kine Weekly is also believed to have produced a manual in 1911, though I have seen only the 2nd edn (1913). Muddle quotes at length from an American article (1911: 46–8). An early 'The Picture Playwright' page can be seen in Bioscope 29 Aug. 1912: 631.

19 See Macdonald 2007, 2010.

20 For example, Muddle (1911: 48). See also John Cabourn (c.1927: 5). The Rise of the 'Plotter'.

21 Elliott may have written this during his first year of writing. He claimed to have studied the technique of photoplay writing 'for six months while working as a writer and journalist' (1915a), so this might have been an early exercise, and/or one of his rejections, albeit one kept by Hepworth (as it appears in the Nettlefold collection of Hepworth studio papers in the British Film Institute National Library).

22 Adrian Brunel later recalled his first efforts at writing 'bioscope plays', presumably around the early 1910s and 'carefully typed on half-quarto sheets' (1949: 20).

23 See Staiger (1985: 110, illustrations 12.10, 12.11, 12.12).

24 I have referred to these as Format A and Format C respectively (Macdonald 2007).

25 Adrian Brunel produced various definitions of film terms for the British Standards Institution in 1939, in which he describes a Scenario as 'the actual film story complete and written in sequences suitable for filming'; the Continuity as 'a detailed form of scenario giving a complete description of each scene'; and under Shooting Script is merely noted '(see Scenario)' (Brunel 1939).

26 Bramble and Stannard's The Laughing Cavalier (1917) is typed in a continuity style (which I have designated Format B) as a list of 'scenes', a few of which are shot variations within the master scene, e.g. scenes 137–9. This is similar to a US example

The Raiders (1913) given in Staiger (1985: 110–11). The 'English style' of script format (Format B) usually referred to shots when included in master scenes, but where they stood alone they were 'scenes'. See Macdonald (2010).

27   See Brunel (c.1911).

28   Gledhill notes (2003: 93) Jon Burrows's PhD thesis showing it was the policy of the Hepworth Company to work with distinguished screen actors; Henry Edwards had an arm's-length but productive relationship with Hepworth, as actor, writer and director. See also Brown (1986: 143–54).

29   See Gunning's essay (1990: 56–62), and Thomas Elsaesser's commentary on it in his introduction to Elsaesser and Barker (1990: 13–14).

30   'Picturization' was indeed a term used generally to describe the process of turning a written text into a scenario.

31   'Plant' was one of Stannard's most common instructions in his scripts (Macdonald 2008: 231).

32   This also bears a resemblance to what Christine Gledhill calls Maurice Elvey's 'flicker-book' approach to editing (2003: 108–11).

33   See Stannard's five articles in 1918 for Kinematograph and Lantern Weekly: 21 May: 76; 30 May: 79; 6 June: 97; 13 June: 81; 20 June: 87. See also Stannard (1920).

34   Gifford (2000): item 00484.

35   See Gledhill's account of 'a cinema of intertitles' (2003: 160–2). Gledhill notes Gertrude Allen's article in *Kine Weekly* in 1921, describing a film without a subtitle to it being like 'a wonderful box of bon-bons without a ribbon-bow' (2003: 161).

36   For example, Brunel was involved in a preliminary meeting of the 'Society of Scenario Writers' on 20 Nov. 1918 (letter from Frank Fowell, 1918).

37   These comments appear as anonymous typewritten notes about the script of The Vortex in the Adrian Brunel Special Collection at the British Film Institute National Library, item 43/4. There are four distinct documents, only one of which appears complete. I base my conclusions here on the assumption that these documents are indeed Brunel and Stannard exchanging comments (though they were possibly typed up by others), and that I have correctly identified which writer is speaking. This cannot be confirmed, although there is a letter from Stannard to Brunel after The Vortex was written, in which he refers to the 'awful difficulties' of The Vortex, and that Brunel 'may not see eye to eye with [him] always' (Stannard c.1927).

References

Archer, William (1913) *Play-Making: A Manual of Craftsmanship*, London: Chapman & Hall.

Barr, Charles, ed. (1986) *All our Yesterdays: 90 Years of British Cinema*, London: British Film Institute.

— (1999) *The English Hitchcock*, Moffat, Scotland: Cameron & Hollis, 6–31.

— (2009) 'Before *Blackmail*: Silent British Cinema', in Murphy (2009: 145–54).

Bennett, Colin N. (1913) *Handbook of Kinematography*, 2nd edn, London: Kine Weekly.

Bioscope (1921a) 'What's Wrong with the Films?', 28 July, p. 33.

— (1921b) 'The Author and the Film. Cecil Hepworth States the Producer's Case', 18 Aug., p. 6.

Bordwell, David, Staiger, Janet and Thompson, Kristin (1985) *The Classical Hollywood Cinema: Film Style and Mode of Production to 1960*, London: Routledge & Kegan Paul.

Brewster, Ben (2004) '"Traffic in Souls" (1913): an experiment in feature-length narrative construction', in Grieveson and Kramer (2004: 226–41).

Brewster, Ben and Jacobs, Lea (1997) *Theatre to Cinema*, Oxford: OUP.

Brown, Geoff (1986) '"Sister of the Stage": British Film and British Theatre', in Barr (1986: 143–67).

— (2008) 'Life among the Rats: The Cineaste-Writer in British Film Studios 1926–36', *Journal of British Cinema and Television* 5(2) (Nov.): 242–61.

Brown, Simon (2008) 'Blanche MacIntosh: First Lady of Screen Crime', paper at 11th BFI/Broadway Cinema Silent Cinema Conference, Nottingham, April.

Brunel, Adrian (c.1911) 'Random Jottings and Rough Notes', unpublished typescript, Brunel Special Collection, item 161/4, British Film Institute National Library.

— (1921) Letter to the Editor, *The Cinema*, 28 July, unpublished typescript, Brunel Special Collection, item 170, British Film Institute National Library. 2pp.

— (c.1922) '*Bitter Thoughts from a Scenario-Editor's Chair*', unpublished typescript, Brunel Special Collection, item 11/3, British Film Institute National Library. 9pp.

— (1927) '*The Vortex: Comments on Initial Continuity*', unpublished typescript, Brunel Special Collection, Item 43/4. British Film Institute National Library. 5pp.

— (1939) '*BSI Technical Committee CM/7 Glossary of Cinematograph Terms: List B The Studio-Production*', unpublished typescript, Brunel Special Collection, item 150/4, British Film Institute National Library. 2pp.

— (1949) *Nice Work*, London: Forbes Robertson.

— (n.d.) 'Past History', unpublished typescript, Brunel Special Collection, item 216, British Film Institute National Library.

Burrows, Jon (2003) *Legitimate Cinema: The Theatre Star in Silent British Films, 1908–1918*, Exeter: Exeter University Press.

— (2009) 'Big Studio Production in the Pre-Quota Years', in Murphy (2009: 155–62).

Burton, Alan and Porter, Laraine (2003) *Scene-Stealing: Sources for British Cinema before 1930*, Trowbridge: Flicks Books.

Cabourn, John (c.1927) '*1906–1927 and After*', unpublished typescript, Brunel Special Collection, item 29/1-2, British Film Institute National Library.

Clarendon Films (1913) Letter to Adrian Brunel, 31 July, unpublished typescript, Brunel Special Collection, item 170, British Film Institute National Library. 2pp.

De Beaurepaire, Gerald (1961) Unpublished letter to Denis Gifford 25 April 1961,.Denis Gifford Special Collection, British Film Institute National Library.

Elliott, William J. (1915a) 'The Picture Playwright', *Bioscope* 20 May, p. 793.

— (1915b) 'The Picture Playwright', *Bioscope* 10 June, p. 1059.

— (1915c) 'The Picture Playwright', *Bioscope* 23 Sept., p. 1409.

Elsaesser, Thomas and Barker, Adam, eds (1990) *Early Cinema: Space, Frame Narrative*, London: BFI.

Elvey, Maurice (1919) 'How does Maurice Elvey Make a Picture?', *Stoll's Editorial News* 2(6), 25 Dec., p. 1.

— (1920) 'Why there are No British Made Stars', *Stoll's Editorial News* 3(12), 5 Aug., p. 7.

Fitzsimmons, Linda, and Street, Sarah, eds (2000) *Moving Performance: British Stage and Screen 1890s–1920s*, Trowbridge: Flicks Books.

Fletcher, Tony (2003) 'The Evolution of the Story-Film in Britain 1896–1909: Some Observations', in Burton and Porter (2003: 29–35).

Foss, Kenelm (1920) *The Work of a Film Producer*, London: Standard Art Book Co.

Fowell, Frank (1918) *Letter to Adrian Brunel*, MS, Brunel Collection, British Film Institute National Library, item 216, unpublished typescript, Brunel Special Collection, Item 216, British Film Institute National Library. 1p.

Fullerton, John, ed. (1998) *Celebrating 1895: The Centenary of Cinema*, Sydney: John Libbey.

Gifford, Denis (1986) 'Fitz: The Old Man of the Screen', in Barr (1986: 314–20).

— (2000) *British Film Catalogue*, i. *Fiction Film, 1895–1994*, London: Fitzroy Dearborn.

Gledhill, Christine (2003) *Reframing British Cinema 1918–1928: Between Restraint and Passion*, London: British Film Institute.

— (2009) 'Late Silent Britain', in Murphy (2009: 163–76).

Grieveson, Lee and Kramer, Peter (2004) The Silent Cinema Reader. London, Routledge.

Gritten, Daniel (2008) '"The Technique of the Talkie": Screenwriting Manuals and the Coming of Sound to British Cinema', *Journal of British Cinema and Television* 5(2) (Nov.): 262–79.

Gunning, Tom (1990) 'The Cinema of Attractions: Early Film, its Spectator and the Avant-Garde', in Elsaesser and Barker (1990: 56–62).

Hayward, Lydia (1927) 'Concerning Scenarios', *Bioscope* 18 June, p. 155.

Hepworth, Cecil M. (1897) *Animated Photography: The ABC of the Cinematograph*, London: Hazell, Watson & Viney.

— (1951) *Came the Dawn. Memories of a Film Pioneer*, London: Phoenix House.

Higson, Andrew, ed. (2002) *Young and Innocent? The Cinema in Britain 1896–1930*, Exeter: University of Exeter Press.

Kember, Joe (2006) 'The Cinema of Affections: The Transformation of Authorship in British Cinema before 1907', *The Velvet Light Trap* 57 (Spring): 3–16.

Kine Weekly (1907a) 'The Inner Side of Film-Making: The Requirements of the Film Plot', 20 June, p. 85.

Kine Weekly (1907b) [Untitled article], 27 June, p. 98.

— (1909) 'Film Plots on Slides', 1 April.

Loughney, Patrick (1990) 'In the Beginning Was the Word: Six Pre-Griffith Motion Picture Scenarios', in Elsaesser and Barker (1990: 211–19).

Low, Rachel (1949) *The History of the British Film 1906–1914*, London: George Allen and Unwin.

— (1950) *The History of the British Film 1914–1918*, London: George Allen & Unwin.

— (1971) *The History of the British Film 1918–1929*, London: George Allen & Unwin.

— and Manvell, Roger (1948) *The History of the British Film 1896–1906*, London: George Allen & Unwin.

Macdonald, Ian W. (2007) 'The Struggle for the Silents: The British Screenwriter from 1910 to 1930', *Journal of Media Practice* 8(2): 115–28.

— (2008) '"Mr. Gilfil's Love Story": The Well-Made Screenplay in 1920', *Journal of British Cinema and Television* 5(2): 223–41.

— (2009) 'The Silent Screenwriter: The Re-Discovered Scripts of Eliot Stannard', *Comparative Critical Studies* 385–400.

— (2010) 'Forming the Craft: Play-Writing and Photoplay-Writing in Britain in the 1910s', *Early Popular Visual Culture* 8(1) (April): 73–87.

Marlow-Mann, Alex (2002) 'British Series and Serials in the Silent Era', in Higson (2002: 147–61).

McFarlane, Brian (1996) Novel to Film. An introduction to the theory of adaptation. Oxford, Clarendon

Montefiore, Victor (1915) *A Few Hints on How to Write a Picture-Play: Reprinted from Pictures and the Picturegoer*, London: The Pictures Ltd.

Morris, Natalie (2008) 'The Early Career of Alma Reville', *Hitchcock Annual* 15 (2006-07): 1–37.

Muddle, E. J., ed. (1911) *Picture Plays and How to Write them*, London: Picture Play Agency.

Murphy, Robert, ed. (2009) *The British Cinema Book*, 3rd edn, Basingstoke: Palgrave Macmillan.

Newey, Katherine (2000) 'Women and Early British Film: Finding a Screen of Her O'wn. in Fitzsimmons and Street (2000: 151-65).

Olsson, Jan (1998) 'Magnified Discourse: Screenplays and Censorship in Swedish Cinema of the 1910s', in Fullerton (1998: 239–52).

Raynauld, Isabelle (1997) 'Written Stories of Early Cinema: Screenwriting Practices in the First Twenty Years of France', *Film History* 9: 257–68.

Reville, Alma (1925) 'Alma in Wonderland', in Morris (2008: 35–7).

Rowson, Harry (*c*.1951) '"Ideals" of Wardour Street', MS, 196pp. (author's collection).

Rushton, Richard (2004) 'Early Classical and Modern Cinema: Absorption and Theatricality', *Screen* 45(3): 226–44.

Salt, Barry (1992) *Film Style and Technology: History and Analysis*, 2nd edn, London: Starword.

Staiger, Janet (1985) 'The Hollywood Mode of Production to 1930', in Bordwell *et al.* (1985: 85–153).

Stannard, Eliot (1917) 'The Use of Symbols in Scenarios: The Coming Film Version of "Justice"', *Kinematograph and Lantern Weekly* 12 July, p. 108.

— (1918) 'An Open Letter to my Godfather: Should Dickens be Modernised?', *Kinematograph and Lantern Weekly* 18 April, p. 66.

— (1920) *Writing Screen Plays*, London: Standard Art Book Co.

— (1921a) 'Advice to Authors Submitting Work to Film-Manufacturing Companies', *The Author* (July): 139–41.

— (1921b) 'The Bachelors Club', TS, Fred Lake Special Collection, British Film Institute National Library.

— (*c*.1927) [Letter to Adrian Brunel], unpublished typescript, Brunel Special Collection, item 112/5, British Film Institute National Library. 3pp.

Stannard, Eliot, and A. V. Bramble (1917) 'The Laughing Cavalier', TS, Fred Lake Special Collection, British Film Institute National Library, 38pp.

Stoll's Editorial News (1919) 31 July, p. 3.

The Times (1958) 'Obituary: W. P. Lipscomb', 31 July.

Tom-Gallon, Nellie (1920) 'The Dramatist and the Screen', *Stoll's Editorial News* 2(21), 8 April, p. 7.

Turvey, Gerry (2003) 'Enter the Intellectuals: Eliot Stannard, Harold Weston and the Discourse on Cinema and Art', in Burton and Porter (2003: 85–93).

Weston, Harold (1916) *The Art of Photo-Play Writing*, London: McBride, Nast & Co.

Part II

Development, craft and process

Chapter 5

An impossible task?

Scripting *The Chilian Club*

Andrew Spicer

Introduction

This chapter will explore the multifarious drafting and redrafting of scripts and full screenplays for a film based on George Shipway's controversial political satire *The Chilian Club* (1971), the story of a quartet of elderly assassins – former army officers – who believe they are saving their country from Communist subversion. Although *The Chilian Club* was never produced, ten complete adaptations were written involving four different hands – writer-directors Peter Collinson and Mike Hodges, Benny Green, the well-known radio scriptwriter and broadcaster, and Michael Klinger who was to have been the film's producer – over a six-year period (1972–7). As discussions of screenwriting often emphasize (Rilla 1973: 12–16; Cook and Spicer 2008: 213–16; Maras 2009: 11–15), it is important to establish what is understood to be the object of study. Thus, although there will be a detailed examination of the scripts themselves and the aesthetic difficulties of realizing Shipway's novel, the chapter will also pay close attention to the fluctuating nature of the collaborations involved and contextual factors that shaped them. This was a period of exceptional volatility and uncertainty in the British film industry, and Klinger, as an independent producer, faced extreme difficulties that had a direct bearing on his attempts to film *The Chilian Club*.

Figure 5.1 The strapline for *Klinger News* with a typical headline; courtesy of Tony Klinger

My analysis of the deeper forces at work in attempting to realize *The Chilian Club* will be based on hitherto unused material in the University of the West of England's Michael Klinger Papers that shed light on the convoluted relationships between screenwriters, distributors, potential investors, public bodies and large corporations, all pivoting round the figure of Michael Klinger as the producer. This material has been supplemented by articles in the trade press and a detailed interview with Klinger's son Tony, who worked as an assistant to his father from 1972 onwards and was thus intimately involved in the project himself.

George Shipway's *The Chilian Club*

Shipway's novel forms part of a minor subgenre in British fiction, the assassination thriller. Its most influential forerunners include J. M. Barrie's *Better Dead* (1896), Edgar Wallace's *The Four Just Men* (1905) and its sequels, G. K. Chesterton's *The Man Who Was Thursday* (1908) and Jack London's *The Assassination Bureau, Ltd.*, begun in 1910, but completed by Robert L. Fish in 1963 and filmed in 1969. Wallace's novel, filmed in 1921 and 1939 and broadcast as a television series in 1959, was the closest prototype, depicting an international quartet of assassins dedicated to punishing wrongdoers who are beyond the law. The four just men are not animated by partisan political motives but fighting for justice, acting to prevent what they perceive as a threat to the moral health of society.

Shipway's novel is unmistakably right-wing, the product of his classically English upper-middle-class education, attending Clifton College and Sandhurst before serving in the Indian Imperial Cavalry from 1928 to 1947. On retirement from the army, Shipway became a teacher at a boys' school in Berkshire and gradually established a reputation as a writer of action-packed historical novels, including *Imperial Governor* (1968) and *Knight in Anarchy* (1969) (Fisk 2003: 4–5). As a political satire, *The Chilian Club* was a departure that Shipway subtitled 'A Diversion', but it has an important historical dimension, beginning with a lengthy prologue detailing the bloody farce of the battle of Chilianwala in India (1849) in which the 6th Hussars, a cavalry regiment commanded by Viscount Cardross, disgraced itself. In the aftermath, Cardross converted his London house into a club as a refuge for his blackballed officers who had been ostracized by polite society as the 'Chilianwala cravens'. Over time, the Chilian (a contracted form of Chilianwala) Club became

> a haven for elderly men who found shelter there from the disconcerting ferment of a modern, alien world; men with the outlook and manners of a vanished age, moulded by the confines of their caste, disciplined by a lifetime's service, arrogant, intolerant – and often ruthless.
>
> (Shipway 1971: 10)

This is Shipway's great theme, men at odds with the modern world, adrift in a present-day England that has become paralysed by strikes and left-wing political activism resulting in race riots, food rationing, transport chaos and rampant inflation. The four Club members who decide to 'rescue' their country from becoming a communist state and a 'Russian satellite' (ibid., 23) – General Sir Henry Mornay, Lieutenant-Colonel Hugo Mayne-Amaury, Brigadier Charles Cotterell and Major Jimmy Curtis – use information gleaned from Mornay's nephew, Group Captain Geoffrey Emtage now in Intelligence, to execute a series of assassinations of both hard and soft left leaders. Courtesy of Sergeant-Major Spragge, the eavesdropping batman at their Club, the quartet recruit a younger man, Captain Nicolas Audenard, a mercenary killer and fellow anti-communist, to dispose of three communist student union agitators. There is an extended subplot involving Mayne-Amaury's niece Sally and her student lover. In a surreal denouement, the co-conspirators forestall the attempt of the Prime Minister – recognizably Harold Wilson – to sell a new super-weapon, ENEMA (the Electronic Neutralization of Earth's Magnetic Attraction), to the Russians. However, they cannot prevent Stonehenge, the target chosen to prove ENEMA's power to his paymasters, being sent into orbit. Blithely unaware that their actions throughout have been manipulated by Emtage and his controller, Sir Nigel Penworth, to dispose of 'undesirable elements', the three remaining 'crusaders' – having blundered, Curtis kills himself rather than jeopardize the others – discuss plans for further assassinations.

Shipway maintains a light tone by emphasizing that the assassins succeed as much through lucky blunders as daring and military precision and he intersperses the plotting and killings with comic scenes in the Edwardian elegance of Mrs Arbuthnot's superior brothel in Half Moon Street, where the vivacious Coralie Cordell plies her trade. However, the overtly farcical elements never obscure Shipway's underlying purpose to delineate the frustrations and blighted hopes of a particular class and generation emasculated by the loss of empire: 'old men nurtured in the disciplines and traditions of a vanished age. They were young when England ruled the world; their manhood saw her empire shredded, her glory tarnished' (ibid., 207). The most powerful moments in the novel tap into this emotional core, as in Mornay's diatribe to the others about the meaninglessness of their existence (ibid., 61) and in the flashbacks during individual assassinations when each of the four recollect the blunders that tarnished their Second World War service, the particular ghosts they are trying to exorcize.

The Chilian Club was successful: published in America (as *The Yellow Room*, an allusion to the windowless chamber in the Club where the four men meet) and reissued as a Granada paperback in 1972. It tapped into a deep stratum of right-wing thinking in post-war British culture that harboured genuine cold war fears of increasing Soviet power and influence and the need for extraordinary measures to combat this (see Hewison 1988; Shaw 2001) that was most popularly displayed in Ian Fleming's James Bond novels and some of the earlier film adaptations (see Bennett and Woollacott 1987). The currency of its central ideas can be indicated by Chapman Pincher's article 'The Secret Vigilantes' in the *Daily Express* (1 Feb. 1974), which stated that a secret group has been set up 'to combat the Reds' who had been infiltrating unions, workplaces and universities. There were also strong rumours of a right-wing *coup d'état* against Wilson in 1974 in which the Intelligence services were involved.[1] However, *The Chilian Club*'s politics were highly controversial: lauded by reviewers in the Conservative press but vilified by those of a left-liberal persuasion.

Genesis of the first screenplay: Peter Collinson, August 1972

Even before its re-publication in paperback, the rights to Shipway's novel had been bought, for £7,750, on 31 May 1971 by Tigon Films.[2] Tigon was part of a group of companies controlled by Laurie Marsh, a shrewd and opportunistic businessman who had made his millions in property as managing director of Star Holdings before moving into the film industry in the late 1960s (Hamilton 2005: 49, 124). Peter Collinson was contracted by Tigon (for £5,000) to direct and also to write the first screenplay.[3] The production was advertised in *Today's Cinema* on 8 October 1971. Collinson retains the novel's central structure of a succession of assassinations, but, either through inexperience – although an established director, this was his first screenplay – or to keep within Tigon's modest projected budget of £150,000 (ibid., 294), Collinson excises entirely the novel's historical prologue that actually explains the origins and significance of the Chilian Club. Collinson substitutes a title sequence depicting a strike-bound, paralyzed London through a montage of black and white photographs 'showing dole queues and the broken faces that go with being out of work … Student sit-ins, empty railways, strikes, empty docks, empty roads, race riots.' Also cut, almost entirely, are the scenes in the bordello that provided Shipway with a rich source of comedy. Collinson is more even-handed politically: one of the victims is right-wing; another a progressive free-thinker rather than communist sympathizer. He retains the surreal/sci-fi denouement on Salisbury Plain, but the three remaining protagonists are killed along with the Prime Minister. The script ends on a sardonic note, Audenard commenting that 'old soldiers never die – they only float away …', an indication that Collinson rather lacked a real feeling for the material, an understanding of the potential of the central characters as engagingly misguided protagonists.

However, by the time Collinson's script had been completed in August 1972, Marsh had severed his ties with Tigon and had asked Michael Klinger to produce.[4] Klinger, who had given Collinson his first break as a director with the low-budget absurdist thriller *The Penthouse* (1967), was rapidly establishing himself as the most important independent producer in Britain (see Spicer 2010). Although a Jewish socialist whose ideological perspective and values were antithetical to Shipway's, Klinger adored the anarchic idea that formed the basis of *The Chilian Club* and recognized its potential as an Ealingesque comedy whose politics could be recast (Klinger 2009). His extensive comments on Collinson's script show Klinger's frustration with its aesthetic limitations, especially the ponderous literalism with which expository openings to numerous scenes are lifted wholesale from the novel, and its lack of pace and action. Even more significantly, Klinger judged that Collinson had failed to reproduce Shipway's adroit mixing of comedy – in several places he wrote 'lighter' in the margins – with a depth of characterization that invites audience involvement.[5] In particular, he wanted the novel's historical opening to be retained, Mrs Arbuthnot and Coralie firmly established as important characters and the killings to be more imaginatively handled. Overall, Klinger was convinced that Collinson's script could not be the basis for a film version and argued for a major rewrite.[6]

The second script: Benny Green, November 1972

As often during this period, Klinger turned to his friend Benny Green, a jazz saxophonist who had transmuted into a broadcaster and prolific writer, especially of radio documentary scripts, and who was renowned for his wit and erudition as film critic for *Punch* and literary critic for *The Spectator* (Gammond 2004). The pair had met while both were members of the West Central Jewish Lads Club, enjoying 'its beguiling amalgam of English manners and immigrant anarchism' (Green 2000: 112). As noted, it was the anarchic element of Shipway's novel that fundamentally attracted Klinger, and Green was similarly attuned to that mode as a connoisseur of English eccentricities and humour – he later wrote a perceptive biography of P. G. Wodehouse (1981). Although Green worked on his own at this point, he was entirely conversant with Klinger's reservations about Collinson's version and rewrote the script accordingly.

Green's script not only reinstates the novel's historical prologue but also enlarges it by offering a conspectus of British military glories shown on a map before alighting on the Chilianwala disaster. A series of vignettes follows, charting the disgraced officers' social exclusion and the establishment of the Club. By setting the story slightly in the future (the country is in the sixth year of strikes), Green is able to accentuate the current chaos where there is fighting, rioting and looting on the streets, and exaggerate the comedy – as in Mornay's Rolls being drawn by horses as he makes his way to the Club. Green also extends the political even-handedness present in Collinson's script by making the third victim overtly fascist (Walter Shorthouse, Chairman of the National British Committee) and having the Prime Minister sell out to an international consortium rather than the Russians. All the assassinations are funnier and more inventive, notably those of Sidney Rinker the union leader and Abdul Sharif the head of the Black Power movement. For both Green and Klinger, these figures are legitimate targets because they are anti-democratic rather than because they are left-wing (Klinger 2009). Green makes the Half Moon Street bordello central to the plot, and introduces Vandenkatz, an American ambassador, who assails Mayne-Amaury's niece Sally, mistaking her for one of the prostitutes. At this point the script turns into something of a sex romp as she rushes around semi-naked before being rescued by Audenard. Mrs Arbuthnot is now in league with Emtage and Penworth and the emphasis on the quartet's manipulation becomes more overt. Shipway's denouement on Salisbury Plain is retained, but the ending is much more upbeat with all four protagonists surviving, toasting the empty coffin of the Prime Minister (who has been sent into orbit rather than Stonehenge) as it passes the Club in an ironic state funeral.

Klinger clearly thought Green's script a major improvement aesthetically on Collinson's, finding it more crisply focused on the central characters, swift-moving and funnier, but he expressed a number of reservations.[7] Some of these were items of detail. For instance, Klinger noted that Shorthouse's death – blown up as he kicks a ball to start a football match – was not original as it had been used before in *The Green Man*.[8] He thought Shipway's device of a super weapon 'needs changing for something else more believable'. However, he was more exercised by the overall tone. Klinger judged the sex scenes possibly overdone, that Sally's character had been coarsened, and that some of the comic scenes were 'over the top … it's almost Monty Python'. He argued that the comedy 'should be blacker' because 'there are more serious overtones such as famine etc. which could be touched upon to give credibility to our anti-heroes'; he wanted an additional counter-argument against the murders, thus lending greater weight to their decision to proceed. Above all, Klinger felt that Shipway's slow-building understanding of the men's desperation and the poignancy of the mournful future that faces them had been lost in Green's adaptation and urged that the flashbacks to war be retained to give the characters greater depth. Klinger concluded his comments by insisting: 'it must be emphasized that these people aren't fanatic Right wingers or Socialists or Liberals but as De Gaulle once said are above politics'.[9] This comment may offer a central clue as to Klinger's interest in Shipway's novel: that he identified with aspects of the protagonists' rage and frustration with British society as a fellow outsider and the need for drastic action.

Some of Klinger's reservations about the revised script were echoed by Marsh: 'I feel that the first 30 pages have taken the view which is too extreme as to the extent of the effect on the country to an almost farcical level i.e. a strike for 3 yrs. and de-valuation down to approx. 1/50th of value is so far-fetched that it would be unbelievable'; he urged Klinger to make the story more credible.[10] However, although Marsh stated that he was 'personally very keen' to have *The Chilian Club* made and wants to be 'more involved than usual' in its production, he was in the process of withdrawing, like so many others, from participating in film production (Hamilton 2005: 232; see also Higson 1994: 219–21). For his part, Klinger had become increasingly exasperated by Marsh's reluctance to pay the negotiated fees.[11] Convinced of the film's potential, Klinger went his own way, eventually purchasing the rights from Marsh.[12] Klinger took the unusual step of co-writing a third script (December 1972) with Green that incorporated most of the changes he had suggested, in particular extending and deepening the characterization of the four protagonists. Shipway's ending was in fact retained but with the final moments focusing more emphatically on 'our old heroes' who are pleased to see 'everything moving again'.

This shift from entrepreneur to active creative agent indicates the importance of the project for Klinger. However, the new script was something of a compromise – one that would haunt the entire project – between fidelity to Shipway's conception (though with the politics changed) and a broader, more farcical comedy. James Mason, an obvious choice to play Mornay, succinctly summed up the problem when he wrote to Klinger expressing his dislike of the 'irrelevant sex adventures' because they undermined 'the basic situation [that] is a very real one and could be dramatized in a very realistic manner which lends itself to plenty of grim humour'.[13]

Rejections of the Green–Klinger screenplay and an intermission

Mason echoed Klinger's own misgivings, but Klinger was acutely aware of the problems of finding an audience for his film and was anxious to press ahead with a production. *The Chilian Club*'s projected budget was now around £400,000, significantly more than Marsh's original figure, but in line with Klinger's ambitions as a producer and his conviction that the film would only work with top-line British stars and an experienced director.[14] However, having severed his ties with Marsh, Klinger had to obtain funding in what had become an exceptionally hostile environment; one in which the medium-budgeted film that could be expected to make a modest profit in the domestic marketplace had almost vanished as British film production contracted and cinema-going declined (Wood 1983: 3–5). In addition to these general problems, Klinger faced specific difficulties with *The Chilian Club* because of its subject matter: too parochial and too political. John Heyman at World Film Services declined to become involved because: 'I really do feel that this is too British for a territorial sales organisation, and I don't think the script is as good as you seem to think it would be.'[15] Danton Rissner, United Artists' Vice President in charge of East Coast and European Productions, also rejected *The Chilian Club* because although he thought it was 'an interesting idea and reminiscent of "Kind Hearts and Coronets"',[16] he judged Klinger's intended film would not be 'commercially viable outside of the United Kingdom. Since the market here in the U.K. and Commonwealth is so restricted, it's a really tough job to recoup any film that costs more than £2–300,000.'[17]

Rissner's comments underline the general difficulties British producers faced in a rapidly shrinking domestic market and thus the necessity to appeal to an international audience, but he also judged that it was *The Chilian Club*'s explicit politics rather than its Britishness that constituted the major obstacle:

> I also wonder whether in fact one can poke fun or dissipate [sic] national institutions – i.e. Black Power figures, Union leaders etc., without making the movie less than a quasi-political film. By dealing with a country in the throes of economic disaster, it may turn the movie around from an overtly comic milieu to one that purports to be making a comment on the political climate of today. If anything, 'Coronets' dealt with a more passive structure – that of a man whose birthright was taken away from him, and who attempted to retain it by way of a series of murders … which I believe is much more

simplistic and does not take on the afore-mentioned political and nationalistic movements.[18]

Rissner and Klinger were on first-name terms and it is clear that he would like to support the project, but he would also have been mindful that United Artists had backed Klinger's previous black comedy, *Pulp* (1972), whose financial returns had been relatively poor, hence the need to be cautious about a property that did not fit existing marketing categories and whose politics, especially the animus against Black Power leaders, might create significant problems for American audiences. Although Rissner would have been well aware of the potential of Ealingesque comedies which had succeeded in America despite their Britishness (see Street 2002: 154–7), this was outweighed by *The Chilian Club*'s problematic politics.

Turning to indigenous sources that might be expected to support a resonantly British film, Klinger fared no better; in fact their attitude was noticeably cooler. In May 1973, F. S. Poole, managing director of the largest British production company, Rank, judging *The Chilian Club* inferior to *The League of Gentlemen*,[19] wrote to Klinger saying that he could not commit the company to a project 'in which you were asking for complete participation'.[20] Eighteen months later, in December 1974, Sir John Terry, chairman of the National Film Finance Corporation, wrote stating that this government body was not prepared to finance either the film or its pre-production and expressed reservations about the script.[21]

Figure 5.2 Michael Klinger in his pomp: on the set of *Gold* (1974); courtesy of Tony Klinger

During this period Klinger had become preoccupied with three demanding and complex international productions, *Rachel's Man* (1974), *Gold* (1974) and *Shout at the Devil* (1976). A further eighteen months elapsed, by which time post-production had been completed on *Shout*, before Klinger was ready to resume serious work on *The Chilian Club*. Klinger now judged that it would be a suitable project for Mike Hodges. Klinger had given Hodges his first opportunity to direct a feature film (*Get Carter*, 1971) and had supported him as *Pulp*'s writer-director, which, despite its poor performance at the box office, Klinger felt had almost worked brilliantly, a strong indication that he could make a success of *The Chilian Club*. Klinger was also conscious that Hodges had had a rough ride with his American films and was anxious to give him an opportunity to re-establish his career in Britain (Klinger 2009). Hodges was hired by Klinger's company Metropic and by October 1976 had completed his draft script.[22]

The Mike Hodges's scripts

Although Hodges was a friend, he considered himself an *auteur*, and, dedicating his script to 'Billy Wilder and Alfred Hitchcock', was prepared not only to ignore the existing script but to be much more free-ranging in his approach to Shipway's original. Hodges noted on the title-page of his draft that it is 'loosely based on a book of the same name'. Although Hodges' erudite script is more literary – making reference to Gilbert and Sullivan, Kipling and Somerset Maugham – he appears to have had little interest in the men's cause or their motivations, reconstructing *The Chilian Club* as a lightweight farce with an underlying theme of violence and sexual deviance. London is depicted as being in complete confusion and chaos: looting and street robberies are commonplace and police battle routinely with gunmen. The historical element is given parenthetically by a guide explaining the origins of the Club to a group of Japanese tourists being flour-bombed by Spragge from an upstairs window of the Club. The main characters become broad caricatures: Curtis is stone deaf and cannot get batteries for his hearing-aid during the privations, Mayne-Amaury has an eye-patch and is a closet homosexual known as Gladys, while their victims are a motley collection of disparate figures some of whom, including Curtis's turf accountant, are killed because they are personally inconvenient, not linked to any cause. The deaths, which are often bizarre, include several that are a case of mistaken identity, including the Bishop of Camberwell, killed in Arbuthnot's brothel. However, the conspirators reflect that, because he was a fetishist who wore women's underwear, his killing is excusable, even justifiable. Hodges, aware of the film's topicality, makes several of the victims readily identifiable with their real-life counterparts, including Taffy Williams, an obvious caricature of Clive Jenkins, the leader of the Association of Scientific, Technical and Mangerial Staffs. There is a protracted joke about the hordes of 'commie' waiters interviewed by the police as suspects in the American Ambassador's death whose broken English creates endless confusion, and rather coarse incidental humour including Emtage's wife deserting him for a fishmonger:

'I think it was the smell that attracted her.' In keeping with the absurdist nature of Hodges's approach, the ending is bathetic: Mornay dies of a heart attack as Emtage breaks the news to him that the Prime Minister is their next target.

At Klinger's instruction, Hodges prepared a second draft, completed by 10 December 1976, but the only major change was the ending in which the old soldiers capture the Prime Minister and place him in Madame Tussaud's. However, Hodges's broad-brush absurdist treatment was at odds with Klinger's fundamental conception of *The Chilian Club* and Klinger sent a very extensive set of notes on the second draft.[23] In reply, Hodges made a number of minor alterations and expressed his satisfaction with the revisions: 'For myself, I now find the script concise, fast, zany and exactly the right length for a farce. Hopefully it is also funny!'[24] Klinger was far from satisfied with Hodges's 'zany' version and again intervened directly in the actual scripting. The new screenplay (the sixth overall), co-written by Hodges and Klinger, opens with a voiceover that recounts the Club's history, makes the central characters more rounded and believable and establishes that they have a recognizable cause; Hodges's grosser jokes are eliminated.

The return of Benny Green

Klinger remained deeply dissatisfied with the co-written script and turned again to Benny Green. Unsurprisingly, the joint Hodges–Klinger–Green script (version seven) shifts back decisively to Green's earlier conception. The historical prologue shown in animated sequences is reinstated, the central characters given more credibility and the deaths became an amalgam of those in Green's earlier version and some of Hodges's inventions, but with a far greater stress on the old soldiers' even-handedness in their choice of victim because of their 'sense of fair play'. Their victims, in their various ways, all deserve to die. However, Hodges's stress on lubricity and a variety of sexual practices is retained. It is now the homosexual Dapier Bennett-Hamilton who is fomenting trouble at the universities and although the ENEMA device is reintroduced, Owen Morgan, the corrupt and venal Prime Minister, collapses and dies after a sex orgy at Mrs Arbuthnot's. Klinger no doubt judged that this was a shift attuned to the sensibility of the times: the plethora of sex romps that dominated the British box office with Klinger's own 'Confessions Of …' series (1974–8) a highly successful example. Even respected established filmmakers, such as the Boulting Brothers (with *Soft Beds, Hard Battles* in 1974), had gone down this route. Green's earlier upbeat ending is restored. Two more versions of this triple-authored script were produced. The first tightened the focus on the central action and made the narrative thread clearer. The second strengthened the descriptions of the protagonists and specifically set the action in 1987, 'ten years hence'.

However, the 'collaboration' on these changes appears to have been between Green and Klinger, with Hodges, preoccupied by trying desperately to sustain his directing career in America, increasingly sidelined. Eventually, there was an acrimonious parting of the ways. While Hodges maintained that he had 'written numerous drafts for a pittance', Klinger responded that it was Hodges who had chosen 'to totally discard the previous scripts and write your own version', had only fitted rewriting in when other tasks permitted and that the overruns had become insupportable: 'a few days had become months'. The upshot was that Klinger had had to 'discard virtually your entire script because it was clearly designed for your own highly personal style of direction'.[25] Klinger's frustration is understandable, but Hodges was a known quantity who had gone his own way on *Pulp* and was therefore someone who would be expected to write something idiosyncratic. It was more that, in this instance, Klinger felt that Hodges was not *simpatico* with what he perceived to be the merit of the original and the strengths of Green's existing script.

Anticipating Hodges's departure, Klinger had already employed an American 'fixer', Lester Goldsmith, to compare the scripts. Goldsmith reported back that, as it now stood, the elements directly attributable to Hodges were sixteen pages 'and a few odd lines' and that these '16 pages comprise only four original scenes and contain no structural contribution'.[26] A tenth script, dated 14 March 1977, was therefore prepared with credits for Green and Klinger only. This script, written very rapidly in a few weeks, reintroduced many of Green's jokes as well as strengthening the characterization. Although the final script closely resembled

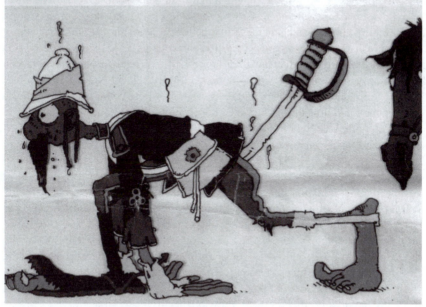

Figure 5.3 A still from the animated titles that had been produced for *The Chilian Club*; courtesy of Tony Klinger

the version that Green had prepared two years earlier, it had become more of a sex comedy, retaining Hodges's emphasis on a plurality of sexual practices and his ending in which the PM collapses during a sex orgy at the brothel after the assassins have bungled several attempts on his life.

The deal that never was: Rank and the NFFC

Despite the departure of Hodges, Klinger was determined to press on because *The Chilian Club* was the most advanced project in a four-picture deal that Klinger – now recognized as the leading British independent producer on the strength of his international success with *Gold* and *Shout at the Devil* – believed he had negotiated with the Rank Organization in August 1976.[27] In a major shift from its earlier position, the NFFC had also now committed itself to providing 25 per cent of the finances, around £300,000, on the understanding that Rank was contributing £400,000.[28] Klinger received warm encouragement from John Trevelyan, the former Secretary of the British Board of Film Censors (he retired in 1971), who admired Klinger as 'one of the few people who can keep cinema alive'. Trevelyan opined that the 'subject is now even more topical' than it was when the novel was first published, 'what with troubles at Leylands and Fords and elsewhere', and looked forward to a film with an all-star cast 'of older actors': Ralph Richardson, John Gielgud, Laurence Olivier, Alec Guinness and Trevor Howard. However, he urged Klinger to avoid any extreme right-wing stance as this 'would be liable to produce antagonism'.[29] After receiving the draft screenplay on 15 April, Trevelyan wrote again to congratulate Klinger on 'getting over the political problems' by accentuating the farcical elements, adding, 'this could be a great film'.[30]

Klinger had tried to recruit Richard Lester as a possible director but he was already committed on other films.[31] Klinger had written earlier to Terry that he was in 'active negotiations' with Guinness, Howard, David Niven and Kenneth More.[32] Although Peter Sellers had expressed an interest in appearing as all the victims but could not commit himself to the project at that point, Klinger pressed ahead, anxious to cement the Rank deal.[33] Film Finances Ltd had already written a completion guarantee, for £1,250,000 on 22 December 1976 with filming scheduled to begin on 18 April 1977.[34] An upbeat edition of *Klinger News* (undated but probably March 1977) announced *The Chilian Club* as one of five projects 'in advanced pre-production stages', named Rex Harrison, David Hemmings, Lionel Jeffries, James Mason, Kenneth More and Peter Ustinov as slated to appear in this 'hilarious and highly pertinent black comedy', as well as 'the lovely Gayle Hunnicut', presumably to play Coralie, and identified Peter Collinson as the director. Collinson is quoted as being enthusiastic about a film depicting 'the British at their best, doing something for themselves ... not a serious movie at all. It's like a cartoon ... [the old boys] try to kill the Prime Minister eight times, but he finally dies in a brothel doing his duty for Britain!'[35]

However, the anticipated funding from Rank did not materialize. Klinger wrote to the then head of Leisure Services at Rank, Edmond Chilton, urging

Figure 5.4 Rank's advert in *Klinger News* (courtesy of Tony Klinger)

him to confirm its financial commitment and emphasizing that *The Chilian Club* was 'designed to be – and will be – an entirely international comedy in the style of, and hopefully the success pattern of, "PINK PANTHER"', an indication that Klinger was now convinced that the film's success depended on its casting and in accentuating the non-political elements.[36] However, no such undertaking was forthcoming from Rank. At the same time, Terry wrote to Klinger introducing a new condition for the NFFC loan: that an American or 'other international distribution deal' had to be negotiated beforehand. Arguing that the film's budget had tripled since the NFFC first became linked to the project, Terry added that his Board 'did not accept your view that the film would command a wide international market'.[37] Klinger, stunned and outraged by this complete change of tack, and the imposition of a requirement that was at variance with the NFFC's standard practice, wrote back stating that the NFFC had been fully aware of the revised budget figure when it had committed itself to quarter-financing the film in January and that there had been no mention of a pre-sales condition at that point. Klinger observed witheringly that it would have been unnecessary for him to approach the NFFC if he had secured international funding, and protested that the NFFC was 'totally ignoring the fact that I am the only United Kingdom based producer with his own, well established, worldwide selling organisation ... You pay lip service to the financing of British films from British sources until it comes to it.'[38] Klinger understood only too well that the NFFC's requirement almost completely undermined his bargaining strategy with potential foreign financiers.

Klinger had good reason to be bitter as he had never succeeded in raising any production finance in Britain and because neither Rank's nor the NFFC's attitude can be explained by purely economic logic, although both may have been ultimately unconvinced that the film would succeed internationally. What had caused this major shift in attitude in the space of six months? According to Klinger's son, Sir John Davis, Rank's chairman, was having a purge of senior staff, including Chilton, and was not prepared to honour any agreements that had been made, thereby undermining his executives' position and divesting them of power (Klinger 2009). Davis had used this tactic before in order to impose his authority (see Spicer 2006: 138–9). It was also part of Davis's longer term strategy to withdraw Rank entirely from active film production. Without Rank's commitment, the NFFC would have felt exposed financially and the agreement would have further added to the increasing pressure the Corporation was under during this period (see Porter 1979: 222–3, 266; Smith 2008: 70). Terry's imposition of a pre-production distribution agreement reads as the action of someone looking for a way out of a commitment that had become onerous and potentially embarrassing, both financially and politically. Klinger, as a working-class Jewish socialist, was never a figure who found favour with the British establishment (Klinger 2009).

Klinger continued his denunciation of the NFFC in the pages of *Screen International*, which reported his trip to the United States to obtain American finance.[39] These efforts proved abortive. John D. Eberts, representing the Canadian Oppenheimer Group, was typical in rejecting *The Chilian Club* because 'I have been unable to elicit any interest in this project from my institutional sources. I think most people feel the subject is too parochial or too "British"'.[40] In Britain, Michael Deeley, the Managing Director of EMI, rejected Klinger's film because 'I don't believe the political background of 1987 that the script prophesies and thus cannot accept the essential justification within the script of the activities of the Club members'.[41] Klinger's health had been permanently damaged by a heart attack suffered on location in Africa making *Shout at the Devil* and he no longer had the same energy and drive to sustain projects. The subsequent rejections of *The Chilian Club* – by Rank (again, 28 February 1978); the Film Finances Group Limited (17 April 1978); Sandy Lieberson at Twentieth Century-Fox (21 February 1979); Verity Lambert at Euston Films (8 June 1979); and Linda Morrow, Program Development Manager for MGM TV (13 June 1979) – were cursory.[42]

Klinger made one final effort to mount the production in the early 1980s, paying Rory MacLean to revise the script.[43] Klinger started negotiations, in July 1980, for Benny Hill to play the eight assassinated characters, with filming to begin in March 1981.[44] Dick Brand at MGM expressed his enthusiasm for using Hill, but nothing came of this.[45] After further rejections by Rediffusion (7 July 1982); Jeremy Isaacs for Channel 4 (12 July 1982); Sandy Lieberson now at Goldcrest (22 June 1984); and by Handmade Films (12 December 1985), the attempt to film *The Chilian Club* finally ended.[46]

Conclusion

The Chilian Club's right-wing politics and its mode of black comedy presented significant problems for Klinger's attempts to produce a film version and this is reflected in the numerous rewritings. They reflect a fundamental uncertainty as to whether the satirical or farcical elements should be accentuated and how much sex and nudity should be presented. Klinger remained dissatisfied with all of the scripts, unconvinced that any of the various collaborations had succeeded in balancing the anarchic comedy with a sense of the humanity of the central characters who were 'above politics' and their underlying frustrations with British society. Though he worked quite effectively with Green, Klinger lacked the defining input from a director at the scripting stage. This was not Collinson's strength and the anticipated collaboration with Hodges turned out to be a mistake, though not one that could have been predicted, given Hodges's obvious talents and the example of *Pulp*.

However, the aesthetic difficulties and the occasionally fraught nature of the various collaborations on the scripts do not explain the project's ultimate failure. Essentially *The Chilian Club* fell between several stools. It was not simply a low-budget sex comedy that could have recouped its money even in a reduced domestic market and by 1973 the medium-budget British film was no longer being produced. *The Chilian Club*'s combination of a parochial Britishness, its overtly political subject matter and the age of its protagonists made it a problematic proposition for international investors who remained unconvinced of its appeal; it was neither a whimsical Ealing comedy nor *The Pink Panther*. However, even an understanding of these commercial factors does not completely explain Klinger's difficulties. In early 1977, when Klinger's own reputation had increased and *The Chilian Club* was actively in pre-production, Rank reneged on its agreement to invest in the film's production as did the NFFC through its imposition of a pre-sales agreement. This double blow, the result of internal corporation politics and Klinger's position as a Jewish outsider rather more than a sense of the film's commercial potential, effectively ended any real hopes of its production. Subsequently, with Klinger's career in decline, it was never seriously considered as a viable proposition in either North America or in Britain. Scripting a successful version of *The Chilian Club* had become an impossible task.

What I hope this detailed study of *The Chilian Club* has shown is the central importance of scrutinizing the industrial, commercial and cultural context in analysing a screenplay. In this instance and, I submit, in any other, one cannot understand either the nature of the detailed changes that were made or the reasons why the film could not be made simply through an examination of the various drafts. The detailed correspondence referred to shows how significantly the scripting process was affected by aesthetic differences among the collaborators, by the attitudes of potential investors, by structural changes in the British film industry and by the career trajectory of Klinger himself. Any serious study of screenwriting, I suggest, must take full cognizance of these contexts if it is to produce a satisfactory account of the processes involved.

Acknowledgements

I should like to thank professors Brian McFarlane, Robert Murphy and Vincent Porter for their comments on a draft version of this chapter.

Notes

1 See *The Plot Against Harold Wilson*, BBC2, 16 March 2006.
2 Information contained in a letter from Richard Odgers representing Spokesmen lawyers to Michael Klinger, 27 Aug. 1975; Michael Klinger Papers, University of the West of England (MKP).
3 Information contained in a letter from Raffles Edelman, solicitor, to Klinger, 13 March 1973; MKP.
4 Letter from Marsh to Klinger, 29 Aug. 1972. Klinger's fee was £10,000; MKP.
5 Marginalia on Collinson's script and accompanying notes; MKP.
6 Letter from Klinger to Kamal Pasha at the Laurie Marsh Group, 23 Oct. 1972. Klinger requested £1,500 for the new script.
7 Five pages of comments are attached to Green's script, dated Nov. 1972; MKP.
8 *The Green Man* is an amiable Launder and Gilliat farce released in 1955 starring Alastair Sim as a professional assassin foiled by an innocuous vacuum cleaner salesman (George Cole).
9 Accompanying notes to Green's script, Nov. 1972; MKP.
10 Letter to Klinger, 6 Dec. 1972; MKP.
11 Letter from Klinger to Marsh, 1 Jan. 1973; MKP.
12 *The Chilian Club* Schedule, dated 31 March 1973; MKP.
13 Letter to Klinger, 3 Jan. 1973; MKP.
14 See Klinger's letter to Marsh, 1 Dec. 1972; MKP.
15 Letter to Klinger, 27 Feb. 1973; MKP.
16 *Kind Hearts and Coronets* had been released by Ealing Studios in 1949, directed by Robert Hamer. It was based on Roy Horniman's 1907 novel *Israel Rank: The Autobiography of a Criminal*. It experienced considerable problems with American censors – see Street (2002: 134–5).
17 Letter to Klinger, 22 May 1973; MKP.
18 Ibid.
19 *The League of Gentlemen* (1960), directed by Basil Dearden, with a screenplay by Bryan Forbes, was based on John Bolan's 1958 black comedy about a group of disaffected war veterans with criminal pasts who are manipulated by Colonel Hyde (Jack Hawkins) into committing a series of robberies that will restore meaning to their lives.
20 Letter to Klinger, 24 May 1973; MKP.
21 Letter to Klinger, 4 Dec. 1974. The film had also been rejected by Warner Bros., 12 March 1974, without reasons being given; MKP.
22 Contract agreement dated 18 June 1976. Hodges' agreed fee was £3,000; MKP.
23 Letter to Mike Hodges, 18 Jan. 1977; MKP.
24 Letter to Klinger, 24 Jan. 1977; MKP.
25 Letter of Hodges to Klinger, 9 March 1977; letter of Klinger to Hodges, 14 March 1977; MKP.
26 Letter from Goldsmith to Klinger, 9 March 1977 with comparison attached; MKP.
27 See the letter from F. S. Poole to Klinger, 19 Aug. 1976; MKP.
28 Letter from Terry to Klinger, 12 Jan. 1977; MKP.
29 Letter to Klinger, 31 March 1977; MKP.
30 Letter to Klinger, 24 April 1977; MKP.
31 Letter from Klinger to Lester, 16 March 1973; MKP. Tony Klinger, interview, Dec. 2009.
32 Letter from Klinger, 21 Feb. 1977; More's agents, Denis Van Thal, had already written to Klinger on 19 Nov. expressing his keen interest in playing Mayne-Amaury; MKP.
33 Handwritten note to Klinger, 31 Jan. 1977; MKP.
34 The budget was finalised on 9 March 1977 at £1,241,467; MKP.

35 *Klinger News*, pp. 1 and 3; MKP. There are also copies in the British Film Institute Library.
36 Letter to Chilton, 10 March 1977; MKP.
37 Letter to Klinger, 21 March 1077; MKP.
38 Letter to Terry, 15 April 1977; MKP.
39 'Klinger flies out to save film', *Screen International* 81/2 (April 1977): 1.
40 Letter to Klinger, 25 April 1977; MGM had already rejected *The Chilian Club* on 28 July 1976 because it was 'too British in tone for our production schedule'; MKP.
41 Letter to Klinger, 14 Nov. 1977; MKP.
42 Letters in MKP.
43 Letters from Klinger to MacLean, 27 Sept. 1985 and 17 April 1986; MKP. There is no MacLean screenplay in the Klinger Papers; perhaps it was not completed.
44 Letter to Hill's agent, Robert E. Stone, 29 July 1980; MKP.
45 Letter to Klinger, 21 July 1980; MKP.
46 Letters in MKP.

References

Anon. (1977) 'Klinger Flies Out to Save Film', *Screen International* 81(2) (April): 1, 7.
Bennett, T. and Woollacott, J. (1987) *Bond and Beyond: The Political Career of a Popular Hero*, Basingstoke: Macmillan Education.
Cook, J. R. and Spicer, A. (2008) 'Introduction', *Journal of British Cinema and Television* 5(2): 213–22.
Fisk, A. (2003) 'The Cavalryman Rides Again: The Historical Novels of George Shipway', *Solander* 7(1): 4–6.
Gammond, P. (2004) 'Bernard [Benny] Green', *Oxford Dictionary of National Biography*, Oxford: Oxford University Press.
Green, B. (1981) *P.G. Wodehouse: A Literary Biography*, London: Pavilion.
Green, D. (2000) *Benny Green Words and Music: A Biography*, London: London House.
Hamilton, J. (2005) *Beasts in the Cellar: The Exploitation Career of Tony Tenser*, Godalming: FAB Press.
Hewison, R. (1988) *In Anger: Culture in the Cold War 1945–60*, London: Methuen.
Higson, A. (1994) 'A Diversity of Film Practices: Renewing British Cinema in the 1970s', in B. Moore-Gilbert (ed.) *The Arts in the 1970s: Cultural Closure?* London: Routledge, pp. 216–39.
Klinger, T. (2009) Interview with Andrew Spicer, Shenley, Herts, 3 Dec.
Maras, S. (2009) *Screenwriting: History, Theory and Practice*, London: Wallflower Press.
Porter, V. (1979) 'Film Policy for the 80s: Industry or Culture?', *Sight and Sound* 48(4) (Autumn): 221–3, 266.
Rilla, W. (1973) *The Writer and the Screen: On Writing for Film and Television*, London: W. H. Allen.
Shaw, T. (2001) *British Cinema and the Cold War*, London: I. B. Tauris.
Shipway, G. (1971) *The Chilian Club*, London: Peter Davies.
Smith, J. (2008) 'Glam, Spam and Uncle Sam: Funding Diversity in 1970s British Film Production', in R. Shail (ed.) *Seventies British Cinema*, London: BFI/Palgrave Macmillan, pp 67–80.
Spicer, A. (2006) *Sydney Box*, Manchester: Manchester University Press.
Spicer, A. (2010) 'The Precariousness of Production: Michael Klinger and the Role of the Film Producer in the British Film Industry during the 1970s', in L. Forster and

S. Harper (eds), *British Culture and Society in 1970s Britain: The Lost Decade*, Newcastle: Cambridge Scholars Publishing, pp. 188–200.

Street, S. (2002) *Transatlantic Crossings: British Feature Films in the USA*, London: Continuum.

Wood, L. (1983) *British Films 1971–1981*, London: BFI Publishing.

Chapter 6

Boards, beats, binaries and bricolage

Approaches to the animation script

Paul Wells

Thinking about the nature and definition of 'script' for animated films is particularly problematic. The form accommodates so many diverse approaches to creating animated narratives that any one case might be unique to that project, and equally, any broad generalizations may be misrepresentative of the form as a whole. It is, nevertheless, the particularity of 'animation' as a model of expression that necessitates an enquiry about what constitutes a 'script', as this offers specific clues about the distinctiveness and attractiveness of the form to artists.

Arguably, in many cases, the piles of sketches, storyboards, materials, artefacts and data files left at the end of the process in making an animated film, are 'the script', but this is to merely acknowledge the complex development of the process, and not to identify how scripts function in animation. It is my intention in the following analysis then, to look at various forms of animation script, both from the perspective of identifying different models, and to evaluate how such scripts are actually defined by the specific use and application of animation as a particular language of expression.

From the outset, then, it is pertinent to loosely define some terms which inform my discussion, as essentially, I wish to ultimately suggest that the term 'script' as it is primarily understood in live action film and television, may operate slightly differently in animation, and further, that 'script' may ultimately be an unhelpful or misrepresentative description in animation practices, *or* must be viewed in a broader light to accommodate animation processes. So, initially, then, I would like to define 'script' as a *language text* determined by the traditional conventions of layout, the descriptors of location and context, the introduction of characters, and exchanges of dialogue (see Frensham 1996: 16–30). Equally, one might use Syd Field's definition of a screenplay: 'A Screenplay is a story told with pictures, in dialogue and description, and placed within the context of dramatic structure' (Field 2005: 2–3). There is some irony in such a definition, of course, as no 'pictures' are actually present, merely words which suggest them. In my discussion, thereafter, other kinds of writing and development process key to animation will be taken into account; principally, 'storyboarding', the process by which the narrative is visualized on an action-by-action basis in the drawn form, anticipating the frame-by-frame process of artificially creating the physical motion in characters and environments (see Wells *et al.* 2008: 84–9); and 'micro-narrativisation', the identification of the minutiae in story expression, particularly on visual and conceptual terms, as the core principle in animated narrative development and accumulation. Micro-narratives function as the core principle of much animated film because of its intrinsic ability to amplify small-scale incident. A conversation, a singular event, a motif or iconic image, a cycle of metamorphosis, the extrapolation of a visual source, a spot gag, etc., becomes a concentrated 'narrative', intensified by the way in which all the aspects of the imagery carries with it the specific weight of 'deliberate choice'. There is no 'accidental' imagery in animation, and consequently, all of its elements take on associative weight, accumulating into a mode of storytelling which self-consciously constructs its formal idioms to work as *saturated* image forms, where character, colour, context and choreography all simultaneously and equally *signify* meaning. These micro-narratives provide the context for my address of 'beats', 'binaries' and 'bricolage'.

Karsten Killerich, executive producer at A Film in Denmark, reports his frustration that it is uniformly the case that in seeking funding to develop his company's animated films, prospective sponsors expect to see a traditional script common to live action, noting 'this does not really represent what an animated film is, or could be, because we would really like to show storyboards-in-progress which actually give a real indication of how the story will work visually, through animation'.[1] This is a common frustration for those in the industry, and indeed, in the academy, who wish to demonstrate both the distinctiveness of the process in animation, and in its potential outcomes as a language of expression. It is slightly different for those studios working in features, whose commercial success, and business partnerships, enable them to devise their own working practices. Dave Sproxton, one of the co-founders of Aardman Animation, has described what he calls the 'kernel' model, in which a studio takes a very small point of departure in developing a feature narrative, citing, for example, Dreamworks' *Shrek* (Dir. Andrew Adamson and Vicky Jensen, US, 2001) where the film was prompted by William Steig's very short, largely pictorial, children's book – the 'kernel' – but which only became the full 'nut' of the movie, once it was decided to contextualize the story in an extended parody of fairytales through contemporary topical subjects.[2] Essentially, what Sproxton alludes to here is the core concept or inciting incident which prompts the development of the story through a range of processes – story meetings, prose treatments, provisional sketches, character models, layout and storyboards, dialogue scripts, animatics and shooting scripts. Andrew Stanton, one of the leading directors at Pixar Animation, has described this as an 'excavation' process, where the bones of the narrative are drawn out of the earth, with the hope that the right bones constitute a correct story skeleton that may be muscled and fleshed with the animation itself, but underpinned with the anxiety that the right 'dinosaur' will emerge.[3] Such is the emphasis on pre-production in animation, this 'excavation' can take a long time, and may be subject to adjustment right until the point where there is a commitment to the production process. Even then changes can be made. Sometimes major revisions or complete rewriting is required to address processes which do not resolve their issues and problems. Supervising animator on *Bolt* (Dir. Byron Howard and Chris Williams, US, 2008), Mark Imrey, notes, for example, the key intervention of John Lasseter halfway through the production of what was at first called *American Dog*, ultimately secured the clarity of the narrative in the eventual film,[4] while Pixar's Mark Walsh, credits Brad Bird with focusing the story in *Ratatouille* (Dir. Brad Bird, US, 2007), when there were seemingly too many characters and sub-plots.[5]

The 'excavation' process, thereafter, can use the classical narrative and mythic structures suggested in the work of Syd Field (2003) or Christopher Vogler (2007), deploying three-act structures, Aristotlean elements, and 'the hero's journey', but this is still all subject to the particular processes required by, and available to, animation as a form. It is curious, for example, that Vogler, a story consultant for Disney animation, does not really consider what animation as a distinctive model of creative expression offers to traditional storytelling processes. Vogler advised on the treatment of *The Lion King*, for example, and in recognizing elements of 'the hero's journey' mythic structure, suggested particular narrative and conceptual interventions, but ultimately, he feels:

> that the movie is weakened by the turn it takes in Act Two. The almost photographic realism of the Act One animal scenes is replaced with a more old-fashioned Disney cartoon style, especially the comic rendering of Timon and Pumbaa. Simba is a growing carnivore and there is nothing realistic about him subsisting on a diet of bugs. I feel the movie missed a big chance to follow through on the promise of the first act with a realistic series of tests, leading to a life-enhancing ordeal near the midpoint … I advocated creating a scene where Simba is truly tested. A real ordeal in which he discovers his mature power in a battle with a crocodile, a water buffalo, a leopard, or some other formidable foe. The development of Simba from a scared little cub into a jaunty teen-aged lion is handled too quickly, in my opinion, with a few quick dissolves of him growing older as he crosses a log bridge. A montage of scenes of him learning to hunt, first comically, and then with greater assurance, would have been more effective storytelling.
>
> (Vogler 2007: 264)

One could easily replace the word 'effective' in the last sentence, with the word 'realistic' or 'logical', to make the point, and at one level, Vogler's critique is persuasive, especially as it chimes with what is both a conceptual and creative issue I have identified in my own work, which I have termed 'the *Madagascar* problem' (Wells 2009: 19–23). This 'problem' emerges when the coherence of story logic is undermined by confusing a range of discourses in the representation of animals, particularly, when the 'real' behaviour of an animal conflicts with broader cartoon expectations and principles. In this instance, though, I wish to suggest that what Vogler actually neglects to take into account is the way in which animation can freely oscillate between and mix registers, without *apparently* undermining narrative coherence. This is essentially because the imagery – quasi-realistic or more abstract – functions on the same representational terms and conditions. It is this fundamental condition which means that the 'metamorphosis' of Simba from cub to young lion remains plausible because it is one of the codes and conventions of animation itself. The obvious and overt illusionism of the form enables seemingly radical shifts in representational style and performance, but only when measured against photo-realistic, physical and material expectations.

This has implications for the writer because the scriptwriter for live action can write descriptors of contexts, actions and environments with the assumption that they exist and function in the concrete world, and possess a logical meaning and affect for directors and performers, *and must be evidenced, as such, in their representation.* The writer for animation must write descriptors for contexts, actions and environments with the knowledge that animators will translate and interpret these ideas, *and may not relate to natural laws or material reality.* The 'script' in animation then, only really functions when the principles of animation as a visual mediation are applied to it. Jeffrey Scott suggests:

> a script [for animation, therefore,] describes the entire story, including a description of all the environments in which the scenes take place, all the action that happens in those environments, and all the dialogue spoken by the characters. In television animation, unlike live action, the cartoon script lays out every detail of the story.
>
> (Scott 2002: 21)

Even with this level of detail, however, it is only when the storyboarding process begins that the actual dynamics and principles of working in animation are properly taken into account and revealed.[6]

Storyboarding is fundamental in bridging the idea, concept and any written treatment or provisional script to the dramatization and choreography of the visual elements. Janet Blatter has suggested, therefore, that 'storyboards are effective because they mediate cognitive, productive, and social processes of animation practice', and operate as a creative tool, a planning tool and a production tool. Storyboarding thus mediates between the production and the different stages in the development of a visual narrative. Ultimately, then, the storyboard works as a model of an 'intended film', as 'a hypothetical world', and as 'a future activity' (Blatter 2007: 4–13). First used by the Disney studios during the 1930s, the working storyboard, played out across huge wall areas, enabled the narrative to develop with a visual immediacy that facilitated collaborative interventions, and a collective understanding of the evolving narrative.

The boards – essentially hundreds of small, ordered sketches – could also help record verbal and textual additions through basic drawings and notation. Though animation is notoriously labour-intensive in its production phase, the script development period, both as text and as storyboard, is necessarily subject to intense periods of review and negotiation as numerous voices – everyone from

Figure 6.1 A story meeting for Halas & Batchelor's production of *Animal Farm* in 1953, featuring the 'script' as it existed in storyboards for a range of sequences

the director to sequence animators and layout artists – speak to an ongoing, and increasingly team-based experience of production. Though there will always be a final directorial choice in the outcome, and as with any production ongoing consideration of economic and time constraints, the freedoms of this kind of *pre*-production process, before any commitment is made to animation itself, also merely reflects the openness of the possibilities when working with the form. Almost whatever might be imagined can probably be animated, but this is in some senses as much of a drawback as it might be a benefit, if the core principles of that which is needed in the narrative, or the clarity of the message, for example, are neglected. It is sometimes the case that stylistic or aesthetic preoccupations can distract from the focus of the story. This is partly because, in animated productions, imagination is not necessarily compromised by economy, since as Scott points out, 'in [drawn] animation it costs the same to have a character jump out of bed or jump off the Titanic' (2002: 14). What is important to remember, however, is that whether a character does indeed jump out of bed or leap from the Titanic, these have to become highly specific creative decisions, that emerge from the ongoing visualization of the narrative, and crucially, represent the intrinsic 'mining' of the particularities of the *action* suggested, as this, to use Field's terms, is both the intrinsic context *and* content for the animation (Field 2003: 160–4).

In typical models of devising and creating 'live action' stories there is, for the most part, what might be termed an 'expansive' model, which seeks to build and accumulate story in an outward direction, organically growing its construction, but in the first instance, at least, animated narratives must address what I wish to term the 'micro-narrativization' – the compression of context and content – which is the intrinsic condition of any one aspect of animation production. A 'micro-narrative' is any one action, choreographic principle, visual motif, or single scenario, and is a conscious creative choice with an embedded or imposed narrative, metaphoric and symbolic agenda, and which thereafter must be *animated*, not merely recorded.

This is why Blatter's point about storyboarding being a 'future activity' is especially important, because storyboarding the micro-narrative is fundamental to the script development process. Storyboards are not an *illustration* of a script but another *iteration* of script, working as a model of editorial and creative construction in the same way as rewriting text, or using the proverbial 'blue pencil' to edit or cut scenes. Each iteration, then, is essentially an ongoing consolidation of the depiction of micro-narratives, and their ultimate particularity as an animated film, either as a single 'scene' in its own right; as the facilitating elements of 'beats' or 'binaries' (and potentially, the 'acts' in a three-act structure); the accumulating agencies of bricolage; or as part of a recognizable relationship to now traditional, 'classical' or 'anti' narrative models. I will seek to address all of these principles, the boards, beats, binaries and bricolage of my title – what I would describe as the key scriptwriting 'building blocks' by which to 'think animation' – in the rest of my discussion.

Aaron Springer, one of the core writers on the hit crossover series, *Spongebob Squarepants*, is constantly engaged with thinking through how ideas and concepts become aspects of story, and may be translated into, and depicted through, animation. Initially, a *Spongebob* episode is itself first developed from an improvised, verbal ideas session summarized into a treatment by a lead writer. Some of these verbal ideas might work like Sproxton's 'kernel' principle – Spongebob and Squidward compete for employee of the month, for example – or be a more extended idea with a number of possible scenarios – the invention of Mermaidman and Barnacleboy as underwater superheroes, for instance, as characters which recur in the series. Springer notes, though, that any one sentence in an agreed narrative treatment for an episode must necessarily be interpreted in regard to its visual execution, its blocking and choreography, and in regard to what must be animated. If we return back to Scott's bedroom scene, for instance, this may be the blink of an eyelid as a character awakens, for example, or a character performing a complex, twisting somersault from the deck of the Titanic, into a swirling whirlpool populated by objects and sea creatures. Springer notes that it is crucial to take into account the *shift* from narrative suggestion in the treatment to narrative interpretation, noting:

> This is maybe one page or two pages long. You read this stuff and it might change a lot from what you finally get. You ask yourself, how am I going to communicate these ideas? They may or may not work. I now have to translate

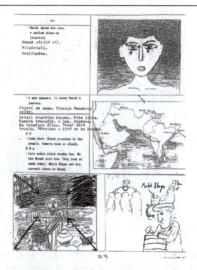

Figure 6.2 Storyboard: A working storyboard from *Animated World Faiths: The Story of Guru Nanak*, in which different graphic stylings, possible character choreographies, and story based camera moves and composition are still being worked out.

these into something that is going to be entertaining. A lot of that comes into play during the storyboarding of it. Here is a line from a treatment for example. 'That night Mr Crabs and Spongebob funnel all the hideous grease out of the trap and into a big dumptruck outside' All you're getting is one sentence that is describing this process. When I read that, I think, that's not funny in and of itself, so what happens ? OK, I think, they siphon it out. You hear about people who put a hose in a gas tank, and start siphoning the gas out. So, I thought, they do that, but it doesn't work at first, and Mr Crabs ends up saturated. That's the challenge because that isn't in the treatment, so the real writing takes place in the storyboard.[7]

In being predicated so much on visual choreographies and the conscious meaning imbued in the motion of characters and objects themselves, animation is not reliant on the word, and its 'script' increasingly functions as a pictorial form the more it develops. It is important to stress this point because, in essence, most animation is effectively determined in the *pre-production* phase, while most 'live action' narratives are ultimately created in the *post-production* phase. Animation, in being so labour-intensive and complex in its construction, requires much more detailed planning in relation to its execution, since to get things wrong in the actual animation production phase is both costly and time-consuming. More importantly, it is technically difficult to correct, as no 'extra' footage is available to save the narrative 'in the edit' or through post-production interventions. The front-ended, pre-filmic aspect of animation production is one of its defining features, even in the digital era when production processes and pipelines are

Figure 6.2 Plates: Storyboard plates from Geoff Dunbar's work on *Rupert and the Frog Song*, an animated music video by Paul McCartney, in which great care is taken to adapt the original illustration style by Mary Turtel and Alfred Bestall, and to dramatise each motion.

potentially more flexible. It places considerable stress then on making sure the concept, narrative and visualization process is well conducted, and prompts a range of procedural engagements with the intended outcome that come to define 'script' in the animated form.

While major studios like Pixar Animation have been celebrated for their storytelling prowess – over half the production period being dedicated to the 'excavation' process Stanton describes above, in ultimately 'locking down' the story before any animation itself is done – there has often been concern shown by festival juries, commissioning editors and university and college tutors, that persuasive storytelling remains a challenging issue in animated film. This is partly because issues of technique or pure aesthetic expression distract animators from constructing a persuasive world – however fantastical or surreal – with a consistent 'inner logic', which defines and supports its characters and contexts. As screenwriter Blake Snyder has noted, even in more loosely determined or experimental structures of storytelling, or 'I wish' movies in which out of the ordinary magical outcomes occur, 'out of the bottle' solutions to narrative development and resolution seem unsatisfying, and undermine what has been created previously, inevitably prompting questions like 'if that can happen now, why couldn't it happen before?' (Snyder 2005: 29–31). Even in animation, where the form affords particular kinds of expressive freedom, it is still necessary to create the conditions by which the characters and contexts are part of a specific 'world'. This remains a major difficulty in many animation scripts, as the mere ability to magically animate solutions, simply because the vehicle in which the narrative is produced can facilitate that, seemingly as part of its creative function, undermines many potentially fulfilling works.

Fundamental to the animation script then, is the reconciliation of its capacity for freewheeling image-making and the construction of a narrative context, with a determined inner logic. This process essentially becomes a concentration upon the dynamics of each 'micro-narrative'. The establishment of one core narrative event, one story principle or one mode of visual representation, is fundamental in defining the 'inner logic' of an animated story world. One of the most famous examples of managing such a micro-narrative remains Chuck Jones's nine rules, which define every cartoon in the 'Roadrunner' series (see Jones 1990: 225). Though Jones's cartoons are effectively 'chase' narratives – one of the most common micro-narratives, in which one adversary merely pursues another – their rules essentially define the limitations of the ostensible story, yet also provoke and justify 'impossible' choreographies and action. The micro-narrative is intrinsically related to what I have termed elsewhere as 'condensation'. This is essentially the maximum degree of meaningful storytelling and symbolic suggestion in the minimum of iconic imagery (see Wells 1998: 76–80; 2007: 24–5). By working outward from this core storytelling principle, each element of the visualization and blocking of action becomes a story 'condition' with its own narrative and technical specificity. Thus, the Roadrunner cannot harm the Coyote, for example, except by going 'beep beep!' – itself the only 'dialogue' Jones allows in the films – but more significantly, Coyote cannot be harmed by any external force. He is undone purely by his own ineptitude or the failure of the ACME products he uses – the only materials, tools, weapons and machines Jones permits – but crucially, by his own fanaticism, and the central character trait of his inability to stop his obsessive pursuit. The location remains the same – a road in a southwest American desert – and the Coyote is most often defeated by gravity, and throughout, more humiliated than harmed by his intrinsic failure. It is this latter characteristic that informs Jones's more psychologically and emotionally charged approach to the chase cartoon, also readily evidenced in his interpretation of the later Tom & Jerry cartoons, which he rendered more lyrical than violent. Jones's rules effectively determine the codes and conventions of the storytelling in the cartoons, simultaneously providing a structure, yet creating the premises to determine the freedoms of expression in the animation itself. Such 'rules' also become the defining characteristics of micro-narrative, and are similar to the mere plot lines Springer was working from in *Spongebob* treatments, prompting thematic as well as choreographic imperatives. What is at the heart of both Jones and Springer's work, then is the concentration upon small, detailed, limited scenarios, that either remain self-contained in the short form, or stimulate related scenes in the longer form. I now wish to explore how certain works function in the short form, and become the parameters by which the longer form is constructed.

The most immediate way I can illustrate this is to give some examples of dominant 'micro-narratives' in animation, and some indication of the ways in which their 'script' emerges from the conditions of devising determined by technique and condensation. One of the most common ways in which animators devise scenarios is by using animation to redefine 'the everyday' by reassigning

Figure 6.4 Squashing tomato in *Western Spaghetti* (2008)

the meaning or function of a particular animal, object and environment. This often emerges from the use of associative thinking in which 'associative relations' inspire links, connections and bonds between common visual forms, functions and concepts (see Wells 1998: 93–7). This can operate in a highly literal or symbolic way, and one of its best exponents is PES (full name, Adam Pesapane), whose narratives are defined by the reconfiguration of objects (see Wells and Hardstaff 2008: 168–9). A good example is *Western Spaghetti* (Dir. Adam Pesapane, USA, 2008), in which PES takes as his 'script' a recipe for Spaghetti Bolognese, playing out the process of making the meal through the novelty of reinventing foodstuffs as a range of everyday objects. Interestingly, Syd Field uses the idea of a 'recipe' as an example of why a scriptwriter must necessarily know the ending of a proposed script before it has begun, noting, 'When you cook something you don't throw things together and then see what you've got! You know what you're going to cook before you go into the kitchen; all you have to do is cook it!' (Field 2003: 115). Animators must necessarily know the ending of their works because of the necessity of knowing what must be animated. PES uses animation to innovate in how he moves to the inevitable conclusion of preparing a meal. An unseen chef lights a hob with flames made from orange sweets, and places a pan of water on the cooker. A frying pan is 'oiled' with tin foil. Dolls' eyes 'season' the water; rubic cubes are chopped into the pan as pieces of meat; red pin-cushions serve as tomatoes, pulped into a woollen Bolognese sauce.

Wooden Pixie-sticks are placed in bubble wrap water, emerging cooked in a colander as brightly coloured elastic bands – the spaghetti. Dollar bills are plucked like leaves and chopped into the Bolognese sauce, along with Post-It 'butter' slivers and melted garlic depicted in ever-dissolving dice. The dish is served with grated cheese 'string' and sprinkled with sparkling 'pepper' from a kaleidoscope.

Figure 6.5 Grating cheese in *Western Spaghetti* (2008)

The script here is effectively extrapolating from and reimagining the process of cooking a meal by interrogating and revising the form and function of the ingredients and the process involved. By substituting novelty objects for key foods, the film impresses with its invention, and draws attention to the ways in which the animation of such objects, in itself, is used to discover and reveal a 'micro-narrative' embedded in everyday experience. The recognition of a recipe and an everyday activity as a creative practice, as models of micro-narrative, becomes the organizational principle, which determines the aspects of the animation itself.

Indeed, many animated micro-narratives emerge from core organizational principles, for example, the list. Many animators make lists around a core theme, idea and preoccupation, and find a way to animate the single idea in various ways – again this works as a set of structuring principles and implicit methods by which the narrative is both executed and accumulated. Simply, a list of related ideas and concepts can be interpreted and visualized as singular narrative vignettes. These individual actions constitute *beats* which in essence move and advance the overall narrative, and promote a model of anticipation and escalation. Identifying the beats – the essential 'rhythm' of the piece – in all animated narratives of any length is fundamental to the success of the motion itself, and the timing of action. An efficiently constructed piece of choreography carries with it the imperative of the narrative and its inherent meaning.

Often this is readily seen in the 'spot gags' that essentially underpin and determine traditional cartoons, but may also be the set of core incidents and concepts which define and inform animated documentaries like *The Darra Dogs* (Dir. Dennis Tupicoff, Australia, 1993) or *The Luckiest Nut in the World* (Dir. Emily James, UK, 2002). The role for the scriptwriter in these circumstances is to determine a persuasive order of events that might peak and climax in a satisfying way, and to find devices which enhance the agency and focus of the narrative. *25 Ways to Give Up Smoking* (Dir. Bill Plympton, USA, 1989) is, as its title suggests, 25 methods by which to give up smoking (see Wells 1998: 172–4), most, excessive interpretations of psycho-therapeutic suggestions like 'over-indulge' or 'empathize with the cigarette', or exaggerated sight gags about making it hard to light up, or facing up to the harmful consequences of smoking, most strikingly revealed through the use of metamorphosis as a youthful face shrivels into a haggard and sallow visage. Plympton carefully structures his narrative with a running gag in which a sumo wrestler arbitrarily falls out of the sky crushing the main protagonist. This occurs at the beginning, halfway through and at the end, and helps provide a building rhythm to the piece, which unsurprisingly also saves its best jokes until last. It also often places a weaker joke against a strong joke, anticipating the resonance of amusement which passes from one to the other, or the continuing enjoyment of one joke, which means the next joke might not necessarily be taken in. The sumo wrestler joke also works as a way of noting that, whatever precautions we may take in the protection of our health, our lives may yet still be taken in the most arbitrary and unanticipated way. Crucial to this 'list' method is the specific way in which the animation is used to deliver each gag. Plympton reverses the anticipated anarchy and speed of an Averyesque cartoon, and makes his central protagonist a static, middle-aged, be-suited man, his every action a slow, micro-narrative of behavioural response to the act of smoking.

As I suggested earlier, micro-narrative in animation is essentially a compression of content and context, and in much animation, 'metamorphosis' is used as a theme and a crucially 'script' technique. Marina Warner has identified that metamorphosis works in a number of forms – mutating, hatching, splitting and doubling (see Warner 2002) – all fundamental aspects of animated narratives from features like *Hulk* (Dir. Ang Lee, USA, 2003) to animated documentaries like *Legacy* (Dir. Will Vinton, Joan Gratz, USA, 1979), to personal shorts like *Gagarin* (Dir. Alexei Kharitidi, Russia, 1995). Kharitidi's film is remarkable in many respects. While many might feel that Field's defining principles of a three-act structure might only be applied to full-length features, this fundamental approach is also possible in animation as an accumulation of micro-narratives, and readily demonstrated in *Gagarin*.

In the first act, a brown caterpillar, marked out as different from a chorus of three green companions, demonstrates his aspiration to fly by mimicking the flight of a helicopter, and staring helplessly to the skies. As this establishing act closes, a shuttlecock from a nearby park badminton match lands nearby. The second act begins with the caterpillar taking the opportunity to fly by entering the space-capsule shaped shuttlecock, and finding himself in wild patterns of flight as the badminton match continues. The second act is essentially, therefore, a tour-de-force of point of view choreography as the metamorphosing blurs of the lines, shapes and forms of the park environment pass the caterpillar's implied gaze. The act ends with the shuttlecock once more landing on the ground, spilling the caterpillar, who, dazed and confused, crawls behind a leaf to be sick. The third act begins with the caterpillar's companions sprouting wings and flying away – their metamorphosis from caterpillar to butterfly complete – but the main character, 'Gagarin', having gained his wings, finds he cannot fly because he is airsick! A sly parable about the failings of Russia in the space race, the short uses metamorphoses as its micro-narratives, condensing the storytelling agenda into key motion scenarios.

The shifts in *Gagarin*'s micro-narratives often function as *binaries*: stasis to movement, ascending and descending, right to left, hope to disappointment, fitness for purpose to failure. Beats and Binaries are often key elements in focusing the minimalist parameters of the storytelling while enhancing the dynamics of what actually requires animation, and how choreographic choices determine meaning and affect. Such beats and binaries often feature as aspects of developing 'storyboards', though, these in the first instance, might be 'mood' boards, identifying how colours, textures, photographic compositions and so forth might work as binaries in a visual script, or as 'tension' boards, matching colour, music, sound, story events, and animation sequences to the mood and emotional outlook of the piece. This is not the work of 'text' then, in the traditional model of dialogue and descriptors, but a set of micro-elements advancing narrative through visualization and its aural complement.

Consequently, then, one 'metamorphosis' might constitute a micro-narrative in animation, but such concentration on the microcosm – the 'small' world – is but one example of the ways in which any of the staple and constituent elements of traditional scriptwriting can be interrogated and reinterpreted. A single scene in an extended live action story, for example, may operate as a convincing micro-narrative in animation. Traditional scriptwriters in soap operas and features often have to write what might be viewed as stock scenes – such as the proposal, the apology, the deception, the postponement, the confession – and though the inventive writer can refresh such scenes they are often hidebound by their naturalistic and domesticated context and content. Such scenes are also localized and intimate conversation pieces, and though, as Blake Snyder has claimed, these kind of expositional exchanges can be subject to a 'Pope in the Pool' strategy – effectively dressing a necessary but mundane and undramatic dialogue with unusual action (Snyder 2005: 123–5) – animation inherently affords 'difference' to these scenes, and makes them dramatically viable as narrative vignettes in their own right. As Syd Field points out, 'The scene is the single most important element in your screenplay. It is where something happens – where something specific happens. It is a specific unit of action and the place you tell your story' (2003: 197). The overt artifice of animated practices allows the reinspection and amplification of the narrative detail intrinsic to such 'units of action', making them focused story events and complete micro-narratives. This becomes clear when looking at a typical scene which might occur in a live action feature or soap, but which becomes a short narrative in its own right by the way in which animation facilitates a different approach to its content and context.

By recasting an apology scene between John and Karen in *John and Karen* (Dir. Matthew Walker, UK, 2007) as an exchange between a massive polar bear and a tiny penguin in an ordinary domestic living room, Matthew Walker allows the anticipated conversation to be refreshed by using the everyday preoccupations of animal life as the subject of the apology, and the incongruity of the animal sizes to underpin the characterization (see Wells 2009). Crucially, though, as well as invigorating the dramatization of the scene, it also allows a concentration on the eating of a ginger biscuit during the exchange to operate as a symbolic subtext, which might have remained unnoticed, or mere dressing in a naturalistic live action exchange. Micro-events inform and become micro-narratives. This is further accentuated when motifs become the intrinsic story points in an animated film, becoming highly concentrated micro-narratives by virtue of their accentuation as foregrounded narrative events. This can service a film composed of personal symbols and memories like Yuri Norstein's *Tale of Tales* (Dir. Yuri Norstein, Russia, 1979) (see Kitson 2005), or a reworking of superhero texts and subtexts in Saturday Night Live's *The Ambiguously Gay Duo* (Dir. Robert Smigel and J. J. Seidelmaier, USA, 1996), or accumulated across a whole feature, like *Monsters vs Aliens* (Dir. Rob Letterman, Conrad Vernon, USA, 2009), in which numerous 1950s B movie icons and signifiers, including motifs from *Attack of the Fifty Foot Woman*, *The Blob*, *The Fly*, are condensed and conflated into an extended narrative.

This kind of accumulation of micro-narratives in animation, I wish to term *bricolage*, in that the fluid and flexible nature of the animated form enables seemingly variable modes of visual expression to work together in a cogent and acceptable way, even though they do not function as a 'classical' or 'anti' narrative in the traditional sense. To conclude my discussion, I wish to illustrate this by looking at the Disney series, 'Phineas and Ferb', created by Jeff 'Swampy' Marsh and Dan Povernire. I wish to stress here that the concepts and ideas that underpin the 'script' of the series facilitate the storyboarding process, the animatics and the final animation process. The 'bricolage' assemblage of the piece constantly demonstrates how content and context are compressed in the micro-narratives, as they themselves function as concepts. This becomes one method, for example, by which when I am teaching about the specificity of the animation 'script', I suggest that 'theory' and 'practice' combines, as each idea or concept often works as a literal pictorial suggestion.

For example, the opening song both sets the scene for the show itself and for the issues I wish to consider. The two boys, brothers Phineas and Ferb, play in a band, and sing:

> There's a 104 days of Summer Vacation
> And School comes along just to end it,
> So the annual problem of our generation is
> Finding a good way to spend it.
> Like maybe …
> Building a rocket or fighting a Mummy
> Or climbing up the Eiffel Tower
> Discovering something that doesn't exist,

Giving a Monkey a shower.
Surfing a tidal wave, creating metal bots,
Locating Frankenstein's brain.
Finding a Dodo bird, Painting a Continent,
Driving our sister insane.
As you can see there's a whole lot of stuff to do
Before school starts this Fall,
So stick with us,
'Cos Phineas and Ferb are gonna do it all!!

At the conclusion of which, Phineas and Ferb's sister, Candace, like many siblings, seeks to get her brothers into trouble by saying, 'Mom, Phineas and Ferb are making a title sequence …' – simultaneously signalling the knowing self-reflexivity of the programme, but also one of the show's ongoing motifs, which is Candace's repeated attempt to expose her brothers' impossible and often spectacular schemes to their mother, only to be constantly foiled by the fact that on every occasion mom witnesses an event, everything seems back to normal. In her mother's mind, this merely confirms Candace's sibling rivalry, and that whatever Phineas and Ferb had actually been doing was nothing more than an act of imaginative play.

As might be expected in animation, elements of the song in the title sequence are illustrated literally – the boys build a rocket, fight a Mummy, climb the Eiffel Tower, but crucially, the sequence establishes the core premise of the programme, namely, the boys' attempts to fill the time in their three-month summer holidays, but equally, the activities which might be undertaken to do this. Such activities are immediately facilitated and legitimized by the animated form, and in themselves operate as micro-narratives, but become justified by the following conditions – an echo of Jones's 'rules', which establish the inner logic of the accumulated narrative:

- The boys undertake impossible tasks and projects as if they were normal play activities. On the one hand, then, intrinsically 'imaginative', but on the other, made literal within the illusionist context of the cartoon form.
- The boys engage with mythic or imaginary worlds as if they were as real as the everyday material world in which they live. The ontological equivalence of the animated text readily facilitates this uniformity and commonality.
- The boys are often participating in surreal scenarios, but at all points, there is a plausible reason for their occurrence, however, seemingly 'illogical' in orthodox live action scenarios.
- The boys access 'real-world' adult activity not accessible to or executable by children, but this is ready evidence of the way in which all cartoonal forms speak to adult audiences.
- The show creates a parallel sub-plot of events featuring pet Perry the Platypus, working for 'O.W.C.A.' (Organization Without a Cool Acronym), fighting the evil mad scientist, Dr Heinz Doofenshmirtz, thus exploiting all the generic 'motifs' from established spy and science fiction narratives.

- The show uses self-reflexive and reflexive use of narrative form, comic events and the language of animation as specific and complete 'units of action'.

Having established these structural and thematic norms, the episodes work as a series of micro-narratives, based on singular *beats* (single story aspects), *binaries* (narrative based on the dramatic tension caused by parallel and opposing story elements suggested above) and *bricolage* (the combination of different but related story modes: songs, self-conscious exchanges, spot gags, genre-based scenes).

These three dynamics of micro-narrative are readily evidenced in the visual materials developed to determine the 'script' and as the focus of the storyboarding process in the creation of the final animation in many productions. The engagement with the suggestiveness and associative relations of single ideas, motifs, objects and limited units of action, insists upon looking at the intrinsic narrative elements embedded in the minutiae of experience, and encourages a rethinking of their expressive representation through animation. The animation script is principally concerned with this 'thinking' of animation as a language of the ways in which motion represents meaning, and artificially conceived moving imagery can create material illusion and emotional affect. From a singular micro-narrative to the accumulation of micro-narratives in the long form, animation facilitates the most intense degree of storytelling resonance in the most limited and selective of moving image practices.

Notes

1 Killerich, personal interview with the author, Oct. 2009.
2 Sproxton, personal interview with the author, Jan. 2010
3 Stanton, personal interview with the author, July 2008.
4 Imrey, personal interview with the author, Jan. 2009.
5 Walsh, personal interview with the author, Jan. 2007.
6 For a TV animation series, there is often a 'bible', including descriptions and model sheets for all characters; a description of the 'laws' of the story world, with images of its principle locations; and some of the key story arcs over the duration of the series. This means that different directors, writers and production personnel can work on the series over time without disrupting continuity. See Wells 2006.
7 Springer, personal interview with the author, Oct. 2009.

References

Blatter, J. (2007) 'Roughing it: A Cognitive Look at Animation Storyboarding', in M. Furniss (ed.), *Animation Journal*, vol. 15, Santa Clarita, CA: AJ Press, 4–23.

Field, S. (2003) *The Definitive Guide to Screenwriting*, London: Ebury Press.

— (2005) *Screenplay: The Foundations of Screenwriting*, New York: Bantam Dell/Random House.

Frensham, R. (1996) *Teach Yourself: Screenwriting*, London: Hodder & Stoughton.

Jones, C. (1990) *Chuck Amuck*, London & New York: Simon & Schuster

Kitson, C. (2005) *Yuri Norstein and Tale of Tales: An Animator's Journey,* Eastleigh and Bloomington, IN: John Libbey.

Scott, J. (2002) *How to Write for Animation,* Woodstock and New York: Overlook Press.

Snyder, B. (2005) *Save the Cat: The Last Book on Screenwriting You'll Ever Need,* Chelsea, MI: Sheridan Books.

Vogler, C. (2007) *The Writer's Journey: Mythic Structure for Writers,* 3rd edition, Studio City, CA : Michael Wiese Productions.

Warner, M. (2002). *Fantastic Metamorphoses, Other Worlds,* Oxford and New York: OUP.

Wells, P. (1998) *Understanding Animation,* London and New York: Routledge.

— (2006) *Fundamentals of Animation,* Lausanne: AVA Academia.

— (2007) *Scriptwriting,* Lausanne: AVA Academia.

— (2009) *The Animated Bestiary,* New Brunswick, NJ: Rutgers University Press.

Wells, P. and Hardstaff, J. (2008) *Re-Imagining Animation: The Changing Face of the Moving Image,* Lausanne: AVA Academia.

Wells, P., Quinn, J. and Mills, L. (2008) *Drawing for Animation,* Lausanne: AVA Academia.

Chapter 7

The flexibility of genre
The action-adventure film in 1939

Ken Dancyger

Genre is perhaps the most misunderstood of narrative tools. In this chapter my goal is to set out my own views on one particular genre, but also to disabuse the reader about the misleading mythologies surrounding genre in general. By doing so I hope to clarify how flexible and useful genre can be in the writing of a screenplay.

One of the most frequent misconceptions about genre is the limiting view that a genre film has a policeman, detective, gangster or cowboy in it. Another misconception is that a road movie, a buddy movie, a drama, a comedy and a documentary each are distinct genres. To my mind these notions are either too general and/or too limiting to be useful to the writer. A documentary can be personal, political, educational, or cinema verité. A comedy can be a farce, situation comedy, romantic comedy, character comedy, screwball comedy or satire. Each of these 'subcategories' has different shapes, tones and character arcs. A road movie can be a gangster film, a western, a fable, even a science fiction film. A film such as *The Road Warrior* (1981) is a mix of the western and the action-adventure film. The overly general description is not terribly useful to the writer facing the writing challenge.

Also limiting is the view that only particular story forms – the gangster film, film noir, the detective story, the western, and the horror film – are genre films while all others are not. Subtextually this interpretation implies that a style alone, as opposed to particular approaches to character and structure, constitutes the genre film.

Nor is the term 'genre' applicable only to the stylized camera angles and lighting of film noir, for example, or the exaggerated colour and art direction of Douglas Sirk's melodramas. These stylistic choices can be characteristic of particular genres such as film noir, but from the writer's point of view the poor choices made by the desperate main character of film noir are far more central to distinguishing film noir from other genres.

Equally limiting is the view that only particular types of stories such as the gangster film and film noir are genre films. It is my contention that every film is one genre or another. It may be a classical genre or a voice-oriented genre. It may mix two genres, with one dominating the plot layer of the structure and a second dominating the character layer of the structure. My key point here is that every film is a genre film and that the nature of the character arc, the dramatic arc and the tone are the characteristics that distinguish one genre from another.

Genre flexibility

Genre flexibility over time is a reflection of the change in the makeup of audiences as well as an effort by producers to retain or regain audience. This is best illustrated by the western, classically represented by John Ford's *Iron Horse* (1926) in the 1920s, *Stagecoach* (1939) in the 1930s, and *She Wore a Yellow Ribbon* (1949) in the 1940s. By the 1950s an adult western, sometimes referred to as a 'neurotic western', joined the classical western. Anthony Mann's series of films, culminating in *Man of the West* (1958) (his version of *King Lear*), exemplifies this style of western. Early in the 1970s the use of the western to criticize contemporary America joined the earlier styles of western. Arthur Penn's *Little Big Man* (1970) is a good example of this tendency. By the 1990s the western was almost extinct. However, Clint Eastwood contributed what I will call the anti-western in his film *Unforgiven* (1992).

Other genres have not been quite as adaptive as the western, but they too have changed over time. The 1930s version of *Scarface* (1932) by Howard Hawks, and the 1980s version of the same story by Brian de Palma, sees a shift in the immigrant origins of its hero from Italy to Cuba, and a presentation of the main character as far more violent and less heroic, although some may argue with my interpretation (the latter having become a contemporary cult favourite).

More extreme examples of genre flexibility, however, have joined the already mentioned examples. Tonal variations in the western range from a primitive darkness, as in John Hillcoat's *The Proposition* (2006) and Clint Eastwood's *High Plains Drifter* (1973), to the lightness of Burt Kennedy's *The War Wagon* (1967) and Mel Brooks's *Blazing Saddles* (1974). I would include Sergio Leone's spaghetti westerns as more stylized and lighter in tone than the classical western.

Tonal variation and narrative ambition are significant factors in the war film. Narrative intentions vary depending on when the film was made and which war America was fighting. The heroism of the main characters dominates the Hawks films about the First World War (*Sergeant York*, 1941) and Second World War (*Air Force*, 1943). Both films, made during the Second World War, set out to characterize the conversion of the citizenry into effective, even heroic, fighting men. This is hardly the case for the Vietnam films of Oliver Stone and Stanley Kubrick. Too often the characters of *Platoon* (1986) and *Full Metal Jacket* (1987) are victims and victimizers.

We turn now to the action-adventure genre, a genre that has become far more prominent and ongoing since the success of *Star Wars* in 1977. Many of the action-adventure films have gone serial, including the *Indiana Jones* films, *Superman* (1978), *Spider-Man* (2002), *X-Men* (2000), *Batman* (1989) and *The Lord of the Rings* (2001, 2002, 2003). Along the way, other series that began as police stories or war stories have moved in their later iterations into action-adventure films. They include

Lethal Weapon (1987), *Die Hard* (1988) and *Rush Hour* (1998). Periodic period films from China have also evolved into action-adventure films. They include *Crouching Tiger, Hidden Dragon* (2003), *Hero* (2002) and *Red Cliff* (2008).

The elements of the action-adventure film are as follows:

1 A main character, whose initial goal may be modest but who ends up wanting or needing to save the world.
2 An antagonist so powerful that, if overcome by the main character, the success elevates the main character to superhero.
3 The plot is nothing short of threatening the world as it is known. The threat could be criminal (*Batman*), or supernatural (*Lord of the Rings*).
4 The journey will threaten the values of the main character.
5 A key struggle in the plot is between an idealized world (pastoral values) and a cynical world (material values or power).
6 The main character's pastoral values will be questioned in the course of the story.
7 Goodness is communal and positive, while self-interest is individualistic and self-serving, evil.
8 The main character goes through a journey where his values are tested.
9 Narrative exaggeration, superstition, evil are manifest and take the narrative away from realistic narrative choices and characters.
10 The action-adventure film is a genre of wish fulfilment, and in the film good tends to triumph over evil.
11 The tone of the action-adventure film is generally enabling, although in *The Dark Knight*, it becomes quite dark.
12 Stories can have a past, present or future setting. Imagined worlds are the most frequent setting for the action-adventure film.

I have chosen 1939 because it is the greatest year of Hollywood production. Never before or since has there been so many enduring films produced. *Stagecoach*, *The Wizard of Oz*, *Gone with the Wind*, *Ninotchka*, *Wuthering Heights*, are just five of the films produced in 1939. The four action-adventure films discussed in this chapter were also produced in 1939. Each of the four is an action-adventure film, and yet they differ vastly from one another. I turn now to these four films.

Every genre is distinguished by its approach to the main character, the role of the antagonist, its deployment in its structure of plot and character layers, and its tone. In the faces of the action-adventure film, the main character's goal is to save his world. This may mean a national goal as in *The Adventures of Robin Hood* (1938), or something more global as in *The Lord of the Rings*. The nature and powers of the antagonists, the Sheriff of Nottingham and King John in *The Adventures of Robin Hood* and Saruman in *The Lord of the Rings*, will determine how much of a superhero the main character will become.

The plot layer is elaborate and implies the end of the main character's world as he has known it and wished it to be. The character layer establishes the journey for the main character, and the journey can be considerable. For Frodo in *The Lord of the Rings,* it is a journey from innocence to the knowledge that evil exists in the world. By the end of the films, Frodo is forever changed and must leave his homeland. Although the action-adventure is a plot-driven genre, the character layer remains very important. The journey of the main character is what emotionalizes the experience of the film.

The tone of the action-adventure film is generally enabling in order to make credible the success of the all-too-human main character. Because the supernatural plays so predominant a role in many action-adventure films, the tone has to be able to embrace fantasy as well as more realistic narrative characters or events. We have to be able to believe that Indiana Jones on a horse can prevail over a truck manned by soldiers transporting the Ark of the Covenant in *Raiders of the Lost Ark* (1981). We also have to believe that a team of astronauts led by an oil rigger can destroy a dangerous and large meteor plunging toward Earth in *Armageddon* (1998). The tonal range is flexible here, with an emphasis on the belief that the main character can carry out his mission regardless of what he is up against.

The classics of the action-adventure range from the early Douglas Fairbanks films through the recent comic book characters awash on the movie screen. The four action-adventure films we will focus upon in this chapter are *Gunga Din, The Four Feathers, Northwest Passage* and *Only Angels Have Wings.* The first two suggest the adolescent appeal of the genre, while the two latter films are more complex and ambitious in the audience they seek.

The tone of *Gunga Din* is exactly the opposite of the tone of *Only Angels Have Wings.* The character level in *The Four Feathers* and *Northwest Passage* is far more developed than is the case in either *Gunga Din* or in *Only Angels Have Wings.* Each of these films is an action-adventure film and yet each offers its audience a very different experience.

Gunga Din

Gunga Din was an RKO project with disaster written all over it. A large budget of $2 million, the decision for location shooting and a late change in directors all plagued the production. Nevertheless, *Gunga Din* has become the gold standard for the sophisticated action-adventure film.

Gunga Din falls classically into the kind of adventure narrative that appealed to adolescent boys brought up on the novels of Robert Louis Stevenson (*The Man in the Iron Mask*), Alexander Dumas (*The Three Musketeers*), H. Rider Haggard (*King Solomon's Mines*) and Rudyard Kipling (*Kim*). Faraway places and times, stories of explorers and adventurers, and noble main characters and dastardly foes distinguished these stories. The future of an empire could hinge on the behaviour of one character. Great riches and enduring love were in the reach of the main character, but only if he overcame the likes of Cardinal Richelieu or Prince John. And at their core these were idealized narratives, focused on morality played out against a large canvas. Comradeship and loyalty to principle was expected on the level of that of the Knights of Arthur's Round Table. Indeed, this behaviour was as important as the mission itself. The adventure tested character and friendship, and if the behaviour of the main character did not disappoint, all would be well in his world and in our own.

Gunga Din is set in nineteenth-century northern India. The plot follows the British army's effort to defeat a Thuggee uprising. The main character, Gunga Din, provides the film with its emotional arc. A water boy (Sam Jaffe) aspires to be more, a soldier in the King's army, but his low caste prevents him, at least until he dies to save his regiment. He is granted in death what he has been denied in life.

In the foreground, the film's plot is carried by three British sergeants, McChesney (Victor McLaglen), Ballantyne (Douglas Fairbanks, Jr.) and Cutter (Cary Grant). For purposes of carrying different narrative strands, Cutter is the anti-authoritarian who acknowledges Din's goal and helps him. He is also the most physical and the source of a good deal of the humour in the film. Ballantyne carries the romance in the film. He is to leave the army to marry (Joan Fontaine). McChesney is the lifer, the army's man, who wants both his fellow sergeants to remain comrades, buddies in the army. His actions also provide humour in the film. It is the three sergeants together with Din who save the British regiment from being trapped and destroyed in the plot of *Gunga Din*. For the most part, the antagonists, the Thuggees and their leadership are presented as cartoon-like characters. Consequently they do not pose a level of threat to make the sergeants more than fun-loving heroes. Only Din, because he is not a soldier and because he sacrifices his life to save the regiment, is an authentic hero.

What is striking about the tone of *Gunga Din* is that it is effective emotionally as well as quite humorous. The humour helps emphasize the entertainment values of the film. In a sense the best way to understand the tone is to compare it to a number of more recent action-adventure films. The Spielberg–Lucas film, *Indiana Jones and the Temple of Doom* (1984), has many location and plot commonalities, but it is the humour of the Indiana Jones series from *Raiders of the Lost Ark* onwards that captures the fun, even the playfulness, that originated with *Gunga Din*. John Huston's *The Man Who Would be King* (1975) also bears the same mixture of emotion and humour, as well as being based upon Kipling original materials. The Spielberg–Lucas and the Huston films treat their adult main characters as if they are boys playing at being men. In each case this approach is key to our affiliation of the tone with 'having a good time'. Adventure dominates the action dimension of these films. Consequently, the action sequences of the plot are set pieces.

There are two set pieces that are notable in *Gunga Din*: the lead-up to and the final battle at the Temple, and the attack on the village at Tantrapur. Each is between the British and the Thuggees. To illustrate how the enjoyment of what is otherwise a violent battle is emphasized, we look at the battle in the village of Tantrapur.

Here McChesney, Ballantyne and Cutter have led a patrol to repair the telegraph and to discover what happened to the British detail that had manned the village. Ballantyne discovers a group of men in one building. They are sullen and he is forceful. Meanwhile, Cutter looks around. In the deep background, one of his men is strangled to death. Ballantyne's intervention quickly descends into a fight. He is outnumbered ten to one, but exhibits no fear. When he is found by McChesney, the big man wades into the fray. He acts as if his presence to aid Ballantyne means they outnumber the enemy. They don't. Nevertheless, the two men quickly subdue the hostiles, but the leader of the enemy calls on his followers, and hundreds of Thuggees attack the village.

The three sergeants call on their men to join them in a building where they will jointly defend their position. What ensues is a defence, but often it feels like an offensive. Dynamite, the sword, as well as pistols are used to meet the enemy, who are superior in numbers and weapons. In spite of vigorous and inventive action, the three sergeants and their men must jump from the building and into the adjacent river to save themselves and escape. The battle is great fun for the three sergeants, and for us. The tone of 'men will be boys' successfully merges adventure, humour and feeling in *Gunga Din*.

The Four Feathers

The Four Feathers, first filmed in 1939, has been remade twice, most recently in this decade. It is a great epic action-adventure film in the tradition of Griffith's *Intolerance* (1916) and Ford's *The Iron Horse*. In short, it is a huge-scale spectacle, framing a more personal story of honour lost and regained. The film was produced, designed and directed by the Korda brothers, who had earlier produced quality epics such as *The Private Life of Henry VIII* (1933) and *Elephant Boy* (1937). Their work was notable for its scale, its action and its great characters.

The main character, Harry Faversham, scion of a military family, is overwhelmed by the expectations family tradition place on his shoulders. Harry and his three friends, Lt. Peter Burroughs, Captain John Durrance and Lt. Willoughby, are graduating as officers. They learn that they are to go to the Sudan to fight under General Kitchener. That night Harry's engagement to Ethne Burrows is announced. John Durrance, also a suitor, is deeply disappointed but gallant about it. The next day Harry submits a letter of resignation from the army. His father's death six months before and his engagement with the orders to ship out prompted him to withdraw from the army.

His friends and fiancée send/give him a white feather, the accusation of cowardice. The wedding is off. The balance of the film is devoted to Harry's effort to get his friends to withdraw the four feathers. He begins in Egypt. There he decides to take on an Arab disguise. The members of the Sengali tribe, having had their tongues cut out, are mute. Thereby he avoids speech which he doesn't have in any case. They are also branded on the forehead. He has himself mutilated, his skin color altered by a dye, and he proceeds to pass himself off as a Sengali.

He joins Kitchener's army as a slave helping drag the British transports down the Nile toward Sudan. He escapes and joins the Sudanese army as a slave, and he waits. As Kitchener's army sends out companies and patrols to find the Sudanese lines, one such patrol runs into trouble. That company includes Harry's three friends. On patrol Captain Durrance spots Dervishes but has an accident and is injured. His injury leads to blindness. His patrol warns of trouble. That night they are attacked by a larger Sudanese force and overtaken. Harry tries to warn them. Lieutenants Willoughby and Burroughs are taken prisoner. Durrance has been left for dead, as has Harry. But both survive.

Harry doesn't speak. When he realizes Durrance is blind, he tries to help him. They survive the desert and finally find the river. On a makeshift raft they make it to a British post. There, Harry deposits Durrance, and while he is placing the feather in his diary, British soldiers capture him. They believe he is stealing from a British officer. Later, Harry escapes.

While Durrance recovers and courts Ethne Burroughs, he shares with her and Dr Sutton the story of the slave who saved him and tried to rob him. He tells them only her last letter to him kept him alive. He shows them the letter. There they find the feather Harry left. They know now Harry is alive. The Captain, blind, doesn't see their reaction to the feather.

Back in Omdurman, Harry connects with Lts. Willoughby and Burroughs. Making contact with them he is found out, beaten and imprisoned. While the battle between Kitchener and the Sudanese forces goes on outside, the prisoners overthrow their guards and fight against their captors.

Kitchener wins the battle. The Sudan is retaken. And the prisoners and Harry are free. Harry reunites with Ethne. The film ends as Harry Faversham returns the white feather to Ethne.

Honour

Honour can be viewed in many ways. It can be foolhardy, it can be public, or it can be private. The Korda version of the A. C. W. Mason novel opts for honour as an internal, private issue. Harry Faversham, as presented, is a shy, fearful teenager, frightened not so much of the world before him but rather by the long shadow of accomplished ancestors. In his mind, he could never match their achievements, their courage.

Positioning his fear as he does, Mason has placed the issue where every boy's fear resides. Can I live up to my father and my father's expectations of me? Or will I fail? By doing so, the writer has made *The Four Feathers* an internal issue of honour rather than the more public versions of honour. This is important because it seeds Harry's journey to regain his honour in personal terms. From a dramatic point of view, this vests the main character's goal as one of achieving or regaining self-respect rather than public glory. The latter, if it were the goal, would make *The Four Feathers* a political film about the heroism and the resourcefulness of the British officer, and implicitly a celebration of British imperialism, exactly what this version of *The Four Feathers* is not.

The other aspect of Harry Faversham's sense of honour is that it embraces the other. Harry cares what his friends think of him. But he also cares about his friends, and they feel as strongly about him. And so the honour that is at the core of *The Four Feathers* is a complex mix of self-respect, duty, responsibility and friendship. It is about personal behaviour as well as personal psychological makeup. To be honourable means extending the self, and taking risks for the other. In this sense the code of honour at the core of *The Four Feathers* is noble, worthy of admiration. The success of *The Four Feathers* is embedded in this idealized sense of honour.

Country

As the world moved towards its second worldwide war of the century, nationalism ran high. In America this translated into films such as *Confessions of a Nazi Spy* (1939), *Man Hunt* (1941) and *Flying Tigers* (1942). In England it meant films such as *That Hamilton Woman* (1941) (about Horatio Nelson, the national hero of the Battle of Trafalgar) and *In Which We Serve* (1942). By 1939, the widespread feeling was that there would be war. And so it is natural that one of Britain's past wars, in this case, the war for the Sudan in the late nineteenth century, could easily be framed as a nationalistic tale.

The fact that it was not is one of the most interesting things about *The Four Feathers*. The presentation of the military tradition in *The Four Feathers* is represented by the second scene in the film, the reunion of the Crimean war veterans at the Faversham estate. The ostensible occasion of Harry's birthday seems unimportant in comparison to the characterizations of the British military tradition in the scene.

The two key figures in this characterization are Generals Faversham and Burroughs (C. Aubrey Smith). General Burroughs talks about a lost tradition and the battle of Balaclava, a turning point in the war with Russia. The general elaborately describes his battle plan using fruit to illustrate. There is also an emphasis upon the brutality in the battle. By affiliating nationalism and national pride with the older generation, the writer and director dissociate Harry's actions from nationalism. I will return to Harry and the nationalism of the previous generation momentarily, but before doing so we need to look at the presentation of warfare once the setting shifts to Egypt and the Sudan.

The presentation of King and country in this phase is the presentation of Kitchener, the British general, and the British army and navy once engaged in battle. Kitchener is presented in a sense as a figurehead rather than as the embodiment of British imperialism. If we look at the presentation of General Gordon and Kitchener in Basil Dearden's *Khartoum* (1966), or of British officers and the class system in Cy Enfield's *Zulu* (1964) (films from a similar historical period to *The Four Feathers*), we immediately appreciate that Kitchener is presented as a military man in *The Four Feathers*. The army, including Captain Durrance and Lieutenants Burroughs and Willoughby are not presented as gung-ho imperialists but rather as decent chaps trying to fulfil their duty. In terms of strategy and professional comportment the army and navy is confident and professional. This is the extent of their representation in *The Four Feathers*.

Personalize the story

The great strength of *The Four Feathers* is that it manages to make personal an epic plot. The epic dimension is the battle for the Sudan. How to make such a large-scale campaign meaningful on the personal level is the challenge the writer faces. The points of comparison are to action-adventure films such as *King Solomon's Mines* (1950) and to war films such as *Black Hawk Down* (2001). The plot of *King Solomon's Mine* is the search for a white man missing in the African interior, lost in search for a fabled mine. The journey inland focuses on an experienced white guide and a mysterious tall black man who is a king seeking to reclaim his crown. In *Black Hawk Down,* the plot is a military campaign gone bad in Somalia. The conflict between American forces and a Somali warlord's guerrillas pits modern against traditional forces and poses questions about the limits of technology. Plot is crucial in each of these films. Yet by focusing upon a white man's inner sense of responsibility to Africa in *King Solomon's Mines,* and to the personal responsibility American soldiers have towards their comrades in *Black Hawk Down,* each of these films finds a way to make a big plot have personal resonance.

In *The Four Feathers,* the personal goal for Harry Faversham is to have each of his four friends rescind the feather that brands him a coward. Although the military battles between the British and Sudanese forces are spectacular, it is the positioning of Harry Faversham, first with the British forces as a slave, then with the Sudanese forces as a slave, that enables Harry to be in a position to effect a rescue of his friends. Unlike Din in *Gunga Din,* Harry does not save the troop and thereby influence a battle's outcome. Instead, Harry focuses on his friends.

In the first battle, all goes badly for the British. Lieutenants Burroughs and Willoughby are captured and Captain Durrance is left for dead. Harry earlier interceded directly to prevent Durrance from being killed. He himself is injured in the effort. Both survive and Harry's effort to rescue Durrance begins. Since it is only the two of them, an Arab slave and a blind British soldier, the personal struggle to survive replaces the military struggle. When Harry deposits the feather in Durrance's diary, it is a moment of personal triumph. It is also a moment of personal threat as Harry as slave is overtaken and beaten for being a thief. Misunderstood once more, Harry's personal triumph is incomplete.

Harry, in organizing the prison rebellion, joins the ongoing battle for Omdurman, but only to help him and his friends to survive the battle that is ongoing outside the city. His only action that impacts the progress of the battle is to raise the British flag over the fort. This stops the British bombardment of its own position. Again, the main character hasn't saved the day for his side but he has saved the day for himself and his friends. By staying with the personal goal of giving each of his friends a personal reason to withdraw the white feather, the story has remained very much Harry's personal story with the more epic struggle proceeding as the context – the background for the personal story.

Epic action-adventure films

The contemporary analogue to *The Four Feathers* is Ridley Scott's *Gladiator* (2000). *Gladiator* is both a personal story of revenge as well as the epic struggle for control of the Roman Empire. The power of this narrative is the personal story enhanced by the epic struggle in the background. Forty years earlier, Anthony Mann told the same story in his *The Fall of the Roman Empire* (1962). In that film the plot – the corrupt struggle of Commodus to succeed his father, Marcus Aurelius – was the foreground story. Without the personal story that film was all spectacular plot, without the emotional base that a personal story provides.

The Four Feathers has a main character whose personal journey from coward to hero is immense and emotional. At the same time, the British military campaign of 1895–6 to regain the Sudan after its loss at Khartoum in 1885 is epic in the scale of the challenge. The presentation of that campaign, although it forms the backdrop of the story, is powerful in the scale of the combatants.

In the action-adventure, the presentation of the main character and the plot can move towards the cartoon if the antagonist, as well as the set pieces, are unrealistic. This isn't the case in *The Four Feathers*. Harry Faversham's motivation for action is clear and psychologically plausible. So too is the behaviour of the various combatants. But nothing acts to convince us more than the fact that Harry is his own antagonist. As in *Lawrence of Arabia* (1962), he is struggling with a personal issue. His choice to resign is his decision. His choice to go to Egypt is his decision. He is seeking by his actions to redeem himself. It is true that the Caliph of Sudan is the enemy. And that the Sudanese soldiers and guards at the prison give a face to the enemy. But they are not the primary antagonist here. It is Harry himself who has created an intolerable situation for himself. And it is for him to extract himself from his self-made dilemma.

In this sense, *The Four Feathers* has many of the attributes of the epic. But because it is always infused with a sense of boyhood challenge and adventure, I consider it an action-adventure film with epic qualities.

Northwest Passage

What makes *Northwest Passage* different from *The Four Feathers* and *Gunga Din* is the seriousness of the premise. Adolescent adventures and codes of personal behaviour are displaced by the issue of leadership. What is leadership? How important is it? What is personally sacrificed for the public behaviour of leadership? These are the questions that emanate from King Vidor's *Northwest Passage*.

Leadership has always been a critical subject for films, particularly periods of political uncertainty or grave threat. 1939 was such a year, and a number of the films of the year are principally about leadership: *Juarez*, *Mr Smith Goes to Washington* and *Northwest Passage*.

I haven't so far defined the purposefulness or importance of 'leadership'. There is moral leadership, political leadership, economic leadership, leadership of the family unit or of the community or of an even larger group. But most of the films that have focused on leadership have focused upon war as a milieu where leadership is defined. It can be presented positively or negatively, it can be strategic or it can be about maintaining or saving life. Since leadership in *Northwest Passage* is presented in wartime, it is appropriate to look at other war films.

The modern film that is thematically similar to *Northwest Passage* is Peter Weir's *Master and Commander* (2003). Although Jack Aubrey is the captain of a ship, whereas Rogers commands a colonial militia, the plots have similarities: the French–British struggle on the seas for primacy in the early nineteenth century in *Master and Commander,* and the Seven Years' War (between the British and French, 1756–63) again focuses on primacy. Will the British or French control the Americas and the colonies in the Far East in *Northwest Passage?* Each film focuses on the power and cunning and cruelty of the enemy. And in each film it is the leaders, Rogers and Aubrey, who make the difference between victory and defeat and death. In each case the leader is courageous but also disciplined in his approach to the mission. In each his strategic resourcefulness makes the difference between victory and defeat. And in each case the leader is concerned about the fate of his men, but not to the detriment of the larger goal: to prevail against the superior force of the enemy.

The balance of films about leadership focus on two goals: the responsibility and fate of the men under the leader's command; or the larger goal, victory. Steven Spielberg's film *Saving Private Ryan* (1997) is all about saving one's men but adds the subtextual question, 'is anything worth the loss of the men or the leader's own life?' Robert Aldrich often focuses on leadership, but as often as not, good and bad leaders occupy opposing positions. Jack Palance is the good leader in *Attack* (1956) while Eddie Albert, his commanding officer, is the irresponsible, dangerous leader. Aldrich replicates this dichotomy in *Too Late the Hero* (1970), with Cliff Robertson as the effective leader and Denholm Elliott as the dangerous leader. The theme is also explored in *The Dirty Dozen* (1967) and *The Flight of the Phoenix* (1965). For Aldrich, leadership issues go to the heart of the outcome in the battle. Leadership is a life or death issue, just as it is in Kubrick's war films, *Full Metal Jacket* (1987) and *Paths of Glory* (1957).

The second kind of film is all about the nature of the great leader who is victorious in war. Whether this means eccentricity and a touch of madness (as in Schaffner's *Patton,* 1970), or military skill (the great warrior notion in Hathaway's Rommel film *The Desert Fox,* 1981), whether it is the narcissism of the colonel (Alec Guinness) in *Bridge over the River Kwai* (1956) – whatever the reason, in each case, leadership has results.

Robert Rogers is such a leader. He's central to the outcome of the raid on St Francis and the survival of his men consequent to the raid. But as Rogers himself says to Huck Mariner, 'I'm a soldier and a commander of men. If you should meet me (in a civilian life) I'm just a man ... you may have to use a little charity ...'

Only Angels Have Wings

Only Angels Have Wings, written by Jules Furthman, directed by Howard Hawks, is another adult action-adventure film. Unlike *Northwest Passage*, it does not focus on a specific theme such as leadership, but rather opts to explore masculinity as a state of being. A character has to prove himself. In this sense *Only Angels Have Wings* is a virtual rite of passage for its male characters.

The story

Only Angels Have Wings takes place in Barranca, a fictitious South American location. The proximity of mountains suggests the foothills of the Andes. The ever-changing weather isn't so much equatorial as variable, suggesting a distance south of the equator. Aside from the Spanish inhabitants, Barranca seems to have an abundance of American expatriates; the men are flyers, the women former entertainers – pianists or chorus girls. In short, they are people with a past and a penchant for escape. The owner of the hotel bar and the local airline is Dutchy, an allusion to his accent and his disposition. The plot focus is on flying airplanes to deliver/pick up the mail. Barranca is subject to lots of weather, rain and fog, and so flying is a challenge. Bonnie Lee (Jean Arthur) is a pianist who arrives for a ship stopover in Barranca and decides to stay when she falls for Jeff Carter (Cary Grant), the manager of the airline. Jeff is a flyer as well as the manager.

Aside from the progression of the Bonnie Lee–Jeff relationship, the focus is on flying, or more specifically, the dangers of flying. The first flight of the film ends in the death of a pilot.

The plot gets complicated by the arrival of a new pilot named McPherson (Richard Barthelmess). He's changed his name because of his reputation; he bailed out leaving his co-pilot to die. There are complications. The co-pilot who died was the younger brother of the Kid (Thomas Mitchell) who is Jeff's best friend and fellow pilot. Another complication is that McPherson's wife, Judy, is Jeff's former flame.

McPherson proves himself through a number of dangerous flights including the last in which the Kid, as his co-pilot, breaks his own neck. The film ends when Jeff and another pilot, both with arms in slings, take up the next mail flight (the weather has cleared). Bonnie decides to stay in Barranca and in the relationship with Jeff.

The existential story

The plot of *Only Angels Have Wings*, if taken literally, makes no sense. There are relationships, there are losses and there is danger, but connecting the dots requires seeing the film as more metaphor than reality. The existential sense of the story begins with the idea that all of these characters seem to have a traumatized past that they are running away from. Their gathering in Barranca, which seems the edge of the world, can't be understood as a flight to paradise. In fact it may be just the opposite. As Bonnie describes it, 'Barranca is far from Brooklyn.'

Men and women

The men and women in *Only Angels Have Wings* seem very lonely, or in existential terms they seem alone. Jeff, as the boss, makes decisions, distancing himself from his personnel. He grounds the man closest to him, the Kid, when the Kid tricks him into the revelation that his eyesight is failing. He sends others up to fly knowing the danger. And he is constantly a man with a chip on his shoulder, given his burden of responsibility.

Nevertheless, men talk of love for one another. And their behaviour is that of a group of gladiators awaiting the arena and possibility of death. Consequently, as they wait they seek female companionship, or male. Each moment is experienced knowing they may die as soon as they re-enter the arena (in this film, flight).

The women are sad, emotional and frustrated. Both Bonnie and Judy are devoted to their men but they seem to settle for their lot, albeit with an attendant resentment that they cannot have more. Drink, an acerbic sense of humour and guilt that they cannot save their men gives these women an all but untenable situation: commitment without security, an unspoken tension and anger that never goes away. Like the men, these women speak and act as if the moment is all they have or will ever have. Their men are going off to a symbolic war, to prove they are men. The test, too often lethal, doesn't end the threat to the relationship. Before the test has ended, the next test looms. And the men and women both know it.

Values

The values expounded in *Only Angels Have Wings* are that life is temporary, fleeting. You can be whole one minute and die having broken your neck in the next. If this is the case, you have to be alive in the moment. This means that in that moment a man has to validate his existence in a ritual test. For flyers this means to fly. The test is to fly in dangerous conditions. For women such a temporary view of living means you need a relationship to prove you are alive. And having a relationship means to accept its temporariness and to enjoy the moment. It also means that relationships that come with a history and imply a future mean not ruminating on the past. Stay in the present; accept its parameters and you can have a kind of happiness.

The surround to both of these present moments suggests flashes of happiness surrounded by a sea of anxiety. This is the state Jeff, the Kid, McPherson, Bonnie and Judy find themselves in. For that reason there is a sadness that pervades *Only Angels Have Wings*. The film is far from the optimism and wish fulfilment of the more conventional action-adventure film. It is as if the writer and director accept the Freudian notion that all that is valuable in life emanates from work and love or relationships. However, the writer and director also embrace thanatos, the death instinct, as well as eros, the life force. And the presence of thanatos in *Only Angels Have Wings* makes its characters more reflective than the group of characters we tend to meet in the action-adventure.

Art

Before we move on to the action-adventure story form, I'd like to suggest that the existential overlay or metaphorical treatment of the story in *Only Angels Have Wings* is an approach that has provided film with a number of its richest and most enduring experiences.

In the USA, films such as *Godfather II* (1974) and *Apocalypse Now* (1979), although genre films, focus on a character who is alone. The actions the character takes against family in *Godfather II* and against a fellow American soldier in *Apocalypse Now* only deepen that sense of aloneness for the main character.

In Europe, *Wages of Fear* (1953) and the Kieslowski trilogy *Blue*, *White*, and *Red* (1994) focus on the aloneness of their characters. Whatever the nature of the plot or the relationship in the films, the focus is on their transitory nature, and it is clear in each film that relationships end suddenly and once again the character is left alone.

Why this approach?

Why do writers and directors opt to tell a story in this rarified manner, and when they do, how do they make the story entertaining as well? The existential/metaphorical approach to story is ambitious, and perhaps this is the appropriate moment to look at the popular/commercial to art grid in filmic storytelling. In a sense, the broader the approach to the material, the more popular/commercial it will be. *Gunga Din* has humour and an ironic tone that lightens the action sequences and their consequences for the main characters. At the other extreme, we have the rarefied approach taken in *Only Angels Have Wings*. There is plot, dangerous airplane action, but essentially the action is dangerous and the tone acknowledges the abundance of potential negative outcomes. The austerity of the tone is intended to zero in on one basic instinct – fear of death – just as the single instinct in focus in the Von Sternberg–Dietrich films was sexuality. Going back to *Gunga Din* for a moment, there the focus was on fun, friendship and social/caste ambition. The difference in tone results in a vastly different experience for the films' audience.

It is clear that the focus on fear, the state of the characters, mostly alone, and the enormous power of fickle nature makes *Only Angels Have Wings* an intense, different kind of experience. This was the goal of Jules Furthman, the writer, and Howard Hawks, the director. It's interesting that Hawks was the director hired for *Gunga Din*, but that he left the project to make *Only Angels Have Wings*. The elemental character of the latter was central to Hawks's view of men.

A last word on the 'why' of it. The sensibility of *Only Angels Have Wings* is one that is associated with Ernest Hemingway and his literary sorties into being a man in the twentieth century. By setting *Only Angels Have Wings* in sybaritic South America, with its mix of romantic notions of manhood and the lurking suspicion that life was more pure there than in the materialistic United States, Furthman and Hawks are able to explore whether men can still be men in the post-First World War world. Or have they lost their independence and now seek adventure in an effort to find their manhood again? By going to the metaphor, Hawks and Furthman sharpen the search for this modern American male, an issue that is artistic in its goal, rather than commercial.

The action-adventure film

The action-adventure genre was as popular in 1939 as it is today. What is different now is that for the most part cartoon characters have replaced real-life main characters, characters such as Jeff Carter in this film or Robert Rogers in *Northwest Passage*. *Batman* and *Spider Man* do struggle with everyday issues that make them more available to identify with, but the scale of the antagonist and the nature of the plot, taking over whole cities, make these films more cartoon, more adolescent, than these earlier action-adventure films.

Whether we call *Only Angels Have Wings* a serious or more adult action-adventure film, we see the primary difference in the realism, the all-too-human main character. Jeff has been hurt by relationships before and he is again in this film. The loss of the Kid brings Jeff to cry; his tears and Bonnie's concern over those tears make Jeff almost too human for the genre.

A second characteristic that makes *Only Angels Have Wings* so very different from the traditional action-adventure film is the total absence of a clear antagonist. Unless we consider the weather the antagonist, there are no other candidates. The consequence is that, although there are dangerous flights, there are no single opposing characters raising the bar against the main character. The result is to flatten the effect of the plot, to leave us alone with the characters. The result is a more relaxed sense of the progression of the film, more episodic than traditional rising action.

A third characteristic that differentiates *Only Angels Have Wings* is its tone. Generally the tone of the action-adventure is light and enabling. The genre tends to brim with wish fulfilment – the heroic main character, the super-evil powerful antagonist, the journey of transformation for the main character, essentially, the plot. All combine to provide a hopeful heroic outcome; let's call it the perfect adolescent fantasy. We certainly could not say the same about the tone in *Only Angels Have Wings*. Instead we get almost a post-apocalyptic film. It is always raining and foggy, and for the most part the film takes place at night, a tone more appropriate for film noir than for action-adventure. Darkness and fog are more sinister than enabling. This tone strips away the obvious romanticism of the traditional action-adventure.

Finally, the absence of an antagonist, and the tone, together make this action-adventure far less of a journey for the main character. If you think of the journey in *Northwest Passage* as the transformation from effective military leader to heroic leader, the plot does transform Roberts. If you think of the journey in *Four Feathers,* it is the journey from cowardice to heroism for Harry Faversham, its main character. In *Gunga Din*, the transformation/journey for Din is from low-caste water boy to military hero. Each of these films presents the more typical case. The lack of transformation in *Only Angels Have Wings* supports a different view of Jeff Carter. He is a survivor. He has the drive of the action-adventure main character, but his actions take place in a centre of despair, Barranca, rather than in an environment where one can imagine a future. He has cheated Bonnie into staying by using a two-headed coin, again not so much a declaration of change as an avoidance of declaring a commitment to a future. He is tentative but smiling when we leave him. What we have then is an action-adventure film where the main character does not journey but simply carries on, doesn't change so much as prevail. This is an existential view of the action-adventure main character. His world is a dark place and he'll have none of that hero stuff – he's just doing his job, and he'll go on doing his job, as long as he is able. It's a pretty different take on our main character, here.

An exploration of masculinity

Instead, we are left with a thorough exploration of masculinity. In the traditional action-adventure film the main character, generally male, tends only to look at the heroic aspect of being male – being capable, having a specific gift, having the heart to rescue whoever needs rescuing in the story. Instead of taking this definition of being masculine, Furthman and Hawks seem interested in defining being a man rather differently. Instead of fulfilling one's genetic destiny, as in *Star Wars*, or the circumstance of being an innocent, as in *The Lord of the Rings*, the Furthman/Hawks version of being a man embraces the need to prove and prove again that you are a man. This testing is integral to being a man, but it is not the only quality on show. Being a man also means being able to express love towards men and women. The heroic Hawks male struggles with this issue but prevails. And the Hawks male is a great companion. He believes in the company of men and that camaraderie is as vital to being a man as breathing.

A man is boy, man, and old man all wrapped into one package. He is son, lover, husband, caretaker, and caregiver. A man is all of these things. For Hawks/ Furthman, the journey is to accept the different male components. The more you incorporate, the more man you are. And that's the heroic goal, an internal goal – to be a man in all its phases and layers.

Conclusion

In this chapter we have examined four action-adventure films released in 1939. My purpose has been to illustrate how flexible one particular genre, the action-adventure film, can be, ranging from the light-hearted fun of *Gunga Din* to the heavy, unanswerable existential anxiety of *Only Angels Have Wings*. All the films share a reliance on plot to test the character. Whether an outer journey for the characters or an inner journey, these four films illustrate that, although genres have recognizable common qualities, those qualities are only a template for the audience. Quite where the writer wants to take us depends upon their willingness to amend the genre, and their courage to push the genre to its limits. Their efforts, and their achievements in these four films made 70 years ago, should encourage today's writers. Genres are not fixed forms. They are no more than templates for audience recognition and interest. Where today's writers will choose to take us depends upon their vision and their willingness to courageously amend the genre.

Filmography

Aldrich, Robert, *Attack*, 1956
— *Flight of the Phoenix*, 1965
— *The Dirty Dozen*, 1967
— *Too Late the Hero*, 1970
Bay, Michael, *Armageddon*, 1998
Bennett, Compton, *King Solomon's Mines*, 1950
Brooks, Mel, *Blazing Saddles*, 1974
Burton, Tim, *Batman*, 1989
Capra, Frank, *Mr Smith Goes to Washington*, 1939
Coward, Noël, *In Which We Serve*, 1942
Coppola, Francis Ford, *The Godfather II*, 1974
— *Apocalypse Now*, 1979
Curtiz, Michael, *The Adventures of Robin Hood*, 1938
Clouzot, Henri-Georges, *Wages of Fear*, 1953
Dearden, Basil, *Khartoum*, 1966
Dieterle, William, *Juarez*, 1939
Donner, Richard, *Superman*, 1978
— *Lethal Weapon*, 1987
Eastwood, Clint, *High Plains Drifter*, 1973
— *Unforgiven*, 1992
Enfield, Cy, *Zulu*, 1964
Flaherty, Robert, *Elephant Boy*, 1937
Fleming, Victor, *The Wizard of Oz*, 1939
— *Gone with the Wind*, 1939
Ford, John, *Iron Horse*, 1926
— *Stagecoach*, 1939
— *She Wore a Yellow Ribbon*, 1949
Hathaway, Henry, *The Desert Fox*, 1951
Hawks, Howard, *Scarface*, 1932
— *Only Angels Have Wings*, 1939
— *Sergeant York*, 1941
— *Air Force*, 1943
Hillcoat, John, *The Proposition*, 2006
Huston, John, *The Man Who Would Be King*, 1975

Jackson, Peter, *The Lord of the Rings*, 2001, 2002, 2003
Kennedy, Burt, *The War Wagon*, 1967
Kieslowski, Krystof, *Blue, White, and Red*, 1994
Korda, Alexander, *Private Life of Henry VIII*, 1933
— *Four Feathers*, 1939
— *That Hamilton Woman*, 1941
Kubrick, Stanley, *Paths of Glory*, 1957
— *Full Metal Jacket*, 1987
Lang, Fritz, *Man Hunt*, 1941
Lean, David, *Bridge over the River Kwai*, 1956
— *Lawrence of Arabia*, 1962
Lee, Ang, *Crouching Tiger, Hidden Dragon*, 2003
Litvak, Anatole, *Confessions of a Nazi Spy*, 1939
Lubitsch, Ernst, *Ninotchka*, 1939
Lucas, George, *Star Wars*, 1977
McTiernan, John, *Die Hard*, 1988
Mann, Anthony, *Man of the West*, 1958
— *The Fall of the Roman Empire*, 1962
Miller, David, *Flying Tigers*, 1942
Miller, George, *The Road Warrior*, 1981
Nolan, Christopher, *The Dark Knight*, 2008
Penn, Arthur, *Little Big Man*, 1970
Raimi, Sam, *Spiderman*, 2002
Ratner, Brett, *Rush Hour*, 1998
Scott, Ridley, *Gladiator*, 2000
— *Black Hawk Down*, 2001
Spielberg, Steven, *The Indiana Jones* Films, 1981, 1984, 1989, 2008
— *Saving Private Ryan*, 1997
Stevens, George *Gunga Din*, 1939
Stone, Oliver *Platoon*, 1986
Weir, Peter *Master and Commander*, 2003
Woo, John *Red Cliff*, 2008, 2009
Zhang Yimou, *Hero*, 2002

Part III

Alternatives to the conventional screenplay form

Chapter 8

'Let the audience add up two plus two. They'll love you forever.'

The screenplay as a self-teaching system

Adam Ganz

A successful film could be described as a self-teaching system, which teaches you how to watch it as you watch. The story reveals itself through a series of observed behaviours about which the audience speculates. What are the underlying motivations and pressures which manifest themselves through these actions? As we watch we come up with theories and test those theories against our understanding of the unfolding narrative. This surely is what Billy Wilder meant when he gave as rule 7 in his rules of screenwriting what he claimed was a tip from Ernst Lubitsch 'Let the audience add up two plus two. They'll love you forever.' (Crowe 1999: 168).

As psychologist Jerome Bruner has written:

> The accounts of protagonists and events that constitute a narrative are selected and shaped in terms of a putative story or plot that then 'contains' them. At the same time, the 'whole' (the mentally represented putative story) is dependent for its formation on a supply of possible constituent parts ... a story can only be 'realized' when its parts and whole can, as it were, be made to live together.
>
> (Bruner 1991: 8)

As film is a time-based medium this information has to be gained in real time and within the context of the story. Any story-specific information must therefore be dynamically learned *through the act of reassembling the story.* Indeed one might describe the process, not as the screenwriter telling a story, but as the audience assembling the story from the clues and traces they find. The story is created through the audience's active speculation about the meanings of those traces. The task of the screenwriter is therefore not to write the story, but to give the audience the tools to imagine the story for themselves.

What we observe in a film is how objects in space change over time. Through the narrative we explore cause and effect, to say, 'this happened because of that'. The better we are at predicting the rules, the better we become at predicting the trajectory of the story and understanding what the forces are acting on the characters. In a satisfying film this information is deduced rather than stated explicitly and the film retains an ability to surprise us, by offering a more satisfying theory, which nonetheless is consistent with all the observed behaviours we have witnessed.

The screenwriter's task is to write scenes in such a way that the audience can figure out not only how story develops, but be actively engaging with the stories that *might* develop. And the screenwriter attempts to build those speculations into the screenplay, to create a route through the events of the narrative so that the audience will arrive at the desired outcome. If we consider a film as a set of interactions, one of the tasks of the screenwriter is therefore that of interaction design, predicting the journey the reader will make through the script and the subsequent film, and giving all the background necessary to make that journey. Moreover the more the audience feels that they have made these deductions for themselves the more they feel they own the discovery. We need to make sure that the audience knows any information – we might call it metadata – which is necessary to understand the context in which the story occurs. It's as if the audience has a different emotional relationship to things they have taught themselves.

The analysis and practice of this kind of speculation has been developed and theorized in the discipline of interaction design (also known as interface design or human computer interaction). As computers started to develop from a central mainframe accessed only by a few to the personal computer on every desktop, the discipline of interaction design was born. As the technology moved from what David Liddle has called an 'enthusiast' to a consumer technology (Moggridge 2007: 245) it needed to reinvent its modes of communication in order to be usable by everyone.

This involved applying advanced design techniques both to computers and the software that they ran. Bill Moggridge (2007) defines the discipline as

> dedicated to creating imaginative and attractive solutions in a virtual world where one could design behaviors, animations and sounds as well as shapes. … Like industrial design, the discipline would be concerned with subjective and qualitative values, would start from the needs and desires of the people who use a product or service, and strive to create designs that would give aesthetic pleasure as well as lasting satisfaction and enjoyment.
>
> (Moggridge 2007: 14)

These techniques were developed at the XEROX PARC research labs at Palo Alto in the 1970s, where some of the most significant developments in computer design were brought into being, including the Graphic User Interface (GUI), the mouse and the WYSIWIG (What You See Is What You Get) text editor. The goal in computing was to develop a self-teaching system, which teaches you how to use it as you use it.

The Graphic User Interface was an immense breakthrough which, by finding metaphors which allowed computers to display their processes visually, enabled humans to interact with their computer and the mathematical processes it was performing in a completely different way and reinvented the computer as a consumer technology, leading to the development of the Apple Mac and the Windows interface. We could describe it as the first attempt to theorize the way in which users of a system process information in real time. Moreover this theoretical approach might draw on a range of different approaches and technologies and use analogies from many different human activities. The desktop and office metaphors of files and folders came from visually representing the world in the room which surrounded the majority of computers in their early days. Finding a visual way of representing the act of saving and storing text created in the computer proved much easier when the user had a way of visualizing and naming what they were doing. (The fact that I had to correct myself after writing 'document' shows how universal the metaphors of 'document', 'folder', 'file' and 'desktop' have become.)

It rapidly became apparent that in a user-friendly system the most important thing was not the actual way in which data were stored, but the presentation of this data in a form which the user would understand. Interface design was no longer dealing with ergonomics but with metaphors. Spatial and narrative concepts became the norm as it became apparent that it was through a symbolic world that humans could best process and understand information in a virtual space.

Moreover the techniques developed at PARC were not only a set of heuristic design principles and products, but a supporting science for the design of human computer interactions. Interaction design made use of psychological analysis that studied how people learn and process information and linked this to the creative work of designers of hardware and software.

Alan Kay, recognized as the father of the laptop, was strongly influenced by Jerome Bruner, whose work on narrative I refer to above. He describes the three distinct stages in the learning process as enactive, iconic and symbolic:

> Bruner convinced me that learning takes place environmentally and roughly in stage order – it is best to learn something kinesthetically, then iconically and finally the intuitive knowledge will be in place to allow the more powerful but less vivid symbolic process to work at their strongest. ...
>
> (Moggridge 2007: 161)

How, Kay asked, can a user interface best cater to these human cognitive approaches? The most important thing was to reconceive the design process with the user at the centre. Google's first design principle is 'Focus on the user and all else will follow' (Moggridge 2007: 481).

The first interaction designers (like the first filmmakers) came from a wide range of disciplines – in the former case they might include computer science, product or graphic design, engineering or cognitive or visual psychology – and there was an attempt to synthesize the scientific and analytical techniques of these areas with creative and imaginative approaches to improve the process of design, measure human response and work out best practice. This, for example, was how the decision was taken to choose the mouse as opposed to the trackball or the joystick as the way of navigating around the screen (see Moggridge 2007: 28–9).

When interaction design began, almost a hundred years after the development of cinema, a wide range of techniques were available to find ways to make human interaction with the machine as intuitive and effortless as possible. This involved theoreticians and creative people working together to solve problems, which might be solved narratively or conceptually by changing the design of hardware or software.

Interaction design as a discipline has from the very start sought to theorize its practice and combine creative and scientific approaches to achieve its results. Team-working meant that the designer, the engineer, the psychologist and the information architect might all be in the same room together, sharing information and approaches and working as equals, without the division of labour which has existed in the cinema for much of its existence. Moreover applying theoretical techniques to practice was seen not as a discrete activity but was valued by all involved as a way to improve the understanding of how interaction design worked in order to improve the finished product. As Stu Card, author of *The Psychology of Human Computer Interaction*, says in an interview with Bill Moggridge:

> ... the idea was that any science worth its salt should have practical applications ... If this was going to work at all, you had to have something that could be used as you were designing. This did not mean that you could do all of design from science. You could have the equivalent role to that of structural engineering in relation to architecture. You could have a technical discipline that would support the design activity.
>
> (Moggridge 2007: 42)

This might entail using cognitive and visual psychology, developmental theory, rigorous analysis and user feedback. In developing heuristic approaches to good practice and finding ways to draw on a range of analytical approaches which were simply not available or in their infancy at the early stages of the cinema (and some of which have been only possible through the ability to record and analyse human behaviour which cinema has allowed) and to integrate them with the invention and inspiration of individual designers, interaction design has developed ways of describing and predicting viewer response to arguments and processes represented through sound and image. It would be foolish for those involved in designing screenplays, which prefigure narrative audiovisual experiences, not to benefit from the insights that this work can offer in analysing and improving our understanding of what we do.

A key text in the history of information design is Harry Beck's London Underground map of 1933. Beck, an electrical draughtsman, based the map on the circuit diagrams he drew for his day job, Beck realized that what was important to the traveller was not the actual relationship between stations but only the journey as he or she perceived it. The journey was measured not by actual distances or landmarks but by stations and intersections. What was necessary for the traveller was to know the key intersection points of the journey. To make those as visible as possible, much extraneous information was removed in order to simplify and accentuate the crucial moments of decision. Actual geographical information was not necessary to enable a traveller within the system for any particular journey. Story space – the way the traveller described the journey to themselves in their own mind – replaced actual geographic space. The journey was reconceived not in terms of distance, or landmarks, but in terms of interactions.[1]

Here already we can see an analogy with the process of screenwriting, in which key narrative trajectories, their points of intersection and moments of decision, are made visible to the audience as they journey through the narrative. If we reconceive the screenplay as the directions for a journey to be made through a storyspace we can take a different approach to the problems of screenplay structure and exposition, drawing on some of the techniques and approaches of interaction design.

The screenplay is often described as a 'blueprint' for a subsequent film. Where I think this metaphor breaks down is that a 'blueprint' is something conceived of as complete, which needs only to be constructed from the paper plan in order to exist in the world. A screenplay on the other hand is better thought of as one side of a dialogue with an audience. An interaction design approach can help us to consider it as a program for a sequence of interactions between the reader and the text as a way of prototyping the interactions between a future audience watching the film to be realized from that text. The audience will respond to a story told in a sequential series of images and sounds whose aim is to produce understanding and affect in its audience. The pleasure of the film lies in the interactions the audience will have with it. One of the tasks of the screenplay is to indicate as far as possible the future pleasures of the film. The interaction design or journey approach puts the audience or user at the centre of the process. The film cannot exist separately from its audience.

Design was defined by Charles Eames as a 'plan for arranging elements in such a way as to accomplish a particular purpose' (Moggridge 2007: 648). In a visual narrative, then, design consists of how elements of information are arranged visually on the screen and chronologically, before or after other elements, for the purpose of telling a story. Screenwriters have often recognized that the correct placing of information chronologically is essential to writing the screenplay. One could say that Billy Wilder is talking about information design when he says: 'If you have a problem with the third act, the real problem is in the first act' (Crowe 1999: 168).

'Information consists of differences that make a difference', writes Edward Tufte in his seminal text *Envisioning Information*. And one of the differences is that information is non-commutative: that's to say, the order in which we learn things changes their meaning. In film the order in which things happen transforms not only how we see, but even what we see. John Berger makes this point tellingly in *Ways of Seeing* (1972: 27–8) when he shows the interrelation between information and image. At the bottom of page 27 we see a representation of a painting by Van Gogh. It's described as 'a landscape of a cornfield with birds flying out of it'. We are asked to 'Look at it for a moment. Then turn the page.' When we do we discover the same picture on the next page: with a note in a handwritten typeface. 'This is the last picture that Van Gogh painted before he killed himself.' As soon as we read this we are no longer looking at a cornfield but the black crows that swoop above it.

The picture hasn't changed, but the informational context through which we perceive it has, and that changes our perception. We therefore need to have information ordered so that we have access to the right things at the right time. The audience needs to know all the necessary information about any given situation to understand the dramatic and emotional significance of the events. The audience also needs to be able to distinguish those bits of information which are crucial for the understanding of the story and those which are purely decorative.

Let us take, for example, the moment in the film *Sideways* when Miles (played by Paul Giamatti) is telling Maya (played by Virginia Madsen) about his interest in wines. In order to understand the emotional significance of the moment we need to understand what wine means to each of the characters. We need to distinguish between those elements of the discussion which set the mood and those which are directly pertinent to the narrative, and we need to be able to understand the significance of the wine-related story elements when they reappear later in the film.

William Goldman, in his book *Which Lie Did I Tell*, in discussing the failure of his own wine movie *The Year of the Comet* in 1992, says: 'The moviegoing audience has zero interest in red wine. They felt ignorant and they hated us' (Goldman 2000: 57). A film about wine lovers has an in-built problem, as Goldman points out. Wine is not a topic of mass interest and there's a prejudice against wine lovers as a snobby bunch. Moreover, unlike in a film about other high-brow activities, music, say, or art, it's not possible for the audience to share the sensory pleasures of the wine directly.

Maya and Miles discuss wine as his travel companion Jack is seducing Maya's friend Stephanie in the other room. We need to understand the information about the wine kinesthetically, then visually and finally symbolically.

The first task of an information designer is to make the audience want to know the information which is necessary for them to understand the system. The strategy of *Sideways* is to introduce us not to the world of wine, but to the characters:

> What you do at the start when you write a movie is this: *you set up your universe.* The audience needs to know what world it's entering.
>
> (Goldman 2000: 56)

In *Sideways* we don't enter the universe of wine straightaway. Instead we enter the universe of the main character, Miles. Eventually we understand why wine matters to him. Nothing else does. He's a loser, recently divorced, and reduced to stealing money from his mother. His best friend doesn't read his novel. For this guy wine is not aspirational. It is the only thing that keeps him from committing suicide. We certainly don't aspire to be like him. Miles is a writer who can't sell his work, his friend is an insensitive boor who, despite being about to get married, wants to spend a week away getting laid.

We don't meet people who are better than us, but people who are worse. This counter-intuitive introduction to the world of wine means that, when Miles first meets Maya and talks to her about wine with passion and humanity, we see a different side of him. We cannot be introduced to the wine kinaesthetically (in that we cannot taste it), but we are introduced to it emotionally. We experience the effect that Miles's love of wine has on him. We see him transformed from the tongue-tied and stumbling man unable to talk about his unpublished novel, to a poet who speaks about his love of wine with passion and enthusiasm. Maya, familiar with this world, enables us to distinguish Miles's real appreciation of wine for itself from her 'phony' ex-husband who didn't love wine for itself but for its value as a status symbol.

We don't just have to learn about wine in general. We are introduced to a very specific bottle, the 1961 Cheval Blanc, through which we will understand Miles's transformation in one of the final scenes of the film. This, we're told, is the wine he was saving for a special occasion – his tenth wedding anniversary. Then his wife left him. Maya tells him (and us): 'The day you open a '61 Cheval Blanc, that's the special occasion.' The wine has been transformed for us, into an indicator through which we'll comprehend how Miles has changed when he does finally allow himself the pleasure of the Cheval Blanc, at the end of the film, from a polystyrene cup in a burger bar. In so doing we understand that drinking wine has become for Miles not an act that stands for something else, but a thing in itself.

This is both deft writing and an equally deft piece of information design, which ensures that we comprehend the significance of Miles opening the treasured bottle through the information we have been given, both factual and emotional, about the wine, and its symbolic meanings

It may be argued that writers and storytellers have always had to find ways of linking the end with the beginning, but there are significant changes when the narrative is transmitted visually. Not only is the language assembled differently and associatively but theories are always tested against what the audience has been able to see 'with their own eyes'.

Let's take as an example the film *Witness*, which tells the story of a young Amish boy who is the only witness to a murder as he passes through Philadelphia with his mother Rachel after the death of his father. In order to understand the film we have to understand the nature of the pacifist Amish community, who do not use machinery or telephones. We need to know the rules of Amish society not only in order to understand how foreign this situation is for young Samuel but also to understand what rules of behaviour are expected of John Book, the Philadelphia policeman who takes refuge on the Amish farm when he realizes that both their lives are in danger.

Some viewers will know of the existence of the Amish community. They are unlikely to know the details of its history – let alone that they mostly share the same surname. The Amish filmgoer by definition is not a significant demographic. In order to understand the narrative and to appreciate whether this will be a sanctuary for him and when he will be in danger, we need to know what the rules of the community are, and when he is breaking them, whether in teaching young Samuel about guns, dancing to forbidden dance music from a forbidden car radio, or in punching a tourist who smears him with ice-cream, thus revealing his hiding place and bringing about the end of the film.

But the only mechanism the film has to convey this information is the film itself. It has to teach us how to watch it – in the same way that a good interface design teaches us what to expect and thus how to get to what we want. How does this film solve this apparent paradox? It sets up a set of disjunctures. We are told something which doesn't make sense. We are given an image which seems to date from the nineteenth century or earlier, yet a title is superimposed on the screen which tells us it is 1984. Our first understanding of the situation (that we are watching a period drama) is proved incorrect. We need to find an alternative solution to this apparent disjuncture between what we see and the information we've been given. We are forced to come up with an alternative solution, which fits these facts – that there is a group of people living in Pennsylvania in the late twentieth century who choose to live as if they were in the previous century. We imagine something and its existence is then confirmed to us. We're learning both the rules of the world in which the story takes place and the rules of the telling of this story.

We are given visual confirmation – feedback – that our speculations are correct. At the conclusion of the opening sequence we see in the same frame the Amish buggy stuck behind a lorry: we are given what Shakespeare calls 'the ocular proof' that these two worlds do coexist. But because we have made the series of deductions for ourselves we also have a personal relationship to this material. Our theory has been proved correct.

As an audience we try to deduce the story from the traces and clues the characters leave behind them. From these observations we try to deduce what the rules and motivations are, and thus what the outcomes will be. This is like a piece of visual detective work – a kind of forensic deduction which relies on Sherlock Holmes's remark to Watson in *The Sign of Four*, 'How often have I said to you that when you have eliminated the impossible, whatever remains, however improbable, must be the truth' (Conan Doyle 1890, 111). This relationship between visual evidence and textual speculation is something which is part of visual narrative. The screenwriter creates a set of images to be scrutinized and deduced from. We produce a series of possible explanations to be observed in time, which become authorized when the audience receives confirmation – visual proof that their speculations were, or were not, correct. We can see it, with our own eyes. Speculation is followed by visual evidence.

In film we need to know things at the right time. First we face the danger of information overload so the user may not necessarily be aware of the key elements in a busy or overcomplicated image. Take by contrast the Google web homepage, which, as Google co-founder Sergey Brin describes, was deliberately minimal:

> It actually matters when you go to the homepage of a search engine; you don't want to spend time trying to find the search box. You want people to come there and right away use it for what they want ... We made a conscious decision that we were going to take things off that page.
>
> (Moggridge 2007: 482)

The search engine should begin searching right away. In the same way that viewers don't want to spend time watching the interminable menus logos and warnings of early DVDs, search engine users want their journey to find information to start immediately. Rob Haitini, responsible for designing the user interface for the Palm operating system developed four guidelines for design practice, which seem generally useful to apply when looking at the design of a screenplay (Moggridge 2007: 213):

1 Less is more.
2 Avoid adding features,
3 Strive for fewer steps
4 Simplicity is better than complexity.

But screenplays not only need to avoid the problem of giving the audience too much information in general, there is also the fact that we absorb visual narrative as soon as we see it and the visual information will have a bearing on our understanding of the narrative. We can know too much too soon. If everything is visible there is no tension, if too little is visible there is no story.

Sir Arthur Conan Doyle complained to the editor of the *Strand Magazine* about the placing of illustrations which accompanied his stories:

> My whole object is to give the reader a stunning shock by Napoleon lying dead at the crisis of the adventure. But the story is prefaced by a large picture of Napoleon lying dead, which simply knocks the bottom out of the whole tin from the Storytellers [sic] point of view.
>
> (Conan Doyle 2007: 516)

The more the act of acquiring the necessary information becomes a dynamic and active process for the audience the more enjoyable it will be, and the more involved the audience will be with the information they have gained.

The screenwriter can make a productive use of the audience's desire to scrutinize and speculate about what they are watching so they follow a set of predesigned interactions and come to the conclusion that the filmmakers intend. This process can be compared to someone invited to pick a card from the proffered selection fanned out by a conjuror – believing the card is freely chosen.

Take for example the beginning of *To Be or Not To Be*, the comedy about a group of actors in Nazi-occupied Warsaw who use their uniforms to imitate the Nazis and escape to England. Directed by Ernst Lubitsch, about a troupe of actors who use their abilities at disguise and acting to fool the occupying troops, it was adapted by Lubitsch (uncredited) and Edwin Justus Mayer from the story by Melchior Lengyel.

The film begins with an image of Hitler looking through the window of a Warsaw delicatessen – the voiceover asks how this came to be and we flash back to the actors' troupe rehearsing their play about Hitler. But we don't know that we are watching a play within a play until the actor playing Hitler comes onto the stage with the line 'Heil Myself'. After a debate about whether or not he looks like Hitler he goes on the street to prove it.

This sequence not only locates the action precisely – to Warsaw immediately before the Nazi invasion but introduces the audience to the fact that it is difficult to tell the difference between Hitler and a small fellow with a moustache. It established the ability of the actor playing Hitler to play Hitler later in the film and that the troupe has access to Nazi uniforms. Moreover, right from the start we are introduced to the pleasure of not knowing whether we are watching a performance or not, which is the theme of the play.

Good information design gives the audience what they need to make sense of a story world by giving them the right information in the right order in a form that is clear and distinctive. But the most important thing is that the audience want to know what you want to tell them.

As Terry Rossio (n.d.) writes in his online journal Wordplayer:

> here's the stunning truth about exposition. You don't need it. 'But the audience needs to know this, that, and the other thing –' says the screenwriter. Not true. The audience does not need to *know*. The audience needs to *wonder*.) Because wonder creates interest. Instead of exposition, think in terms of situation –

Screenplays involve the audience gaining any information necessary in order to tell themselves the story *as the story is told*. In order to understand a story we need to know both the events of the story and any cultural information necessary to understand its significance. We may learn this from our knowledge of the world, from the rules of the genre, or from the film itself. But films don't come with a manual. Therefore films which are set in unfamiliar situations or genres need to find new way of informing the audience of what the rules and parameters in any particular situation might be. So, for example, to appreciate the film *The White Balloon* (1995), set in Iran during New Year, you need to know about the importance for a child of having a goldfish at New Year. But the film also needs to work for an Iranian audience who would find this information redundant. In order to appeal to the widest possible audience we have both to learn the necessary contextual information and the developing story: what it means for Razieh, the 7-year-old heroine whose quest for a goldfish leads the audience through the narrative.

In a fantasy film – like for example James Cameron's film *Terminator* (1984) – we have to learn information which can't be dependent on shared cultural knowledge since we are dealing with an entirely invented world and characters. Our only possible information source about the behaviour of Terminators is the film itself.

Groundhog Day (1994) is a particularly interesting problem of information design. Until the film was released Groundhog Day was just an obscure festival in Pennsylvania. Since the film 'It was like Groundhog Day' is a phrase that has entered the language. A websearch reveals that it is used to describe the experience of being a Sheffield Wednesday fan,[2] dealing with customer services[3] or being kidnapped by the Colombian FARC Guerrillas.[4] So the concept in its current form was more or less invented by the film. I want to look at the way in which the audience understands the meaning of Groundhog Day, given that they had no pre-existing screen model or genre to compare it to. In an early draft of the film Phil Connors has a spell put on him by a jilted girlfriend. In the screenplay as realized there is no explanation for the events. The audience are forced to try and deduce both what is happening to him in order to understand what he can do about it. The absence of a classic protagonist in the realized version of *Groundhog Day* means that Phil becomes his own protagonist and antagonist. Why does it happen to him in the final draft? There is no explicit reason. He's stuck in Groundhog Day because he deserves it. He's full of contempt. He's full of hubris. And he's egocentric. It's his 'defining characteristic', as Rita points out to him. 'People are morons', he claims as he sets off to cover Groundhog Day for the fourth time.

There are many metaphors for Groundhog Day. It has been seen variously as a Buddhist metaphor, as a call to faith, or as a film about depression. There may be doubt about how the film should be interpreted. But we are in no doubt at all about what happens, because the film very successfully teaches us what the phenomenon of Groundhog Day is, what its parameters are and ultimately how it might be solved. It does this by following the design principles outlined in Gillian Crampton Smith's foreword to Bill Moggridge's book: giving a clear mental model, reassuring feedback, navigability and consistency.

We can understand what Groundhog Day is, the same thing happening over and over again. Phil Connors can change each individual action he performs but cannot escape his fate. Each of the individual steps are concentrating on questions rather than explanations. By making the various stages in Connor's understanding of what he is doing apparent, the audience is deeply committed to deducing the story and attempting to work out its solution.

Why is this happening from the main character's point of view? By choosing to forego the why we are forced to experience what is happening from a very different place. *Groundhog Day* becomes a journey to understand the why.

Donald A. Norman's *The Design of Everyday Things* outlines a set of design principles. A designer, he says (1998: 199), should ensure the user can 'determine the relationships

- between intentions and actions.
- between actions and their effects on the system.
- between actual system state and what is perceivable by sight sound or feel.
- between the perceived system state and the needs intentions and expectations of the user.

Phil Connors acts on behalf of the user to help us deduce the rules of the world and the way in which he interacts with it. Rather than having his transformation explained to him (or to us) we have to deduce it. But we are given very clear feedback about the state of his knowledge, and his speculations. On the first day he leaves the bed and breakfast arrogantly describing his chance of departure as '100%'. On the second day, after he has been forced to return to Punxsutawney and live the same day for the first time, he describes his chances, as '80%, -75, 80'. We laugh at the joke and understand his growing uncertainty.

On the evening of the second day he breaks a pencil in order to understand whether he is really waking up all over again (which is becoming the only possible explanation to the combination of events that have occurred). When he wakes up the next day the pencil is whole. We can easily determine the relationship between the action of breaking the pencil and the intention of proving that this is 'really happening'. Moreover it is clear that the action of breaking the pencil has no effect on the system. In the Rubin/Ramis script Connors paints his room – for no reason – to prove this point. We also get feedback on the way his character is starting to change. Because the process is transparent and the feedback clear we can learn why he has done what he's done, and what the rules of his character are. The user learns about a piece of design through the feedback they are given. Good story design means good feedback. And feedback serves to reinforce and clarify the rules with increasing precision and consistency as the story progresses.

Later on in the Rubin/Ramis draft of the screenplay, Phil Connors breaks the rules of his character's behaviour by robbing a bank. In the film he observes the moment when the security guards aren't paying attention, and helps himself to cash; he's a smart and egotistical chancer but he's not a violent criminal. The fact that he has observed so carefully to find the opportunity to grab the cash also adds an additional piece of story information – it shows us how long he has been there.

The first phase of the story establishes the phenomenon of Groundhog Day (the same day repeating over and over again). The story becomes how Connors comes to understand the phenomenon, to explore it, and how he finally returns to normality. This is dependent on a complicated set of feedback loops, between him, the other characters and the situation in which he finds himself. We can easily understand what is being tested, and the effects of Connor's actions. Once he has established that Groundhog Day exists he immediately starts to ask other questions. How far can he go? Are there really no consequences? He asks two regular guys from Punxsutawney, over beers at the bowling alley: 'What would you do if you were stuck in one place and every day was exactly the same, and nothing that you did mattered?' This is funny – we see the analogy to their lives before they do but it also clearly feeds back to us how he is now viewing his situation. When he asks them 'what would you do if there was no tomorrow?' he gets the answer that there would be no hangovers and no consequences and they could do whatever they wanted. It's not exposition, it's a 'situation', as Rossio terms it, but it's also an opportunity to test the boundaries of the situation through action.

He refuses to live by 'their rules anymore' and that's not just the irritating laws of normal behaviour. It includes 'not riding on the railroad track'. What will be remembered the next day? Just to be sure he asks the landlady in the bed and breakfast if there has been a state official looking for him. When he learns that he is free he kisses her on the mouth. During the sequence, in another necessary piece of feedback whose significance we won't learn until later, we see him, briefly, in a cell. This makes clear that the spell doesn't end at midnight. In another example of action as information, the prison scene sets clearer boundaries to his condition.

Each moment in Connors's journey, from waking in the bed and breakfast to see the groundhog at Gobbler's Knob, is delineated very clearly, so we are absolutely sure of where we are in the narrative. There are very clear and specific visual and aural beats that we can relate to – the clock/radio blasting out 'I got you babe', DJ and sidekick, fat man on the stairs in the bed and breakfast, the hostess, the beggar approaching him for cash, insurance guy Ned Ryerson, stepping in the puddle in the gutter, and then filming the groundhog appearing, and going to the diner. Each of these is a familiar navigation point which enables us to map the narrative territory. Because we know where we are at any given moment we speculate about how each moment will be interpreted. How will he treat Ned Ryerson this time? What will happen with the puddle? We test our theses against the coming events of the script. In the diner he approaches an attractive woman sitting on her own and asks her name, which high school she went to and the name of her English teacher. We may or may not guess what he has in mind the next day; more important than knowing what he has in mind is knowing that he has *something* in mind which is dependent on realizing that he will wake up the next day knowing this information and being able to exploit it. When he meets the woman we now know to be Nancy Taylor and we see how he uses the knowledge he has gleaned the previous day to seduce her we are in on the joke and eager to test the boundaries with him, in every sense.

Where the script outwits us is that, when he is in the romantic firelit room with Nancy, he says Rita's name. And now his goals are redefined and the trajectory of the story is more clear and more specific. He will continue to use the same techniques to win Rita, until he is forced into another paradigm shift and sees the fact of being trapped in Groundhog Day in a different light. He stops seeing the condition as a curse and becomes devoted to others and not himself. When Rita 'buys' him at a charity auction for everything she has in her purse she breaks the spell and he is cured.

But at the very end of *Groundhog Day* we are deliberately led into a 'wrong' assumption, when we hear 'I've got you babe' yet again as he wakes up, before the film corrects our error by revealing that Rita is now lying beside him and telling us it is a practical joke by the DJ.

Groundhog Day has become a cinema classic, a funny and profound film which Stanley Cavell has described as:

> A small film that lives off its wits and tells a deeply wonderful story of love. It creates a vision of the question I ask here – of what will endure. Its vision is to ask how, surrounded by conventions we do not exactly believe in, we sometimes find it in ourselves to enter into what Emerson thought of as a new day.
>
> (Cavell 1996)

I think the sophistication and clarity of *Groundhog Day* as a film is due in part to its elegance as a piece of design, which make it so clear in conveying an unfamiliar concept with precision, wit and wisdom.

David Mamet describes the essential nature of the dramatic interchange as 'to engage the audience in *wondering what happened next*' (Mamet 2007: 129; original emphasis). Using the analytical approach and tools of interaction design can help us to understand the screenwriting process from a different angle. If the screenplay is considered as not a text, but a prototype which attempts to anticipate the interactions between the audience and the future film made from the script, then the insights of interaction design have a great deal to offer the practice and theory of writing for the screen. By opening ourselves to the tools of a new discipline which is attempting to make new forms of communication as transparent and user-friendly as possible we can reinvigorate our own way of making stories.

Notes

1 All the London Underground maps from 1889 to the present can be accessed at : http://homepage.ntlworld.com/clivebillson/tube/tube.html
2 http://www.sheffieldtelegraph.co.uk/sportstalk/OWLS-BLOG-Stop-groundhog-day.4803984.jp
3 http://www.wired.co.nz/Blog/default.asp?blogid=12
4 http://news.bbc.co.uk/1/hi/scotland/1430309.stm

References

Berger, John (1972) *Ways of Seeing*, London: British Broadcasting Corporation and Penguin Books.

Bruner, Jerome (1991) 'The Narrative Construction of Reality', *Critical Inquiry* 18(1) (autumn): 1–21.

Card, Stuart, Moran, Thomas P. and Newell, Allen (1983) *The Psychology of Human Computer Interaction*, Englewood Cliffs, NJ: Lawrence Erlbaum Associates.

Cavell, Stanley (1996) *New York Times Magazine* 29 Sept.

Conan Doyle, Arthur (1890) *The Sign of Four*, London: Spencer Blackett.

— (2007) *Arthur Conan Doyle: A Life in Letters*, ed. Jon Lellenberg and Daniel Stashower, New York: Penguin.

Crowe, Cameron (1999) *Conversations with Wilder*, New York: Alfred A. Knopf.

Gardner, Martin (2008) *Origami, Eleusis, and the Soma Cube*, Cambridge: CUP.

Garland, Ken (1994) *Mr Beck's Underground Map*, London: Capital Transport.

Goldman, William (2000) *Which Lie Did I Tell? More Adventures in the Screen Trade*, New York: Random House.

Groundhog Day (Ramis, 1994; screenplay, Rubin Danny, revised Ramis Harold, Jan. 1992).

Mamet, David (2007) *Bambi vs Godzilla: On the Nature, Purpose and Practice of the Movie Business*, New York: Random House.

Moggridge Bill (2007) *Designing Interactions*, Boston, MA: MIT Press.

Murch, Walter (2001) *In the Blink of an Eye*, Los Angeles: Silman-James.

Norman, Donald A. (1998) *The Design of Everday Things*, Boston, MA: MIT Press.

Rossio, Terry (n.d.) 'Situation-Based Writing', Screenwriting Column 49, URL: http://www.wordplayer.com/columns/wp49.Situation-Based.html (accessed April 2010).

Sideways (Payne 2004).

Terminator (Cameron 1984)

To Be or Not To Be (Lubitsch 1942).

Tufte, Edward (1990) *Envisioning Information*, Cheshire, CT: Graphics Press.

White Balloon, The (Panahi 1995).

Witness (Weir 1985).

Chapter 9

The screenplay as prototype

Kathryn Millard

Introduction

The most common models for the screenplay have traditionally been drawn from literature: from the nineteenth-century novel to the 'well-made play'; from historical narrative to Aristotle's *Poetics*. I would like to discuss some alternatives drawn from design and digital media. After all, as Lawrence Lessig notes, our very understanding of what it means to write is shifting. 'Writing with text is just one way to write ... The more interesting ways are increasingly to use images and sound and video to express ideas' (Koman 2005).

In this chapter, I shall explore some alternative approaches and methods of script development and visualization from projects as varied as Neil Blomkamp's sci-fi thriller *District 9* (2009), Terrence Davies's essay film *Of Time and the City* (2008), Francis Ford Coppola's dreams of electronic cinema, the Disney Corporation's storyboards and Leica reels of the 1930s, Pixar's *Toy Story* (1995) and Gus Van Sant's *Elephant* (2003) – projects from across the filmmaking spectrum: studio animations and thrillers, independent and art-house cinema, documentary and the essay film. More specifically, I will consider the advantages in conceiving of screenplays (or, at least some of them) as design prototypes, rather than solely literary documents. By way of context, I introduce a recent project of my own which played a significant role in developing this interest.

In 2008, I completed a feature-length essay film, *The Boot Cake* (2008), about the transnational appeal of Charlie Chaplin's Tramp, with a particular focus on his Indian manifestations. I initially planned a film that would trace Chaplin imitators around the globe, from silent cinema to the internet and from cartoons to curry westerns and Hong Kong action films. In so doing, I hoped to shed light on the way a global figure had been adapted and transformed to become a local character in many places around the world. After several years of exhaustive research, of proposal and treatment writing, the project was on the verge of being financed via a jigsaw of international broadcaster pre-sales, distribution guarantees and government subsidies. No sooner had I approved the draft press release announcing funding that had been drawn up by the major government investor, however, than the local broadcaster withdrew and the film's financing

Figure 9.1 Dr Aswani and the Charlie Circle with the boot cake from *The Boot Cake* (2008)

collapsed. The project seemed doomed. I decided to make a virtue of necessity and focus on what was achievable rather than what was not (Millard 2008). After all, as Adrian Martin notes, New Wave filmmakers often shaped projects around resources. Jean Pierre Gorin, one of Godard's collaborators in the 1960s and 1970s, described Godard's creative process as 'working out what film could be made with this much money, this many friends and a few interiors' (Martin 2006). Looking back even further, in an interview Charlie Chaplin described the process of making his own early silent film comedies as 'writing with a camera' (Robinson 2001: 628). Since I no longer needed script and editorial approval from the many and various commissioning editors and film agency investment managers, I was free to write, devise and produce the film in a looser, more improvisational way than would otherwise have been possible.

Shifts in writing practices: the big picture

In advocating new forms of writing that use images and sound as well as text, Lessig echoes theorists and practitioners concerned with the shifts taking place in writing in our digital era. Lanham, for example, argues that print is a particularly limited mode and that multi-modal texts, which can incorporate images, text and sound, allow writers a fuller range of expression (Lanham 1993: 77). Starke-Meyerring places these shifts in writing practices within the larger context of digital literacy. She observes that for the past several hundred years, writing has primarily been centred around print technologies and that, consequently, writing has settled into a set of stable practices and norms. The rise of new technologies and networks means that writing now happens primarily in digital environments: on screens, personal computers, netbooks and myriad mobile devices. We compose digital texts for websites, blogs, wikis and interactive media, opening up alternative practices to those established around print. 'Digital writing spaces ... enable, constrain, challenge, reproduce, or question established practices, social orders and hierarchies rooted in print materialities' (Starke-Meyerring 2009: 508).

In this new order, the serious novel – and prose fiction more generally – no longer enjoys its undisputed place at literature's top table. An order in which non-fiction, poetry and playwriting are all further down the hierarchy, while screenwriting – which has always had an uneasy relationship with literature – is the late arrival, desperately trying to crash the party. The novel is now increasingly being challenged by non-fiction forms of writing, such as biography, memoir, the essay, the blog and forms which combine images and text such as the graphic novel, manga and video game. It is in fact the screen, with its increased emphasis on images, that dominates our contemporary writing landscape. Many of the film industry's gatekeepers, however, seem oblivious to the opportunities these rapid changes offer screen media writers and practitioners. Many remain fixated on rigid 'one size fits all' script development processes, seemingly determined to do their very best to ensure that moving pictures join the growing pile of obsolete entertainment forms called 'heritage media'.

Writing as design

In his discussion of digital writing spaces, new media theorist Jay Bolter observed that 'we may come to associate text with the qualities of the computer (flexibility, interactivity, speed of distribution) rather than those of print (stability and authority)' (Bolter 2001: 3). Gunther Kress proposed: 'We have moved from literacy as an enterprise based on language to *text-making as a matter of design*' (2003: 105; my emphasis). These new conceptualizations of writing suggest a more fluid set of processes than traditional models of script development employ or allow. Such models typically involve the writer progressing through a series of clearly delineated stages (such as Outline, Treatment and First, Second and Third Draft), with each stage requiring 'notes' and formal approval from investors or funding agencies before proceeding to the next stage. In the light of these contemporary shifts in writing practices, how is the screenplay being reconfigured and reshaped? And to rewind for a moment, how did the development processes of film and television (media which incorporate moving images, performance, dialogue and narration, text, music and sound) become so strongly tied to what has become an outmoded form of print media, i.e. the traditional screenplay? For, while the novel, short story and essay have continued to evolve and change, incorporating new structural approaches, styles of syntax and expression, even sketches, photographs and notes, much of the film industry still insists on a rigidly prescribed document formatted in Courier 12 – a font designed in the 1950s to resemble letter forms from the late nineteenth century, when the typewriter was invented. This symbolic linking of the development of film ideas and stories with the typewriter tries to suggest that screen media have always been devised or written in one way – and always will be (Millard 2010: 11–25). This is despite the fact that many screenwriters and filmmakers have long used alternative methods of scripting that draw on improvisation, images and words (Millard 2006; Murphy 2007; Wells 2007).

In the early twenty-first century the industrial screenplay has come to be a technical document specifying not only a particular font and size, but the one-page-to-one-minute-of-screen-time rule, organized into scenes with 'big print' written in the third person and present tense summarizing the dramatic action and dialogue. Enshrined in all these rules is not only an authorized version of layout and presentation but a dramatic structure outlined in Syd Field's influential *Screenplay: The Foundations of Screenwriting* and the avalanche of screenwriting manuals that followed its late 1970s publication. 'Dramatic films follow a basic paradigm the three-act structure corresponding to beginning, middle and end. This is the foundation of dramatic structure' (Field 1979: 12). 'Classical design means a story built around an active protagonist who struggles against primarily external forces of antagonism to pursue his desire, through continuous time, within a consistent and causally connected fictional reality, to a closed ending of absolute, irreversible change', adds script guru Robert McKee (1997: 45). These handbooks serve the needs of particular cultural interests: the United States/Hollywood view of the world and filmmaking. Writer/Director Hal Hartley recalls that he was taught 'a classical American film was to have 64 scenes with everything in its place. Introduction, exposition, inciting incident, false climax, true climax, reversal, and denouement. It was math' (Murphy 2007: 98).

Improvisation and writing

By contrast, writer and director Paul Schrader describes screenwriting as part of an oral tradition. 'It's like telling a story. It's not like literature. So what you have to do is you have to start telling your story' (Schrader 1998). Tracing this lineage, Adam Ganz proposes oral storytelling, and in particular the ballad, as one productive model for screen practitioners. 'Oral storytelling not only stretches back much further than a European dramatic literary tradition but it is more improvisational, adaptable, collaborative, as opposed to the model of the screenplay-as-a-text, envisioned as separate from the film which arises from it' (Ganz 2009). Writing always has an improvisational aspect, notes creativity theorist Keith Sawyer. Typically, writers begin with a phrase or an image rather than a fully fleshed-out plot and progress their works through successive stages of drafting and writing. That is, most creative writers use a problem-finding style (Sawyer 2009: 176). Digital composing practices have only made improvisation, adaptation and hybridization of forms and genres more central to writing. Consequently, terms like story design and digital composition are finding increased acceptance across a range of media.

The digital jigsaw

The traditional screenplay is a document that exists as a carry-over from a pre-digital era in which the industry norm was for projects to proceed through script development, pre-production, production and post-production. Yet filmmaking rarely occurs in these discrete stages. Keith Griffiths argues:

> Live-action footage is now inevitably only the first phase of a production process, during which all images can be digitised, then composited, animated and morphed ... What were once defined as 'post' or 'end' processes have been fundamentally shifted to the very heart of the production of motion picture images. The conceptual structure of production has collapsed and the ordering of images, their surface and manipulation has now become part and parcel of the same digital jigsaw.
>
> (Griffiths 2003: 18)

Like Paul Wells, Griffiths argues that animation is becoming increasingly important to cinema, as it was in the era of silent film.

What is a prototype?

In the light of these reconfigurations of our writing and media ecologies, the prototype might be one useful way to conceptualize the screenplay as it continues to evolve, one pathway towards injecting a spirit of creative exploration and 'play' back into the often rather misnamed 'screenplay' and a means of highlighting the development of screen ideas as a design process. But first: what is a prototype? Improvisation is the key to fostering innovation in the development laboratories of a range of industries including manufacturing, computing and entertainment. Prototypes and simulations are the two major methods of turning ideas into physical objects early in the design process, thus contributing to the improvisation process. Schrage suggests: 'Prototypes tend to be physical models of a product while a simulation is a mock-up of a process' (2000: 7). Design management theorist, Bettina Von Stamm categorizes prototypes as either informal or formal, or rough versus polished. Prototypes can be made in order to create opportunities or to manage the risks inherent in the research and development stages of designing products. They can be made for internal or external audiences. That is, for collaborators or participants in the development process as opposed to those who will sign off on the production or are potential audiences and end-users (2008: 192).

'Prototypes are concrete representations of the to-be-designed product', notes Apple designer Thomas Erickson. 'A number of different prototypes will usually be created during the design process, often for different purposes' (Erickson 1995). In other words, while polished prototypes might be used to 'sell' a concept, crude, roughly built prototypes more successfully capture ideas early on. For example, one of the most famous 'quick and dirty' prototypes in the design world is the cardboard model that introduced the Dynabook personal computer to the world in the 1960s. Although it never proceeded into production, the Dynabook, which looked very much like a contemporary netbook, had a significant influence on the evolution of the personal computer and the laptop. Dyson's three-dimensional cardboard model helped capture people's imaginations.

In addition to their widespread use in product design, prototypes are also frequently used in the development and testing of advertising, computer software, games and interactive media products. The essence of prototyping, says designer Tom Kelley, is expressing the idea quickly and cheaply (2001: 103–18). In the entertainment and media industries, this often takes the form of animations, trailers and software trial versions of games. Prototyping materials in the manufacturing and engineering industries may once have been foam, cardboard and sticky-tape, or whatever could be repurposed from the shelves of the local dime store. In recent years, prototyping, like writing, has migrated across to digital spaces. Translating this to film, scripting *The Boot Cake* we sketched and shot three rough versions of one mock archival scene, reviewed and discussed them before deciding which version to go with.

Iterative and waterfall design cycles

Many designers distinguish between two kinds of design processes; on the one hand, *iterative* methods and, on the other hand, *waterfall* or cascading methods. Waterfall design methodologies involve a series of incremental development stages, each of which are successively reviewed, perfected and approved by management as the software or product moves closer to production. One of the limitations of waterfall methodologies, particularly in a climate of uncertainty and rapid change, is their lack of flexibility. I first read about waterfall design cycles with a shock of recognition. For me, they described almost perfectly the slow and careful script development processes of the Australian government agencies and public broadcasters with whom I have worked. By contrast, iterative design methodologies are based on cycles of prototyping, testing, analysing and refining works-in-progress. 'In iterative design, interaction with the designed system is used as a form of research for informing and evolving a project, as successive versions, or iterations of a design are implemented' (Zimmerman 2003). Games designer Eric Zimmerman notes that it is common practice to develop games by creating rough software versions of proposed games throughout the design and production process. While computer software prototypes are often accompanied by short pitch documents, the design and development process rarely takes place primarily on the page (Zimmerman 2003: 12). Filmmakers who produce graphic novels, short trailers, animations and websites as part of the development stage are using a similar methodology.

From pencils and pixels – and back to pencils

The last decade has been characterized not only by a shift to digital tools and thinking spaces but a renewed interest in drawing and sketching with pencils as well as pixels. Pixar, for example, the producers of critically acclaimed and commercially successful feature animations like *Toy Story* (1995) have developed a formidable reputation for fostering a culture of innovation. The company's innovation strategies extend to holding regular drawing classes for everyone – 'creatives' and 'suits' alike and regardless of individual skill levels – in order to promote visual thinking. Unlike most studios, Pixar does not have a story department but assembles cross-disciplinary teams to generate new ideas. The role of its development division is not to come up with ideas for films but instead to assemble small incubation teams (Catmull 2008: 6). The teams, which typically include writers, artists, storyboard personnel and directors, are filmmaker-led. From the very early stages of development, the creative teams draw storyboards, digitize and edit them and add dialogue and temporary music to create story reels. 'The first versions are very rough, but they give a sense of what the problems are, which in the beginning … are many. We then iterate, and each version gets successively better and better' (Catmull 2008: 5–6). While 'script notes' from management are not part of the company's culture, project teams are encouraged to constantly discuss 'rough' unfinished ideas and solicit feedback from as many colleagues as possible. The intention is to encourage people to take risks and try new approaches; their work is not expected to be perfect the first time. Pixar executive Ed Catmull explains that these methods are part of a problem-solving approach to the development and production of animated films.

Digital remix as a writing practice

Paul Wells suggests that visualization has always been a more significant aspect of developing concepts and scripts for animation films than live action. Visualization can involve preliminary sketches, narrative drawings, designs, storyboards or preliminary animatics (Wells 2007: 63). As an example of some of the differences between traditional language-based scripts and visualization strategies, he details the way in which filmmaker, Chris Shepherd adapted David Shrigley's graphic narrative *Who I Am And What I Want* (2005). Shepherd scanned selected drawings and then ordered them into a sequence. Shrigley and Shepherd next exchanged ideas and sketches and opinions with the aim of creating sequences with a sense of narrative movement. The original graphic novel relied on a series of 'stand alone' gags or observations, rather than a cause-and-effect narrative (Wells 2007: 77). Lessig argues that the digital remix, or the capacity to assemble, juxtapose and sample images, text, music, sounds and animation using computers, is now a contemporary form of writing on the scale of a mass cultural practice (Koman 2005). He suggests that some of these modes of writing include: remixing clips from films to create trailers for imaginary movies, adding music and text to edited film and television clips, combining found and original images to explore an idea (with or without text) and mixing animations and texts to create cartoons or satirical clips. The remix did not emerge with digital technologies and the modes of thinking they enable, but has a long tradition in the form of music sampling, visual arts assemblage and collage, Dada performance and compilation and essay films. The availability of prosumer tools (low-cost, professional equipment that can now be purchased by consumers who are also media producers) and digital culture, however, have led to the remix's current status as a mass cultural practice.

Mapping ideas and stories

Cartographer Denis Woods (1998) says we live in an age of maps (with 99.9 per cent of the world's maps produced over the last one hundred years). Not only are tools like Google Earth accelerating map-making as a way of making sense of the world but more and more cultural geographers and artists are devising maps that incorporate subjective experience (Jackson 2009: 117–20). All stories are maps of a kind, says Peter Turchi, involving decisions about inclusion and order, shape, form and a balancing of intuition and intention (2004: 25). A number of screenwriters have made use of maps to record their ideas and stories. Many of Wim Wenders's most successful films are road movies. It is not surprising then that he says 'A lot of my films start off with maps instead of scripts' (2001: 226). Michael Winterbottom's semi-improvised *In This World* (2002) records the journey of two young Afghani refugees. Screenwriter Tony Grisoni wrote the outline from which the film was shot by mapping out the geographical spine of the story then adding notes on character and possible lines of dialogue. According to Gus van Sant, he worked from a written outline rather than a conventional script on *Elephant* (2002), his critically acclaimed film about a school shooting. As locations were locked down and the project moved into production, his prose outline morphed into a map: 'The sentences became, actually, lines on a map. And the map was the footprint of the school' (Murphy 2007: 163). Van Sant's script maps suggest another possible approach to prototyping for screenwriters. Commenting on the differences between the novel and cinema, he notes 'Going from Point A to Point B can't hold a novel together. But movement can hold a film together' (Klosterman 2008). It is worth noting that, in all these examples, the creative teams worked with both story outlines and maps, side-by-side. Maps and their symbols did not replace written documents but freed writers and directors to devise new forms of scripts more suitable as a basis for improvisation.

District 9: the script as graphic novel

In an interview writer/director Neil Blomkamp and producer Peter Jackson described the package of script materials for their feature film *District 9*. It included Blomkamp's short film which inspired the project, a graphic-novel style presentation of the script and its production design, and a 10-minute test scene shot on location (Lee 2009). An article in the *Wall Street Journal* described the genesis of this project.

> In 2006, filmmaker Peter Jackson hired a small team to illustrate a script in development about aliens stranded in South Africa. Meanwhile, Neill Blomkamp, who was co-writing the screenplay with Terri Tatchell, travelled to Johannesburg to shoot photographs. The results were packaged into a graphic novel-style treatment to attract potential investors.
>
> (Jurgensen 2009)

Only 10 copies of the book were ever published. There was no star, script or budget but the graphic novel presentation provided ample data on which investors could base their decisions (Jurgensen 2009). Working with illustrators on his book also helped Blomkamp confront creative challenges. An example: he had originally envisioned menacing creatures similar to those in the *Alien* movies. On reviewing the early sketches, however, he realized that audiences may not empathize with the creatures and so he gave them more human-like eyes. The graphic novel also sketched out the wider world of *District 9* and featured elements that did not make it into the final film, but helped lay the groundwork for the film's viral marketing campaigns. That campaign included online videos that showed glimpses of the alien culture. One page of Blomkamp's graphic novel, for example, describes an alien commercial with the lines like: 'Learn to talk human! Better jobs at the mine!' Blomkamp's document mixed elements from the traditional screenplay, the graphic novel and literary fiction. *District 9*'s colour artwork is not presented in panels (graphic-novel style) but illustrates the text. Technical information usually provided in screenplays is minimized for ease of reading. All of these strategies create the overall impression of a document aimed at investors and key collaborators rather than intended for on-set use.

Proof of concept videos

Writer/director Roberto Rodriguez, who started his career in comics and graphic novels, regularly uses 'proof of concept' videos as part of what he describes as a scripting process. In press interviews, the writer/director has told the story of convincing Frank Miller to allow him to adapt *Sin City* (2005) by producing a 'fake trailer'. In the hope of convincing Miller to give the project his blessing, Rodriguez shot a 'proof of concept' adaptation of the *Sin City* story. 'The customer is always right.' Miller was reportedly happy with the results and the footage was later used as the opening scene for the completed film. The 'fake trailer' that he produced then became a template for other films including *Grindhouse* (2007). 'It makes more sense than just going around with a script, because it is a visual medium', claims Rodriguez (Kelly 2009). 'As cross-functional, cross-disciplinary teams become the dominant medium for managing innovation, prototypes and innovation can promote awareness and empathy between collaborators', Michael Schrage suggests

(2000: 211). That is, viewing trailers, short videos and websites is more likely to foster discussion across disciplinary boundaries with their varied strengths and thinking styles than text-based documents alone. Yet it is not enough, he suggests, for prototypes and models to act simply as a shared means of communication. In order to drive innovation, models must invite people to step out of their everyday roles and view projects from different perspectives. While development processes like those of *District 9* and *Sin City* are increasingly common, the real challenge they pose is in thinking of them as legitimate scripting processes rather than as creative pre-production.

Electronic cinema

In the 1970s, Francis Ford Coppola embraced with a vengeance the new video recording and editing tools of his era to create 'Electronic Cinema'. Fundamental to Coppola's vision was that these technologies would provide new thinking tools. In preparation for the production of *One From the Heart* (1982) he set up the Silverfish, a bus fitted out as a mobile studio with taping, editing and special effects facilities. This mobile studio was to assist him in creating a more fluid method of scripting and visualizing his films. 'That was the idea behind *One From The Heart*: that we were going to try to make live cinema. And it was to combine a lot of elements of theatre and television and cinema …' (Schwartz 2006). In an article based on extensive interviews with Coppola during this production, Lillian Ross described the process:

> The pre-visualisation was accomplished by means of tapes of the actors reading, videotaping rehearsals, Polaroid stills, artists' sketches, and a filmed walk-through of the story in the real Las Vegas (as opposed to the studio version designed by Coppola and his team) all of which enabled Mr. Coppola to rewrite and edit the script while the movie was still being shaped and before actual filming had begun.
>
> (Ross 2004 : 63)

Ross went on to observe with some astonishment that more than 1300 Polaroids were taken before the movie had even begun shooting. Not so extravagant by today's standards, I suspect. Arguably, though, electronic cinema made more of a contribution to the film's striking visual style than its narrative shape or momentum. *One From the Heart* went wildly over budget and received mixed critical and audience responses. Coppola was undeterred and continued to refine his electronic cinema, however, on future productions including *The Outsider* (1983) and *Rumblefish* (1983).

One From the Heart provides a good example of some of the challenges confronting those using models and prototypes as part of a story design or script development process. What happens when the tools themselves start driving the modelling process? That is, when people begin producing more and more models or pre-visualizations simply because they can? Who are the prototypes for? How many should be produced? And over what time frame? Did the sheer mass of Coppola's video sketches and mock-ups, for example, distract him from more urgent issues facing his massively overbudget production? It is now clear that, unfortunately, his experimentation on *One From the Heart* did not help clarify the film's narrative structure or story design. What it did, however, was make a significant contribution towards the development of the non-linear editing systems that are now standard in the screen media industries, demonstrating that experimentation goes together with risk and the discoveries made are not always those anticipated.

Walt Disney and the Leica Reel

Long before Pixar and their story reels, Disney developed a technique known as the Leica reel in which rough storyboards were filmed and edited to the music intended for the film's soundtrack. These methods preceded the now widespread use of animatics by many decades. (Anamatic is a video-recorded version of a hand-drawn storyboard with limited motion to convey camera movement and a soundtrack.) Tracking the history of film animation, Bendazzi criticizes Disney's production methods in this era as following a Taylorized rationalization of labour. 'Specialised teams worked at either animation, scene design, special effects, lay-out or scripts; inking, colouring and filming were also separated. The storyboard, a sort of drawn script, helped to keep the theme of a script under control' (Bendazzi

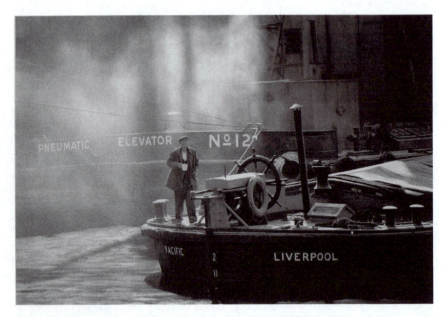

Figure 9.2 Writer/director Terrance Davies, *Grain Barge* (2007) from the exhibition series 'The Long Walk' (2007), Liverpool Museum

2001: 66). He suggests that the primary reason why Disney preferred his studio's cartoons to be visualized was so that he could imprint his own style on them. Again, this raises a number of issues discussed in the literature of design and innovation. Who are prototypes for? Collaborators? Team members? Bosses? Management? End-users? These are all questions that can usefully be addressed by screenwriters and filmmakers creating prototypes as part of a development process.

Of Time and the City: digital video prototype

In interviews, Writer/Director Terrence Davies described making what could be called a prototype for his critically acclaimed essay film – both a love song and a eulogy to Liverpool – *Of Time and the City* (2008) Davies trained at art school and his strongest films have been poetic narratives such as *Distant Voices, Still Lives* (1988) and *The Long Day Closes* (1992), in which patternings of images, memories and songs form the story design. Davies's initial proposal for the low-budget feature initiative Digital Departures consisted of a written sketch accompanied by a six-minute digital video trailer. The trailer 'already had the architecture of the film', says Davies (Badt 2009). Once the project was green-lit, this first draft was rewritten and refined in the editing room as Davies and editor Liza Ryan-Carter worked with the mass of archival materials and texts that make up *Of Time and the City*. Describing the genesis of the project, Davies says that the nature of memory is associative, non-linear, emotive, we remember the intense moment rather than

Figure 9.3 Writer/director Terrance Davies, *The Long Walk* (2007) from the exhibition series 'The Long Walk' (2007), Liverpool Museum

the things around it. He found the key to the film's structure in the editing room. The emotional arc of the film, he decided, would depict the streets of Liverpool coming to life as generations of kids played in them, women popped in and out of each other's houses, adults made their way to and from work, and went on outings to the pub or the cinema. This is a discovery that perhaps could only be made as the director and editor worked together with the images and sounds – watching, listening, juxtaposing, assembling, writing and recording text, placing it in the mix and re-viewing, rather than via the words on a blank screen or page required by a traditional script. This is because the materials that we work with are fundamental to our thinking processes.

Objects as prototypes

When I began working on the new version of my Chaplin project, transforming it from a broadcast documentary to an essay film, I did not have a script. Instead, I showed my collaborators a 10,000 word print essay, a four-minute trailer combining pre-shoot footage and key archival moments, a DVD of Chaplin's *The Gold Rush* (1925) and various objects from a grab-bag of Chaplin related relics that I had assembled over the term of the project's incubation: a talcum powder holder in the form of Charlie Chaplin from Adipur in India, a flexible bamboo cane, a hat from a theatrical supplies store in Rio de Janeiro, a publicity still of Chaplin posing with a doll of his alter-ego The Tramp, a hand-coloured photograph of a Japanese imitator from the early 1920s and a melancholy-looking Chaplin puppet from Czechoslavakia. Funding agencies were no longer involved and our ultra-low budget allowed us the freedom to shape the film in production, moving more fluidly between shooting, editing and writing than would otherwise have been possible. As I worked with a small team of collaborators, we came up with ideas for scenes based around some of these objects. (At fine cut, *The Boot Cake* attracted post-production funds from a government film funding programme with a brief to support innovation.) In retrospect, it seems that in addition to the usual promos and pre-film trailers, objects such as the Chaplin figures and costumes had an important role in bringing the film to life. For me, working from this collection of clips, objects and a personal essay – rather than a screenplay – helped preserve a sense of discovery throughout the shooting and post-production of *The Boot Cake*. To borrow an example from design: creativity theorist Mark Runco suggests that, of the myriad sketches and drawings developed in graphic design processes, those that are most useful are nearly always 'rapidly hand-drawn sketches made at the front end of the process when ideas are still tentative and designs are partial and conditional' (Runco and Pritzker 1999: 535) In the case of *The Boot Cake*, there was never a sense of simply executing a pre-planned story and set of decisions, instead we were finding our way, step by step.

Figure 9.4 Dr Aswani and the Charlie Circle with a life-sized cut-out of Charlie Chaplin from *The Boot Cake* (2008)

Conclusion

Design theorist, Donald Schon proposes: 'Design is a dialogue that the designer conducts with his or her materials' (Runco and Pritzker 1999: 525). Gestalt psychologist Rudolf Arnheim writes that we think in particular media. '*Visual thinking* is distinct from *linguistic thinking* because it takes place in media such as ink, paint, stone, plaster, and clay – or in video, film, and digital images in contemporary work' (Marshall 2007: 23; my emphasis). Perhaps it is not so surprising then that more and more filmmakers write with images, sound and text. In proposing the prototype as one direction for the screenplay in a digital era, I am not suggesting a 'one size fits all' model. I am suggesting, though, that the prototype may provide a model for thinking about the screenplay that:

1 places the emphasis firmly on the creative process and the generation and development of new ideas rather than pre-determined templates;
2 privileges visual and sonic thinking;
3 assumes that the materials that projects are generated in impacts their design;
4 encourages 'cheap and dirty' solutions and rapid iteration and thus liberates screenwriters from the pursuit of the 'perfect script';
5 promotes collaboration across different specializations within filmmaking.

Throughout the more than one hundred years of the history of the medium, many screenwriters and filmmakers – in art-house and independent cinema, animation and non-fiction – have developed their ideas off the page. Never as rigid as claimed, the boundaries between writing and production are increasingly stretched in a digital era, thereby offering new possibilities for collaboration and new modes of screen storytelling. As the very notion of writing shifts to embrace multi-modal texts (texts which incorporate images, sound and words), scriptwriting is being reimagined and repositioned.

References

Badt, K. (2009) 'Paradise Betrayed', *Bright Lights Film Journal*. URL: http://www.brightlightsfilm.com/61/61daviesiv.html (accessed Dec. 2009).

Bendazzi, G. (2001) *Cartoons: One Hundred Years of Cinema Animation*, Bloomington and Indianapolis, IN: Indiana University Press.

Bolter, J. (2001) *Writing Spaces: Computers, Hypertext and the Remediation of Print*, 2nd edn, Englewood Cliffs, NJ: Lawrence Erlbaum.

Catmull, E. (2008) 'How Pixar Fosters Collective Creativity', *Harvard Business Review* (Sept.): 64–75.

Erickson, T. (1995) *Notes on Design Practice: Stories and Prototypes as Catalysts for Communication*. URL: http://www.pliant.org/personal/Tom_Erickson/Stories.html (accessed Dec. 2009).

Field, S. (1979) *Screenplay: The Foundations of Screenwriting*, New York: Dell Publishing.

Ganz, A. (2009) 'Leaping Broken Narration: Oral Storytelling and the Cinema', Re-Thinking the Screenplay Conference, University of Helsinki Arts and Design.

Griffiths, K. (2003) 'The Manipulated Image', *Convergence: The Journal of Research into New Media Technologies* 9(4): 12–26.

In This World Production Notes (2001). URL: http://www.milestonefilms.com/pdf/InThisWorld.pdf (accessed Dec. 2009).

Jackson, M. (2009) *Distracted*, USA: Prometheus

Jurgensen, J. (2009) 'The Fellowship of Peter Jackson', *Wall Street Journal*, 8 Aug. URL: http://online.wsj.com/article/SB10001424052970204908604574332481205990114.html (accessed Dec. 2009).

Kelley, T. (2001) *The Art of Innovation*, London: Profile.

Kelly, K. (2009) 'SDCC Interview: Robert Rodriguez', *Cinematical*. URL: http://www.cinematical.com/2009/07/29/sdcc-interview-robert-rodriguez/ (accessed Dec. 2009).

Klosterman, C. (2008) 'On The Road', *The Believer* (March/April). URL: http://www.believermag.com/issues/200803/?read=article_klosterman (accessed Dec. 2009).

Knobel, M. and Lankshear, C. (2008) 'Remix: The Art and Craft of Endless Hybridization', *Journal of Adolescent and Adult Literacy* 52(1): 22–33.

Koman, R. (2005) 'Remixing Culture: An Interview with Lawrence Lessig', O'Reilly Network. URL: http://www.oreillynet.com/pub/a/policy/2005/02/24/lessig.html (accessed Dec. 2009).

Kress, G. (2003) *Literacy in the New Media Age*, London: Routledge.

Lanham, R. (1993) *The Electronic Word: Democracy, Technology, and the Arts*, Chicago and London: University of Chicago Press.

Lee, P. (2009) 'Peter Jackson on Why District 9 Breaks the Sci-Fi Mold', *Sci-Fi Wire*. URL: http://scifiwire.com/2009/07/peter-jackson-on-why-dist.php (accessed Dec. 2009).

McKee R. (1997) *Story: Substance, Structure, Style and the Principles of Screenwriting*, New York: Regan Books

Marshall, J. (2007) 'Image as Insight: Visual Images in Practice-Based Research', *Studies in Art Education* 49(1): 23–41.

Martin, A. (2006) 'Kind of a Revolution and Kind of Not: Digital Low-Budget Cinema in Australia Today', *Scan* 3(2). URL: http://scan.net.au/scan/journal/display.php?journal_id=76 (accessed Dec. 2009).

Millard, Kathryn (2008) Australian Screen Production Education and Research Association 2008 Conference Papers. URL: http:// www.aspera.org.au/node/29 (accessed Dec. 2009).

— (2010) 'After the Typewriter: Screenwriting in a Digital Era', *Journal of Scriptwriting* 1(1): 11–25.

Murphy, J. J. (2007) *Me and You and Memento and Fargo: How Independent Screenplays Work*, New York and London: Continuum.

Robinson, David (2001) *Chaplin: His Life and Art*, London: Penguin.

Ross, L. (2004) 'Some Figures on a Fantasy: Francis Coppola', in F. Coppola, G. Phillips and R. Hill (eds), *Francis Ford Coppola Interviews*, Jackson, MS: University Press of Mississippi, 63–105.

Runco, M. and Pritzker, S. (1999) *Encyclopaedia of Creativity*, vol. 1, Berkeley, CA: Academic Press.

Sawyer, R. (2009) 'Writing as a Collaborative Act', in Scott and James Kauffman (eds), *The Psychology of Creative Writing*, Cambridge: CUP, 166–79.

Schrader, P. (1998) Quoted in M. Colville-Anderson Interview, *New York Conversations: Paul Schrader at Hotel Chelsea*. URL: http://zakka.dk/euroscreenwriters/screenwriters/paul_schrader.htm (accessed Dec. 2009).

Schrage, M. (2000) *Serious Play: How the World's Best Companies Simulate to Innovate*, Cambridge, MA: Harvard Business School Press.

Schwartz, D. (2006) 'A Pineword Diallogue with Francis Ford Coppola'. http://www.movingimagesource.us/files/dialogues/2/45024_programs_transcript_pdf_254.pdf

Starke-Meyerring, D. (2009) 'The Contested Materialities of Writing in Digital Environments: Implications for Writing Development', in R. Beard, D. Myhill, M. Nystrand and J. Riley (eds), *Handbook of Writing Development*, Thousand Oaks, CA: Sage, 506–26.

Turchi, P. (2004) *Maps of the Imagination: The Writer as Cartographer*, San Antonio, TX: Trinity University Press.

Von Stamm, B. (2008) *Managing Innovation, Design and Creativity*, 2nd edn, Chichester: John Wiley.

Wells, P. (2007) *Basics Animation: Scriptwriting*, Lausanne: Ava Publishing SA.

Wenders, W. (2001) *On Film: Essays and Conversations*, London: Faber & Faber.

Woods, Denis (1998) 'Mapping', *This American Life*, Chicago Public Radio. URL: http:// www.thisamericanlife.org/Radio_Episode.aspx?episode=110 (accessed Dec. 2009).

Zimmerman, E. (2003) *Play as Research: The Iterative Design Process*, URL: http://www.ericzimmerman.com/texts/Iterative_Design.htm (accessed Dec. 2009).

Chapter 10

A similar sense of time

The collaboration between writer Jon Raymond and director Kelly Reichardt in *Old Joy* and *Wendy and Lucy*

J. J. Murphy

It can be argued that two distinct attitudes exist towards the screenplay within American independent cinema. One strand has tried to find ways to move away from the written script through a variety of alternative filmmaking strategies, which include improvisation, psychodrama and visual storytelling (Murphy 2010: 175–96). The other response is more firmly rooted in the primacy of the screenplay as an essential feature of dramatic film production. This latter strain of indie cinema has been the legacy of two major institutions created in the early 1980s. The first of these was the Sundance Institute, a laboratory workshop experience specifically targeted to independents with more commercial ambitions.[1] The second was the PBS-backed *American Playhouse* television series, which provided funding and showcased independent feature work.[2] Both the Sundance Institute and American Playhouse placed a major emphasis on the screenplay (and working with writers) as a key factor in developing stronger independent films that could compete more successfully within the marketplace.

Most independent film directors choose to write their own screenplays rather than work with screenwriters. One reason for this is that indie cinema, like art cinema, tends to be *auteur*-based, reflecting a desire on the part of directors to maintain complete artistic control over their productions.[3] Jim Jarmusch, Hal Hartley and Andrew Bujalski, for instance, write their own screenplays. With the exception of *I'm Not There* (2007), which he co-wrote with Oren Moverman, Todd Haynes has written the screenplays for his films. David Lynch has written the scripts for some of his most critically acclaimed films, notably *Eraserhead* (1977), *Blue Velvet* (1986), *Mulholland Dr.* (2001) and *Inland Empire* (2006), but he has also worked with screenwriters such as Barry Gifford on *Lost Highway* (1997) as well as directed *The Straight Story* (1999) from a screenplay by Mary Sweeney and John Roach. Some other indie directors appear to be equally flexible. After writing and directing her first feature *River of Grass* (1995), Kelly Reichardt has worked with writer Jon Raymond on her last two films, *Old Joy* (2006) and *Wendy and Lucy* (2008).

In this chapter, I explore the collaboration between Kelly Reichardt and Jon Raymond in these films. *River of Grass* will serve as a point of reference in order to compare and contrast it with her two later collaborations with Raymond. In my discussion of *Old Joy* and *Wendy and Lucy*, I examine Raymond's published short stories, the co-written screenplays, various published interviews with both the writer and director, and personal correspondence with Jon Raymond. I also analyse the films themselves in order to understand what makes this such a unique and successful collaboration. I am especially interested in how their collaboration straddles the divide between the two different views towards the screenplay within American indie cinema. I hope to demonstrate that having a clearer sense of character and story as a result of working with a fiction writer allows Reichardt greater flexibility to concentrate on aspects of visual storytelling. This includes developing strategies for engaging the viewer more fully and for how the story will unfold in time.

I take the notion of creative collaboration between Raymond and Reichardt at face value. My interest here is not in the thorny issues of authorship, but in the significant benefits of writers and directors working collaboratively. Although Reichardt and Raymond develop the screenplays together, their roles remain somewhat traditionally defined, even if their working methods are not. Raymond views himself primarily as a writer. His contribution is clearly in developing the story – structure, characterization, tone, locations and dialogue – while Reichardt's role, when she switches to that of director, involves not only choosing and working with the actors, but visually rendering the written material on the screen.

Not all collaborations between independent directors and writers have gone smoothly. Some have been fraught with discord, such as Andy Warhol's stormy relationship with the playwright Ronald Tavel in the 1960s. Warhol had Tavel write scenarios – *The Life of Juanita Castro* (1965), *Horse* (1965), *Vinyl* (1965), *Kitchen* (1965), *Space* (1965), and so forth – which Warhol then proceeded to undercut in various ways. During the filming of *The Life of Juanita Castro*, for instance, the film's star Marie Menken, a notorious alcoholic, was permitted and encouraged to become inebriated, causing her to rebel against saying certain lines of dialogue in the script. Warhol encouraged actors not to learn their lines for *Kitchen*, forcing Tavel to hide the script in various places on the set and to whisper the dialogue to the actors during production, while in *Horse* huge placards with the dialogue were held up off-screen for the performers to read. For the most part, the resulting films exhibit some resemblance to Tavel's scenarios, but *Space* bears almost no relation to Tavel's written text. Some of actress Edie Sedgwick's friends who appear in the film became involved in an unscripted food fight during the shooting that caused the screenwriter to walk off the set in disgust (Tavel 1965: 1–8).

If the Warhol and Tavel collaboration, which included disputes about authorship,[4] can be viewed as 'strained', the one between Reichardt and Raymond could stand as exemplary. Raymond and Reichardt work very closely. This was even truer on *Wendy and Lucy*, where the two of them actually developed the initial story idea together. Although Raymond and Reichardt communicate regularly, even when she's in the midst of production, Raymond is not on set, nor does he contribute to the visual aspects of the film beyond what is written on the page.[5] Yet he has hardly been rendered 'invisible' in the process. Reichardt, at least in interviews, has gone out of her way to credit Raymond's substantial contributions to the two films as writer, and has even suggested that her collaboration with

Raymond has been so fruitful that she can no longer think of making a film without him. She comments, 'I feel like it's a perfect match, in that he [Raymond] writes these really interior kinds of characters, and then the challenge for me is just figuring out how to physicalize that in turning things over into a script' (Jones 2008: 45). In discussing why he thinks their collaboration works so well, Jon Raymond emphasizes that it has to do with the temporal aspect of both his writing and Reichardt's filmmaking: 'I think one thing that makes our process work is a similar sense of time. Our inner metronomes are both kind of slow. Neither of us seems to mind letting certain moments expand, and we don't need too much narrative activity to keep us interested' (Raymond 2009a).

Reichardt's debut feature *River of Grass*, a regionally inflected, feminist riff on genre set in the area between Miami and the Everglades, brought her attention within independent film circles, but received limited theatrical distribution. *River of Grass* offers a revisionist take on a number of genres – the crime film, the road movie and the love story – which Reichardt manages to subvert at nearly every turn. A crime-scene detective named Jimmy Ryder loses his gun. The person who finds it gives it to a loser friend named Lee Ray Harold to sell. One night Lee meets Ryder's daughter, Cozy, a bored and lonely housewife, at a bar. After a night of drinking, he persuades her to go swimming at a 'friend's' house. At poolside, Lee places the gun in Cozy's hand but it accidentally goes off when they are surprised by the owner. Thinking they've killed a man, Lee convinces Cozy to flee, and they hole up at a cheap motel. Returning to the crime scene, Lee discovers that the owner is very much alive, but he keeps this a secret from Cozy. When the two run out of money, they set out on a road journey, but only get as far as the first toll booth. While a trooper runs a check on them and they struggle over the whereabouts of the gun, Lee is forced to tell Cozy they haven't killed anyone. As they drive back and the camera focuses on her face, Cozy shoots Lee and dumps his body out of the car. *River of Grass* provides a feminist twist on what are essentially male film genres by deflating the romance associated with crime, violence, the open road and heterosexual love.

Reichardt subsequently made a super 8mm film *Ode* (1999), as well as a couple of shorts. It would be over ten years before her collaboration with Portland-based fiction writer Jon Raymond, who published *The Half-Life: A Novel* (Raymond 2004), provided the unexpected spark that reignited her feature-film career. Both of the Jon Raymond short stories on which Reichardt's last two films are based have been published in a collection entitled *Livability: Stories* (Raymond 2009b: 1–21, 206–60), providing us with an opportunity to understand their connection to the films. *Old Joy* managed to become a major critical hit and to gross ten times its $30,000 production cost. *Wendy and Lucy*, produced for $300,000, grossed over $1 million worldwide and was named the best film of the year in the *Film Comment* 2008 annual critics' poll (*Film Comment* 2009: 36). The film not only fulfils the promise of Reichardt's earlier work, but pushes her into the forefront of major independent directors. *Old Joy* evolved from Raymond's initial collaboration with photographer Justine Kurland (Kurland and Raymond 2004), to a 21-page short story, to a co-written 50-page screenplay, to a 76-minute film. Raymond and Reichardt's story concept for *Wendy and Lucy* dealt with a vulnerable young woman in dire economic straits post-Katrina and her dog. Raymond transformed the idea into a 54-page short story, entitled 'Train Choir', and he and Reichardt simultaneously co-wrote a 68-page script that eventually resulted in an 80-minute film.

Old Joy tells the story of a camping trip between two thirty-something friends whose lives have taken strikingly different trajectories. *Old Joy* begins with shots of nature. After sounds of a meditation bell, a bird on a gutter flies off. We see Mark (Daniel London) meditating outside his house, followed by a shot of swarming ants. The tranquillity to which Mark aspires is punctured by the grinding of an electric blender and the sound of music indoors, as his pregnant wife, Tanya, makes some type of green smoothie. The phone rings. The film cuts to Mark meditating with the sounds of neighbourhood kids in the background. The answering machine plays a message from Kurt (Will Oldham), who announces he's in town. Tanya comes into the room and stares at the answering machine. A pan over telephone lines to a bird serves as a transition to Mark's conversation. As Mark talks with Kurt, Tanya paces back and forth in the background. When she sits down, there's obvious tension between them. Tanya resents Mark seeking her permission to go camping with Kurt, and the two of them argue briefly, suggesting either that they have marital problems, which have been exacerbated by their impending baby, or that it is directly connected to the message from Kurt.

While Mark drives to meet Kurt, we hear *Air America* on the radio, which situates what transpires within a political context. Jon Raymond and Kelly Reichardt share a similar interest in the relationship between characters and landscape, and in personalizing the political. Reichardt remarks: 'His [Raymond's] writing leaves so much space for people to bring their own experience, which I'm really interested in as a filmmaker. There's all this space in his stuff, and it ties people very much into their environments – the landscape. And he's also really good at making the political super-personal' (Jones 2008: 45). Photographed by Peter Sillen, *Old Joy* provides us with a sense of nature and physical place, not only as indicated by the opening scene, which I've described at some length, but through long tracking shots of neighbourhoods and extended shots of the natural landscape that convey the texture of the Pacific Northwest. After Kurt and Mark get lost while searching for a remote hot spring, the pair end up camping overnight in a garbage-strewn area in the forest. As the two shoot empty tin cans with a BB gun in front of a golden bonfire, Kurt, stoned and drunk, discusses his theory of a falling tear-shaped universe and then has a sudden emotional outburst over their changed relationship. The two eventually make it to a hot spring in the Cascade Mountains. While Mark lies blissfully in the hot spring, Kurt gently massages his shoulders – the meaning of which (sexual or fraternal) is left open to interpretation.

Reichardt's characterization in *Old Joy* and *Wendy and Lucy* is much more complex than in the genre-based *River of Grass*, where she employs recognizable character types, voiceover narration and expository dialogue to delineate the characters of Cozy, Lee and Jimmy Ryder. In *River of Grass*, coincidence plays a major role in the plot, and fate rather than agency provides the primary motivation for Cozy's actions in the film. Cozy's shooting of Lee has been foreshadowed by her early voiceover narration in which she expresses fascination about the woman who murdered her husband. In both *Old Joy* and *Wendy and Lucy*, on the other hand, Reichardt buries the motivation. Unlike *River of Grass*, Reichardt never explains the characters to us. Their actions are much more ambiguous. Exchanges between characters, such as between Mark and Kurt, rely heavily on subtext.

In *Old Joy*, for instance, what is the nature of the relationship between Mark and Kurt? In Raymond's short story, which is narrated by Mark in the first person, the friendship between Mark and Kurt was close at one time, but they have drifted apart in recent years. Mark comments, 'There was a time, back before Kurt was set wandering in the world, before he had finally burned too many bridges with his regular breakdowns and tantrums, that we had been very close, and there was still a certain duty from those days that bound us' (Raymond 2009b: 2). He's actually anxious rather than ambivalent (as he is in the film) to go camping with Kurt. Mark adds, 'My friendship with Kurt was a point of some pride in my mind, after so many people had written him off over the years' (Raymond 2009b: 3). But after the two come together, Mark is suddenly reminded of Kurt's downside: 'I had forgotten the mild struggle we fell into every time we found each other again' (Raymond 2009b: 4). In both the script and film, Kurt gets Mark to use his car for the trip, buy the gas and bear the burden of driving. In addition, Kurt hits him up for money to buy a bag of pot for the trip.

The two key scenes in *Old Joy* that define their relationship are the camping scene and the one at the hot spring. At the campfire, Mark suddenly becomes aware that Kurt is crying.

The scene, as written in the script, is very close to what appears in the film:

Figure 10.1 Kurt and Mark at the campfire, in *Old Joy* (2006, Kino International)

Kurt leans back on the love seat moaning, his shoulders heaving up and down and sniffling sobs pour out of his mouth.

He looks up at Mark.

> KURT (CONT'D)
> I miss you Mark. I miss you so much. I want us to be real friends again. There's something between us now and I don't like it and I want it to go away.

Kurt stares at Mark with tears streaming down his face. Stunned, Mark watches from across the fire.

> MARK
> Hey, man. What are you talking about? We're fine.

Kurt drops his head between his knees and continues to cry.

> KURT
> Are you serious? Do you really think that?

Mark crosses over to Kurt's side of the fire and hugs his shoulders.

> MARK
> Of course. Of course, I do. We're fine. We're totally fine.

> KURT
> I don't know . . .

Mark keeps his hand on Kurt's shoulder, staring into the fire.

Then, out of nowhere, Kurt makes an immediate recovery. His shoulders become still and the mucousy noises fade away.

(Reichardt and Raymond 2009: 27)

Because it is not clear in the short story, screenplay or film why Kurt cries over his relationship with Mark, the situation is rich in ambiguity, and the fact that it is never explained gives the viewer an opportunity to piece together various clues. Kurt indicates he misses Mark, but what has come between them? Is it some past unresolved incident?

Reichardt added two important elements to the screenplay and film that are not in the original short story, namely the character of Tanya (Mark's wife, who seems to have an almost jealous reaction to Kurt) and his impending fatherhood. Is it Mark's marriage and his family responsibilities that have come in the way? Marriage usually represents a major change in male friendships, especially when one person has remained single like Kurt, who doesn't have the same attachments. In relation to Mark becoming a father, Kurt actually verbalizes this by calling Mark 'so fucking brave' for having a child and remarking, 'I've never gotten myself into anything that I couldn't get myself out of. It's just having a kid is so fucking for real.' Although we never see Tanya again after the opening scene, she does maintain contact with Mark twice through his mobile phone, and the fact that the two guys get lost creates pressure on Mark because it extends the length of their camping trip and the amount of time he spends away from home.

In the short story, the morning after Kurt's tearful outburst, Mark vows, 'I would try harder to find some way to connect' (Raymond 2009b: 12). Mark later fills Kurt in about some of the things he's become involved in lately: community gardening, befriending a homeless woman and letting the neighbourhood kids use his backyard as a playground. In the script, these activities have been changed to spending time woodworking with teenagers and community gardening. When Kurt compliments Mark for his community activities, Mark takes a dig at Kurt in both the script and film by responding, 'It's nothing you couldn't do if you felt like it, too.' This point is emphasized by the use of italics in subsequent description in the script, which also suggests that Mark has a cruel side. In an interview, Reichardt remarks, 'I thought of the film as a western in that way, with a new kind of competitiveness, a competitiveness that challenges each other's openness. Which comes to a head at the tubs' (Rowin 2006).

Reichardt refuses to take sides in terms of her own identification with the characters. The criticism of Kurt is obvious, but she also offers a critical perspective on Mark. She told James Ponsoldt in *Filmmaker*, 'I think of Mark as this guy who really wants world peace, but at the end of the day he can't even be totally forthcoming and honest and giving to his wife or to a good old friend' (Ponsoldt 2006: 132). Raymond's short story is told from Mark's subjective point of view, but the screenplay and film alter that perspective. In the short story, it is Mark who explains the title of the film, while walking towards the hot spring: 'What is sorrow? I thought. What is sorrow but old, worn-out joy?' (Raymond 2009b: 14). Somewhat strangely given its significance, the line doesn't appear in the screenplay, but in the film it is Kurt who relates the line to Mark at the hot spring when he tells a very convoluted and seemingly improvised story about an incident with a female cashier in a store that merges with a dream. Raymond, however, explains the omission of the line in the script as the difficulty in transforming a thought into believable dialogue:

> That was a big, ongoing question leading up to the shoot. In the story, the title sentiment appears as a rumination in Mark's head while hiking. But it was hard to figure how to get those words out of his mouth. For awhile, the sentence kind of fell out of the script. We just couldn't figure out how to

make it natural. I think it was only on set that the decision was made to give the sentence to Kurt, and incorporate it into a re-written tub-side speech. I do believe that Will [Oldham] improved the speech on the spot, with that sentence as an anchor.

(Raymond 2009a)

In a dream, the same woman tries to console Kurt. He tells Mark, 'She just put her arms around me and said, "It's okay, you're okay. Sorrow is nothing but worn-out joy."' Mark merely stares ahead blissfully and doesn't respond. Right after this, Kurt comes behind Mark and begins to massage his shoulders. Mark immediately gets uptight and resists, but Kurt tells him to relax. The camera focuses on Mark's hand with his wedding ring resting on the edge of the tub. His hand slowly slips into the water. Reichardt cuts to a closeup of Kurt as he kneads Mark's shoulders, then to Mark's face as the tension releases, and finally to a closeup of water draining from the tub.

Despite its ambiguity, the scene at the hot spring has distinct sexual overtones. When asked specifically about this, Reichardt responded:

The two things that are somewhat inherent in [a story about] going into the mountains alone with someone, especially if they're going to a hot spring, are the loneliness and desertedness or whatever it is of being in the forest and then sexuality. They're either going to kill each other or they're going to fuck each other – one of those things is bound to happen! A lot of that is just the anticipation that people bring with them from a million years of movie watching.

(Ponsoldt 2006: 99)

The relationship between sexuality and nature is evident in the initial collaboration between Jon Raymond and Justine Kurland, whose brownish photographs of lush, barren and burned landscapes – many with naked figures of men and women communing with nature – were the source of inspiration for Raymond's story (Kurland and Raymond 2004). Raymond writes about Kurland's photographs:

Her landscapes could be a Garden of Eden or a Romantic 'wilderness of the soul'. Her naked figures could be Old Testament heroes, or transcendentalists, or hippies. I figured a good accompaniment should have these kinds of resonances. I ended up doing what I think of as a kind of contemporary Cain and Abel story. Or a Cain and Abel story in reverse. Two estranged brothers traveling back into a primeval garden and reuniting.

(Raymond 2006)

The estranged friends do reunite on the camping trip, but in the film at least, the shared intimacy between the two men appears to carry with it a sense of finality. Dave Kehr underscores this point when he writes: 'And so the ultimate subject of

Old Joy is not friendship but betrayal; not nostalgia but the impossibility of reliving times past; not generational solidarity but lonely individualism' (Kehr 2006: 54). Raymond, however, offers a different interpretation: 'I think the story leaves their future friendship a little more uncertain. But in any case, the moment they share in the tubs is a form of intimacy, even if it means a deeper future estrangement' (Raymond 2009a).

In discussing the character of Kurt in *Old Joy*, Reichardt asks, 'At what point do you become a wanderer, and at what point do you become homeless?' (Ponsoldt 2006: 99). That same question is taken up in Reichardt and Raymond's next collaboration, *Wendy and Lucy*. Reichardt has always gravitated to vulnerable characters who seem to exist on society's margins, such as Cozy and Lee in *River of Grass* and Kurt in *Old Joy*. *Wendy and Lucy*, in fact, begins and ends in a train yard, as if deliberately conjuring up the past – the mythic figure of the hobo – in order to suggest that the Great Depression of the 1930s is back again. As such, the film easily can be read as a searing indictment of the Bush economic legacy. In working on the screenplay for *Wendy and Lucy*, the story began with two essential elements. It would involve a young woman, whose life was on the skids without a safety net, and the director's dog, Lucy, who also appeared as Mark's dog in *Old Joy*.[6] Raymond describes the process of how they developed *Wendy and Lucy*:

> That was more intentionally written to be a film. It was written first as a story, and Kelly and I had had lots of conversations about themes and possible narratives and influences and things like that. The story was written with her serving as an editor, and then she adapted it with me as an editor. It was a strange process, unlike anything I had done before, but it worked.
>
> (*Films in Focus* 2009)

In *Wendy and Lucy*, Wendy (Michelle Williams), a young woman in her twenties, is down on her luck. She is hell-bent on making it to Alaska, where she believes she'll be able to earn enough money to start her life over. En route from Indiana, Wendy's car breaks down in a small town in Oregon. With a tight budget and food running out for her pooch, Lucy, Wendy attempts to pilfer some cans of Iams from a nearby grocery store. On her way out the door, she gets stopped by a young worker. With a silver cross around his neck, he's strictly Old Testament, demanding retribution for her petty crime. After vacillating, the spineless boss lets the worker call the cops, and Wendy gets hauled away, fingerprinted and booked by an inept officer, before she's forced to pay a fine she cannot afford. By the time Wendy returns to the grocery store hours later, Lucy has disappeared from the parking lot where she was left tied to a post outside the store. Wendy's search for her missing dog takes up most of the film and involves a series of episodic incidents, mostly with the people Wendy happens upon in the vicinity where her car has broken down. By the end, she's so beaten down by events that she can no longer even think straight. When Wendy finally gets word that Lucy has been

Figure 10.2 Wendy talks to Lucy through the fence, in *Wendy and Lucy* (2008, Oscilloscope Laboratories)

located, she goes to retrieve her. But, with her life in a tailspin, she impulsively ends up abandoning her beloved companion.

The tragedy of *Wendy and Lucy* is rooted in Wendy's decision regarding Lucy. Her motivation in the film is deliberately left ambiguous. In Raymond's short story, however, it is much clearer. Wendy is named Verna. When Lucy disappears, Raymond describes the effect on Verna: 'The ache of Lucy's absence was like a limb being severed over and over again' (Raymond 2009b: 230). She goes to the backyard where Lucy is being temporarily kept with the intention of taking her. But Verna suddenly gets confused when she ponders her own future. After playing with Lucy, she begins to rationalize: 'A dog could love anyone, she thought. A dog could be happy almost anywhere. They just needed food and water and affection. They were not picky about who delivered it. And by the same token, a dog could forget anyone, too. They were loyal, but only to whoever was around' (Raymond 2009b: 258). Wendy's motivation in the screenplay is quite different – she more clearly realizes that Lucy is better off now than with her:

Scratching Lucy's head, she becomes overwhelmed with a
sad recognition.

                         WENDY (CONT'D)
        It's nice here isn't it, Lu? You've got a
        yard -

Tears roll down her cheeks.

                         WENDY (CONT'D)
        That lady seems nice.[7]

Wendy realizes she is saying good-bye.

WENDY (CONT'D)

I'm sorry, Lu. I lost the car.

Their years of caring for each other, for living for each other, are coming to an end. The one creature she truly loves in the whole world is no longer her own.

WENDY (CONT'D)

You be good. I'll be back. I'm gonna make
a little money and I'll be back. Okay?

(Reichardt and Raymond n.d.: 66–7)

In the film, Wendy's conflict remains an internal one. We can only understand her behaviour through her actions and Reichardt's reliance on visual storytelling. When Wendy sees Lucy, who sports a new leather collar, the dog runs over and licks her face. We view Wendy from Lucy's side of the fence. As Wendy leans down and talks to Lucy – the scene described in detail above – Reichardt's closeup framing and camera placement suggest that Wendy is really the one in a cage. As in the script, she tries to explain that she has lost the car and will come back for her when she makes some money. Once Wendy's fingers let go of the chain link fence, Reichardt cuts to a closeup of Lucy whose eyes remain riveted on Wendy. From Lucy's POV, we watch the back of Wendy as she walks away and hear the sounds of a distant train and Wendy crying.

In *River of Grass*, Reichardt provides psychological explanations for her characters. Through Cozy's narration, we learn certain aspects of her backstory, such as the fact that her mother deserted the family when she was 10 in order to join the circus. Her father's profession explains her fascination with the gory details of the woman who murdered her husband in the house that she and her husband, Bobby, bought at auction, foreshadowing her own violent actions later on. Her husband, whom she doesn't love, works all the time, while Cozy remains stuck at home. We see her doing cartwheels in her house and spinning around in the yard like a child. That she leaves her kid asleep on the couch to go to a bar reveals a lot about her character. All of these traits – broken home, a loveless marriage, detachment from her kids, boredom and loneliness – serve to motivate why she might take off with Lee.

In their initial meeting at the bar, Lee tries to impress Cozy with the new tattoo on his shoulder that says 'Mom', but she points to a photograph of his mother he's placed on the counter and tells him, 'Mom? But we already have Mom here'. In the motel room, where Cozy and Lee get stoned by passing around a joint they hold with their toes, Lee talks about his past. He reveals that his mother collects husbands. His real father, who married her twice, committed suicide on their second honeymoon by walking into the ocean. His mother married the mortician who buried him. Lee adds that it was 'very creepy living with that guy!'

By contrast, in *Old Joy* and *Wendy and Lucy*, we know almost nothing about Wendy or the previous issues that haunt the friendship between Mark and Kurt. In terms of backstory, we glean limited information about Wendy from her phone call to her sister. Although it's not made explicit in the film what has left her in such a dire predicament, she elicits no sympathy from her sister, who prefers to let her husband talk to Wendy. The short story, on the other hand, provides more exposition. Raymond writes of the $5000 Verna would make in Alaska: 'For her, that would be enough to put a good dent in the Visa bills she'd racked up since her apartment had flooded in the winter, and possibly even get the collection agency goons off her back' (Raymond 2009b: 207). He even provides her ultimate goal: 'The dream of a house with a fenced-in-yard and rosebushes would wait for another time' (Raymond 2009b: 207). Yet that specificity is lacking in both the screenplay and film.[8]

In employing a type of narration more often found in art cinema than in classical Hollywood, Reichardt, like Todd Haynes in *Safe*, deliberately creates gaps in our understanding of these characters (Murphy 2007: 62).[9] This not only gives more space to the viewer to extrapolate 'character' from a number of cues, but it gives a certain freedom to the performers as well. Michelle Williams has admitted to being in awe of the 'mystery' that shrouded Will Oldham's portrayal of Kurt in *Old Joy*. It's also what made her to want to play the part of Wendy after she was first given the short story and then the actual script to read. The two friends in *Old Joy* represent a striking contrast. In terms of performance, Oldham communicates Kurt's restlessness through the awkwardness of his jerky body movements, whereas we register Mark's feelings largely through the anguish on London's expressive face – he's virtually a walking reaction shot. Because Reichardt works from a more bare-bones screenplay (that doesn't follow the convention promulgated by the manuals that one page equals one minute of screen time), she's able to give her actors the freedom to improvise, such as Oldham's story and dream that contains the reference to the title. In a similar vein, it's impossible to talk about *Wendy and Lucy* without discussing the understated performance of Michelle Williams. Critics and scholars sometimes talk about acting as if it were somehow unrelated to the script. Yet if Wendy's motivations are not always defined in the script, this gives an accomplished performer like Williams even more creative room, including an opportunity to utilize gesture as part of her characterization.[10] In her interactions with others, the character Wendy, as played by Williams, has a tendency to turn completely away from them (and the camera) as an innately defensive response. It's only with Lucy that Wendy is able to exude any warmth or spark, which is why her decision about Lucy, her only real friend, will no doubt haunt her forever.

Raymond's spare short stories 'Old Joy' and 'Train Choir' are essentially character studies. They provide Reichardt with basic plot elements and locations, but most importantly, they spell out the motivations of the characters. This allows Reichardt an opportunity to visualize these characters without relying on the type of expository devices she employed in *River of Grass*. Other than through performance, we understand Wendy through certain character traits. Wendy is a loner. It's Lucy who brings her into contact with the gutter punks at the bonfire at the beginning of the film. Wendy appears to have some degree of OCD. She keeps detailed records of her spending by writing the cost of everything in her notebook. Despite being homeless, Wendy meticulously washes at the gas station and changes her undergarments, even if she's forced to wear the same plaid blouse, brown pedal pushers, blue hoodie, and distressed sneakers throughout the film.

Reichardt is a visual stylist, which is already evident in *River of Grass*. All of Reichardt's characters in *River of Grass* are defined by the desolate sun-drenched landscape they inhabit. She uses frontal, postcard-like compositions, as well as tracking shots of depressed areas of South Florida – a vast wasteland of bars, record shops, convenience stores, strip malls, single-storey dwellings, desolate palm trees, flat terrain and intersecting highways. Shots of passing freight trains and a jet flying overhead create a striking contrast to the inertia of the aimless main characters, whose life on the run remains largely confined to a motel room. And the lone jukebox in the bar Ryder frequents becomes a recurrent motif – a sad and alienating image of Americana that we associate with the photographs of Robert Frank.

In *Old Joy*, dialogue is deliberately kept to a minimum. Reichardt's penchant for long takes and letting scenes slowly unfold, includes everything that would be cut out of most other films in the service of succinct storytelling. When Mark drives to Kurt's house, for instance, we watch him park, get out of his car, and walk all the way to Kurt's front door. In one memorable scene from later in the film, the camera frames Kurt smoking a joint inside the car, as we watch Mark studying a map through the windshield. Mark heads away from the car down the road. His mobile phone rings. We watch him jog back to retrieve it, and then amble back away from the car. We can't hear Mark's conversation with his wife as he paces, but we can sense her irritation, as can Kurt, no matter how dulled his senses have become by being stoned. The next morning, as the two have breakfast in a diner, Mark's mobile phone rings once again. He leaves the table and goes outside, which suggests it is Tanya. A simple reaction shot of Kurt is enough to convey a sense of unspoken tension.

In one of the most striking visual scenes in *Wendy and Lucy*, Wendy visits the local pound in her search for Lucy. Reichardt's camera tracks past the various cages of dogs, suggesting the inside of a prison. Through her compositions and mise-en-scène, Reichardt creates rectangles within rectangles, evoking all the ways that Wendy manages to get herself boxed in, which serves as a visual motif in the film. There is a shot of her inside a phone booth and another of her framed in the window of a doughnut shop. Afterwards, Wendy is positioned in the centre rectangle of an exterior wall as she attaches the sign about her lost dog. Not much later, the camera follows Wendy as she walks in front of a brown building. She turns the corner, but the camera stops abruptly, dividing the space of the frame in half. Instead of music, Reichardt relies on a symphony of train sounds and Wendy's humming to create emotional resonance. She uses a palette of muted colours, especially various shades of denim and dark blue and maroon and brown.

Examples include the consecutive boxcars of a train in the opening shot, Wendy's brown Honda, and the faded blue house in the background behind her stalled car, which provides the backdrop for Lucy's separate (metallic blue) food and (maroon) water dishes. Wendy's blue blanket matches the colour of the security guard's shirt, as well as the colour of the doors and painted trim on the gas station. With its carefully chosen colour schemes, rusting metal and grey skies, *Wendy and Lucy* manages to create an overall sense of melancholy that seems to reflect its protagonist's bruised psyche.

Creative collaboration is always a complicated endeavour, especially between writers and film directors. As writer and filmmaker Kathryn Millard suggests: 'Collaboration involves reading and re-reading, notes, discussion and redrafting, creating and recreating something that represents a common understanding' (Millard 2010: 14–15). Raymond and Reichardt have developed a unique approach to working together in order to achieve this mutual understanding, which, in the case of *Wendy and Lucy*, involved their simultaneously co-writing a screenplay and Raymond turning the story concept into a short story. Reichardt offers her own explanation for why their method of working makes this such a good collaboration:

> Working with him [Raymond] definitely makes my films better. He's a great partner. He gives me notes and comments and if we disagree on something, I get my way for the film and he gets his way for the short story. But, the idea of doing this story is that you get more depth than if you go straight to the script. He writes from a very interior point of view. He doesn't have to think about how it's going to look on screen. He can just plunge into someone's mind.
> (Jenkins 2009)

In a *Filmmaker* interview, Reichardt indicates that she prefers to work from a short story precisely because it provides her with more detailed characterization (Gross 2008: 126–7).

Once she has that sense of detail, as I have tried to show, Reichardt attempts to create space for the viewer. She buries the motivation of her characters, allows gifted performers like Will Oldham and Michelle Williams the freedom to improvise and add to their characterizations, and finds ways to interpret the story visually. Working from Raymond's short stories and their co-written screenplays allows Reichardt even more latitude to do this. What's interesting about the collaboration between her and Raymond in these two films is that Reichardt, in working with a fiction writer, enters production with a screenplay, even if the way she uses it more closely resembles Millard's notion of 'an open text that sketches out possibilities and remains fluid through the film-making process' (Millard 2010: 15). This fits the Sundance and American Playhouse model to some extent, but it also relates to the alternative one by employing limited improvisation and relying on visual storytelling rather than an overdeveloped dialogue-driven screenplay, which still remains the industry norm.

Notes

1 After nearly two years of planning, the Sundance Institute, the brainchild of the Hollywood actor Robert Redford, opened its doors in a converted ski lodge resort in Park City, Utah, during the summer of 1981. The purpose of the Institute was to provide a remedy for the two perceived weaknesses of most independent narrative projects: the direction of actors and the screenplay. The Institute was intended to be a place for independent filmmakers to develop and improve such skills under the tutelage of industry professionals. Ten scripts were chosen for development, and selected scenes were then shot on video and polished in a workshop setting, so that the commercial potential of the material could be further enhanced. See Peary 1981.

2 The purpose of American Playhouse, which began in 1980, with Lindsay Law as its executive producer, was to provide a forum for the kinds of voices ordinarily neglected by both mainstream television and film. Besides giving independent features much-needed funding and exposure on public television, American Playhouse developed the innovative strategy of also granting its feature film projects the possibility of showing theatrically before they actually aired on television. The programme proved highly successful. Within its first five years of existence, American Playhouse had its hand in approximately 100 independent productions, including five that saw theatrical release. See Stein 1986.

3 In her article on the screenwriter Tonino Guerra, Riikka Pelo provides a detailed discussion of the influence of the auteur theory in privileging the role of the director in art cinema. See Pelo 2010: 114–15.

4 When asked whether it bothered him that he did not receive proper credit on the films he made with Warhol, Tavel responded: 'Of course it bothers me. Look at the credits on this pirated edition of *Kitchen*. Nowhere on the dust jacket am I mentioned, even though I wrote, directed, and appeared in it. That was intentional on Andy's part – to write me out of history' (Krasowska 2002: 45).

5 In an email correspondence, Jon Raymond clarified his role during production: 'I tend to keep off set. I wasn't there for any of *Old Joy*. And I only came on set during *Wendy and Lucy* when they were shooting within a block of my house. My role during production is usually more of outside confidante and commiserator. Kelly and I talk on the phone most days at least once and I more or less serve as a sounding board for whatever she needs to get off her chest' (Raymond 2009a).

6 Because Reichardt's dog, Lucy, is always with her, even when she's directing films, there's a practical consideration in making Lucy a part of the last two films. Reichardt, however, actually credits Raymond with writing the dog into *Wendy and Lucy*. See Gross 2008: 60.

7 In the film, the person who is boarding Lucy has been changed from a woman to a man.

8 In an interview about *Wendy and Lucy*, Jon Raymond minimizes the importance of backstory in terms of audience identification with a character by suggesting that 'we can fill in the blanks for ourselves'. See Kern 2009.

9 For an extended analysis of art-cinema narration, see Bordwell 1985: 205–33.

10 In response to a question about how well Michelle Williams was able to convey the ideas contained in the script regarding the character of Wendy in *Wendy and Lucy*, Raymond told an interviewer: 'To me, the incredible thing she accomplished, and which I can only imagine is like the black belt of acting, was somehow to express the idea that she was, in fact, withholding expression. Somehow, she managed to give the impression of blocked feelings, which to me seems almost impossible. How do you express that you are not expressing something? It seems really hard'. See Kern 2009.

References

Blue Velvet (Written/dir. David Lynch, USA, 1986; 120 mins).

Bordwell, D. (1985) *Narration in the Fiction Film*, Madison, WI: University of Wisconsin Press.

Eraserhead (Written/dir. David Lynch, USA, 1977; 89 mins).

Film Comment (2009) '20 Best Films of 2008' (Jan./Feb.): 36.

Films in Focus (2009) 'Jon Raymond's Portland' (27 Feb.). URL: http://www.filminfocus.com/article/jon_raymond_s_portland (accessed Jan. 2010).

Gross, L. (2008) 'Animal Rescue: With *Wendy and Lucy*, Kelly Reichardt Finds a Parable for Contemporary America in the Story of a Woman and her Dog', *Filmmaker* 17(1) (fall): 60–4, 126–7.

Horse (Written Ronald Tavel, dir. Andy Warhol, USA, 1965; 66 mins).

I'm Not There (Written Todd Haynes and Oren Moverman, dir. Todd Haynes, USA/Germany, 2007; 135 mins).

Inland Empire (Written/dir. David Lynch, France/Poland/USA, 2006; 179 mins).

Jenkins, D. (2009) 'Interview: Kelly Reichardt', *Time Out London* (3 March). URL: http://www.timeout.com/film/features/show-feature/6962/interview-kelly-reichardt.html (accessed Jan. 2010).

Jones, K. (2008) 'Time Out: The Quiet Beauty (and Radiant Desperation) of Kelly Reichardt's *Wendy and Lucy*', *Film Comment* (Nov./Dec.): 44–5.

Kehr, D. (2006) 'End of the Road: Kelly Reichardt's *Old Joy* Sifts through the Ashes of a Friendship Gone Dark', *Film Comment* (Sept./Oct.): 50–4.

Kern, D. (2009) 'An Interview with Jonathan Raymond, Screenwriter of *Wendy and Lucy*', *Into the Hill* (13 Feb.). URL: http://www.intothehill.com/film-reviews/an-interview-with-jonathan-raymond-screenwriter-of-wendy-lucy/ (accessed Jan. 2010).

Kitchen (Written Ronald Tavel, dir. Andy Warhol, 1965; 66 mins).

Krasowska, D. (2002) 'Collaborating with Warhol: An Interview with Ronald Tavel', *Cabinet* 8 (fall): 43–5.

Kurland, J. and Raymond, J. (2004) *Old Joy: Photographs by Justine Kurland, Fiction by Jonathan Raymond*, San Francisco, CA, and New York: Artspace Books.

Lost Highway (Written David Lynch and Barry Gifford, dir. David Lynch, France/USA, 1997; 135 mins)

Millard, K. (2010) 'After the Typewriter: The Screenplay in a Digital Era', *Journal of Screenwriting* 1(1): 11–25.

Mulholland Dr. (Written/dir. David Lynch, France/USA, 2001; 141 mins).

Murphy, J. (2007) 'The Passive Protagonist in *Safe*', in *Me and You and Memento and Fargo: How Independent Screenplays Work*, New York and London: Continuum, 46–64.

— (2010) 'No Room for the Fun Stuff: The Question of the Screenplay in American Indie Cinema', *Journal of Screenwriting* 1(1): 175–96.

Ode (Written/dir. Kelly Reichardt, USA, 1999; 48 mins).

Old Joy (Written Jonathan Raymond and Kelly Reichardt, from a story by Jonathan Raymond, dir. Kelly Reichardt, USA, 2006; 76 mins).

Peary, G. (1981) 'Sundance: What Happened When Robert Redford Brought Hollywood Cattlemen and Independent Sheepherders Together?', *American Film* (Oct.): 46–51.

Pelo, R. (2010) 'Tonino Guerra: The Screenwriter as a Narrative Technician or as a Poet of Images? Authorship and Method in the Writer–Director Relationship', *Journal of Screenwriting* 1(1): 113–29.

Ponsoldt, J. (2006) 'Sound of Silence: James Ponsoldt Talks with Kelly Reichardt about *Old Joy*, her Intimate Story of Two Friends' Search for a Hot Spring and the Self-Discoveries they Find', *Filmmaker* 15(1) (fall): 98–101, 131–2.

Raymond, J. (2004) *The Half-Life: A Novel*, New York and London: Bloomsbury.

— (2006) 'Old Joy Notes: The Creation', http://www.kino.com/oldjoy/pages/creation. html (accessed Dec. 2009).

— (2009a) Email correspondence with the author (31 Aug.).

— (2009b) *Livability: Stories*, New York: Bloomsbury.

Reichardt, K. and Raymond, J. (2009) Screenplay: *Old Joy*, from a story by Jon Raymond (unpublished 9 Jan. draft). Quoted material reproduced with the permission of the authors.

— and — (n.d.) Screenplay: *Wendy and Lucy* (unpublished). Quoted material reproduced with the permission of the authors.

River of Grass (Written/dir. Kelly Reichardt, USA, 1995; 100 mins).

Rowin, M. (2006) 'Q & A: Kelly Reichardt, Director of *Old Joy*', *Stop Smiling Magazine* (22 Sept.), http://www.stopsmilingonline.com/story_detail.php?id=655 (accessed Dec. 2009).

Shadows (Written John Cassavetes and Robert Alan Aurthur, based on an improvisation (second version), dir. John Cassavetes, USA, 1958, 1959; 81 mins).

Space (Written Ronald Tavel, dir. Andy Warhol, USA, 1965; 66 mins).

Stein, E. (1986) 'Quality Time', *American Film* (Jan./Feb.): 46–51.

Tavel, R. (1965) 'Introduction', Screenplay: *Space* (unpublished), http://www.ronald-tavel. com/pdf/013.pdf, pp. 1–8 (accessed Jan. 2010).

The Life of Juanita Castro (Written Ronald Tavel, dir. Andy Warhol, USA, 1965; 66 mins).

The Straight Story (Written John Roach and Mary Sweeney, dir. David Lynch, France/UK/ USA, 1999; 112 mins).

Vinyl (Written Ronald Tavel, dir. Andy Warhol, USA, 1965; 66 mins).

Wendy and Lucy (Written Jon Raymond and Kelly Reichardt, from a story by Jon Raymond, dir. Kelly Reichardt, USA, 2008; 80 mins).

Chapter 11

On screenwriting outside the West

Sue Clayton

Introduction

As a feature film screenwriter and director I have been strongly influenced by what we generically call 'world cinema' – films from countries with long-established traditions of filmmaking like Japan and Brazil, to those regions more recently arrived on the global stage like Iran, Indonesia and Mexico, and the central Asian states of Nepal and Bhutan. I have also worked first-hand with writers from Bhutan, Belize and Indonesia, as I will detail below. In this chapter I will examine more closely some of the notions of writing, and writing practices, adopted by world cinema screenwriters, and how these might challenge our own views of both screenwriting and the critical approaches we use towards the screenplay.

My own writing and directing has always been concerned with how our identity is shaped by our relation to our geographical, cultural and political landscape, and with an acute sense of how that landscape – and so our values – shifts and changes. This approach is developed in my drama-documentaries – like *Commodities* (1986), a TV series which chronicles the global shifts of people and cultures resulting from the production of commodities like coffee, sugar, opium and gold; *Turning Japanese* (1987), a film about the cultural intervention in the Northeast of England by Japanese companies in the 1980s; and *Japan Dreaming* (1991), which explores how Japan exported its cultural values along with its fifth-generation soft-technology products. For me, the latter two films were particularly significant as they suggested that widely held notions of Western hegemony over commerce and culture were becoming eroded as the world order changed. My ideas were reflected back in films like Gitai's *Bangkok Bahrain* (1984) and O'Rourke's *Yap – How Did You Know We'd Like TV?* (1980), both of which speak from the so-called 'periphery' – the perspective of Pacific islanders who had US cable TV foisted on them and disenfranchised Asian guest-workers in the Middle East – while questioning that very concept.

I continued to work in this territory, with further literary, musical and landscape references, in my fully fictionalized works, which often feature transient peoples, gypsies, migrants and refugees as central characters and themes. My short film

Heart Songs (UK/Canada, 1992) references the lament of the Acadian people who were expelled from Canada in the eighteenth century; and *The Last Crop* (UK/Australia, 1990) the Irish and Greek communities who found a home in the brash new towns of Australia. *The Disappearance of Finbar* (UK/Ireland/Sweden, 1996) plays on the trope of the legendary Irish wanderer, paralleling the migrant culture of the Lapps, and of Mongolian refugees who have adopted Sweden as their home. These references are scripted but in indirect and allusive ways – influenced in part by films like Mikhalkov's *Urga* (USSR, 1991) and Tran Anh Hung's *The Scent of Green Papaya* (France, 1993) which work intensively with visual and musical allusions. This transnational, post-modern approach to the accretions of culture prompted Michael Wayne to write:

> *The Disappearance of Finbar* has a white diasporic structure of feeling, an atunement to the sort of hybridities of identity and culture usually associated with black and Asian cinema in the UK. . . . (the film) is shot through with translated elements of popular culture while largely rejecting the clear generic markers of the Hollywood paradigm.
>
> (Wayne 2002: 74)

Working in this mode, across borders and boundaries, led me into various practical collaborative projects – with Riri Riza, director of *Three Days to Forever* (2007) and *The Rainbow Troops* (2008) in a project to develop local Indonesian fiction into feature scripts; with Belizean writers such as Melanie Springer, author of *Pearl* (2009), to find ways to generate and define a local film culture; and more extensively in Bhutan where I co-wrote a feature film screenplay *Jumolhari* (2007) with various writers, directors and actors there, about the two-way fascination between Bhutan and the West; and co-founded Ricebowl, an online group for developing new Bhutanese screenwriting work, with Donald Ranvaud, producer of the breakthrough Brazilian film *City of God* (2002).

Out of my experience of viewing new world cinemas, collaborating with international writers, and producing my own film work in the kind of cross-boundary context described above, I have made three important observations. First, I have become aware of a proliferation of countless new and different narrative structures, styles and approaches to the practice of writing in diverse cultures, from which we, with our more formulaic and classically based, prescriptive models of screenwriting, have everything to learn: the Bhutan collaboration that I describe later is a case in point. Secondly, I became aware that traditional methods of analysing world cinema in terms of, for instance, post-colonial models, are scarcely adequate to examine what are increasingly complex networks of authorial and cultural influence, production and consumption of cinema. Shohini Chaudhuri makes a case for a 'network dynamics' model, which:

> allows us to theorize cinema within and beyond the nation-state, highlighting the important cultural dynamics which both the binary of Hollywood versus

World Cinema and the closed hermeneutics of national cinema served to obscure.

(Chaudhuri 2008)

Such a model would take account not only of the cross-currents and influences of global film production, but also of the influences and experiences of writers and directors – it is in this spirit that I present some case studies below.

My third observation also relates to film criticism. I have noted how surprisingly little has been researched or written by world cinema critics and theorists on screenwriting issues in comparison with, say, directing, cinematography, issues around production, audience and censorship. For instance a standard web search of articles on *City of God* yields over 40 profiles and interviews with director Fernando Meirelles, but only one article on its Oscar-nominated screenwriter Bráulio Mantovani. World cinema criticism also tends to treat world cinema writer-directors as directing *auteurs*, underestimating the importance of the screenwriting process as a mediation, a crucial stage in constructing the film through specific conventions of writing – staging, scene-making, montage, flashback and so on. In the case of Bhutanese monk and teacher Khyentse Norbu, the *New York Times* (2000) refers to him as a 'born film maker' and implies his early film *The Cup* (1999) appeared as a spontaneous expression of cinematic talent, though it was in fact fully scripted by Norbu who had attended film school in the USA. One wonders whether some critics are tempted to romanticize and exoticize the notion of the *auteur* who somehow simply 'creates' from experience, and is imagined to be free of the industrial stages and conventions under which we in the West operate – or indeed of literary or other aesthetic conventions in their own culture.

However this lack of attention to writing practices may also be due in part to the paucity of critical frameworks and reference points in the field of screenwriting. In comparison film direction tends to be perceived as part of an overt technical and aesthetic process, with its language of the angle, the shot and the cut understood universally by both critics and practitioners, screenwriting remains an oddly 'virtual' practice. The screenplay texts are not as readily available as the films themselves; the writing process is less visible than that of the shooting process. The only systemic context we have is the raft of Hollywood 'how-to' books which are oddly unconcerned with content or with the relation of the screenplay to other aesthetic forms, but focus almost entirely on structure. These texts, as I have argued elsewhere (Clayton 2007b:1–3; 2010) propose an Aristotelian structural model apparently derived from classical Greek theatre, which is paradoxically claimed to have universal application, and is proselytized around the world by McKee, Root, Field, Seger *et al.* These influential gurus (McKee works as a consultant to Disney and Nickelodeon) propose a 'three-act' model of the flawed or 'conflicted' hero who follows a linear arc of character progression from stasis to destabilization (the 'inciting incident'), crisis and resolution. In this way they characterize classic Hollywood and European cinema, and advocate its structural principles and narrative values as a set of rules to writers globally. Even proposed variants on the familiar 'three-act' model such as Linda Seger's (2006) commentary on non-chronological narratives in recent Hollywood films like *Pulp Fiction* (1994) and *Memento* (2000) and Christopher Vogler's incorporation of Joseph Campbell's anthropological archetypes (Campbell 1949; Vogler 1992, 2006), still advocate the same story shape, with its overdetermined use of the single linear – one might say Oedipal – structure, which prescribes the trajectory of the hero, his conflict, his fight to overcome the symbolic threat or adversary, and his attendant growth in wisdom and stature.

I would argue that both the narrative organization as described and the model of the human subject in this type of narrative propose – characters who are self-willing, self-aware, able to affect and change their world in an uncomplicated linear continuum of cause-and-effect – is not shared by all cultures. In many Southeast Asian countries, for instance, there are circular or repetitive elements to cinema storytelling. For instance in Buddhist cultures, as I discuss later, there is a different concept of the human subject-self, where the notion of ruthlessly pursuing a personal goal in the face of other spiritual or societal considerations may be regarded as the very opposite of 'heroic'.

However, in the absence of other articulated models of cinema storytelling, the three-act transformative character-arc model continues to dominate. Arguably only nations with large-scale domestic film production and highly developed home markets – countries like China and India – are economically secure enough to resist the pull of this 'formula'. For every other nation, the spectre of Hollywood story values and their associated high production-values hover over debates around the promotion of indigenous and national cinema, offering both a familiar structural model and the lure of a global market, or at least the consolation prize of an expensive remake of local films in Hollywood (Xu, 2004; Fox Searchlight 2008). The model thus could be seen to devour difference and homogenize global diversity.

It is in the context of the above history and terms of argument that I have started to ask specific questions of 'world cinema' writers. Do screenwriters work differently in other countries and cultural contexts? From what sectors do they come and what kind of skills and influences do they bring to the filmmaking process? What are their creative preoccupations, and the processes by which they bring these into productive collaboration? Do they see the Hollywood, or any other dominant national cinema, like Bollywood, as presenting values which conflict with their own? For what audience or market do they see themselves as writing? These questions are of course unrealistically broad, and there are as many answers as there are countries and filmmakers in the non-Western world; but I pose them precisely because there is so little written on world cinema screenwriting, and yet so much on what a (Hollywood) screenplay ought to be, that it seems important to lay down some simple markers in this little-explored territory.

Makhmalbaf Film House

In the West, we increasingly regard feature film screenwriting as a learnt trade or profession rather than an artistic activity. With the demise of the US studio system there is no longer 'in house' employment and training for staff writers, and with the decline in writing 'apprenticeships' offered by broadcasters like the BBC, the task of educating screenwriters is increasingly seen as the provenance of film schools and universities. In Iran, Mohsen Makhmalbaf, celebrated screenwriter and director of *Salaam Cinema* (1995), *Gabbeh* (1996) and *Kandahar* (2001), proposed to the Iranian Ministry of Culture a radical new approach.

In the years after the Iranian Revolution of 1979, most American cinema was banned from exhibition (see Akrami 1987), and this provided greater opportunity for Iranian writers and directors to come to the fore. By the early 1990s, Makhmalbaf was as excited by the possibility of educating a new generation of filmmakers as by making his own films. As well as what he saw as the inadequacy of university film training, he claimed that his own education had been the hardship of many years as a political prisoner, and that other eminent Iranian filmmakers had benefited by coming from diverse disciplines – Kiarostami from graphic art, and Mehrjui philosophy. He saw his concept as intrinsic to the values of his culture:

> In the West the system is complex, but the human beings are simple. They have all acquired specialised skills to perform different functions, like parts of a complex machine … But in the East the system is simple and the individuals are complex … Easterners are of a more poetic, mystic and philosophic temperament and tend to adopt more comprehensive world views. In the East if you were to ask a porter or a pedlar about poetic or mystic subjects, he wouldn't hesitate to expound his own views, but he may know nothing about the scientific principles governing his own work tools. Our film-making is also more or less like that. They write scripts, direct, design the sets, edit, and occasionally act and compose music. They are like that even at home. In Iran people change professions fifty times in their lives.
>
> (Makhmalbaf and Herzog 1994)

Thus he proposed to the Ministry of Culture his plan for a school for a hundred students, who would be taught painting, photography, poetry and music, film economics, production, programming, screenplay writing, acting, camera operating, editing, sound mixing, decoupage, history of cinema and film analysis – alongside driving, travelling alone outside the country, urban navigation, cooking, computer science and foreign languages, plus sports such as cycling, swimming and skating (Makhmalbaf 2000). The plan was rejected but in 1996 he created his own school in his home in Tehran, calling it Makhmalbaf House, and teaching the above subjects each intensively for a month, with days of eight hours that often became sixteen (Makhmalbaf 2000). His three children Samira, Maysam and Hana Makhmalbaf were students at this school, where Mohsen taught and wrote the outlines and screenplays for his daughter Samira's directing successes *The Apple* (1998) and *Blackboards* (2000). A founding theme of Makhmalbaf House was collectivity, and it is significant that he and Samira are each variously credited with the authorship of the final-version screenplays, even on the Makhmalbafs' own web pages. For a period from 2001 both the family and the school relocated to Kabul where they made *Kandahar* (2001) and *At Five in the Afternoon* (2004). In 2001, the house was sold to pay off the debts caused by Mohsen's film *A Moment of Innocence* being withheld by censors (on the grounds that it referred to and appeared to condone an incident in Mohsen's own past when he attacked a police guard). Makhmalbaf Film House became no longer a literal house or a school, but effectively a production company which owned all the scripts and films.

As a writer, Makhmalbaf credits his inspiration for stories to fleeting moments of observation, of his own life and those around him. Though he speaks of comparison to Italian neo-realism, his is not a world of edgy or gritty social observation but something more philosophical and reflective, often a world of contrasts and oppositions. Stillness is found in war; humour in tragedy. *Blackboards* is the story of newly trained young teacher Said who walks the mountains, blackboard strapped to his back, looking for pupils. He falls in with a group of Kurdish refugees trekking over the mountains, back towards Iraq, and falls in love with one of them, Halaleh. The humour in *Blackboards* – the illiterate Halaleh oblivious to earnest Said's chalked messages of love, her old father cursing the world because he can't urinate – offsets a story of otherwise intolerable suffering as the refugees make their way to certain death as they trudge exhausted toward their homeland. The screenplay was written in first draft as a simple 20-page story, primarily visual (Makhmalbaf 2010). Makhmalbaf comments:

> Of course Iranian cinema . . . has more focus on reality. Because, more than anything else, it's life that changes, that moves. But the more life confronts danger, the more it reveals its true character. When someone is living in danger as a result of . . . an earthquake, a flood, or civil war, that person cherishes life just like when one opens a pomegranate and tries to savour every single seed in it. So . . . Iranian cinema praises life and is hopeful.
>
> (Walsh, 1996)

Samira Makhmalbaf too sees the redemptive qualities of realism, as she argues against Western films where characters are given fixed moral or character values by the author. Of the real-life situation that prompted *The Apple* – a couple who locked up their two daughters for their whole childhood in a fit of overprotectiveness – she says 'I don't judge it, and I don't find any guilt in it, and I can just see different people's reasons for doing what they've done. I can go into a dark heart, a bad situation, and find a little brightness and happiness' (Hattenstone 1998).

Hana Makhmalbaf talks in similar vein about the film she directed, *Buddha Collapsed out of Shame* (2009), written by Mohsen's wife Marziyeh. By working on a low budget the production was able to go back and film some characters across a year, rough-editing as they went, to precisely avoid the kind of simple character and event closure Mohsen and Samira criticize in Hollywood storytelling (Hattenstone 1998). This collective strategy allows events to simply unroll, and the focus is instead the poetry of the image; for instance in *Blackboards* the symbolic blackboard serves variously and poignantly as shelter for Said and his new wife, a wedding gift, a place for expressing words of love, and a symbol of literacy and learning. Overall Mohsen Makhmalbaf's writing is stylistically distinctive, signifying directly in the story text a complex arrangement of symbolic objects and meanings perhaps only matched in the West by a handful of films, such as those of Tarkovsky and Mallick; this more complex visual grammar changes our spectator role, engaging us in a wider aesthetic and philosophical view rather than one driven by the cause and effect of action, which seeks to steer us into an overdetermined ending.

Structurally, the scripts of both *The Apple* and *Blackboards* end just before what might be more conventionally seen as the resolution of the climax. In *The Apple*, the screenplay ends not on the cathartic scenes of the sisters' new freedom, but on their blind mother who, now also free of confinement, makes her way along a street teased by a boy bobbing an apple in front of her, which she angrily tries to grasp. We see that her life is changing, that she is free of her own self-imposed imprisonment, but that she is still angry with the world outside. There is the hope of a better life but it remains, like the apple, tantalizingly out of reach. The last line of the final scene is given to a passing street crier. Thus life goes on, and the street crier represents history, continuity, community and, it could be said, sublime indifference to the tempestuous highs and lows of our 'heroes'.

Bráulio Mantovani – *City of God* and *The Elite Squad*

Another screenwriter who structures his script work through visual metaphors, creating this kind of visual syntax which guides us through the narrative exposition, is Bráulio Mantovani, who wrote the Oscar-nominated screenplay for *City of God* (2002) directed by Fernando Meirelles, and *The Elite Squad* (2007) by José Padilha. The Makhmalbafs' work, as I have discussed above, distills both landscape and character journey to give a reflective, almost 'empty' quality often reminiscent of the work of Japanese director Ozu, whom Makhmalbaf claims as an influence (Makhmalbaf and Herzog 1994). This strategy is seen elsewhere in Iranian cinema, such as in the work of Abbas Kiarostami (*Taste of Cherry*, 1997; *Shirin*, 2008). In their case we might speculate that such a style may also be related to working in the face of political censorship (see Margulies 2007); with minimal use of dialogue, yet inscribing the narrative with visual symbolism, the films allusively comment on for example the persecution of the Kurds (*Blackboards*) and women's rights in Afghanistan (*At Five in the Afternoon*). In *City of God*, Mantovani too tackles a political topic – the rise of drug-related violence in the *favelas* (shanty-towns) of Rio de Janeiro. However what he faces in the context of Brazilian culture is not censorship or the absence of open debate, but almost the opposite challenge: in Brazil the visual media have undergone an explosive growth in recent years (see Reis 2010). With over 200 TV channels available, and the recently government-incentivized local film market benefiting from US investment and tie-ins with the larger Brazilian broadcasters like TV Globo, this visually sophisticated audience navigates a host of local and global styles and influences; films adapted from crime writing and news reportage, avant-garde fiction, graphic novels, comics, satire and powerful traditions of music and dance, with influences from the European *nouvelle vague* its own *Cinema Novo*, from the very Hispanic *telenovela* to the Hollywood mafia blockbusters of Tarantino and Scorsese. Mantovani has spoken of the challenge to find a screenwriting language or register that will find a voice through these competing influences, and organize the material in a unique way to serve the subtextual needs of the story (Mantovani 2009).

Mantovani adapted *City of God* from Paulo Lins's iconic novel *Cidade de Deus*, the name of a shanty-town notorious for drug crime. Lins himself grew up amid its violence and deprivation, and the novel's reception in Brazil was based on its perceived values of authenticity and veracity. Thus at first glance, the adaptation might be seen as requiring an unrelenting realism like that of Matteo Garrone's Italian *Gomorrah* (2008), a film also based on factual memoir. However the book's opening is highly poetic and dramatic, employing, as Lucia Nagib details, arcane and alliterative poetic language, including a first-person injunction for the success of the novel – a kind of prayer – to the Muse of poetry:

> [The] tranquil river, on the banks of which the characters recollect a past crushed underneath houses and the other buildings of a new *favela*, then begins to turn red, a colour that precedes the appearance of human bodies – corpses from the war that is now being waged. At that point, the narrator stops dead, in order to make a comment in the first person: 'Poetry, my benefactor, illuminate [...] the shades of my words', he pleads, before plunging headlong into a prose that will have 'bullets flying into phonemes'.
>
> (Nagib 2007: 103)

In Nagib's view 'the extreme linguistic sophistication that is obvious from even the opening lines of the novel, leads us to reject the idea that Lins is using direct register'. (Nagib 2007: 103). The novel's 700 pages of rapid-fire reportage, covering literally hundreds of plots and subplots, are interspersed with these kind of non-narrative lyric injunctions. Mantovani and director Meirelles also saw a further potential structure that appealed: they were aware that the book had come about as a product of a comprehensive research project led by sociologist Alba Zaluar on crime and criminality in working-class communities, in which Lins was a participant.

> I decided to do the film ... not because of the action, because I don't like action films at all. But because of this anthropological approach. To show

how these societies are organized, how they took the first steps which led to where they are today.

(Meirelles 2010)

Mantovani thus needed to solve two issues in constructing the screenplay – first, he needed to not simply chronicle one violent incident after another but to somehow account for the systemic historical invasion of gang culture into *favela* life, and its infrastructural effects; and secondly, he sought to locate a poetic quality, a philosophical reflective mode which would reference an authorial voice that the lyric parts of the book suggest, but which for the most part is buried beneath an 'unreliable narrator' figure as cynical as any character in *Goodfellas* or *Pulp Fiction*.

His solution to the first problem was to structure the story historically, moving from the late 1960s before the drug lords had taken over – the almost pastoral place of Lins's childhood; to the 1970s, with youth's ambition circumscribed by the ghetto; then the early 1980s, by which time gang affiliations had made the *favela* a war zone. But there is no linear progression between these eras, instead a series of *bravura* cuts back and forth which highlight the changes between them, and suggest a reality (or realities) more complex than a single chronology could. I have written elsewhere, as have others, about the notion of non-chronological time in Latin American fiction (Clayton 2007b), particularly in terms of the magical realism genre and its disruption of linear continuity in favour of cyclical structures, or events connected within more elliptical or subliminal ways. Many critics (D'Haen 1995; Durix 1998) have argued that this type of non-chronology in effect critiques what Monica Hanna calls the 'official national [and one might add, colonial] . . . narratives of linear progress' and can, by a process she calls microhistorical research:

> provide alternative visions of the effects of historical 'progress' and different methods of representing history. It re-casts history, focusing the narrative on the lives of characters that would not normally be considered historically important figures, and … emphasiz(es) alternative spaces in this reconstruction of national history.

(Hanna 2009: 200)

This interest in a different chronology, with its complexifying of the way we read the world of the film, is evidenced in Mantovani's own influences:

> I was seduced by unconventional narrative at the early age of twelve, when I read, in school, the Brazilian novel *The Posthumous Memoirs of Bras Cubas*. Machado is a nineteenth-century writer, influenced by Lawrence Sterne's *Tristram Shandy* (one of my favorite novels, by the way). When I was seventeen, I discovered Marcel Duchamp and Dada, along with Joyce's novels and the Brazilian modernists. I simply loved all of that.

(Mantovani 2009)

Mantovani's eclectic time-line in *City of God* does not have the whimsical anarchy of say García Márquez, but more the deft orchestrating of structural shifts and perspectives as used by novelists like Julio Cortazar (*Blow Up*) and Jorge Luis Borges, whom he also cites as influences (Mantovani 2010a). This structural mapping becomes a tool in his second challenge – to not only distill down the novel's countless narratives but to create within them an authorial point of view or perspective. He foregrounds three central characters, Rocket, Li'l Zé and to a lesser extent Knockout Ned; he also makes Rocket, the main protagonist, a photographer whose loyalties are ultimately split as he chooses whether to offer the press sensational pictures of notorious criminal Li'l Zé's dead body, or instead his pictures of police corruption, which will stir the politics even more. Rocket's dilemmas are ours too, as we are also spectators, voyeurs, who can choose to take sides. But we don't identify only with Rocket, as we might in the ubiquitous McKee 'transformative arc' model: the split-time structure allows us to focus on various characters as protagonists in their own stories, then back-track and pick up the others' progressions:

> When a less important character in Chapter One becomes the protagonist in Chapter Two (like Little Zé), I would then go back to Chapter One so I could show what happened to that character while the focus had been on someone else.
>
> (Mantovani, 2010b)

This technique of creating a complex matrix of identifications, with their attendant time-lines, is at the heart of Mantovani's visual poetics (not left to the director, or to the cinematographer, as so many Hollywood 'how-to' books suggest or infer). An extreme example of this is the way he makes us identify with the chased chicken at the very start of the film.

> In the novel, there's a chapter in which the narrator describes a banquet from the point of view of a rooster (it became a chicken in the film). The rooster understands it will be killed and eaten. It's a funny and clever moment in the novel. I loved it and became obsessed with the idea of 'translating' that in film language. I remembered the famous 'Kuleshov montage effect' and wrote the scene based on that effect: close ups of the chicken/chicken's being slaughtered. I wanted the audience to see what was going on through the chicken's eyes without any verbal explanation. I guess it worked. Fernando loved it.
>
> (Mantovani 2009)

Mantovani adopts a related technique in a subsequent screenplay, *The Elite Squad*, where he restructured the film to tell it from the point of view of a character, police captain Nascimento, who does not appear for the first fifty minutes of the story, but whose voiceover we hear – again this is a subtle issue of perspective and identification.

The combined effect of the strategies discussed above, by constructing hiatuses in time and space, playing with shifts in the point of view to create meaning produces a cinema with definite echoes of early modernism. Duchamp's collages, and not only the Kuleshov experiment, but Vertov's *Man with a Movie Camera* (1929) – which incidentally also creates a character out of the photographer – also have narratives which are to do with rhythm and repetition, the unspoken cause and effect of complex communities. For all the critics' comparisons of *City of God* to Tarantino, to a randomized pop-promo style (Meirelles is also a commercials director), and to a style supposedly 'designed to convey the paranoia of the cocaine-fuelled tension that marks the lives of those hoodlums' (Pasolini 2010), there is something more deeply structural here. The content may be generically familiar; however its organization and attention to temporality and point of view as inscribed at script stage, is something new, or renewed.

Tran Anh Hung: 'Cinema is My Country'

It is worth considering how many world cinema writers and writer-directors live far from their country of their birth, whether by (personal) choice or (economic or political) necessity. Of those discussed here, Khyentse Norbu spends much of his time in religious practice worldwide; the Makhmalbafs now live in political exile in France (Black 2009); and Vietnamese writer-director Tran Anh Hung is also an exile, having left Vietnam in 1974 with his family when he was aged 12; he was subsequently brought up and educated in Paris where he still lives. The reception of Tran's work as a Vietnamese in exile, and his own perception of his cultural identity, complicates any simplistic notion of intrinsic national cinema, and confirms the need to consider the complex network of influences at work in the way we read the screenplay text. Tran attended film school in Paris, training first to be a cinematographer, then after making a number of short films went on to write and direct the highly acclaimed and Oscar-nominated *The Scent of Green Papaya* (1993). The film tells the story of Mui, who as a child is sold as a servant to a rich Saigon family in the 1950s and 1960s (the end of French rule and the beginning of US hostilities). When the family falls into crisis she is sold again, to a family friend, a pianist. Her selfless actions make the pianist fall in love with her and they marry.

What is remarkable about *The Scent of Green Papaya* is that Tran had spent very little of his adult life in Vietnam when he wrote and made the film, which was shot entirely on studio lots in Paris. In it he seeks to recreate the Vietnam of his childhood, and as such he, rather like other writers discussed here, works with a stylized visual poetry or grammar. In this case the story is structured not around the human household but in Mui's absorption in the rhythms and patterns of nature in those tropical gardens of Saigon long ago. The exotic plants and strange fruits, frogs, insects, and birds, seasonally washed by sun and rain, all provide a kind of alternate world for Mui and are not simply 'set dressing' or something added at shoot stage to embellish the script. They are written in like characters in

Mui's daily life, making tolerable for her the restraining verticals of railings and frames of diving doors. Tran has said that his childhood memories are sensual and tactile: 'the smell of fruit coming in through the window; a woman's voice singing on the radio. . . . If I've ever experienced harmony in my life it was then' (Johnston 2001).

Equally allusive, and more sinister, are the scripted references to war-planes heard overhead, along with unexplained dialogue allusions to a 'curfew', both are ready acknowledgement of a Vietnam divided and about to face war with America, but they remain almost subliminal and contained in this careful lexicon of images, underwritten so as to interweave with the subtle rituals of Mui's daily life. According to Tran, this creation of gentle natural rhythms and customs, with the war referred to only indirectly, is part of his strategy to explore and promote the idea of 'Vietnamese-ness', for like Mantovani, Tran sought to counterbalance a global media loaded with sensationalist images, in his case the gritty news footage and melodramatic military-movie scenarios that saturated Western film and television for decades after the Vietnam war was over:

> When you go to Vietnam today the people who have lived through the war with the Americans don't talk about it. It just doesn't come into their minds to do so. And in some ways, possibly subconsciously, I wanted Vietnam to regain her normality.
>
> (Johnston 2001)

Tran's statement may to us sound simply like wish-fulfilment (how can a country in one generation simply stop thinking about its invaders?) but I would argue that, rather, it speaks to the underlying values of Confucianism that I have experienced in my own empirical research in Vietnam (Clayton 2003) and which is echoed in many aspects of Vietnamese culture. Tran himself speaks of Buddhism and its origins in Confucian thought, which I take in the context of conversations with him to have two relevant characteristics: first (he means by it) a kind of fatalism, a view which dictates that worldly events will occur beyond our control, their full significance beyond our understanding; and secondly, (he refers to) a kind of moral code by which we are to negotiate our lives in the face of such unpredictable and unfathomable forces, which requires that the individual respond to, for instance, suffering or adversity with patience and fortitude. Mindful of fate's capriciousness, Confucius preached that 'virtue carried within it its own reward, namely, the wise are free from doubts; the virtuous from anxiety; the brave from fear' (Confucius, *The Analects* IX, 28).

Thus in Vietnamese society many people like Tran himself speak stoically, or not at all, of the war; and thus Mui does not baulk at her servant role, but learns from the cyclical rhythm of her garden kingdom to show patience and tolerance. Her employer's family's fortunes fall as hers rise, so that as she starts her own household she completes, as film critic Gary Tooze describes, a kind of circular rather than linear journey:

The audience sees constant juxtapositions of characters that cruelly shun nature while Mui is amused and comforted by their existence. In an extension of placid Asian philosophy, Mui's quiet observances lead her from her second family home to an evolving one of her own, as she herself enters the 'Circle of Life'.

(Tooze 2003)

Similarly in his later film, *At the Height of the Summer* (in the USA called *The Vertical Ray of the Sun*) (2000), a film about the lives and loves of three sisters in Hanoi, Tran constructs a scene where a wife learns that her husband has had a relationship with another woman. She cries and closes the door on us. He then takes the narrative away from her, following another parallel story, and only picks up the tale of the husband and wife after their crisis has passed. Tran says of this:

What interested me was to look at the idea of the couple in the context of Confucius. In the film, where the photographer tells the truth to his wife, she cries because it is painful to her. It is at this moment that I choose to cut. What I cut out is actually very precious in Western cinema, that's to say the confrontation. In the West confrontation is dynamic, in Asia it is not necessarily so, it is the moment when each character asks, which part of this pain shall I keep within myself.

(Wood 2006)

The 'Confucianism' of Tran's storytelling challenges our own received models in two ways. First, his stories suggest a different narrative shape or structure – one that is not necessarily catalysed by a self-willing hero responding to the inciting moment or 'Call to Adventure' as Vogler would put it, but perhaps more about the building and deepening of bonds, or the cyclical play of life-events, or the slow journey towards accepting one's place in a capricious world. Both his films after *The Scent of Green Papaya*, *Cyclo* (1995) and *At the Height of the Summer,* concern the family, and *Cyclo* in particular uses metaphors of circles and cycles as the eponymous hero, a young bicycle rickshaw driver, embarks on a kind of pattern of journeys around the city, and is embroiled in a number of situations where city life and the well-being of his own family interweave (for instance one of his clients, who seems honourable, is sexually exploiting Cyclo's sister). By the end of the film, having for a time lost his cyclo to the demands of the extortionist, Cyclo is back on the streets, his reconciled family as passengers. However this is seen as only a temporary harmony, not the cathartic linear resolution of the Hollywood plot; furthermore, our focus has not been entirely on the diegetic events – as one review puts it: '*Cyclo*'s excellence comes not in its plot but in its rhythms, and its flawless juxtaposition of dreams and reality, of art and trash, and of pain and pleasure' (Anderson 2004).

This raises the second aspect of Tran's storytelling model. As I have argued earlier, he does not necessarily focus on internal character-conflict to drive his stories forward. To we who are so attuned to the high drama of the cathartic third act, and to the histrionics of reality TV which mimic this model and privilege the moment of the individual's conflict or emotional excess, Tran's approach invites us to reassess the world-view, based on the notion of the self-willing individual able to forge real effects on their own universe, that underpins our model. His approach reassesses the well-worn traditions of establishing identification and point of view, which can limit the viewer's reading of the text to the conscious (and partial) view of the hero. Maybe we should trust ourselves to see more.

I have made much here of Tran's 'Vietnamese' outlook but I would like to end by contextualizing this. Tran is a writer who sees inspiration everywhere, citing the influence of writer-directors David Lynch and Cronenberg, and claiming *The New World* (2005) by Terence Mallick as his most influential film. 'It is like hearing a Buddhist gong struck. – it is the first Buddhist movie' (Tran and Clayton 2009). He is hugely influenced by music, juxtaposing sounds from Velvet Underground with traditional performed Vietnamese songs as source-music in *At the Height of the Summer*, and working with Radiohead on *I Come with the Rain* (2009). He also is a great lover of Bach: 'This music opens doors, takes you to another place but doesn't quite let you in' (Tran and Clayton 2009). His screenwriting grammar or poetics, drawing heavily on both visual and musical tropes, is drawn from his Vietnamese identity but combined with this eclectic and innovative approach to other cinemas and to music, leaving us curious to see how such a writer will combine these elements in his upcoming work for a global audience:

> I do not feel French. Here is not my place. But equally I am not accepted by the French as an 'ethnic' Vietnamese; apparently my films lack the sort of 'veracity' they want from films about Vietnam. I am permanently suspended, uncomfortable ... I wonder where my true self is. Cinema is in a way my nationality . . . Cinema is a language that can be learnt.
>
> (Tran and Clayton 2009)

Tran speculates whether his 'true self' may after all be in Vietnam. 'A life I haven't lived . . . but maybe have lost' (Tran and Clayton 2009). The railings in *The Scent of Green Papaya*, the music that 'almost lets you in'; these speak of a constant theme of reflecting on the immanence of experience; the moment of fully entering our own lives; the fantasy of being truly present to our own experience and understanding. This is maybe something else to learn from cinema from the margins – the precarious nature of the self, without a home in a more complex philosophical universe. Tran's crime film *I Come with the Rain* (2009) filmed in Los Angeles, the Philippines and Hong Kong, has been awaiting final edit and release for several years owing to financial and editorial issues; his new film *Norwegian Wood*, based on Haruki Murakami's Japanese novel, will be released in late 2010. They both are awaited with enormous interest.

Khyentse Norbu and Bhutanese Buddhism

The challenge of navigating two cultures – of triangulating, as it were, one's writing practice and choices across different and opposing value-systems, is something that also inflects the work of Bhutanese writer-director Khyentse Norbu, and indeed my own work with writers, producers and actors in Bhutan. Norbu's story is interesting in the way he began as assistant on a European-American art-movie, then after training abroad, returned to a culture with practically no filmmaking tradition to present what may be 'Bhutanese' values to a world audience, but also to the Bhutanese themselves.

When Bernardo Bertolucci filmed *Little Buddha* (1993) in the tiny Himalayan state of Bhutan, he was the first outsider to gain access. Isolated by choice from even its near neighbours India, Nepal and China, Bhutan had been effectively a religious state (see Clayton 2007a), with few foreign visitors and virtually no access to television and the internet. Music, visual arts and theatre flourished in the monasteries – where the young Bhutanese monk Khyentse Norbu developed an interest in the performing arts. Norbu was employed as Bertolucci's assistant director and also his adviser on matters spiritual – as not only was he a *rinpoche* (teacher) but he is considered by the Bhutanese, who believe in reincarnation, to be a sacred *tulku*, or reincarnate, of a Tibetan saint, and therefore revered very highly. After *Little Buddha* Norbu travelled to America where he studied politics and film in New York. He returned to Bhutan to script *The Cup* (1999), the story of some young monks' quest to find a TV so that they can watch the 1998 football World Cup, its theme that of how such an isolated society might negotiate the new worldly threat of modern media and values. The film was nominated for Best Foreign Film at the 2000 Oscars.

Figure 11.1 Bhutan's largest cinema in Thimpu, where local movies now rival Bollywood imports

Figure 11.2 Khyentse Norbu directs Travellers and Magicians by the painted rocks at Begana, Western Bhutan, 2002; the painting is of Guru Rinpoche

However my own interest in Bhutan and in Norbu's work began with his second film, *Travellers and Magicians* (2003). Where *The Cup* was a simple realist tale (albeit with a powerful subtext about the seductiveness of Western media) *Travellers and Magicians* is stylistically much more complex and its narrative multi-layered. It tells the story of Dondup, a young man from the remote east of the country who plans to leave Bhutan to seek his fortune overseas, but is beguiled instead by old stories told to him by fellow-travellers as they hike towards the border. The narrative cuts back and forth between Dondup's journey and a parabolic story told to him on the road by a monk about a character called Tashi, also a wanderer, who falls in love with a young married woman with disastrous consequences – together they kill her old husband only to be haunted by his ghost. There is another narrative level where Tashi, himself bewitched, begins dreaming a further story. The links of these second and third stories with magic and witchcraft, and the way in which they are intercut with the primary tale, suggest that we are being invited to consider all storytelling – both the monk's tale and Norbu's own authorial spinning of all the stories – as a kind of witchcraft or enchantment. Norbu has written elsewhere about the illusory nature of cinema, and how it echoes a Buddhist concept called *samsara* – that is, all of life as we perceive it is simply an illusion (Norbu 2003). What interested me however was the specific notion of dreaming particular to Buddhist cultures. Tashi is given a message in a dream; Dondup later dreams of the story he has been told. In Western culture and cinema, we are used to considering the dream as the product of an individual's mind or memory. Writing; a dream, as with a flashback, will generally have the effect of increasing or consolidating our sense of being 'inside the head' of the dreamer, and thus seeing and understanding all the events of the film through their eyes. In Bhutanese Buddhist cosmology, however, dreams are not seen as products of the individual psyche but rather direct communication from the divine. Faure (2004: 151) comments:

Figure 11.3 Film posters in a Thimpu store window. Local movies are beginning to advertise

> The Freudian interpretation tends to reduce dreaming to an unconscious monologue. The ancients knew that there are different kinds of dreams, some of which imply either vertical communication with higher spheres or horizontal communication with other human beings. In Buddhism ... revelations are often mediated by dreams or visions.

This approach to dreaming is evidenced in the screenwriting of other Southeast Asian cultures – for instance in Thai writer-director Achipatpong Weerasethakul's award-winning film *Tropical Malady* (2004) and his recent *Syndromes and a Century* (2006) – and implies a more complex approach to dream material, suggesting other layers and levels of reality, which may be only partly available to our conscious minds.

I will describe below how this dream concept inflected my collaborative work in Bhutan. I was invited by local filmmakers and supported by the Ministry of Culture, along with Donald Ranvaud (producer of *City of God* and *Farewell My Concubine*), to give training to screenwriters and to work on a joint feature project. With the doors now open to Western culture, the Bhutanese are acutely aware of the need to both represent their culture to their own new generations, and to interact with ideas and approaches from outside. Thus we were faced with the same challenge as Norbu with *Travellers and Magicians* – how to tell a story that presented the uniqueness of Bhutanese life and culture to the outside world, but also connected to the local audience whose cinema diet had been exclusively Bollywood and then, after satellite, Fox and MTV. Together with documentarist Dorji Wangchuk, producer Pema Rinzin and actress Lhaki Dolma, we agreed a simple narrative which we thought would appeal to both audiences. As I have mentioned, in the last decade the Bhutanese have focused much attention on how to incorporate global culture and media into their national life while struggling at the same time to maintain their unique and long-held Buddhist values. Thus, from originally much discussion about Western and Bhutanese encounters, we developed together a story about an American IT consultant in Bhutan, named Ellis, who hopes to climb Jumolhari, a remote mountain in the west of the country, when the term of his contract has ended. But climbing mountains in Bhutan is forbidden because tribal groups like the Layas consider them to be the home of deities, to be protected. Ellis disregards the restriction and tricks his young Bhutanese guide by saying he'll only trek. However at the base of Jumolhari Ellis declares his intention to climb, and tells the guide to turn back. Ellis makes his ascent but, as the Layas had predicted, storms and avalanches follow. Ellis is trapped in the ice and goes through a number of harrowing adventures in order to escape. A further plot complication is that he has overlooked the fact that the guide, not a trained climber, will feel obligated to rescue him, and thus endanger her own and others' lives.

Thus far, Ellis's story had been an individual quest story, very much along the lines of the classical three-act structure. However the Western notion of the hero as self-willing subject, in control of his/her destiny (a concept which I have

Figure 11.4 A monk passes by a hand-painted poster for a Bhutanese film showing locally in Punakha, Central Bhutan

also discussed in relation to Tran Anh Hung's work and Confucianism) began to appear inadequate as our group debated the notion of *karma*, whereby a person's every action has consequences for himself or others that cannot be avoided. While Ellis makes his linear journey and climbs the mountain, his actions are observed from another perspective or point of view – but of whom? On this the Bhutanese writers were very clear: the principal participant in Ellis's story, whether he knows it or not, is Jumo, the guardian deity of the mountain Jumolhari. For according to Buddhist principles, Ellis's actions are part of a wheel of cause and effect, and the pattern of his journey will be dictated partly by the merit or demerit he may have obtained through previous deeds, and partly by the animist spirits that surround him. Even modern Bhutanese hold these animist beliefs, which come from Bon, a religion on which its Buddhism is founded: 'Happiness in phenomenal things depends on (the lords of) the soil. Fertile fields and good harvests … Although half (of such effects) is ordained by previous action, the other half comes from the lords of the soil' (Anon., quoted in Samuel 1993: 179).

So the simple linear narrative of Ellis's quest that we had constructed and written became enveloped, as it were, by a more complex point-of-view structure where Ellis's past and future deeds, and the deeds of others, are interpolated by Jumo, the organizing spirit who is the dispenser of karma. Jumo's influence has the effect of complicating the tenses and time-structure of our story – rather in the way I have discussed Mantovani's cutting back and forth in the narrative to capture other characters' points of view. This development suggested the need for

Figure 11.5 Film posters outside a store in Thimpu's food market, Bhutan

a device to ultimately bring Ellis and Jumo – in whom he does not believe, and whom he cannot see – into dramatic contact with each other. While Ellis himself regards the final confrontation as just one more in a series of bizarre hallucinations he has had on the mountain, to the Bhutanese he is being seen and judged from another reality – he is more object than subject. The dreamer in Buddhism is seen by the dream (the being from Faure's 'higher sphere' who seeks to communicate), and not vice versa. It is Jumo's gaze, not his, that controls the scene, the camera's look, and thus our identification.

In summary, Bhutanese ideas around narrative cause and effect, and the notion of points of view beyond that of the individual hero, seemed to me to offer important challenges to both the classical and to Vogler's 'monomyth' model of mythic storytelling. What was most inspiring to both myself and Bhutanese colleagues was not the manifest content of our joint myth-making and storytelling; it was beginning to understand the potential of cinema language in expressing these complex and exciting systems of subjectivity.

Conclusion

While the above studies are little more than sketches of some significant screenwriters and their concerns, they do it seems raise many interesting points for further exploration and debate. Two issues in particular emerge strongly. First, it is clear that the Aristotelian model of McKee *et al.* and its Jungian-influenced Campbell/Vogler variant cannot claim, as they do, that their notion of the universal hero and that hero's trajectory (the transformative character arc) is indeed a universal model.

Other cultures – specifically as I argue here the cultures of Southeast Asia – and other religions and value systems do not perceive the role of the hero in the humanistic and individualistic way that we in the West understand from our notions of character drama, emotion and conflict. As well as this, not all cinema may even be perceived to be about the role of the individual hero at all. This has radical effects for how we identify (or not) with characters and where the focus of a story is to be found. It also may disrupt our long-held commitment to the Aristotelian unities of time and place, and (if the self-willing hero is no longer the single subject) the simple linear cause-and-effect way we construct stories.

New international cinema offers us stories that are elliptical, cyclical, meditative; or highly complex, building levels of dream and consciousness, locating our point of view in a more complex way than simple hero-identity.

Secondly, it is telling how all of the writers here – whether or not they also work as directors – privilege the visual elements of storytelling over the verbal, and find their structuring principles in the image and in, for instance, the pace and sequencing of the image, or in the language of the body (Tran Anh Hung, Mantovani) and the landscape (Makhmalbaf, Norbu). The visual image and perspective is coded, as we saw in the 'chicken' example from Mantovani, or the bobbing apple on a string that teases the blind lady back to life in Makhmalbaf's metaphoric story, or the pulsing rhythm and buzz of nature in the lush gardens of Saigon, as described by Tran Anh Hung. As Tran puts it, 'People make the mistake of thinking that the visual language of cinema is a natural language, but it is not – it has to be learnt' (Tran and Clayton 2009).

In many countries, audiences watch cinema that is predominantly in a language other than their own (the effect of the huge Hollywood and Bollywood diasporas). Variable literacy rates complicate even the reading of subtitles, fuelling further the sense of alienation of trying to hear someone else's language. Movements such as Italian neo-realism effectively made the image new, rediscovering the local culture through primarily visual means – vibrant style, less formal dialogue; greater attention to the 'world' of the film, with the texture of real locations and non-actors. Equally the writers of new world cinema seem, in many cases, to seek to create a visual world, of unique characteristics and subtleties – a lexicon or a grammar of images in which to embed their own cultural uniqueness. Speech may be replaced by silences (Makhmalbaf) or music (Tran Anh Hung) or the babble of the community (Mantovani). We should perhaps remember that our own cinema started without words; and that the electronic and digital future (music videos, advertising, the web) is image-led. We in our highly literate and literary culture have much to learn from those who write with images and not just words.

Acknowledgement

Sue Clayton would like to thank Julie Block, a film student at Cornell University, for her assistance in the researching of this chapter.

References

Akrami, J. (1987) 'The Blighted Spring: Iranian Cinema and Politics in the 1970s', in J. D. H. Downing (ed.), *Film and Politics in the Third World*, New York: Praeger Publishing.

Anderson, J. (2004) *Cyclo – The Real Wheels*. URL: www.combustiblecelluloid.com/classic/cyclo.shtml

Black, I. (2009) 'Interview with Mohsen Makhmalbaf' (25 Nov.). URL: http://www.guardian.co.uk/world/2009/nov/25/iran-mohsen-makhmalbaf-sanctions

Campbell, J. (1949) *The Hero with a Thousand Faces*, New York: Harper Collins.

Chaudhuri, S. (2008) 'The Network Dynamics of World Cinema', paper given at 'Multiplicities: World Cinema, Globalised Media and Cosmopolitan Cultures' conference at Manchester University, 16–17 June.

Clayton, S. (2003) 'H'Mong Friends – The Benefits of Ethical Trading in Vietnam', *Guardian* (11 Oct.). URL: http://www.guardian.co.uk/travel/2003/oct/11/vietnam.guardiansaturdaytravelsection

— (2007a) 'Film-Making in Bhutan: The View from Shangri-La', *New Cinemas* 4(3), London: Intellect Books.

— (2007b) 'Mythic Structure Screenwriting', *New Writing* 4(3).

— (2010) 'Flawed Heroes, Fragmented Heroines: The Use of Myth in Cinema Screenwriting', in S. Bahun and V. G. J. Rajan (eds), *Myth and Violence in the Contemporary Female Text: The New Cassandras*, Aldershot: Ashgate.

D'Haen, T. (1995) 'Magical Realism and Postmodernism: Decentering Privileged Centers', in L. Zamora and W. Farris (eds), *Magical Realism: Theory, History, Community*, Durham, NC: Duke University Press.

Durix, Jean-Pierre (1998) *Mimesis, Genres and Post-Colonial Discourse: Deconstructing Magical Realism*, Basingstoke: Palgrave Macmillan.

Faure, B. (2004) *Double Exposure: Cutting Across Buddhist and Western Discourse*, trans. Janet Lloyd. Stanford, CA: Stanford University Press.

Field, S. (2003) *The Definitive Guide to Screenwriting*, London: Ebury Press.

Fox Searchlight (2008) URL: http://www.facebook.com/board.php?uid=7670069196

Hanna, M. (2009) 'Cien años de Participación: Magical Realism and Italian History in Antonio Tabucchi's Piazza d'Italia', *Carte Italiane*, 2(5), Berkeley, CA: University of California.

Hattenstone, S. (1998) 'Interview with Samira Makhmalbaf', *Guardian* (11 Dec.).

McKee, R. (1997) *Story*, New York: Harper Collins.

Johnston, T (2001) Interview with Tran Anh Hung, *The Independent* (London), 19 August.

Makhmalbaf, M. (2000) *Makhmalbaf Film House*. URL: www.makhmalbaf.com/articles.php?a=4

— and Herzog, W. (1994) 'Eastern Mysticism Meets Western Discipline: A Dialogue between Werner Herzog and Mohsen Makhmalbaf'. URL: www.makhmalbaf.com/brrev.php?pa=1&br=120

— (2010) Outline and screenplay of *Blackboards*. URL: www.makhmalbaf.com/books.php?b=38

Mantovani, B. (2009) Email correspondence with Sue Clayton, 1 Sept.

— (2010a) Email correspondence with Sue Clayton, 13 Feb.

— (2010b) Email correspondence with Sue Clayton, 14 Feb.

Margulies, I. (2007). *Abbas Kiarostami*, Princeton, NJ: Princeton University Press.

Mereilles, F. (2010) Interviewed by Terry Keefe. URL: http://thehollywoodinterview.blogspot.com/2010/01/fernando-mereilles-and-city-of-god.html

Nagib, L. (2007) *Brazil on Screen: Cinema Novo, New Cinema, Utopia*, Nagib: Tauris World Cinema.

New York Times (2000) Review of *The Cup* (28 Jan.).

Norbu, K. (2003) *Life as Cinema*. URL: www.landmarktheatres.com/travellersmagicians.html

Pasolini, A. (2010) Review of *City of God*. URL: www.kamera.co.uk/reviews_extra/city_of_god.php

Reis, R. (2010) *Press Reference: Brazil*. URL: www.pressreference.com/Be-Co/Brazil.html

Root, W. (1987) *Writing the Script: A Practical Guide for Films and Television*, New York: Holt (Henry) & Co.

Samuel, G. (1993) *Civilised Shamans: Buddhism in Tibetan Societies*, Washington, DC: Smithsonian Institution Press.

Seger, L. (2006) *Advanced Screenwriting*, New York: Holt (Henry) & Co.

Tooze, G. (2003) *Anh Hung Tran – a Review*. URL: www.dvdbeaver.com/FILM/tran/tran.html

Tran, A. H. and Clayton, S. (2009) Conversation, Paris, 9 Nov.

Vogler, C. (1992, revised 2006) *The Writer's Journey: Mythic Structure for Storytellers and Screenwriters*, Los Angeles, CA: Michael Weise Productions.

Walsh, D. (1996) Interview with Mohsen Makhmalbaf, New York Film Festival 1996 programme.

Wayne, M. (2002) *The Politics of European Cinema*, London: Intellect Books.

Wood, J. (2006) *A Quick Chat with Tran Anh Hung*. URL: www.kamera.co.uk/interviews/
trananhhung.html

Xu, G.G. (2004) *Remaking East Asia, Outsourcing Hollywood*. URL: http://archive.
sensesofcinema.com/contents/05/34/remaking_east_asia.html

Part IV

Theoretical and critical approaches

Chapter 12

Character in the screenplay text

Steven Price

Now you're getting to what screenwriting's all about: *character*.

(Lew Hunter[1])

There *is* no character.

(David Mamet[2])

The extreme polarity between these two statements, the first by the writer of a popular manual and the second by one of the most celebrated of screenwriters, encapsulates a problem with the study of screenplay character. Within film studies, written texts are usually subordinated to or consumed within the analysis of cinema, and there have been understandably few attempts to examine character independently of the actor's performance or other aspects of the film text. (For exceptions, see Sternberg 1997: 108–30; Price 2010: 124–31.) Conversely, in screenwriting manuals, of which Lew Hunter's is a good representative example, discussion of the topic is voluminous, but conducted from the perspective of the practitioner or teacher who is concerned more with the process of developing a character suitable for filming than with retrospective textual analysis; with creative production, rather than critical consumption.

Consequently, manuals often fall foul of one of the basic principles of literary criticism by encouraging the perception of characters as real people. Hunter insists that 'fine screenwriting comes down to the characters' (1994: 71), and reproduces a number of character sketches written by his students. As Michael Hauge observes,

> [m]any teachers recommend writing full biographies of all your characters, or at least the primary ones, before beginning the screenplay itself. At the very least, outline your main characters' lives from birth until their appearance in your story to ensure that you know them at least as well as you know your best friends. Even though much of this background material will never be revealed in the screenplay itself, your characters will function much more consistently, realistically, and effectively if *you* know the details of their lives.

> (Hauge 1989: 39)

Such a passage demonstrates the dangers of using manuals as critical studies, rather than as writing aids. Literary criticism has long insisted that characters are textual constructs, and that no more can be known about them than what the text provides. This approach can be traced back at least as far as the rejection by the 'New Critics' in the 1920s of the kind of naïve assumptions about character encapsulated in A. C. Bradley's then-influential *Shakespearean Tragedy* (1904). New Criticism saw itself as freeing criticism of subjective speculation by focusing on the formal and linguistic properties of the textual artefact. For example, W. K. Wimsatt and Monroe C. Beardsley's (1946) 'intentional fallacy' proposed that it is impossible to reverse engineer a text to arrive at the author's intentions. Arguably, the same holds for character: all we can know about the character is what is present on the page, and from a critical (as opposed to a 'creative') perspective, such exercises as those endorsed by Hunter and Hauge are pointless. The ironic question posed in the title of L. C. Knights's 1933 essay 'How Many Children Had Lady Macbeth?' had the welcome effect of driving the stake through the heart of biographical character study.

Novelistic and screenplay conceptions of character

So successful was this line of reasoning that by 1979, when Richard Dyer published his seminal analysis of *Stars*, it had become something of a problem, because 'in so far as there has been any theoretical consideration of character in fiction (in any medium), it has primarily been directed to exposing its fallacious aspects' (Dyer 1998: 89). What such an exposure failed to account for was the *effect* that characters often give of somehow exceeding the texts in which they appear. Consequently there had been a kind of critical short-circuit: 'having demonstrated that characters are not real people, that they are an effect of the text constructions, critics and theorists have not proceeded to an examination of how this effect, so widely known and understood, is achieved, and just what the rules of construction are' (Dyer 1998: 89).

Some of these 'rules of construction' are evident in the nine 'qualities' Dyer isolates in 'the novelistic conception of character'. These are sufficiently familiar as to require little elaboration here, but collectively they construct what remains the dominant idea of character in Western culture, deriving from the growth of capitalism and the concurrent development of notions of liberal humanism. This ideology was fully expressed in the rise of the novel, in which the character is an autonomous individual, possessing multiple and perhaps contradictory qualities to give an impression of wholeness, roundness and uniqueness, and with motivating desires that help to propel his or her story arc.

Alternative conceptions of character are readily available, of course: among Dyer's examples is the use of 'types' to represent general classes or interests in Sergei Eisenstein's Marxist dramas of class conflict, and we should add here the structuralist understanding of character discussed below in relation to the work of David Mamet. Moreover, the dominant paradigm is not without inherent difficulties. For example, the protagonist is often required to 'develop' and yet to stay, essentially, the same. Most significant from the present perspective of screenwriting is that the novelistic character possesses both 'interiority' (the ability to detail this 'without necessary recourse to inferences from what s/he says aloud, does or looks like' (Dyer 1998: 94) is the novel's trump card), and 'discrete identity', that paradoxical quality of appearing to exist somehow independently of the text. This 'is a problem for any narrative form' (Dyer 1998: 95), presenting the same logical absurdities as the character's 'backstory' that is recommended in screenwriting manuals but that cannot appear in the film.

A partial answer to this problem is simple, if tautological: it is *because* the 'novelistic' character has been constructed as a free agent that s/he appears to have an existence beyond the limits of the text. It is perfectly possible to create texts that do not generate this effect, so differing theoretical notions of character are also tied to generic distinctions between different kinds of text, as well as to different ideological conceptions of the human individual. For example, Leo Braudy, in a discussion of character that Dyer analyses at length (Dyer 1998: 101–3), proposes a distinction between 'closed' and 'open' films. 'Open' films, such as those of Jean Renoir, suggest the character has a life that persists beyond the frame of the film; 'closed' films, like those of Alfred Hitchcock and Fritz Lang, do not. Several years later, the drama critic John Peter argued for a more or less identical distinction between open and closed plays (Peter 1987). He titled his book *Vladimir's Carrot* because that object exemplifies the workings of a closed play: it simply does not occur to an audience of *Waiting for Godot* to ask where Vladimir obtains the carrots he produces on stage, because we do not imagine his world to be an extension of or metonymically related to our own, but recognize it instead as a self-referential structure.

That screenwriting manuals often recommend the creation of characters with a full biography, whose decisions present a further revelation of the self, is a sure sign that the 'novelistic' conception of character has become so ubiquitous as almost to appear beyond ideology altogether: a character is an autonomous individual with the freedom to choose. What is remarkable in the present context is that this novelistic conception is in fact, and almost by definition, very clearly differentiated from what we might call the screenplay conception of character. Arguably, the screenwriter ordinarily has access to *none* of the most common relevant methods of characterization exploited by the novelist: detailed physical description, the ability to describe inner thought and the broader possibilities of omniscient narration.

An accumulation of physical detail, including facial features and build as well as the semiotics of fashion, clothing, hairstyles, designer brands and the like, not only gives some indication of character, but also, through the accumulation of redundant detail, helps to create a reality effect whereby the character appears securely anchored in a finely realized storyworld. Yet the screenwriter is unable to present such detailed physical description, partly because of the need to defer in such matters to directors, designers and actors, and partly due to the sometimes disputed convention that a page of script is equivalent to a minute of screen time. The writer simply does not have the words at his or her disposal to engage in leisurely description of people or places. In short, the screenplay is a structuring document that demands concentration on the shape of the story and the succession of events rather than on redundant physical detail.

Second, the novelist may give direct access to the thoughts and inner life of the character by such means as interior monologue and free indirect speech. The only equivalent techniques available to the screenwriter are the montage signifying a succession of thoughts, and the voiceover. Of these, the montage, besides now being rather clichéd, cannot capture individual voice in the way that prose narration can. Meanwhile, voiceover has often been dismissed in film criticism as a manipulative literary device that falls victim to the 'specificity thesis'. This proposition, associated with Rudolf Arnheim among several other early film theorists, and still influential, holds that the art of cinema consists primarily in camera and editing, since these are specific to the medium, and not in dialogue, which is theatrical. The thesis has itself more recently come under sustained attack from several quarters, chiefly on the grounds that it artificially privileges one element of what has always been a hybrid and synaesthetic medium (see Carroll 1992). Nonetheless, voiceover is still widely viewed with suspicion, and in any case is generally used either in scripts for particular kinds of film, such as the 'art movie' in which there may be a conflation of not only writer and director but also protagonist, or to explain to the audience through narration what could not be satisfactorily achieved by other means. Examples are the introductory, expository voiceovers, with accompanying visual montage, that orient the spectator within what might otherwise be the confusing storyworlds of *Casablanca* (Michael Curtiz, 1941) and *The Third Man* (Carol Reed, 1949). Such a use of voiceover may indicate a perceived difficulty with the screenplay. The introductory narration for *The Third Man*, for example, was developed at a late stage when it was feared the audience would not understand the complicated division of powers in post-war Vienna; the speech does not appear in Graham Greene's original screenplay (White 2003: 7–9).[3]

A third, related novelistic method is authoritative narrational commentary about characters. The problem of narration in *film* is too complex to engage in the present context, but related if simpler difficulties bedevil the screenplay. The clearest approach to this question is perhaps that outlined by Claudia Sternberg, who identifies three different modes in the non-dialogue elements of the screenplay text. '[T]he *mode of description* is composed of detailed sections about production design in addition to economical slug-line reductions' (Sternberg 1997: 71). The *report mode* is the temporal sequence of actions, usually human. Of greatest interest here is the third, *comment mode*, whereby the text offers a commentary on events. As Sternberg observes, such commentary, akin to the authorial narration of prose fiction, is routinely prohibited in manuals. The assumption is that such comments cannot be filmed, and even if they could, they would be the province of the director rather than the writer. Sternberg easily refutes this by pointing out that her sample range of Hollywood screenplays contains innumerable figures of speech and other things that cannot be shown or seen. Indeed, according to Sternberg 'screenwriters rarely miss the opportunity to use the mode of comment' (Sternberg 1997: 74). This final remark seems to overstate the case, however, since most screenplays are sparing at best in direct comment.

To these three novelistic modes of character presentation we may add the freedom generally afforded the novelist to present speech in written forms, either dialogic or monologic, that would sound wholly unnatural if recited orally. An extreme example is Marlow's 'yarn' in *Heart of Darkness*, which comprises virtually all of Joseph Conrad's 1899 novella, and is replete with highly literary techniques in description, characterization and dialogue. Seemingly oral recitation can thereby become conflated with textual narration in ways that are unavailable to any screenplay that attempts to create realistic speech.

A provisional conclusion is that screenplay character is, necessarily, *generically* distinct from novelistic character. For example, the relative lack of access to the screenplay character's inner world, or to its contemplation of the various discourses – legal, religious, educational, etc. – that may construct and define it as a social subject, makes him or her a more consistently existentialist being than an equivalent figure in realist prose fiction. In the screenplay we see only the actions through which the character responds to, and carves out an identity for itself within, this social world. Of course, this is also an illusion: the screenplay character's series of actions is orchestrated by the text, and to say that this character is an effect of structure is only a different way of saying that it is an effect of narration. Nonetheless, the illusion is of a different kind, or possesses a different set of emphases, than that created by the novel.

But there is more than one way of writing a screenplay, and different styles of writing produce different effects of character. To illustrate this we may contrast two celebrated scripts: David Mamet's *House of Games*, which adheres rigorously to the disciplines of screenwriting outlined above, and whose author conceives of screenwriting in structuralist terms; and Graham Greene's *The Third Man*, which not surprisingly retains much of the sensibility of the novelist.

The structuralist conception of character: David Mamet and *House of Games*

In a classically structuralist analysis, there can be no autonomous, individual character. The 'character' has no 'positive' or innate qualities, and instead exists only as one term within a structure of signs, assuming its identity to the extent that it differs from, and operates in relation to, the other terms. The 'hero', for example, acquires definition in relation to the 'villain'. In his *Morphology of the Folktale* (1928), the proto-structuralist Vladimir Propp avoids the ideological connotations of the word 'character' and instead identifies a common structure to the tales he analyses, each of which consists of a selection of 31 possible 'functions', performed in an invariable sequence by the dramatis personae who occupy seven 'spheres of action' (villain, donor, helper, princess, dispatcher, hero and false hero) (Propp 1984: 23). The sequence of these functions remains fixed, though not all would appear in a given tale.

Mamet's comments on writing and film indicate that he views texts and stories in similarly structuralist terms. He admires the work of Joseph Campbell (see Kane 2001: 209), who identifies a 'monomyth' in Western storytelling which in many respects resembles Propp's recurrent tale: 'A hero ventures forth from the world of common day into a region of supernatural wonder: fabulous forces are there encountered and a decisive victory is won: the hero comes back from this mysterious adventure with the power to bestow boons on his fellow man' (Campbell 1949: 30).[4] The fairytale itself is one of Mamet's preferred 'teaching tool[s]', because it is 'told in the simplest of images and without elaboration, without an attempt to characterize' (Mamet 1994: 396). He argues that 'all there is in a movie [is] structure' (Kane 2001: 66), affirming that the task of the writer begins with the creation of a 'logical structure', after which 'the ego of the structuralist hands the outline to the id, who will write the dialogue' (Mamet 1994: 346). Characters themselves are 'nothing but habitual action' (Kane 2001: 40). More broadly, in an essay against realism, he observes that '[i]n general, each facet of every production must be weighed and understood *solely* on the basis of its interrelationship to the other elements' (Mamet 1994: 201; my emphasis). He believes that the audience finds it easier to 'identify with the pursuit of a goal' than with '"character traits"', because 'those idiosyncrasies … *divide* us from [the protagonist]' (Mamet 1994: 406).

This distinction between the protagonist and his or her 'idiosyncrasies' resembles Dyer's differentiation between 'character', which 'refer[s] to the constructed personages of films', and 'personality', which is 'the set of traits and characteristics with which the film endows them' (Dyer 1998: 89–90). Unsurprisingly, both 'personality' and the comment mode are almost completely absent from a Mamet script. This is the case even in his first filmed screenplays, for *The Postman Always Rings Twice* (Bob Rafelson, 1981), *The Verdict* (Sidney Lumet, 1982), and *The Untouchables* (Brian De Palma, 1986). While all of these display a similar authorial method to that in the screenplays Mamet would later direct himself, the work of the other directors, and the performances of the major stars Jack Nicholson, Paul Newman, and Robert de Niro, respectively, give those characters a greater sense of 'openness', in keeping with the Method acting or New Hollywood directorial style with which most of these figures are associated. It is therefore quite possible for a Mamet script to be read or filmed in such a way that a conventional sense of 'character' emerges. For example, in one of the better screenwriting manuals Paul Lucey adopts the figure of Galvin in *The Verdict* as his principal 'character study' (Lucey 1996: 109–37). Lucey's decision may have been influenced by Paul Newman's unforgettable

performance, but it also indicates that character can be, as it were, 'read into' –
or out of – Mamet's words.

When Mamet directs his own films, however, the full consequences of
his theoretical conception of character emerge. This is well illustrated in the
screenplay for his directorial debut, *House of Games* (1987), in which Margaret
Ford, an academic who has just published a book on psychology, is drawn into the
increasingly complex and dangerous world of a team of confidence men headed
by the antagonist, Mike. The drama comes to revolve around the erasure of an
initial structural opposition of Margaret (female, professional middle class, student
of psychology) and Mike (male, criminal underclass, practitioner of confidence
tricks). At the heart of this opposition lie the questions of whether Margaret or
Mike has the better understanding of the mind, and whether or not there is a deep
psychology to be unearthed. In other words, Mamet's first film as writer-director is
an interrogation of what the human – and what the 'character' – *is*.

The script opens with the following sequence:

> People hurrying to work across a crowded plaza. Camera
> moves forward toward a coffee cart in the background.
>
> A young woman walks into the frame in the foreground. She
> takes a book out of her purse, looks down at the book.[5]

The above description simply reports the sequence of events that the imagined
spectator (or camera) is imagined to observe on, or record for, an imagined screen.
It does not comment on these actions, nor does it give any authorial or narratorial
insight into the woman's character, grant her any 'traits', or even provide any
physical description bar the kind of approximation of age – 'young' – that would
occur to any observer.

This method persists throughout the text. The reader does not receive any
direct indication of the age of the protagonist, Margaret, whose autograph the
young woman solicits as the opening scene continues. Mamet is, apparently,
neither creating nor referring back to any visualization or interpretation of
'character'. He is simply describing a series of actions, and it is as if the names
alone are sufficient to distinguish one figure from another. We know the gender,
we are sometimes told that a person is 'about thirty', for example, but otherwise
there is simply a series of actions involving several figures who interrelate in ways
that form the structure that is the screenplay.

Yet it is not quite true that there is *no* comment in the script. Margaret's
apartment, for example, is '[o]bviously the abode of a single woman' (28).
Is that a description, or an interpretive comment? It appears to be a subtle
direction to the readers, or to the designer (who is also a reader), indicating that
the apartment must be set in such a way that the cinema spectator will interpret
the shot as the author intends. At such moments the text is interpretive, but only
so that it can describe the *effect* the reader is to imagine will be generated by the
screen image.

This is more significant than at first appears. Later, once Margaret has been drawn more deeply into the world of the confidence men, the camera adopts her point of view when she and Mike arrive on the scene of a complicated con, in which Mike and his gang attempt to trick a businessman into giving them his money in exchange for a suitcase he thinks contains a fortune. Her involvement in this begins when she sees two men in the street 'conversing, as after a good meal' (42). One of these is the 'Vegas man', whom Margaret already knows to be part of the gang; the other is the businessman. The depiction of how the two men speak ('as after a good meal') is another example of a clause that is both a description and a comment, again with the apparent aim of indicating the required effect on the screen. Then '[t]he cab drives away. But the Vegas man has forgotten his suitcase' (43). Conjunctions such as 'but' should logically be omitted in the rigorously paratactic style for which Mamet strives, because, by providing a connection between the material in two sentences or clauses, they comment on the action. Moreover, there is a trace of interiority in the declaration that 'the Vegas man has forgotten his suitcase'. Once it becomes clear that the businessman is sufficiently greedy to have taken the bait, Mamet will supply another descriptive-interpretive phrase when 'Mike turns to Ford, [and] nods slightly, sadly, meaning you see what human nature is?' (46).

These tiny modifications to Mamet's paratactic style are remarkably suggestive. They can be reconciled with his purist conception of screenwriting by noting that cinema has always been able to signal interior thought through the juxtaposition of shots. The writing at this point in the script implies the use of the Kuleshov effect: the meaning of Mike's nod will emerge on the screen because the businessman has just shown that he wants something for nothing, and is therefore a natural 'mark'. Later in the script, after the businessman has been shot (having been exposed as an undercover policeman), there is an explicit revelation of interiority when memories of the shooting pass as visual images through Margaret's mind, revealing her horror, guilt and anxiety. It seems, then, that no matter how hard Mamet insists both in theory and in practice that there is no such thing as character, the concept cannot finally be dispensed with.

A similar argument could be made about his dialogue. In a self-deprecating preface to the published text, he records that to prepare for directing *House of Games* he used a simple version of Eisenstein's theory of montage 'to reduce the script, a fairly verbal psychological thriller, to a *silent movie*' (p. vii), following the principle that the juxtaposition of two shots creates a third, unspoken and unvisualized idea. Mike's nod provides an illustration, although it also helps to indicate why the comment mode sometimes has to intrude, since otherwise his gesture could appear ambiguous in the written text.

The belief that a film should be directed as if it were a silent movie, with the concomitant devaluation of dialogue, suggests an endorsement of the specificity thesis. Yet a glance at any Mamet script will show that, partly because it attempts to eschew comment, it is dominated by dialogue; and it is hardly surprising that the dialogue of this celebrated dramatist turns out to be essential to our understanding of character. To take a simple example, Margaret first encounters Mike in the otherwise exclusively masculine domain of the title location, in which pool, poker and con tricks are the major currencies. She apparently tries to adopt the idiom of the confidence men, but is comically inept at doing so ('Let's talk turkey, Pal', 13). Such lines indicate things about Margaret's character, particularly in relation to Mike: she is awkward and, in this environment, inferior to him, and although she is an expert on psychology she appears remarkably superficial and inauthentic.

And yet, in the brilliant twists of *House of Games*, such notions are confounded. First of all, despite what the text appears to say, the Vegas man has *not* 'forgotten' his suitcase: he has remembered to appear to forget it, this being the opening move in the con. The text does not reveal what is going on in the Vegas man's mind; it constructs what is going on in the *reader's* mind. This is a clue as to what is really happening in the 'Mamet movie'. We understand quickly enough that the Vegas man did not really forget anything. Only when the businessman is revealed as a police officer, however, do we have to reinterpret Mike's unspoken comment about human nature: the businessman's words in fact reveal nothing at all about human nature because he was only pretending to fall victim to the gang. Even this is not the end of the matter. At the climax of the film, Margaret discovers that the 'police officer' is alive and well and just another member of the gang, that she herself has been the 'mark' all along, and that everything we have seen has been a performance that revealed nothing about anyone's nature save her own. Mike's nod was just another deception. Although there are still further twists to come, the film appears to conclude with Margaret learning something about her own character: she herself is capable of becoming a thief and a con artist, and was latently so from the beginning.

If this were really the conclusion we are supposed to reach, then for all its trickery *House of Games* would be an example of the Aristotelian principles of recognition and reversal that Mamet has frequently insisted lie at the heart of drama. It would not sit easily, however, with the notion that 'there is no character'. That notion transmits itself readily to most spectators who recognize that it establishes something distinctive about Mamet's work. Everyone notices, for instance, that there is something peculiar about the delivery of the lines in a Mamet-directed film: the actor appears to be reciting, rather than simply speaking, the dialogue. This is one of the ways in which a Mamet film never possesses the illusion of reality, but instead calls attention to the film as a record of a script. His celebrated dialogue is not just audible but also, as it were, *visible*. This is literally so in the book cover, diary entries, notebooks, and building signs that pepper *House of Games*, but it is also in a different sense true of the spoken dialogue. One reviewer of the film felt the presence of 'the man, just off-screen, who wrote the screenplay and is monitoring everything the actor does' (Canby 1987); another remarked, 'you feel as if Mamet were in the seat next to you repeating, "This isn't real, this is . . . artifice"' (Hinson 1987).[6]

Although it appears to be a drama played out between Margaret and Mike, these figures have no real substance. The real drama is that between Mamet and the audience or reader. This is absolutely in accordance with Mamet's understanding of film. Exposing character as an illusion created by the structure of the text, he locates the source of meaning not in the character, the actor, or even the director, but in the writer: 'The words are set and unchanging. Any worth in them was put there by the author' (Mamet 1997: 62). His method of working with a familiar ensemble – which may partly explain the absence of description (Margaret Ford was played by Mamet's then-wife, Lindsay Crouse) – means that his actors 'will trust that the line's going to work and read the line as it's written' (Mamet, in Kane 2001: 158). Directing is simply an extension of writing; it is a record of the pro-filmic event, 'the work of constructing the shot list from the script' and of 'record[ing] what has been chosen to be recorded' (Mamet 1994: 349). His ideas about filmmaking therefore protect the writer's voice at the expense of the director's, just as, in John Lahr's words, 'his ideas about acting protect the author's voice at the expense of the actor's' (Lahr 1997: 78).

Character that exceeds the text: *The Third Man*

Mamet's screenplays suggest that the structuralist and paratactic style is not simply one way of rendering character with the aim of eliminating material that cannot be filmed. Instead, it constructs a generically distinct form of characterization that differs from that produced by other approaches to screenwriting, such as Graham Greene's in writing *The Third Man*. Greene's Harry Lime is a criminal racketeer who fakes his own death amidst the ruins of post-war Vienna. For most of the time his deception fools the audience, as well as both the authorities, headed by Colonel Calloway of the British Military Police, and Harry's naïvely innocent friend Holly Martins, whom Harry has invited to join him. Even though Harry does not appear until two-thirds of the way through and is on screen for barely 10 percent of the duration, he famously dominates the film. He therefore provides a fine example of the notion of character as something that appears to *exceed* the textual structure that seemingly confines it, and although Orson Welles's performance and persona undoubtedly contribute to this effect, it is also bound up with the way the character is created in the screenplay text.

One way of demonstrating the difference between the two kinds of screenplay considered in this chapter is by borrowing a distinction developed by Steven Maras between two 'discourses' surrounding screenwriting (Maras 2009). The first sees the text as a blueprint that completes the 'conception' stage; the filming is merely the execution of the idea. Mamet's ideas about the relationship between screenwriting and production offer the starkest possible illustration of this discourse, with the near-total absence of the comment mode in *House of Games* suggesting that the text is a self-sufficient document that requires no further elaboration. The second sees screenplay and filming as a continuous, evolving process that cannot be divided so easily into two stages. For this reason, Maras offers the term 'scripting' as a way of blurring the distinction, and to suggest that filming may itself be seen as a form of writing. The published text of *The Third Man*, which uses parentheses to indicate material from the screenplay that was unfilmed or omitted from the release print, and footnotes to present material found in the film but not in Greene's screenplay, preserves a textual record of this 'scripting' process in *The Third Man*.

Different production practices produce different kinds of script. Mamet worked with his own screenplay and acting ensemble, so the text remained relatively stable, whereas in *The Third Man* Lime's character was altered significantly from Greene's original conception due to the nature of the collaboration. Most significantly, while the producer David O. Selznick initially wanted Noël Coward for the role, in the end the director Carol Reed won the day and Orson Welles was cast (Thomson 1997: 293–4). The resulting 'problem of fit' (Dyer 1998: 116) between actor and character was then partially resolved by alterations in the script, most memorably in Welles's authorship of the 'cuckoo clock' speech, which appears in the published text merely as a footnote, since it formed no part of Greene's creation.

There is a related sense of 'fit' in the relationships between different characters in the text. The casting of Joseph Cotten (rather than Selznick's preferred choice, Cary Grant) as Holly Martins reconstituted an old partnership familiar to cinema-goers from *Citizen Kane* (Welles, 1941), and this adds an extra-textual dimension to the understanding of the film. Even within the text, however, Harry Lime and Holly Martins each derive at least some of their meaning from the structural relationship to the other. Partly this is a matter of narrative, with Harry the object of Holly's pursuit; but it is also an effect of a kind of doubling, whereby each character becomes more complex (more 'realistic', in this sense), either by taking on traits of the other or by coming to be seen as representing conflicting forces in a dynamic between two figures. Originally named 'Rollo' throughout Greene's script, the change of Martins's first name to 'Holly' in the film has the happy effect of suggesting this connection even at the level of sound; indeed, Anna frequently calls Holly 'Harry' by mistake. This is doubly irritating to Martins once he realizes that he wishes to occupy his friend's former position as the lover of Anna, the girl Harry leaves behind.

This drama, in which one character unknowingly begins to take on the characteristics of another who is either dead or presumed to be so, particularly by moving into the physical spaces previously occupied by another, is common in literary fictions of the uncanny or the doppelgänger, such as many of Poe's tales. It is also frequently found in ghost or horror stories, perhaps the best cinematic example being *The Tenant* (Roman Polanski, 1976). Its significance in the present discussion is that it shows how the structural method of distinguishing characters by means of parallels and contrasts does not *only* establish one character's identity as an effect of its difference from others. It also shows how one character *acquires* identity by taking on aspects of the identities of others, and in so doing gains the appearance of greater substance than it would possess if it were really an autonomous and unique individual.

For example, our understanding of the child-like, playful aspect of Harry Lime, so sharply in contrast to the crimes he has committed, is prompted by the likeable Holly entering into and performing Harry's role from the beginning. As with any literary doppelgänger, the doubling presents not contrast but uncanny repetition: like Harry, Holly is a seemingly innocent American, a lover of westerns, wandering through a bomb-shattered Vienna, trying to survive by his wits, and falling in love with Anna. Each figure seeps into the other, so that when Harry finally emerges from the shadows it is as if we have known him already: not because of what other people have said about him, much of which is lies, but because we have already seen Holly acting out a version of the '[b]est friend I ever had' (25).

It is unusual for one character almost literally to *embody* another in this way, but much more common, of course, for the various personages in a screenplay to comment upon one another in ways that contribute to the construction of character. Still, if Mamet is right in arguing that character is 'nothing but habitual action' – a belief derived from Aristotle's *Poetics*, which is an almost ubiquitous authority in screenwriting circles – then oral comment in the screenplay is likely to be minimal compared to the stage play. In *House of Games*, such comment does not take the form of extended reflection; instead, one character may offer a cutting epithet to define another, as when Mike dismisses Margaret simply as 'an *addict*' (61).

But if a character is absent or even dead, as for example in *Last Orders* (Fred Schepisi, 2001), the verbal commentary of others becomes much more significant. This technique is remarkably extensive in *The Third Man* due to Harry's delayed appearance and the conflicting accounts of what has happened to him. Until his emergence from the shadows, he has existed not as an autonomous individual but as a series of verbal or textual stories or ideas created by others. Anna idealizes him as the romantic lover who could not have betrayed her, Holly is convinced of the essential decency of his childhood friend (his changing loyalties an index of the developing drama) and the textual fabric constructed by his underworld associates Kurtz and Tyler (Popescu in the film) slowly unravels under critical interrogation. Even Calloway's revelation of the extent of Harry's criminal depravity, while 'true', is a narrative construct nonetheless. As Holly remarks after hearing it, 'He never existed, we dreamed him' (83). Yet this dream-figure who appears so briefly has a striking tangibility and roundedness, partly because of the rather literary and theatrical method whereby conflicting conceptions of Harry are articulated by different characters.

More subtly, however, two contradictory qualities of his nature are expressed by two different methods that do not require explicit verbalization. The doubling with Holly lends Harry associations of light-heartedness and an essentially American optimism; conversely, a submerged connection to Conrad's *Heart of Darkness*, which is present from the outset, thickens the characters of both Holly and Harry and helps to weave around the unseen Harry the intimations of horror that will be fully redeemed at the children's hospital, where Calloway confronts Holly with the irrefutable consequences of Harry's diabolical trade in diluted penicillin. If Holly's first name is similar to Harry's, his surname, Martins, recalls that of Marlow, Conrad's embedded narrator who is similarly in search of a mysteriously disappeared figure, reports of whom occupy much of the first half of the text, and whose persona becomes no less enigmatic with his tangible yet fleeting appearance towards the end. In *Heart of Darkness* the character Marlow pursues is Kurtz; in *The Third Man* another Kurtz, the phoney 'Baron', contacts Holly to begin the long process of deceiving him. In both texts, Kurtz is associated with a lie about the last words of a dying man: Conrad's Marlow cannot bring himself to tell Kurtz's fiancée the horrifying truth about Kurtz's last words, and tells her instead that he spoke her name; in *The Third Man* Kurtz similarly embroiders the fiction about Lime's death by telling Holly that 'Even at the end his thoughts were of you . . . he was anxious I should look after you' (35–6). The echo is unmistakable. Perhaps because screenplays are rarely considered as literature, perhaps because they are often adaptations of a single privileged precursor text, it is easy to forget that they can participate in intertextual worlds just as readily as novels. In *The Third Man*, the effect is the same as that produced by similar references in more 'literary' texts: the reader who spots the connection, even unconsciously, begins to extend the understanding of character beyond the limits of 'the words on the page'.

The Third Man also exploits various more direct modes of comment that Mamet eschews. Among the most conspicuous and unusual of these is that Greene's screenplay is prefaced by short descriptions of each of the main characters:

```
Harry Lime has always found it possible to use his
devoted friend [Holly]. A light, amusing, ruthless
character, he has always been able to find superficial
excuses for his own behaviour. With wit and courage and
immense geniality, he has inspired devotion both in
Rollo Martins and the girl Anna, but he has never felt
affection for anybody but himself. (7)
```

Although this is a thumbnail sketch, it hints at a backstory of sorts, and certainly predisposes the reader to conceive of Harry in certain ways. It might be objected that this kind of paratextual or supplementary material is not part of the screenplay proper, and that these qualities in Harry should be inferred from the screenplay itself: if they can be, the paratextual materials are redundant; if they cannot, there is a fault in the text. Alternatively, however, this kind of material may act as an interpretive guide for producers or actors: it does not necessarily retain for the writer a privileged interpretation of the character, but instead offers a concession to the collaborative nature of film. In any case, as we saw in *House of Games*, even the most purist approach to screenwriting finds it difficult to eliminate directions about character altogether.

That Harry's character is defined by storytelling is confirmed when he finally speaks: he is less an active agent within the story world than a commentator upon it. Aside from the game of cat-and-mouse in the shadows and the climactic sequence in the Viennese sewers, the only scene in which he makes a substantial appearance is one that does not advance the plot at all, and if anything represents a hiatus in the action. Like the giant Ferris wheel that is its location, it describes a circle, beginning and ending with Holly's conviction of the depravity of Harry, whose own character similarly undergoes no change within the scene. Instead, what make the moment unforgettable are Harry's two speeches about the reduction of human life to dots seen from afar, and about peace and democracy in Switzerland producing nothing more significant than the cuckoo clock. As noted earlier, the routine affirmation in manuals that character is defined by a series of actions and decisions amounts to an ideological belief in the autonomy and freedom of the individual. Such notions certainly inform many contemporary Hollywood genres, among them Holly's beloved westerns. Yet this is quite at odds with the world-view of *The Third Man*, which instead dramatizes the helplessness of individuals in the face of post-war *realpolitik*. One of the reasons why Harry is so memorable, so much more than a cameo, is that he recognizes this and in the Ferris wheel scene expresses it with aphoristic clarity: 'In these days, old man, nobody thinks in terms of human beings. Governments don't, so why should we?' (98).

On the one hand, this speech represents conclusive proof of Harry's psychopathic unconcern for the human individual; on the other, much like the contemporaneous writing of George Orwell, Greene articulates a fear that Harry's understanding of power may be right. One of the ways in which *The Third Man* dramatizes this is by questioning whether the human individual any longer possesses the agency and potential that conventional notions of 'character' ascribe to it. So Holly is an essentially passive victim of Harry's plot; Anna delusionally refuses to act in accordance with what she now knows about Harry, and instead is condemned to life behind the Iron Curtain; Harry dies unheroically in the sewers of Vienna.

House of Games and *The Third Man* both demonstrate that the presentation of character in the screenplay text must be carefully distinguished from that in the dominant paradigm of the realist novel. At the same time, however, these screenplays indicate that diametrically opposed approaches to screenplay character are not just possible but inevitable, not least because of the demands of differing modes of film production. *House of Games* presents character as contained within a closed system, as an effect of structure; *The Third Man* is an open text, acknowledging some of the many ways in which character can appear to exceed this structure to produce something akin to, but distinct from, the reality effect of the novel. In each case, the interplay of character and structure remains a persistent dynamic. That two such radically different approaches have each produced a text that challenges the most familiar notions of screenplay character as autonomous, active and defined by choice is further evidence that the time for a properly critical examination of screenplay texts is long overdue.

Notes

1   Hunter 1994: 71; italics in the original. Hunter has previously discussed ideas for, and outline plotting of, the story. As with Michael Hauge's arguments, the implication is that at least some aspects of character are separable from, or can exist independently of, the story.

2 Mamet 1997: 9; italics in the original. Although expressed in the course of an argument against Stanislavskian notions of inner-directed acting in the theatre, this remark, and the following sentence ('There are only lines upon a page') are wholly consistent with Mamet's views on writing for both theatre and film.

3 The text of *The Third Man* used in this discussion (Greene 1988) was originally published by Lorrimer in 1973. For detailed discussion of the development of the screenplay, see White 2003, and, in particular, Drazin 1999.

4 Not surprisingly, this paradigm has proved influential both in Hollywood and in manuals, most prominently in Vogler 1998 and also in Voytilla 1999.

5 Mamet 1988: 5. Subsequent page references are to this edn. To avoid confusion, I have not retained the italicization of the scene (non-dialogue) text that is used in the printed editions of both *House of Games* and *The Third Man*.

6 For a more detailed discussion of these aspects of the film, and the critical response to them, see Price 2009.

References

Campbell, Joseph (1949) *The Hero with a Thousand Faces*, Princeton, NJ: Princeton University Press.

Canby, Vincent (1987) 'Mamet Makes a Debut with *House of Games*', *New York Times* (11 Oct., sec. 1): 94.

Carroll, Noël (1992) 'The Specificity Thesis', in Gerald Mast, Marshall Cohen and Leo Braudy (eds), *Film Theory and Criticism*, 4th edn, Oxford: OUPress, 278–85.

Drazin, Charles (1999) *In Search of The Third Man*, London: Methuen.

Dyer, Richard (1998) *Stars*, rev. edn, London: BFI.

Greene, Graham (1988) *The Third Man*, London: Faber.

Hauge, Michael (1989) *Writing Screenplays that Sell*, London: Elm Tree.

Hinson, Hal (1987) 'House of Games', *Washington Post* (19 Dec.).

Hunter, Lew (1994) *Screenwriting*, London: Robert Hale.

Kane, Leslie (ed.) (2001) *David Mamet in Conversation*, Ann Arbor, MI: University of Michigan Press.

Knights, L. C. (1933) *How Many Children Had Lady Macbeth? An Essay in the Theory and Practice of Shakespeare Criticism*, Cambridge: Gordon Fraser.

Lahr, John (1997) 'Fortress Mamet', *New Yorker* (17 Nov.): 70–82.

Lucey, Paul (1996) *Story Sense: Writing Story and Script for Feature Films and Television*, New York: McGraw-Hill.

Mamet, David (1988) *House of Games*, London: Methuen.

— (1994) *A Whore's Profession*, London: Faber.

— (1997) *True and False: Heresy and Common Sense for the Actor*, New York: Random House.

Maras, Steven (2009) *Screenwriting: History, Theory and Practice*, London: Wallflower.

Peter, John (1987) *Vladimir's Carrot*, London: Deutsch.

Price, Steven (2009) 'Televisuality in the Films of David Mamet', in Johan Callens (ed.), *Crossings: David Mamet's Work in Different Genres and Media*, Newcastle: Cambridge Scholars, 33–48.

— (2010) *The Screenplay: Authorship, Theory and Criticism*, Basingstoke: Palgrave.

Propp, Vladimir (1984) *Morphology of the Folktale*, Austin, TX: University of Texas Press.

Sternberg, Claudia (1997) *Written for the Screen: The American Motion-Picture Screenplay as Text*, Tübingen: Stauffenburg.

Thomson, David (1997) *Rosebud: The Story of Orson Welles*, London: Abacus.

Towne, Robert (1998) *Chinatown and The Last Detail*, London: Faber.

Vogler, Christopher (1998) *The Writer's Journey: Mythic Structure for Storytellers and Screenwriters*, 2nd edn, London: Pan.

Voytilla, Stuart (1999) *Myth and the Movies: Discovering the Mythic Structure of 50 Unforgettable Films*, Studio City, CA: Michael Wiese Productions.

White, Rob (2003) *The Third Man*, London: BFI.

Wimsatt, W. K., and Beardsley, Monroe C. (1946) 'The Intentional Fallacy', *Sewanee Review* 54: 468–88.

Chapter 13

Realism and screenplay dialogue

Jill Nelmes

Introduction

Screenplay dialogue contributes towards creating the illusion of a real and believable film world and, by giving voices to characters, makes them appear three-dimensional and complex. Dialogue in the narrative film is subject to the codes of realism which have evolved since the early days of cinema and is, therefore, carefully constructed to appear natural. The words spoken are directed at the audience, who view the unfolding drama through the eyes of the characters and are encouraged to identify with them as they talk.

Dialogue has two primary functions in the screenplay; first, to make the storyworld more believable, to create a world in which characters talk, have voices, say what they think and feel, building the illusion of a real world inhabited by real people; and second, to provide narrative information as the film characters express themselves in their fictional world.

This chapter will discuss the role of realism and dialogue in the feature film screenplay by referring to the dialogue in four screenplays: *Billy Elliot* (2000), *The English Patient* (1995), *The Ice Storm* (1997) and *Sideways* (2003). Although these screenplays are very different in subject matter they all use dialogue to draw the audience into the storyworld and to develop character.

Realism and dialogue

Film aspires to verisimilitude by making the audience feel they are part of the action and encouraging identification with the characters in the film. Screenplay dialogue heightens the appearance of realism by making the language used seem appropriate for the setting while at the same time developing the film story. As Sarah Kozloff observes, 'Most American films work hard to encourage the suspension of disbelief; they sustain the illusion that the viewer is observing the action as a fly on the wall' (2000: 47). The sense of realism then is a construct and, guided by conventions the audience have learned to understand, accept the film world as being lifelike in some way. Dialogue is a very important means of encouraging the sense that we are entering a living, transparent world. Ted

Berliner suggests realism can be seen not as 'the authentic representation of reality but rather a type of art that masks its own contrivance' (1999: 5). It is the play between realism and contrivance that I will explore in this chapter.

Real talking

The illusion that we are watching real people in a film is enhanced by the use of what appears to be everyday conversational language. The dialogue works alongside the visual image, often enhancing meaning, undercutting or providing new information while helping us to build up a picture of the characters; their accent tells us where they are from and the tone and tempo of the dialogue discloses mood and what the characters are feeling. The syntax and grammar, the actual words spoken and whether they are contrived or naturalistic, also build detail about the world of the film and differentiate between the characters who inhabit that world.

Because screenplay dialogue is constructed to give the impression of how people talk in real life it often appears to be inarticulate and lacking in complexity, especially in comparison with theatre dialogue which is generally more focused, more 'talky' and more obviously dramatic. Wolf Rilla explains:

> Both the theatre and the novel base their use of speech on articulacy: and again this is where film dialogue differs, for at its most effective it is based on inarticulacy. When two lovers part in a play, they give the fullest expression to their emotion by verbalizing it. In a film what they say to each other is likely to be as banal and inadequate as it would be in real life.
>
> (1973: 89)

Although film 'talk' may appear natural or inarticulate or even banal it is often highly sophisticated in its construction. Film dialogue is a construct in which certain aspects of 'real life' dialogue are drawn upon to aid our acceptance of the screen world. In life dialogue is rather less organized and focused, as Ted Berliner points out: 'A real-life conversation will illustrate not only how unlike real speech movie dialogue really is but also how odd real dialogue would sound in a movie' (1999: 4).[1]

Screenplay dialogue aims to convince the audience of its reality, to help 'fix' the film text as a living, breathing world. The most important of these devices is the style of language used; the appropriate colloquial language, the accent, tone, timbre, rhythm, pace and the sentence construction all help to convey the reality of the characters and at the same time also inform us about the content of the storyworld.

Colloquial dialogue is a particularly powerful device used to draw the audience into accepting the film world. In *Sideways*, for instance, on the first page of the screenplay all Miles says is 'the fuck', 'yeah', 'why' and 'yeah, hold on' (Payne and Taylor 2003: 1); Miles's dialogue could hardly be less articulate. Later in the screenplay we find out Miles actually has great clarity of expression but these minimal first few words give us an insight into his state of mind and, to some extent, his personality. Miles is at odds with life and being forced to take on the outside world from his womb-like apartment.

In *Billy Elliot* we hear the characters talk in the northeastern dialect of the Durham coalfields, which places them geographically and culturally. Phrases are used which we trust are from that region and even though we may not understand every word, we can guess its meaning from the context. For instance, when Billy is a dismal failure at boxing the teacher, George, lambasts him;

> GEORGE
> Ah, no not again. This is man to man
> combat, not a bloody tea dance.

George looks over to Dad who shakes his head.

> What are you doing, man? Hit him!

Billy sees one of the ballet girls and smiles.

> Greavesy, he's jut pissin' about. Now get
> stuck in and give him a belt. He's like a
> fanny in a fit.

(Hall 2000: 7)

The dialogue is humorous and enjoyable – 'fanny in a fit' – for instance is funny and derogatory and seems to fit Billy's background, and colloquialisms like 'man' and 'pissin' about' add to the realism of this world.

Accents also help to define the world of the characters – this is not only important in locating where they are from but also their upbringing – in the *English Patient* we are introduced to characters from a particular background and period. The way the characters talk not only identifies their background but also their emotional reserve, and in this extract there is the added dramatic irony that Katherine's husband, Clifton, has just missed catching Katherine and her lover, Almasy, together:

> CLIFTON
> Darling, I just heard. You poor sausage,
> are you all right?

> KATHERINE
> I'm fine. I got hot.

> CLIFTON
> Lady H thought you might be -

> KATHERINE
> I'm not pregnant. I'm hot. I'm too hot.

```
                              CLIFTON
         Right.

                              KATHERINE
         Aren't you?

                              CLIFTON
         Sweltering.
```
(Minghella 1995: 60)

Words such as 'poor sausage' and 'sweltering' suggest they belong to another era but when Clifton replies to Katherine she interrupts him, the dialogue overlapping as if talking in real life.

Real people

The way characters talk, tell us about their outlook on life, what they want, what they think and what they know about other characters, are all indicated through the dialogue. As Sarah Kozloff suggests, 'on the most mundane level, dialogue helps us distinguish one character from another' (2000: 43) and yet 'the more significant use of dialogue is to make the characters substantial, to hint at their inner life' (ibid.). It is the exposure of the characters' inner life that adds to the appearance of three-dimensionality and makes film characters seem interesting and believable.

In *Billy Elliot* the dialogue reflects the dysfunctional world the eponymous character lives in and expresses the tensions that exist between the main characters, who mostly speak in brief, punchy sentences with sparse conversations that are often argumentative in tone. This mood is enhanced by the rhythm and timing of the dialogue, especially where each line is short, usually less than 15 words. In the first few pages the dialogue sets up the conflict between the key characters; when Billy tries to play the piano he responds to his father telling him to 'Leave it Billy', by replying 'Mam would have let us' (Hall 2000: 5). From these few lines of dialogue we learn much about the emotional tone of the story; that Billy's father disapproves of him playing the piano, his mother did let him play, isn't there any more and, as a result, their home life has changed for the worse; all these factors build up the reality of Billy's world.

Film dialogue also allows the characters to express a range of complex feelings, revealing and clarifying their wants or desires. In *Billy Elliot* for instance, the ballet teacher, Mrs Wilkinson, has spotted Billy's talent and wants him to come back but, rather than say this directly, she asks him to bring the money for the lesson next week and then pretends indifference when Billy doesn't respond positively:

```
                    MRS WILKINSON
         You owe me 50p.

                         BILLY
         I don't.
```

                    MRS WILKINSON
You do. Why don't you bring it back next
week?

                    BILLY
I can't, Miss. I've got to go boxing.

                    DEBBIE
But you're crap at boxing.

                    BILLY
No I'm not.

                    MRS WILKINSON
Shut up. Thought you enjoyed it. Please
yourself darling.

(Hall 2000: 13)

The above dialogue does two important things: it confirms what the audience knows, Billy is not good at boxing and has a talent for ballet and that Mrs Wilkinson is aware of this. The dialogue also adds a slightly argumentative staccato-like tone to their talk and suggests the relationship will be riven with conflict.

Detail about a character is often revealed by another character talking about them. This device not only allows us to see that character from another point of view, but the audience also takes on the point of view of the person being informed, as if they were eavesdropping on a real-life conversation. The beginning of the *Ice Storm* uses dialogue to help the viewer identify with and understand more clearly one of the central characters, Paul, an 18-year-old student. When we meet Paul and his friend, Marge, we learn very little about her. She is not important to the story and we do not see her again, but she reveals crucial details about Paul, not only regarding his nature, but also about his previous behaviour, in effect his backstory. Marge acts as a cypher for his thoughts, intentions and also reveals his character traits. The scene begins with Paul's dramatic assertion that he's in love:

                    PAUL
I'm in love with Libbets Casey.

                    MARGE
Well you've been in love with like every
girl here, I was wondering when you'd get
around to Libbets.

                    PAUL
It's beyond mere attraction.

                    MARGE
That's good because I don't think Libbets
is capable of the sex act.

                              PAUL
          Truly? Do speak.

                              MARGE
          My diagnosis - messed in the
          head.

                                              (Schamus 1997: 7)

The dialogue not only appears to allow interaction between the characters, but their talk is carefully constructed to reveal a great deal of information about Paul. Marge's dialogue tells us that Paul's crush is the latest in a long line of crushes and that Libbets is probably not a good candidate for a girlfriend. The scene lets the audience feel they are part of the action because we know as little as Paul about Libbets; when Marge reveals that Libbets is a 'poor little rich girl', Paul is as surprised as we are. Marge tells him this in a revelatory style and we are placed in his position of ignorance, eavesdropping on details. Marge also acts as adviser, suggesting Paul doesn't tell his friend, Francis, about Libbets because 'he sleeps with every girl you ever show an interest in'. The whole scene works on giving the reader and the audience information about the important characters but also serves to foreshadow the events which are to unfold. Marge, by revealing that Francis is in competition with Paul for every girl he falls for, sets up the later scene when Paul goes to Libbets's apartment only to find Francis already there.

In this short scene the dialogue has provided us with much detail about the central character and his concerns, setting up later issues in the story without seeming to be like exposition, building up the sense that Paul is a three-dimensional and flawed character. The dialogue tells us Paul's love for Libbets is hopeless and that he makes unwise choices, not only regarding his love life but also what he tells his friends. It also helps us enter and believe in the story world, as problems and possibilities are revealed through the dialogue and our curiosity is aroused as to what the outcome will be.

In the *English Patient,* when Katherine and Almasy meet for the first time, their conversation is ostensibly about Almasy's lack of use of adjectives when writing but it is much more than that: the dialogue informs the audience about their differing natures. When Katherine says: 'I wanted to meet a man who could write such a long paper with so few adjectives' (Minghella 1995: 11) she is saying much about his character and that he is to the point, practical and economic in his use of language and ideas, but maybe lacks imagination. Almasy replies: 'A thing is a thing no matter what you place in front of it. Big car, slow car, chauffer driven car, still a car' (ibid.). Almasy appears to see the world in a reductive way. Then Katherine, rather abruptly, brings up the subject of love, 'Love? Romantic love, platonic love, filial love – ? Quite different things surely?' (ibid.). As well as making a point she is foreshadowing the turmoil to come and the very different types of love which are indeed the subject of the film. In this scene we find out that Katherine had wanted to meet Almasy and is an astute judge of character but we learn rather more about Almasy through Katherine; he is revealed by the dialogue to be a character of few words – and has a nature not easily swayed by love.

Dialogue and the believable film world

Dialogue draws the viewer further into the film narrative by developing our knowledge of the world portrayed, allowing us to become more active participants and to understand the rules of a world we may well know nothing about. In *Billy Elliot* the dialogue helps us to enter the 1980s mining community and to contrast this with the feminine world of ballet. In *The English Patient* we are informed about the desert, archaeology, Herodotus's histories and the Second World War. In the *Ice Storm* we learn through the dialogue about growing up in a middle-class New York suburb in the 1970s, key parties and the Watergate scandal. In *Sideways* we enter the world of wine tasting through Miles, a snobbish wine connoisseur, who wants to pass his knowledge onto his friend Jack. The latter acts as the non-informed viewer by receiving information and asking questions:

> MILES
> 100% Pinot Noir. Single vineyard. They
> don't even make it anymore.
>
> JACK
> Pinot Noir? How come it's white? Doesn't
> noir mean dark?
>
> MILES
> Jesus. Don't ask questions like that up in
> the wine country. They'll think you're a
> moron.
>
> JACK
> Just tell me.
>
> MILES
> Color in the red wines comes from the
> skins. This juice is free run, so there's
> no skin contact in the fermentation, ergo
> no color.
>
> JACK
> (not really listening)
> Sure is tasty.

(Payne and Taylor 2005: 10)

The dialogue creates a detailed, specialist world and allows Miles to tell Jack about the grape, but the audience is also placed in the learning seat, and this makes the journey more interesting, especially as Jack is such an entertaining and witty character. At the same time, as they talk, we are also finding out about these two characters – Miles is serious and insecure, uses words like 'ergo', while Jack is a sensualist and more interested in the taste of the wine than learning about its finer points.

In *The English Patient* we are told about classical Greek literature by Almasy's possession of Herodotus' histories. When Katherine asks for his copy so she can read out the story of Candaules and Gyges this not only tells the audience about the extract from the book but also provides a direct link between the two characters. We know something important is happening between Katherine and Almasy and they have been connected in some way, first by the book and then by the content of the story, a triangle in which the servant kills the husband and takes over the throne and his wife:

```
Almasy stares at her, framed by the velvet black sky.
Katherine turns to look at him.

                    KATHERINE
          But then the Queen looked up and saw Gyges
          concealed in the shadows. And though she
          said nothing she shuddered. The next day
          she sent for Gyges and challenged him. And
          hearing his story she said this –

                    CLIFTON
          Off with his head!
```
                                                      (Minghella 1995: 17)

Clifton, Katherine's husband, interrupts the story in a moment of bathos but his words also signpost that he is the king referred to in the story and Almasy is the servant; the tale acts as a foreshadowing of what is to come.

The harsh masculine world of the miners and the gentler world of dance is contrasted in *Billy Elliot* by the dialogue which moves Billy from voyeur to participant as the audience follows his journey through Mrs Wilkinson's words:

```
 Billy watches the class with fascination. One girl,
 DEBBIE, turns and stares at him.

                    DEBBIE
          Why don't you join in?

                    MRS WILKINSON
          Port de bras and up.

                    BILLLY
          Nah.

He glances at Debbie and the girls as they continue to
dance.
```

                        MRS WILKINSON
          Port de bras, forward and up. And hold.

INT. BOXING HALL - LATER

The girls continue to do their exercises at the barre.

                        MRS WILKINSON
          And three, and four, and … Debbie,
          straight leg. Seven, and eight. And one,
          and two, and three …

We see Billy's legs, still wearing boxing boots, dancing.

                        MRS WILKINSON
          … and four, and five, boots off!

Mrs Wilkinson stands on Billy's foot.
          Seven and eight.

To Billy.
          What size are you?

                                              (Hall 2000: 11)

The scene concludes with Billy wearing ballet shoes. The dialogue, with great
economy, builds detail so the audience learn some of the terms used in the ballet
but is also told that Billy is moving step by step into a new world. In one page of
dialogue Billy's life, and the narrative, has changed direction and he has put on a
new mantle – the ballet shoes – while the viewer follows Billy's progress, entering
that world at the same time as he does.

Realism, dialogue and narrative unity

Dialogue helps to unify and develop the screenplay narrative in a natural and
seamless way and is especially important in its ability to integrate the aural with
the visuals, suturing the story so that the audience is drawn into the film world,
rather than acting as observers. A powerful scene in *The English Patient* exemplifies
this point; the dialogue between Hana, one of the central characters, and her
friend, Jan, seems light-hearted and innocuous as they chat to each other about
getting lace to make clothes. The set up of the dialogue tells us much about the
two women's relationship: they're close and there is a relative shortage of clothes
and money; more importantly though, the dialogue serves to lull us into a false
sense of security so that when Jan's Jeep is blown up, and she is killed, the effect is
even more shocking:

A JEEP pulls out of line and approaches the Red Cross
truck containing Hana and the Patient. The horn blows

and Hana looks out to see it contains her best friend
JAN, who sits in the back with a second nurse, BARBARA,
while two young soldiers sit up front, one driving, both
grinning. Jan signals for Hana's attention;

>   JAN
>   There's meant to be lace in the next
>   village - the boys are taking us.

>   HANA
>   I'm not sewing anything else.

>   JAN
>   (mischievously)
>   You don't have any money, do you? Just in
>   case there's silk.

>   HANA
>   No.

>   JAN
>   Hana. I know you do.

Hana leans under the tarpaulin, holding some dollars.
The two hands - hers and Jan's - reach for each other as
the vehicles bump along side by side. They laugh at the
effort. Jan's GOLD BRACELET catches the sun and glints.

>   HANA
>   I'm not sewing anything else for you.

>   JAN
>   (getting the money) I love you.

The jeep accelerates away. Hana sighs to the patient.

Suddenly AN EXPLOSION shatters the calm as the jeep runs
over a MINE. The jeep is THROWN into the air. … Hana runs
the other way, towards the accident.

(Minghella 1995: 3)

The dialogue very economically allows us to find out much about the two
characters and their relationship. In hindsight the final words 'I love you' add
great poignancy, the words spoken embed the visuals and the lightness of the
conversation contrasts with the horrific scene that follows.

Dialogue is often used to unite the narrative by linking scenes and moving the
story forward, keeping the audience engaged while encouraging the semblance
of realism. A character talking may help to elide the transitions from one scene
to the next or link a number of scenes, as in the following example from *Billy*

Elliot. While Billy is learning to dance we follow his progress, moving to different locations which are united by Mrs Wilkinson stirring Billy to do better. The 30 scenes in the sequence are linked as Mrs Wilkinson cajoles, bullies and persuades Billy, guiding him through the ballet moves:

```
INT. BOXING HALL

Mrs Wilkinson stands behind Billy and points out in front
of him.

                    MRS WILKINSON
        … and focus on that spot.

Billy stares in front of him.
            Then whip your head round and come back to
            that spot, prepare.

INT. BATHROOM

We see Billy's reflection in the mirror.

                    MRS WILKINSON
        (off screen) One, and two, and …

Billy breathes deeply and raises his arms.

                    MRS WILKINSON
        (voice over) One, and two, and …

Billy lowers his arms, moves to turn.
                    BILLY
        Fuck it.

INT. BOXING HALL

                    MRS WILKINSON
        (off screen)
        Have you got the spot?

INT. BATHROOM -THE SAME

Billy looks at his reflection, as he prepares.
                    MRS WILKINSON
        (voice over)
        Prepare.

Billy takes up his position.
```

```
INT. ELLIOT HOUSE. BEDROOM - EVENING

Billy stands by the bed and takes up his position.

                    MRS WILKINSON
        Prepare.


INT. BILLY'S ROOM - NIGHT

Billy is lying on his bed.

                    BILLY
        (softly)
        Prepare.
```

(Hall 2000: 25–7)

Each scene shows Billy's progress and his determination to succeed, so much so that he repeats Mrs Wilkinson's instructions in bed. The sequence is made more dynamic and involving for the audience because the imperative is used, the words shortening towards the end of the sequence, adding pace and rhythm until the final series of 'go's build up to the climax. The dialogue seamlessly takes the reader from location to location, giving a framework to the scenes, mostly through Mrs Wilkinson's dialogue providing detail on Billy's progress, first as a novice dancer to finally accomplishing a difficult pirouette.

In the *English Patient* dialogue helps to make the transitions back and forth in time less jarring and more organic to the story, segueing the scenes without pulling the audience out of the story. For instance in one scene Hana's dialogue eases the move back in time to a Christmas party with Katherine and Almasy:

```
                    HANA
        Tell me about this, this is in your
        handwriting - December 22nd - Betrayals
        in war are childlike compared with our
        betrayals during peace. New lovers are
        nervous and tender, but smash everything -
        for the heart is an organ of fire …
        (she looks up)
        I love that, I believe that.
        (to Almasy)
        Who is K?
```

(Minghella 1995: 58)

We know from the link to expect the next scene to reveal more about K – who the reader realizes must be Katherine. But we are also linked in again to the theme of the film, love and betrayal.

Lies, subtext and revelation

In life we frequently do not say what we mean, we do not talk about our feelings openly but tend to mask and disguise them. So it is not surprising that characters in a screenplay frequently do not say what they mean, especially when under emotional pressure. If the holding back of information is a contrivance, it is a believable one. In real life, Karl Iglesias points out, 'Speaking indirectly is the way most of us talk when the emotional; stakes are high, When we deal with intense emotions, like anger, hate, love, or desire we're often afraid to expose ourselves emotionally. So we usually hide our true feelings and motivations' (2007: 44). Characters not saying what they mean and having different underlying motives to the apparent and obvious one is termed subtext; often the audience are aware of the deception and this helps to suggest complex characters with believable motives. For instance in *The English Patient* when Clifton, Katherine's husband, is going away, leaving Almasy and Katherine together, Almasy asks Clifton to take her with him, suggesting the desert isn't good for her. But this scene has a powerful subtext as it follows on from one in which a few pages earlier the Arab has warned Almasy and Katherine to be careful of 'The one who appears not to be moving' (Minghella 1995: 38). The audience already know of the attraction between Almasy and Katherine and we know he is afraid of what might happen if she is left alone with him and without Clifton;

> ALMASY
> Clifton - your wife - do you think it's appropriate to leave her?
>
> CLIFTON
> Appropriate?
>
> ALMASY
> I think the desert is, it's - for a woman - It's very tough. I wonder if it's not too much for her.

(Minghella 1995: 39)

Almasy is not worried because of the reasons he outlines above, rather he's worried because Katherine's not safe with him and he's not safe with her. Ironically, Clifton completely misunderstands Almasy's words of caution, assuming he is threatened by having a female presence in the camp.

In *Sideways* the dialogue in two different scenes shows Miles contradicting himself and indicates his personal confusion; when Miles tells Jack he's waiting to hear if his novel is to be accepted by the publisher he declares wearily 'it's always been a fucking waiting game, I've been through it too many times already' (Payne and Taylor 2003: 7) but he feigns acceptance of this position. Later dialogue sets up that Miles is actually very keen to hear from his publisher even though in this scene he contradicts himself, telling Jack 'I've stopped caring' (ibid., 8) but we, the audience, know he really does care and when his book is finally rejected by his publisher he reacts dramatically. Miles's half-truths make him believable and sympathetic at the same time.

Layering dialogue is often used to mask the real theme or meaning in a scene, and while this is partly to do with a concern that the story world should appear natural this device can make film a very subtle medium. If we were told too clearly about Miles's ambition the lines could seem laboured and boring but an extra layer of humour is added in *Sideways* to avoid this. The scene in which Miles is asked to try samples of the wedding cake is not really about whether he likes the white or dark cake, although this is what the dialogue that concludes the scene suggests. Even though the scene finishes with Miles commenting on his preference what is more important is that the scene reveals information about Miles's character. The cake dialogue is banal and the book dialogue is important, the cake dialogue detracts from the exposition and we are diverted by the entertaining debate about which is the best cake:

> Jack and the Erganians surround Miles as he eats from a
> plate with two pieces of CAKE - one white, one dark.
>
>   MRS ERGANIAN
>   Jack tells us you are publishing a book.
>   Congratulations.
>
>   MR ERGANIAN
>   Yes, congratulations.
>
> Miles shoots Jack a look. Mr Erganian gets some ice cubes
> from the refrigerator door.
>
>   MILES
>   Yeah, well, it's not exactly finalized,
>   yet, but, um, there has been some interest
>   and -
>
>   MRS ERGANIAN
>   Your friend is modest.
>
>   JACK
>   Yesh, Miles, don't be so modest. Indulge
>   them. Don't make me out to be a liar.

Of course Jack is an inveterate liar and he is pressurizing Miles into lying himself. The scene continues with a short discussion about whether Miles's book is fiction or non-fiction which also serves to undercut, somewhat ironically, his authority as a writer;

>   MR ERGANIAN
>   What subject is your book? Non-fiction?

                    MILES
No, it's a novel. Fiction. Although
there's a lot from my life, so I guess
technically some of it is non-fiction.

                    MR ERGANIAN
Good, I like non-fiction. There is so much
to know about the world that I think
reading a story someone just invented is
kind of a waste of time.

The scene then concludes with Christine asking:

                    CHRISTINE
So which one do you like better?

                    MILES
I like them both, but if pressed I'd have
to say I prefer the dark.

(Payne and Taylor 2005: 5–6)

The seemingly innocuous dialogue rounds off the scene by suggesting that Miles is a prevaricator and a diplomatic and not quite truthful himself and, therefore, a much more vivid and believable character. But also there is the sense that he has been forced by Christine to make a choice – to take a path and he has chosen the dark side.

Film characters often withhold information and this is an important way of controlling the flow of the narrative: holding back or gradually revealing information draws the audience into solving the puzzle, hooking us into wanting to know more. In *The English Patient* we are told the story in flashback as the Patient, step by step, reveals to us the dramatic events which led to his near-death, events which it appears he is trying to forget but are brought back by Hana reading his Herodotus out loud:

                    HANA
I will hide you in my room where we sleep.
When my wife comes to lie down she always
lays her garments one by one on a seat
near the entrance of the room, and from
where you stand you will be able to gaze
on her at your leisure …

EXT. BASECAMP AT POTTERY HILL

                    KATHERINE
And that evening, it's exactly as the King

had told him, she goes to the chair and
removes her clothes …

(Minghella 1995: 17)

The present and the past are linked as Katherine continues reading from the Herodotus; the same story segued together as more detail from the Patient's life and his affair with Katherine is revealed to us through flashbacks.

Dialogue as poetry

Paradoxically, although screenplay dialogue aspires to seem real, the language used is often sparse, minimal and economic in its construction and has much in common with poetry, not only because of the stanza-like layout and the reliance on rhythm and pacing. The use of lyrical dialogue engages the audience, eliding the contrivance of realism by being entertaining and enjoyable to hear. Fawell suggests film dialogue:

> is probably most like poetry, in the sparseness of its language, its need for each line to be polished cleanly, its need for hard simple language. … Like lines of poetry, film lines have to be packed with ambiguity and resonance because there are so few of them.

(1989: 44)

In *Billy Elliot* the dialogue may not appear to have a great deal in common with poetry but the speech is expressive and the cadence and rhythm of the language poetic. For example, George the boxing teacher finishes his volley of insults aimed at Billy with dialogue that has such a powerful rhythm it sounds like a poetic refrain:

GEORGE
Jesus Christ, Billy Elliot, you're a
disgrace to them gloves, your father and
the traditions of this boxing hall. You
owe us fifty pence.

(Hall 2000: 7)

At times film dialogue is more directly poetic. In *The English Patient* the drugged state of the Patient allows the audience to accept the evocative description of his heightened senses which would be much too florid for a normal conversation:

… Ask me about the scent of acacia – it's
in this room. I can smell it. The taste
of tea so black it falls into your mouth.
I can taste it. I'm chewing the mint. Is

```
there sand in my eyes? Are you cleaning
sand from my ears?
```
(Minghella 1995: 20)

Fawell discusses the link between dialogue and the musicality of the filmscript, pointing out that the rhythm of the language and repetition of phrases often makes for memorable dialogue, despite the fact that 'The best film lines are often those that taken out of the context of film would seem bland and anonymous' (1989: 44), such as the repeated refrain in *Something Wild* 'You're a really good liar, Charlie', which takes on a slightly different significance each time it is used in the film, emphasizing the characters' changes through the narrative. In film, dialogue which appears insignificant becomes loaded with meaning – as in the earlier example of Katherine saying how hot she is when we know she has just made love to Almasy.

In a similar way 'echoing' helps make a story resonate by linking an idea or an important part of the story into a pattern or a motif. This is often visual but can work through dialogue, as in the *English Patient*, where echoes set up around our knowledge about the Patient are eventually used to confirm his identify to Caravaggio, who has been searching for him. There are three echoes around the Patient's singing, the first in the desert when Katherine tells him, 'You sing. All the time' (Minghella 1995: 40), the second, when Hana tells the Patient, 'Did you know that? You're always singing' (p. 69) and the third time when Caravaggio tells the Patient how he found him, 'You were burned and you didn't know your name but you knew the words to every song there was …' (p. 103). These echoes not only link the threads of the narrative they also connect the Patient to music and make his character appear more rounded.

Metaphor and allegory

Dialogue, akin to poetry, may work on a metaphoric level and in a different way to the film image which is metonymic, appearing to be a literal translation of reality. Spoken language often uses metaphor and simile for comparison, adding greater texture to the film world. In *Billy Elliot* colloquial metaphors are used when George the boxing teacher chastizes Billy, 'this is man to man combat, not a bloody tea dance' (Hall 2000: 7) and Mr Braithwaite tells Billy 'you look like a right wanker to me, son' (p. 29). Metaphor is often used more subtly though, especially at a key point in a film when the dialogue may allude to one of the themes of the film, sometimes in a poetic and profound way. For instance in *Sideways* Miles explains to Maya, the first woman he's dated since his divorce, why he loves the Pinot grape so much:

```
Miles laughs at first, then smiles wistfully at the
question. He searches for the answer in his glass and
begins slowly.
```

<pre>
                          MILES
          I don't know. It's a hard grape to
          grow. As you know. It's thin-skinned,
          temperamental, ripens early. It's not
          a survivor like Cabernet that can grow
          anywhere and thrive even when neglected.
          Pinot needs constant care and attention
          and in fact can only grow in little
          tucked-away corners of the world.
          And only the most patient and nurturing
          growers can do it really, can tap into
          Pinot's most fragile, delicate qualities.
          Only when someone has taken the time to
          truly understand its potential can Pinot
          be coaxed into its fullest expression.
</pre>
(Payne and Taylor 2005: 71–2)

Miles's speech is unusually long and indisputably poetic, his detailed description of the grape as being temperamental and needing care we realize is a metaphor for Miles himself. The scene is also important in revealing his vulnerability to Maya and the dialogue draws in the audience who hope Miles will be brave enough to open up to love.

Stories within stories are often used in screenplays to parallel the main narrative or to create an analogy and describe a situation that the characters are in or could be placed in. Dialogue is important in developing complex ideas which it would be difficult to develop on a purely visual level. Although dialogue may help in fixing the sense of a scene it can also add levels of meaning which the audience has to work at to interpret and understand. In *The English Patient*, an apparently harmless description of hunting an ostrich becomes loaded with innuendo by using language that is sensual in its comparison of a mountain to 'a woman's back' (Minghella 1995: 36). The scene gradually shifts its tone, finally becoming a warning. We now think Almasy has gone from predator in this story to the one who is being told to be careful and an element of danger is brought to the scene, as Almasy translates the storyteller's words to Katherine:

<pre>
     The Arab has more to say. Almasy doesn't respond,
     quietening him with a dismissive gesture.

                          KATHERINE
          What is he saying?

     (Almasy, awkward, shakes his head)
          Come on, what did he say?

                          ALMASY
          He said – be careful.
</pre>

```
                    KATHERINE
      Be careful? You mean you - or me? Who?

                    ALMASY
      (to the Arab)
      Her or me?
```

The Arab speaks again. Almasy speaks without looking at her.

```
                    ALMASY
      The one who appears not to be moving.
```

The scene finishes on an ambiguous note of warning in which the audience are drawn into the idea of the characters being dangerous to each other and a foreshadowing of the tragic events to come.

In *Billy Elliot*, Mrs Wilkinson and Billy listen to Tchaikovsky's *Swan Lake* while crossing the river on a ferry. She tells Billy the story of the swan who falls in love with the prince and while this may not be a direct metaphor of either Billy or Mrs Wilkinson's life it has almost as much resonance. In the previous scene Billy lost his temper, shouting 'Don't pick on me just cos you've fucked up your life.' The mood of the scene is one of loss and regret but also serves to foreshadow Billy dancing in *Swan Lake* at the end of the film:

```
                    BILLY
      So she has to be a swan for good.

                    MRS WILKINSON
      She dies.

                    BILLY
      Cos the prince didn't love her?

                    MRS WILKINSON
      Come on, it's time to go. It's only a
      ghost story.
```

(Hall 2000: 56)

It may only be a ghost story but it is a tragic one and the dialogue ripples through the narrative while the music played in the background adds poignancy to the scene.

Conclusion

Screenplay dialogue in narrative cinema creates the illusion of real people talking in a real world but it also reveals story detail, allowing the characters to give information about themselves and others while at the same time developing the narrative. Characters sometimes say what they mean whilst at other times, either directly or using subtext, misinform and suggest other agendas. Film dialogue is a complex mix of the everyday and the poetic; it creates the illusion of being natural by using colloquial words yet its actual language construction is anything but; each word is carefully chosen, more artifice than natural, a contrivance which aspires to seem real but is not. Dialogue is a central part of the film, drawing the audience further into the storyworld, allowing us to identify with the characters while making the world they inhabit appear as seamless as possible.

Note

1 Berliner's article on Cassavates makes a number of very interesting points about dialogue in the Hollwyood film in contrast to the naturalistic style of dialogue in Cassavates films.

References

Bordwell, D. (2006) *The Way Hollywood Tells it: Story and Style in Modern Movies*, Berkeley, CA: University of California Press.

Berliner, T. (1999) 'Hollywood Movie Dialogue and the "Real Realism" of John Cassavates', *Film Quarterly* 52(3) (April): 2–16.

Fawell, J. (1989) 'The Musicality of the Film Script', *Literature/Film Quarterly* 17: 44–9.

Hall, L. (2000) *Billy Elliot*, London: Faber & Faber

Horne, William (1992) 'Reflections on the Ontology of the Screenplay', *Literature/Film Quarterly* 20: 48–54.

Howard, D. and Mabley, E. (1993) *The Tools of Screenwriting*, New York: St Martin's Press.

Iglesias, K. (2007) 'Subtext in Dialogue', *Creative Screenwriting* 14(3) (May): 44–5.

Kozloff, S. (2000) *Overhearing Film Dialogue*, Berkeley: University of California Press.

Maras, S. (2009) *Screenwriting: History, Theory, Practice*, London: Wallflower Press.

Minghella, A. (1995) *The English Patient*, draft dated 6 June.

Payne, A. and Taylor, J. (2003) *Sideways*, draft dated 29 May.

Rilla, W. (1973) *The Writer and the Screen*, London: W. H. Allen.

Schamus, J. (1997) *The Ice Storm*, New York: Newmarket Press.

Thompson, K. (1999) *Storytelling in the New Hollywood: Understanding Classical Narrative Technique*, Cambridge, MA: Harvard University Press.

Chapter 14

Analysing the screenplay

A comparative approach

Mark O'Thomas

Screenplays are functional objects – they exist to provide a blueprint for filmmakers to construct their films. In this sense, they are not simply screenplays or plays for the screen in the same way as their theatrical counterpart: the play. Plays are written down and often published, which enables them to be read by an interested readership and also serves to authenticate the place of drama in a literary canon. However, the central and most important consequence of plays being documented in this way is that it affords them the possibility of being performed again. The publishing of plays, then, carries with it enormous historical importance in the continuation of a dramatic tradition and enables us not only to reflect on aspects of dramas written long ago but also offers up the opportunity to reproduce such dramas in new and invigorating ways. The screenplay, in contrast, is a frozen entity – published after the fact of its making in celluloid, it serves in this post-production, post-blueprint guise as documentation of the film that already exists. Whereas plays can work hermeneutically in a circle of birth and rebirth, screenplays, post-event, will always figure as a referent to another kind of text entirely.

Plays, which evolved across cultures out of an oral tradition, have been recorded through the process of scribing and transcribing since the beginnings of alphabetic writing (Zarrilli *et al.* 2006: 60) and their genesis is paralleled by the development of theatre and theatre practice itself. The publishing of the first Folio edition of Shakespeare's plays in 1623 remains a landmark event in the history of published play texts – not only in the sense that it circumscribed a corpus of work that is as popular today as it was in Elizabethan times, but also that it imbued the work with a hitherto unknown sense of authorial authority – by placing Shakespeare's portrait on the cover. Play and playwright became inherently bound up with an idea of authorship, despite the collaborative nature of theatre practice where the lines between the roles of writer, actor and director in the creation of a play text can remain somewhat blurred. While differences between styles and the presentation of action and dialogue have emerged and are discernible in terms of both time period and genre, such differences in the overall format of what constitutes a *play* remain comparatively minor.[1]

The development of the screenplay form owes much to its dramatic sister in the theatre and many of the first films produced were adaptations of stage plays

(Stempel 2000: 3). However, from the very beginning the format of the screenplay was dependent on and determined by technology. Silent films could only be shot on one reel at a time which meant that early cinema was characterized by short-story 'scenarios'. While for many, the origins of the modern screenplay form are located in the screenplay of the first sound feature *The Jazz Singer* (1927), as early as 1911, Everett McNeil in a prescient forerunner of Syd Field's *Screenwriter's Workbook*, set down some guidance for budding screenwriters:

> Divide the scenario into scenes, giving each change in the location of the action a separate scene – that is, whenever the plot renders it necessary for the operator to change the position of his camera, as from an interior to an exterior view, begin a new scene. Number the scenes consecutively to the end of the play. At the beginning of each scene, give a brief but clear word picture of the setting of the scene; also the position and action of the characters introduced when the picture first flashes on the screen ... Now carefully study out the needed action for each scene; and then describe it briefly, being careful to cut out every act that does not have a direct bearing on the development of the plot.[2]

Filmmaker and innovator Thomas Ince developed this approach into his continuity scripts which in turn paved the way for the development of the story scenario into a blueprint for filmmaking. His 1914 script for *Satan McAllister's Heir* demonstrates a high degree of similarity with what we now think of as a standard screenplay format:

```
SCENE 1: CLOSE UP ON BAR IN WESTERN SALOON

A group of good Western types of the early period
are drinking at the bar and talking idly - much good
fellowship prevails and every man feels at ease with his
neighbor - one of them glances off the picture and the
smile fades from his face to be replaced by the strained
look of worry - the others notice the change and follow
his gaze - their faces reflect his own emotions - be sure
to get over a sharp contrast between the easy good nature
that had prevailed and the unnatural, strained silence
that follows - as they look, cut.[3]
```

What is most striking about Ince's script is that it is so completely embedded in a relatively new technological process of filmmaking that distinguishes itself from theatre-making in the central innovation of its ability to frame action through the close-up.[4] While the tone veers towards instructional – 'be sure to get over ...' – the essential quality of the screenplay form to describe action through pictures is clearly evident as is the syntactic importance of the narration through film's ability to move focus through the use of shot change – 'as they look, cut'.

With the development of talking pictures, dialogue became much more a feature of the screenplay form and, in a certain irony, it somewhat belatedly moved a step closer to its play text origins. But vital and significant differences have developed and persist until today. Having sketched out, albeit briefly, the antecedents of the screenplay form and its relationship to emergent cinema, I will now address the issue of the fundamental nature of the screenplay form, as it has developed, through a direct comparison with the play text form. My reason for doing this is not to privilege one or the other but simply to attempt to elucidate the nature of the screenplay by highlighting what makes this form unique from other kindred forms.

Patricia Highsmith's novel *The Talented Mr Ripley* can be seen as an archetype of the adaptive text. Published in 1955, the novel is the first of the Ripley series which deals with the sexually and morally ambiguous character of Tom Ripley and his attempts to live by his wits in a world that seems set against him. The novel was adapted into a screenplay as early as 1960 when French film director René Clément made *Plein Soleil*, a highly successful film in its own right which launched the career of Alain Delon who played the sociopathic anti-hero. Almost 40 years later, in 1999, playwright Phyllis Nagy and screenwriter Anthony Minghella quite accidentally both chose the novel to adapt for their own particular disciplines, providing us with a unique opportunity to contrast the two forms.[5]

The novel *The Talented Mr Ripley* tells the story of Tom Ripley a young man of dubious means who is sent to Italy by wealthy shipping magnate Herbert Greenleaf in order to coax his son back home. While in Italy, Tom becomes more and more drawn to the son, Dickie Greenleaf, and all that he represents – wealth, style and power. He eventually kills Dickie and manages to impersonate him, accessing his funds and lifestyle, and eventually escaping to Greece where he inherits Dickie's fortune through a forged will.

Highsmith's novel begins its story in Manhattan where Tom believes he is being pursued by a creditor (who turns out to be Dickie Greenleaf's father):

> Tom glanced behind him and saw the man coming out of the Green Cage, heading his way. Tom walked faster. There was no doubt that the man was after him. Tom had noticed him five minutes ago, eyeing him carefully from a table, as if he weren't *quite* sure, but almost. He had looked sure enough for Tom to down his drink in a hurry, pay and get out.
>
> (Highsmith 1999: 5)

Nagy's theatrical adaptation begins as all play texts generally do with a dramatis personae: a list of characters in the piece, as well as other paratextual information about the first production of the text, its location and its chief personnel. This serves as an attempt to paradoxically fix the text in time and space – the date of the first performance and the place where that occurred – in that the particular choice of words spoken, the particular sequence of the scenes is closest to that particular textual record than any other preceding or future performance. Film, however, serves as a finite documented text of its own single performance (in the final-cut stage), but what is worthy of note here is that, while the opening and closing titles of films do carry similar information about the cast and crew of a production, this is not recorded in the published screenplay format. Films, unlike plays, can never have subsequent performances (beyond their reception) unless they are entirely completely remade and so, while the ability of a text to be remade and reimagined is the very nature and *raison d'être* of the play text, such events remain relatively rare in cinema.[6]

Nagy's play is divided into two acts – a popular form of playwriting which enables an audience to rest and refresh during an interval in the performance – and this demarcation is clearly signposted at the top of her text. She then invokes a range of theatrical signs (sound, lighting, staging) as she describes the entrance of Tom Ripley on to the stage:

ACT ONE

Darkness. The sound of waves and gulls. Gentle.
Languorous. Peaceful. Still. A fishing boat's bell sounds.
Gradually, the sound of the waves becomes more and more
unstable and turbulent until it becomes the sound of a
violent storm at sea – a typhoon, an event of devastating
catastrophe. And just at its height, when it seems it
can't get any worse, the storm sounds are replaced by the
sound of a motorboat at full speed – the sounds of which
appears to come closer and closer and closer until the
lights come up suddenly, the motorboat sound disappears,
and Tom Ripley is there, startling as the storm, to
address us:

                              TOM
              We live happily ever after under cover.
              He tells me this one morning while he
              butters our toast and she prepares the
              espresso. We're at the end of our dock. I
              say to him: it's the first sunny morning
              in months and what do you *mean* we'll live
              happily ever after under cover? Just as
              I'm about to sink my teeth into a slice
              of toast, an adder slithers up my right
              leg. I am not at all startled, but I
              jump. To the left. He drops his toast.
              To the right. On to the dock. The toast
              burns a hole right through the dock.
              We watch it smoulder. She says to me:
              but what about the adder? I say to her:
              don't worry, it's domesticated. But what

about the *toast*? We have no more bread. He
cries. Unstoppable tears. The adder's at
my jugular, preparing for a big bite. And
I'm thinking, no no no. This can't be.
We're going to live happily ever after
under cover. The water rises. Above the
dock. We're knee deep. We're waist deep.
I cannot move. It's his tears, she says,
it's his tears creating a flood. What have
you done? What have you *done*? The adder's
poised to strike. What the hell. We'll
starve anyway. And then I wake.

(Nagy 1999: 5)

Nagy uses the present tense to describe action that is to occur live during the physical performance of the text on the stage – an established convention of dramatic writing which clearly delineates that what is written has not already happened (as in the novel) but is happening *now*. This information amounts to more than mere 'stage directions' – instructions for actors on where to move on and around the stage – and in some ways might be thought to be essentially cinematic in her description of events that move far beyond the locale of a domestically set stage scenario to the open waters. Her invocation of the unfolding narrative of the sound effect signifier remains, however, at the level of signifier: 'the motorboat sound' rather than just the physical entity of 'the motorboat' is registered in the text as one would expect in the screenplay. The use of such descriptions which set out in the present tense detailed descriptions of stage sets and settings predates cinema – for example, Henrik Ibsen's stage directions have been likened to painting in their artful and meticulous thoroughness. When it comes to Nagy's description of the physical body of the actor on the stage, however, the signifier becomes linked to its signified as a metaphor, hence the image of Ripley 'startling as the storm'. This kind of description is one that allows for the collaborative process of director and actor to interpret gesturally what is laid out in the text which must be reproduced and physically enunciated each time it is performed.

Nagy then moves on to place the character of Tom Ripley at the centre of her piece as primary narrator as she creatively responds to the themes of the novel by having him relate a dream which plays with the pivotal event in the story – the murder of Dickie Greenleaf – in an improvisatory and surreal way. This text, which serves as a kind of prologue to the whole play, is stylistically a play text that calls for it to become a *performance* text in that it is inherently performable and speakable.[7] The use of repetition – 'It's his tears, she says, it's his tears. What have you done? What have you *done*?' – augments the tension and serving a poetic purpose that lifts easily from page to stage. The fact that Tom is standing on the stage 'to address us' registers the third element of dramatic writing: the audience. In Nagy's text, Tom talks directly to the audience, not only narrating his own voice but also those of others (just as in the source text, he is shown to be adept at imitating the voices and characteristics of those around him). It is clear that the events and point of view are framed through Ripley's eyes and immediately we see that this view is tormented (the adder coming at his neck) and disturbed: 'What the hell. We'll starve anyway.'

Anthony Minghella, when reflecting on his adaptation of *The Talented Mr Ripley*, wrote that 'the screenplay ... is both an argument with the source material and a commentary on it' (Minghella 2000: p. ix). Clearly, Nagy would say much the same about her argument and commentary which utilizes a different semiotic system altogether. Minghella conceives the opening to the Ripley story through a sequence of short scenes but also, interestingly, chooses to open with a prologue which in this case situates Ripley flashed forward to the end of the film, reflecting back on the chain of events and how they first began:

1958 PROLOGUE: INT. RIPLEY'S CABIN. EVENING

Fade up on RIPLEY, as in the final scene of the film, sitting, desolate in a ship's cabin. The camera rotates around his face, which begins in light and ends in darkness.

RIPLEY (O/S)

> If I could just go back. If I could rub
> everything out. Starting with myself.
> Starting with borrowing a jacket.

EXT. CENTRAL PARK WEST TERRACE. EARLY EVENING

RIPLEY is at the piano, accompanying FRAN, a young soprano.

FRAN (sings)

> Ah, such fleeting paradise,
> Such innocent delight,
> To love,
> Be loved,
> A lullaby,
> Then silence.

The song finishes. Applause. They're the entertainment at a cocktail party to celebrate a silver wedding anniversary. Some partygoers congratulate FRAN on her performance. A distinguished-looking man, pushing his wife in a wheelchair, approaches RIPLEY, offers his hand.

HERBERT GREENLEAF

> Most enjoyable. Herbert Greenleaf.

```
                        RIPLEY
        Tom Ripley. Thank you, sir.

                 HERBERT GREENLEAF
   (pointing at RIPLEY'S borrowed jacket)
        I see you were at Princeton … Then you'll
        most likely know our son, Dick. Dickie
        Greenleaf …

                  EMILY GREENLEAF
        We couldn't help noticing your jacket.

                 HERBERT GREENLEAF
        Yes.

                  EMILY GREENLEAF
        Class of '56?

                 RIPLEY (hesitating)
        How is Dickie?
```

(Minghella 2000: 1–2)

The use of the present tense to describe the unfolding story scenario, as is common practice in the screenplay form, recalls and has evolved out of both the dramatic tradition of writing for the stage as well as the impact of film production techniques on the origins of screenwriting itself, as demonstrated by the work of Thomas Ince. In its hybridized form, it is used to both denote the physical action of the characters – Ripley 'hesitating' before he finally speaks denoting an early subtextual layer and hint of deception – as well as the manipulation of cinematic signs and technological processes – 'the camera rotates around his face, which begins in light and ends in darkness'. Acts and scenes have disappeared from the equation (in a formal, numbered sense) and have been replaced by slug lines which contain information about location shooting and the time of day. Even in its published form, these technological considerations form part and parcel of the fabric of the screenplay form and serve to enhance a sense of the film *as constructed* as well as the film that *has been* constructed to which the screenplay is an unavoidable referent. The characters' dialogue is placed centrally on the page, which facilitates a kind of seamless reading of the screenplay, uninterrupted by divisions of scenes, as one might read a credit roller on screen or a lengthy scroll.

Following the killing of Dickie, Tom Ripley begins to live the life of his acquired friend, taking on many of his attributes, accent, dress and physical gestures. What Dickie had always taken for granted is both celebrated and savoured by Tom. However, his new life of opulence and material pleasure becomes threatened with the arrival of a friend of Dickie's, Freddie Miles, who comes searching for him. In Highsmith's novel, Freddie turns up at the apartment in Rome and is instantly suspicious about Tom's status and the absence of his friend. In Nagy's stage adaptation, the chronology of the narrative is fragmented with the central act of Dickie's murder recurring throughout the piece and Dickie himself remaining as a constant stage presence as he continues to permeate deep into Tom's psyche. However, the arrival of Freddie Miles is used to interrupt a recalling of the murder as:

> The sound of the motorboat is heard coming ever closer. Richard holds out his hand to Tom. Richard very nearly manages to grab hold of Tom's hand, the motorboat is very close when, like a bolt of lightning, the motorboat sound is replaced by a loud and insistent ringing telephone. Lights down very quickly on all but Tom – perhaps he's isolated in a tight bright light. Abruptly startled out of his fantasy, Tom appears to be, for the first time, thrown by a situation.

> TOM (to the audience)
> Can that really be the telephone? Such
> a common means of communication. And
> in any case, nobody has this number.
> Shall I answer? Shall I let it go? Such
> a dangerous decision. Delicious. (Beat,
> then, as Richard:) Pronto. Sono Greenleaf.

> Lights up on Freddie.

> FREDDIE
> You're a hard man to pin down, Greenleaf.
> I'll give you that. Making folks write to
> you care of American Express. Unlisted
> phone number.

> TOM
> Who is this?

> FREDDIE
> Come on, Rickie. You haven't been out of
> the loop all that long. It's me. Freddie.
> Freddie Miles? Long lost so-and-so you
> bumped into not that long ago?

> TOM
> Ah. Freddie. Of course (Beat) How did you
> find me?

(Nagy 1999: 76)

This is a complex scene with shifts of time, character and characters playing other characters as well as a full utilization of theatrical signs. The emboldening of the characters' names on the page adds clarity to the complexity of who is doing what and who is actually who, while there remains a sense of the collaborative nature of theatre-making – 'perhaps he's isolated in a tight, bright light' – by Nagy's script being less of a blueprint for production than a conceptual starting point for options. As the British theatre director Katie Mitchell notes:

> Some directors cut all stage directions from the text because they can predetermine the moves and actions of the characters. They also remove all adjectives that precede lines, like 'angrily' or 'through tears' because these words might put the actor under pressure to deliver slabs of generalised feelings. Others prefer that every stage direction, comma, full stop and adjective that came from the writer's pen is retained in the text.
>
> (Mitchell 2008: 65)

The playwright's directions for the stage, then, can only ever be the formulation of a possibility whereas the screenplay, which is published post-event, will always be determined by a singular source.

The relationship between stage directions (the term is used here generically) and dialogue has in the past been a concern for structuralists working in the area of theatre semiotics. A differentiation between the *Haupttext* and the *Nebentext*, as exemplified in the close textual analysis of Aston and Savona (1991: 71–95) can prove an illuminating tool particularly in locating its privileging of the former (dialogue) over the latter (ancillary text).[8] While contemporary drama has tended to minimalize *Nebentext,* with some dramatists doing away with it altogether (e.g. Kane 2000; Crimp 2007; Stephens 2008), the screenplay tends towards privileging the *Nebentext* over the *Haupttext* – something that has become enshrined in the strict formatting systems that govern and legitimize its existence. Due to the complex staging of Nagy's text where characters appear in multiple time-frames, stage directions remain a critical feature of the play. However, in contrast to the screenplay, these function primarily as indicators that help punctuate the action and present future productions with starting points and possibilities. The actual physical arrival of Freddie Miles is conveyed in Nagy's text simply as '*Lights up on Freddie*'. In Minghella's screenplay, Freddie's arrival is set against a mise-en-scène that confers the kind of comfort and luxury afforded to only an elite few:

```
INT. RIPLEY'S APARTMENT. AFTERNOON.

RIPLEY is in the apartment, fire burning, wearing pyjamas.
There's a small Christmas tree. He kneels on the floor
with some festive, gift-wrapped packages. He opens a
package. It's a marble head of Hadrian. He picks up a
glass, pours himself a drink.

INT. RIPLEY'S APARTMENT. LATE AFTERNOON.

RIPLEY plunges into Bach's Italian Concerto on his new
```

and precious toy, a Steinway grand. His doorbell rings.
He stops playing. He doesn't get visitors. He rises, a
little nervous.

                RIPLEY
   Hello?

             FREDDIE (o/s)
   Dickie?

                RIPLEY
   Who is it?

             FREDDIE (o/s)
   It's Freddie. Let me in.

RIPLEY can't think what to hide, where to hide. He opens
the door.

(Minghella 2000: 87–8)

Nagy's text is both about showing ('Tom *appears to be, for the first time, thrown by a situation*') and telling in equal measure:

           TOM (to the audience)
   Can that really be the telephone? Such
   a common means of communication. And
   in any case, nobody has this number.
   Shall I answer? Shall I let it go? Such
   a dangerous decision. Delicious. (Beat,
   then, as Richard:) Pronto. Sono Greenleaf.

(Nagy 1999: 76)

However, in Minghella's text the showing is privileged and does the work of signalling Tom, seduced by Greenleaf's lifestyle, set against the urgent threat of Freddie's arrival. Thus rather than use a telephone call, he opts for a picture of luxury and opulence – the Steinway piano, the marble bust – where a whole afternoon's experience of these things are relayed in a matter of seconds.

While visually alluring as a film, Minghella's Ripley is far less textually poetic than Nagy's. Aside from the opening voiceover, the viewer is left to discover and unearth from the showing of events the full horror of Ripley's talent, whereas for Nagy he must verbalize it, too:

           TOM (to the audience)
   Fate is on my side. Here is the proof.If I
   was not meant to overcome every obstacle
   put in my path, then why is it all so
   easy? Anyway, I am blameless. The pen was

```
held by Rickie's hand and is still now.
I see him in every café, at every hotel,
under every umbrella. … His whisper in
my ear a caress, a comfort: You are not
alone. You are not alone. You are not.
Tom.
```
(Nagy 1999: 72)

While this could easily become a voiceover in the film adaptation, such a move would not chime so well with the visual form. As Minghella himself notes in his introduction to the screenplay:

> Film grammar, with its unique ability to manipulate images, flexing from the intense close-up to the broadest vistas, is perfectly placed to situate personal behaviour in a public landscape. It can contextualise action, remind us that how we are as individuals in thrall quite literally to the bigger picture.
>
> (Minghella 2000: p. x)

This 'bigger picture', the ability of film to project itself onto our lives and the lives of others, relinquishes the screenplay text from its tight technological and structural constraints into something that makes it a referent for its cinematic other – something that can be enjoyed for itself but like adaptation needs to be experienced *as* a play on the screen to be fully appreciated and fully understood.

That the screenplay and the stage play should respond in completely different ways to the same source is far from surprising. Adaptation theorists have for some time been interested in the different ways in which film, in particular, differs from its various literary sources as a direct result of its differing technological processes (Cardwell 2002: 74). Ever since George Bluestone promoted the idea of an essential ontological difference between the novel and the film – that they represented 'different aesthetic genera, as different from each other as ballet is from architecture' (Bluestone 1961: 5), the specifics of the particular medium has played a central role in critical thinking about adaptations. The evolution of the screenplay form has been one that has paralleled the development of cinema to such an extent that the form has become enshrined in screenwriting software, such as *Final Draft*, which has itself become established as the industry format standard. While different publishing houses such as Methuen, Faber, and Nick Hern Books have their own individual house styles playwrights are expected to conform to, screenwriting styles are generic across the industry and follow a common template of scene headings (slug lines composed of whether the shot is to be filmed in the interior or exterior, its location and its time of day), dialogue and action.

The screenplay form as it has evolved can be seen as structurally limiting in comparison to plays written for the stage. Its form has taken on a generic, rigorous framework that must be adhered to in order for the industry to acknowledge, authenticate and develop the text into production. However, within the constraints of the form, a number of screenwriters have made their names not simply through the authority and creativity of their vision but also the poetry and subtlety of their writing. Many screenwriters started out as playwrights[9] and those who endure as writers for the screen of note, such as Woody Allen, Quentin Tarantino, Sally Potter, David Mamet, do so because of their ability to write poetically *within* the constraints of the form. However, as Potter's screenplay for her film *Yes* (2005) demonstrates, when a writer is moving towards a heightened poetic style (the text is written entirely in iambic pentameter) the screenplay itself moves much closer to the stage play form than is usual. Thus, Potter's screenplay begins with a list of characters or dramatis personae as is common practice in stage writing and while the use of slug lines remains, there is a greater emphasis on characters' intentions than descriptions of visual story scenarios:

```
A tall, dark man, HE, dressed in a tuxedo walks out from
the stark neon-lit kitchens into the candle-lit banquet
hall. HE is heading for the long table laid for dinner,
but then pauses, his attention caught by this elegant
woman standing alone. HE stares at her for a moment and
then approaches her cautiously.

      HE    Forgive my question, but are you
            alright?
     SHE    I'm fine. Thank you.
      HE    Are you sure?
     SHE    Yes, quite.
      HE    A woman left alone … if it was me …
            I wouldn't …
     SHE     - wouldn't what?
```

(Potter 2005: 4)

Not only does Potter eschew the conventional parameters of the screenplay form such as centralizing the character's name on a line by itself, but her use of the deictic 'this' in 'this elegant woman standing alone' as opposed to the unfolding visual narrative of '*an* elegant woman standing alone' locates her text structurally much closer to stage writing than film. Moreover, Potter's screenplay demonstrates the limitations of a comparative approach – that while highlighting differences between screenplays and plays can be illuminating (particularly when they share a common source), to see the two forms in oppositional terms cannot wholly account for the work of those who challenge forms, expectations and accepted practices in their writing.

Notes

1 Elaine Aston and George Savona's study of theatre semiotics is particularly insightful on the history and role of stage directions in theatre play texts (Aston and Savona 1991: 71–95).
2 Quoted in Staiger 1979: 19.
3 Quoted in Norman 2007.
4 The impact of this for acting styles in both theatre and film were extraordinary. See e.g. Pearson 1992.
5 It is interesting to note here that while the homosexual subtext was all but erased by Clément, the passage of 40 years saw both Nagy and Minghella having no qualms about exploring the sexuality of Ripley that is clearly evident in the Highsmith source text.
6 A notable exception here is Gus Van Sant's remaking of the Hitchcock cinematic classic Psycho which attempted to follow its source as close as possible with a new cast of actors and crew. See Donaldson-McHugh and Moore 2006.
7 The notion of the performability or the speakability of an adapted or translated text for the stage has been a major strand of both translation theory and adaptation studies and is a useful way in highlighting the difference between performance writing and other associated genres – see Bassnett-McGuire (1980), Bassnett (1985: 102), Batty (1999: 390). Essentially, the notion maintains that in order for a drama text to work in either its interlingual (translated) or intersemiotic (adapted) form, it needs to change so that the dialogue e.g. can be competently and confidently spoken by actors in a way that sounds completely 'natural'.
8 Aston and Savona (1991) utilize the distinction between dialogue (Haupttext) and stage directions (Nebentext) in play texts made by Roman Ingarden (1973). This distinction offers possibilities for further examination of the screenplay form and the relationship between dialogue and other paratextual information within the script.
9 Minghella is a case in point here who wrote a wide range of plays for both the stage and radio prior to taking up screenwriting.

References

Aston, E. and Savona, G. (1991) *Theatre as Sign System: A Semiotics of Text and Performance*, London and New York: Routledge.
Bassnett-McGuire, Susan (ed.) (1980) *Translation Studies*, London: Methuen.
Bassnett, Susan (1985) 'Ways through the Labyrinth: Strategies and Methods for Translating Theatre Texts ' in T. Hermans (ed.) *The Manipulation of Literature: Studies in Literary Translation*, London: Croom Helm.
Batty, Mark (1999) 'Translation in the Theatre I: Directing as Translating' in S. Chew and A. Stead (eds) *Translating Life : Studies in Transpositional Aesthetics*, Liverpool: Liverpool University Press.
Bluestone, G. (1961) *Novels into Film*, Berkeley, CA: University of California Press.
Cardwell, Sarah (2002) *Adaptation Revisited: Television and the Classic Novel*, Manchester: Manchester University Press
Crimp, M. (2007) *Attempts on her Life*, London: Faber & Faber.
Donaldson-McHugh, S. and Moore, D. (2006) 'Film Adaptation, Co-Authorship, and Hauntology: Gus Van Sant's Psycho (1998)', *Journal of Popular Culture* 39(2): 225–33.
Highsmith, P. (1999) *The Talented Mr Ripley*, London: Vintage.

Ingarden, R. (1973) *The Literary Work of Art: An Investigation on the Borderlines of Ontology, Logic, and Theory of Literature*, Northwestern University Studies in Phenomenology and Existential Philosophy, Evanston, IL: Northwestern University Press.

Kane, S. (2000) *4:48 Psychosis*, London: Methuen Drama.

Minghella, A. (2000) *The Talented Mr Ripley: A Screenplay,* London: Methuen.

Mitchell, K. (2008) *The Director's Craft: A Handbook for the Theatre*, London: Routledge.

Nagy, P. (1999) *The Talented Mr Ripley*, London: Methuen Drama.

Norman, M. (2007) *What Happens Next: A History of American Screenwriting*, New York: Harmony Books.

Pearson, R. E. (1992) *Eloquent Gestures: The Transformation of Performance Style in the Griffith Biograph Films*, Berkeley, CA: University of California Press.

Potter, S. (2005) *Yes: Screenplay and Notes*, New York: Newmarket Press.

Staiger, Janet (1979) 'Dividing Labor for Production Control: Thomas Ince and the Rise of the Studio System', *Cinema Journal*, 18: 2, 16–25

Stempel, T. (2000) *Framework : A History of Screenwriting in the American Film*, Syracuse, NY: Syracuse University Press.

Stephens, Simon (2008) *Pornography*, London: Methuen Drama.

Zarrilli, P., Mconachie, B., Williams, G. J. and Fisher Sorgenfrei, S. (eds) (2006) *Theatre Histories: An Introduction*, New York and London: Routledge.

Chapter 15

Beyond McKee

Screenwriting in and out of the academy

Barry Langford

Amongst the many pleasures afforded the screenwriting theorist by Charlie Kaufman's deliriously reflexive *Adaptation* (2002), pride of place must surely go to the celebrated scene in which screenwriter anti-hero 'Charlie Kaufman', despairing of his prospects of delivering his contracted adaptation of Susan Orlean's *The Orchid Thief*, attends one of screenwriting guru Robert McKee's legendary story seminars. McKee – characterized as a preening if hard-working blowhard, a self-confessed 'opinionated arrogant asshole' (vividly impersonated by Brian Cox in Spike Jonze's film[1]) – delivers himself of a series of truisms and soundbites on the art of the screenplay; cumulatively these strike the initially sceptical but desperate modernist Kaufman with the force of an Exocet. McKee harnesses writing for the screen unapologetically and inextricably to narrative: (86)[2]

                    MCKEE
          Literary talent is not enough. First,
          last, and always, the imperative is to
          tell a story.

With Aristotle's dictum that stories must have a beginning, a middle and an end as his inevitable point of departure, McKee rolls out the familiar dogmas and doctrines of Hollywood screenwriting: drama is conflict, actions not words, character arcs, act breaks. All of this is underpinned by an unstated but unchallenged and unnoticed metaphysics of presence in which the 'trivial' and inherently inauthentic written word threatens the compelling force of the gesture or visual symbol ('God help you if you use voiceover in your work, my friends', warns McKee (87)) and must be corralled by vivid action. Kaufman (the writer, not the character) adds to his hall of mirrors by permitting McKee an extended credo whose own inclusion in *Adaptation* defines this as a script that challenges the very precepts McKee here expounds: (88)

                    MCKEE
          Long speeches are antithetical to the
          nature of cinema. The Greeks called it

```
stykomythia -- the rapid exchange of
ideas. A long speech in a script, say a
page long, requires that the camera hold
on the actor's face for a minute. Look
at the second hand on your watch as it
makes one complete rotation around the
clock face and you'll get an idea of how
intolerable that would be for an audience.
The ontology of the screen is that it's
always now and it's always action and
it's always vivid. Life is rarely vivid.
And that's an important point. We are not
recreating life on the screen. Writers
are not tape recorders. Have you ever
eavesdropped on people talking in a coffee
shop? Then you know how dull and tedious
real conversation is. Real people are not
interesting. There's not a person in this
world -- and I include myself in this --
who would be interesting enough to take as
is and put in a movie as a character.
```

Kaufman's script, and its realization in Jonze's film, have been extensively examined in critical literature. In fact, with its artful reflexive recursions, its consciously undertaken performative contradictions (most notably, the way in which the absurd action climax epitomizes the commercial principles abjured by the factitious 'Charlie Kaufman', but embraced by his – wholly fictitious – brother 'Donald'), and the high degree of critical capability it assumes and requires from its audience. *Adaptation*, like both 'high' modernist (Joyce's *Ulysses*) and playfully post-modern (Martin Amis's *Money*) texts, actively solicits critical exegesis as an integral part of producing its meaning(s).[3] This in itself places *Adaptation* at odds with normative approaches to screenwriting – as embodied in Kaufman's screenplay by McKee – which stress the transparency and the self-explanatory qualities of the ideal commercial screenplay, and accordingly render 'excessive' critical interrogation redundant. Indeed, the requirement for such interrogation would by McKee's standards constitute *prima facie* evidence of the script's inability or, worse, cussed refusal to engage its audience on their own (assumed) terms.

On the other hand, *Adaptation*'s post-modern narrational and representational gamesmanship is precisely what has so successfully recommended it to an academic reader/viewership. To the extent that Kaufman-the-character takes McKee's strictures to heart – fashioning a script that, assuming *Adaptation* to be the film of that script, delivers on propulsive third-act climaxes and an emotionally resonant resolution – he falls short of the astringent standard set by Kaufman-the-writer, whose own *Adaptation* maintains an ironic distance from the McKeevian devices it parodically performs. *Adaptation* and Kaufman's other screenplays – including *Being John Malkovich* (1999), *Confessions of a Dangerous Mind* (2002), *Eternal Sunshine of the Spotless Mind* (2004), and *Synecdoche, New York* (2008) – have joined a select group of other scripts (Quentin Tarantino and Roger Avery's *Pulp Fiction* (1994) and Christopher Nolan's *Memento* (2000) are amongst the more obvious examples)[4] whose ostentatious interrogation of the quasi-Aristotelian mechanisms of conventional Hollywood dramaturgy have rendered them more-or-less instant fetish objects for academic narratology and other critical analysis. In part, this reflects the critical preferences that govern much academic reception of narrative cinema – attitudes that, it could be argued, are in their own way almost as unexamined as the Aristotelian principles they critique.

Since the 'theoretical turn' driven by *Cahiers du Cinéma* (in France) and *Screen* (in the UK) in the early 1970s, academic film criticism has retained a degree of loyalty to the Brechtian models of non-identificatory, non-empathetic, 'epically' distanced drama that informed not only the critiques of hegemonic European cinemas in the pages of those journals, but also certain strains of the contemporary cinematic New Waves (Godard, Straub-Huillet, Kluge, Bob Fosse, etc.).[5] Of course, since the 1980s formal analysis generally and analysis of film narrative in particular has been widely displaced in film studies by film history, reception studies, as well as more broadly 'culturalist' readings that seek to locate films within (rather than identifying or prescribing means of colluding with or opposing) their larger social-historical contexts. Rather remarkably, since Edward Branigan's *Narrative Comprehension and Film* in 1992, only one significant book devoted to the general principles of film narrative has been published, Marilyn Tabe's *Closely Watched Films*, which is essentially her own introductory lectures on the subject in book form. In general, narrative conventions have been more likely to be diagnosed than described. That is, the overdetermination of narrative operations by, for example, ideology has been taken as a starting point for analysis, rather than a conclusion: a celebrated example would be Robin Wood's characterization of some Hollywood films of the 1970s and 1980s (*Taxi Driver, Cruising*, etc.) as instances of the 'incoherent text'. Furthermore, as screenwriting critics and theorists have often lamented, the screenplay itself – and the principles of script construction it embodies – has very rarely been discussed as a separate, or even separable, entity from the completed film.[6] The elements of narrative and character delineated in the script tend to be treated as givens, likely to be considered as the most highly conventionalized and normative elements of the film, which can be foregrounded, interrogated or even belied by mise-en-scène, montage or other aspects of visual style. An extreme example would be the estrangement Douglas Sirk's famously 'excessive' visual style is held to effect upon ingenuously novelettish narrative material in his Universal-International melodramas of the 1950s, such as *All That Heaven Allows* and *Written on the Wind*.

Thus the screenplay is relegated by criticism to the paradoxical status of a 'second-order phenomenon' – paradoxical because, in whatever industrial context, the script (or scenario) has always necessarily preceded and in important ways defined the parameters of the ensuing production. This has various sources within the institutional politics of academic film studies. Partly, as several commentators have noted,[7] it reflects a felt need on the part of the pioneering generation of film scholars to differentiate their nascent discipline from the kinds of literary analysis practised in university English and modern languages departments, in which many film programmes were originally located. The development of a technical vocabulary of film analysis, focused on precisely those dimensions of the cinematic text for which ready analogues in older media could not be found – pre-eminently the image and, less so, sound track – enabled this project of professional differentiation. Speculatively, one might go further and suggest that this process partook of a transferential element in which film scholars came unconsciously to identify themselves with the apparatuses and practices of the industries they studied, especially Hollywood – in which screenwriters endured a notoriously, if somewhat exaggeratedly, subaltern status – as a form of Oedipal aggression against the supremacy of the writer and the written text in their parent literary disciplines. Disciplines which were themselves traditionally notorious for their elision of the industrial and institutional dimensions of literary production[8].

Emergent methodological controversies within cinema studies also played a part in inhibiting critical engagement with the principles of film narrative construction. From the mid-1980s, the perception grew that 'neo-formalist' analysis of film style, of the kind identified with David Bordwell, functioned, whether by design or accident, to exclude the kinds of readings and critical interventions centred on gender, sexuality, race and decreasingly, as the 1980s proceeded, class in favour of a largely uncritical 'historical poetics'. This in turn encouraged more aggressive forms of historicism and counter-reading, all of which tended to regard conventional narrative (as opposed to innovative, or even hysterically disorganized) practices as being of little inherent interest in themselves other than as pretexts for such interventions. It is true that some 'neo-formalist' analyses – Kristin Thompson's (1999, 2007) accounts of contemporary Hollywood storytelling, for example – seem almost wilfully disinclined to locate their objects of study in any kind of larger context, or to do much more than record narrative or industrial practice. But the historically loaded deprecation of 'formalism', echoing the so-called 'Realism Debates' of the 1930s within European Marxist literary theory,[9] has petrified the field of narrative and screenplay analysis between the neo-formalists and the post- or quasi-Brechtian positions: the latter valorizing narrative dislocation, estrangement, reflexivity and so forth, to which much contemporary film analysis still adheres, albeit almost unconsciously.

What seems to me to be missing here is the effort to think film narrative form(s) theoretically, historically and indeed dialectically. Perhaps ironically (given the tortuous relations between English and film studies), one model for such a criticism is to be found in literary theory, in the work of Fredric Jameson, whose 1981 *The Political Unconscious* modelled an understanding of the evolution of literary modes, styles and genres (such as the romance) as neither purely formal analyses, nor as inertly 'historical', but as complexly expressive of and responsive to their social and historical situation. In *The Political Unconscious* and his influential later work on postmodernism, Jameson has become renowned for his undertaking of a kind of immanent criticism where the social and cultural dimensions of a text (a film, a novel, etc.) can be 'read' not merely through its intended purposes and meanings, nor yet the ideologies sedimented within textual *content* at whatever level, but above all, through the characteristic *forms* of genre and narrative that typify a given period. Understanding these forms, Jameson argues, entails not merely a history of aesthetics but an understanding of how the historically specific practices and norms that defined the expressive horizons of literary form available to writers, in a given place and time, themselves responded to, and were part of, larger but comprehensible historical conjunctures (these for Jameson being defined by a Marxist account of social history).

The advantage of applying a Jamesonian methodology to screenwriting would be its potential to move critical approaches to the screenplay away from the futile and frankly bankrupt situation where a reductively formulaic application of quasi-Aristotelian norms, on the one hand, is met with an equally reified valorization of pseudo-Brechtian strategies on the other, and in which the normative, hegemonic tendencies of the former (taken as a given) are challenged by the presumptively insurgent character of the latter. At its worst, this has the tendency to assume that various purely technical devices automatically constitute a 'challenge' to the world-view embodied in conventional styles of narrative, regardless of the specific location of these discourses in culture and history. Thus, fragmented or decentred narratives and complex, non-linear time schemes; direct address to the audience; intrusive impersonal narration; ruptures of naturalistic conventions; and other such elements of non-classical screenwriting can be seen in rather unhistorical ways as 'oppositional' in whatever context, including otherwise very conventional ones. To the extent that academic criticism persists in regarding the inclusion of such devices in screenplays as innovative or challenging, it lags some way behind both contemporary screenwriting practice and mainstream film culture. It regards such devices with an equanimity and treats them as transparent to a degree that would be surprising to devotees of such notions from 1970s *Screen* theory as the 'progressive text',[10] of which these critical assumptions (which are genuinely 'formalist' in the pejorative sense of the word) are limp after-echoes.

To take one obvious example, direct interpellations of the audience[11] by characters, traditionally regarded as intrusively reflexive (hence potentially productively estranging), have become to all intents and purposes a form of unremarked narration in scripts ranging from *GoodFellas* (1989) to *High Fidelity* (2000). In few if any of these instances – Jim Uhls's *Fight Club* (1999) and Michael Haneke's *Funny Games* (in either version) are two clear exceptions – do such gestures accomplish, or for that matter appear to intend, the kind of textual subversion of the self-sufficient individual subject, for example, with which they are traditionally associated. It is notable that Kaufman-the-character (who is identified as the writer of the wildly stylized yet also strongly character-based *Being John Malkovich*) in Kaufman's *Adaptation* attempts to defend his non-Aristotelian/anti-McKeevian narratives not as challenges to hegemonic norms but merely as 'more a reflection of the real world' (90). Another example might be the ways in which non-academic reviewers and commentators widely failed, or perhaps saw no need, to comment on the panoply of formal derangements that constituted the bricolage-like texture of David Veloz, Richard Rutowski and Oliver Stone's *Natural Born Killers* (1994) and persisted in seeing so to speak 'straight through' to the film's ultra-violent content. This is a notable instance of how canonically modernist devices, employed in canonically modernist (parodic, satirical and distancing) modes, largely failed to achieve their purposes for an audience to which such 'avant-garde' techniques have been naturalized by commodified usage, in the 1980s and 1990s, for instance, in music video.

None of the preceding is intended to suggest that, faced with the diminishing efficacy of 'alternative' procedures, either practising screenwriters dissatisfied with the tyranny of the three-act structure, or scholars seeking to understand the screenplay in its historical and cultural contexts, should surrender to the self-evident truths of the well-made script as propounded by McKee or Syd Field. On the contrary, there is surely a strong argument to be made that, if alternatives are to be found to these deadening and ubiquitous contemporary norms, a more complex and rigorous understanding is required of how and why such infantile bromides as Vogler's 'Hero's Journey' achieve hegemonic status. Such an understanding might indicate, for instance, that the invocation of timeless, 'archetypal' cod-mythologies may precisely be expressive of a period which has lost the inclination or capacity for authentic historical understandings. This in turn may enable the discovery of alternatives that speak to a contemporary context in ways that, through no fault of their own, methods devised to address the conditions of mid-twentieth-century capitalism cannot. Equally, it will become necessary to try to understand why Aristotelian prescriptions became integral to the practice and latterly the teaching of screenwriting (in ways that have no real parallel in, for example, modern theatre practice). Nor have there yet been adequate efforts to think the ways in which non-Aristotelian models on character and narrative in non-Western cinemas (notably Indian cinema) may help us reflect back on European and American models and practice. Historical accounts of the institutionalization of screenwriting practices in the evolution of national film industries, such as those offered by Bordwell, Staiger and Thompson (1985), and more recently Steven Maras (2009), are an essential part of this understanding; yet empirical histories on their own may not render the necessary kind of active comprehension.

Much would have to happen both within and without the academy for such a reappraisal of approaches to scripts and screenwriting – not least, the continuing rupture, and at a significantly more rapid pace, of the safety curtain between 'theory' and 'practice'. Perhaps the essential important first step, however, will be to abandon the prescriptive quality that has typified almost all screenwriting teaching, but also too much critical analysis of screenplay and narrative: that is, valorizing and either explicitly or implicitly recommending particular formal choices at the expense of (all) others. In place of this, I propose we commit to *researching* the screenplay – something that can be undertaken by practitioners and scholars alike. To concretize this suggestion somewhat, in the second part of this essay I will explore how two very different screenplays engage with the problems of narration and representation posed by perhaps the central trauma of modern (Western) history and culture, the Holocaust.

Case study: a long film and a short film about a big subject

The Holocaust is both an event, or a series of events, in modern European history, in which regard it recommends itself, at least in principle, straightforwardly to such dominant generic paradigms as the war film or the period drama, and, as numerous writers have suggested, an ontological rupture in the traditions of Western post-Enlightenment discourse. The history of Holocaust film can in good measure be organized around a central antinomy: on the one hand, those films that maintain, with whatever degree of self-awareness, the continuing applicability to this particular subject of the forms of 'received wisdom' embodied in conventional narrative and representational paradigms; on the other, those that insist on the need for the radical historical rupture represented by the Holocaust to find formal expression through the innovation or estrangement of formal procedures – to develop (as Oskar Schindler irritatedly expresses it in *Schindler's List*) 'a whole new language'. I wish here briefly to consider how these contrasting approaches are exemplified in two screenplays: the first, Steven Zaillian's Oscar-winning adaptation of Thomas Kenneally's *Schindler's List*, filmed by Steven Spielberg in 1993, the second my own short screenplay *Torte Bluma*, filmed by Benjamin Ross in 2004.

As I have argued elsewhere, for better or worse *Schindler's List* chooses very visibly to engage with the Holocaust through the readily recognizable paradigms of American film genre(s), an approach that partly testifies to the film's determination to render terrible events widely regarded as beyond representation or comprehension as, ultimately, manageable, recuperable and above all ethically accountable.[12] While it is not relevant or appropriate here to assess the terms or the validity of this understanding of the Holocaust, it is important to note that this ontological confidence is also reflected in writer, Steven Zaillian's, general adherence to the Aristotelian norms of the Hollywood screenplay. Above all, the depiction of the flawed yet ultimately redeemed character of Oskar Schindler as an individual finally compelled into decisive, meaningful and, importantly, effective action by his involvement with the horrors of the Nazi genocide. This not only qualifies Zaillian's script as well-made (and Oscar-worthy) on Hollywood criteria, but bespeaks this conviction of the ongoing relevance of categories like individual agency and redemption, in a context that to say the very least might be thought to challenge them. Exemplifying these assumptions is a climactic scene towards the start of the film's final act, when the female 'Schindler Jews' – whom Oskar has providentially arranged to be transferred from the now-liquidated Plaszow labour camp to his own, salvific rather than carceral, factory camp in Czechoslovakia – are by bureaucratic error transported instead to Auschwitz.

```
EXT. AUSCHWITZ -- DAY

The stunned women climb down from the railcars onto an
immense concourse bisecting the already infamous camp. As
they're marched across the muddy yard by guards carrying
truncheons, Mila Pfefferberg stares at the place. It's
so big, like a city, only one in which the inhabitants
reside strictly temporarily. To Mila, under her breath --

                        WOMAN
          Where are we?

Mila's eyes return to the constant smoke rising beyond
the birch trees at the settlement's western end.

INT. OFFICES -- BRINNLITZ FACTORY -- DAY

Schindler comes out of his office and, passing Stern's
desk, mumbles --

                        SCHINDLER
          They're in Auschwitz.

Before Stern can react, Schindler is out the door.¹³
```

This scene not only typifies aspects of the representation of the Holocaust in *Schindler's List* that many have found problematic (the script's ascription of epistemological and moral authority to Schindler, who answers the question, in place of the bewildered and terrified Jews who ask it), but demonstrates that, faced with the ultimate crisis, the Aristotelian protagonist knows what to do about it. While – once again – his desk-bound Jewish amanuensis is speechless and helpless, Schindler is off to redress the situation.¹⁴ Furthermore, the utterance of 'Auschwitz' here denotes not the unguessable event horizon of European culture discussed by Theodor Adorno, George Steiner, Giorgio Agamben and many others – that is, a definitively unanswerable question in and of itself – but precisely and quite literally the answer to a question: a place, a problem, and a challenge to which the capable protagonist must and will rise.¹⁵ There are obvious pitfalls in comparing the screenplay for a large-scale Hollywood-funded film about the Holocaust, intended for a mass audience, with a script of just 20 pages, with only two central characters. However, *Torte Bluma*, set in the Treblinka extermination camp, based on an anecdote recounted by former camp commandant Franz Stangl to Gitta Sereny and recorded in her celebrated study of the psychology of mass murder,¹⁶ may nonetheless illustrate ways in which dramatic film writing can engage with theoretical issues in ways largely foreclosed on by Hollywood screenwriting paradigms, yet also different from the anti-Aristotelian orthodoxies invoked by many scholarly critiques of mainstream (especially Hollywood) narrative film. *Torte Bluma* dramatizes and expands Stangl's account of one day on which a certain Blau, one of the Jewish slave workers with whom Stangl had established a certain affinity as a fellow Austrian, approached the commandant to inform him that his father, aged 82, had arrived in that day's transport.[17] Unable – for 'practical' reasons that Blau, according to Stangl, fully accepted – to employ an 82-year-old man in the camp workforce, Stangl extended himself to endorse the more pragmatic act of kindness Blau proposed: to save the old man the indignity and horror of the naked race to the gas chambers inflicted on his fellow deportees, and instead to allow Blau to see his father murdered more 'humanely' by means of a bullet in the back of the head at the camp's fake 'clinic'.[18]

Torte Bluma was conceived of as in a sense a 'research project' in screenplay form, whose aims were twofold: first, to explore the possibilities of dramatic representation of the Holocaust on a deliberately limited scale and with a focus on the interpersonal, rather than through epic recreations of historical fact in the mode of *Schindler* or *The Pianist*. Second, and in the present context most important, was to extend the analysis of the theoretical debate around the 'unrepresentability' of the Holocaust on film I had already presented in published academic work[19] into a performative interrogation: specifically, by resituating the concept of 'unrepresentability' away from the spectatorial register into a cognitive dimension of the event itself, one arguably crucial to the ability of both perpetrators and victims to continue to function in the distorted moral and ethical environment of the *univers concentrationnaire*. *Torte Bluma* was thus consciously conceived as in part a rejoinder to the discourse of 'unrepresentability' in Holocaust film: while the film itself avoids graphic horror, seeing and representation are explicitly thematized within the text itself, thus relocating questions of what is, or may not be, 'seen' away from sometimes abstract questions of the ethics of representation into a key dimension of the interpersonal and affective relations that made the Holocaust possible. The complex – and reciprocal – blindnesses of Treblinka commandant Franz Stangl and *Kapo* Blau enact issues around the relationship to the Other that echo philosophical positions explored in relation to the Holocaust by Emmanuel Levinas. The characters themselves – both Nazi *and* Jew – can only survive (however attenuated that survival) by not seeing, and agreeing amongst themselves not to see, the blindingly obvious atrocities in which they are enmeshed.

Torte Bluma's formal challenge consists less in overtly modernist strategies – both the script and the film, in fact, strive to remain within the parameters of an understated naturalism – than in its approach to character, which is conceived in very different ways than the transparent self-sufficiency of screenwriting orthodoxy. Flying in the face of (the real, not Charlie Kaufman's) Robert McKee's neo-Aristotelian dictum:

> why a man does a thing is of little interest once we see the thing he does. A character is the choices he makes to take the actions he takes. Once the deed is done his reasons why begin to dissolve into irrelevancy.
>
> (McKee 1998: 376)

– *Torte Bluma* situates motivation as the principal or indeed *only* focus of dramatic interest, but furthermore denies the characters themselves any insight or moral progression. In Sereny's own words, Stangl's self-serving presentation of this episode (some 25 years after the war's end) represented 'the profoundest example of a totally morally corrupted personality I had ever encountered'.[20] Nor however was Blau innocent of this corruption in his acceptance of the (im)moral (il)logic of the situation. This corruption was itself contextual: a function of the environment Stangl and Blau both inhabited, albeit in the vastly different positions of perpetrator and victim. It was therefore crucial to ensure that Stangl neither did, or could, acquire 'insight' about his actions, *nor* did, or could, Blau function as a voice of outraged victimhood and conscience (as, arguably, Itzhak Stern functions in *Schindler's List*). The point was that this inverted moral environment rendered certain concepts, integral both to Western bourgeois thought generally, as well as to screenwriting orthodoxies, as specific instances of that philosophical tradition in practice, untenable: most notably, individual choice and moral agency, and the potential for self-development. The purpose of the script was to enforce the invalidity of these concepts to this situation upon the audience.

Conclusion

How to enable creative work to function as 'research' is a problem that exercises all of those who find themselves straddling the institutional boundaries of practice and scholarship (and not merely when deciding whether to justify practical work as 'research' for the purposes of the Research Assessment Exercise and its ilk). Without wanting to make overlarge claims for a work of purposely limited scope (and conscious of the element of special pleading that is a perennial pitfall of reflecting critically on one's own work), I have tried in this chapter to indicate some ways in which *Torte Bluma* attempts to articulate complex conceptual and theoretical questions by managing narrative form in ways that do not simply react against mainstream conventions, but work actively, so to speak, to compel those conventions into revealing their own contradictions. While of course *Torte Bluma* may have fallen short in execution of that ambitious agenda, it may serve to illustrate one way at least in which screenplay form can be activated into the necessary project of reading itself against its own historical grain.

Notes

1 In this chapter, unless clearly indicated otherwise in the text it should be assumed that film citations refer to their original screenplays – in the versions/drafts cited – rather than to the film itself.
2 Charlie Kaufman, Adaptation, Second Draft, 24 Sept. 1999. URL: http://www.dailyscript.com/scripts/adaptation.pdf. Kaufman's McKee cites Aristotle to the effect that 'Twenty three hundred years ago, Aristotle said, when storytelling goes bad in a society, the result is decadence' (85), a point made by the real McKee 1998: 13.

3 In which regard it has been highly successful, with a large number of scholarly accounts comparing the film/script to works by Milan Kundera, Julian Barnes and other literary novelists.

4 Dates provided are for the year of production, not script drafts.

5 On 'the presence of Brecht' in Screen theory, see Stam 1999: 140–53.

6 A complaint most recently and elegantly laid out in Boon 2008.

7 See e.g. Easthope 1983: 121–35.

8 I am of course aware that such generalizations by no means hold true historically for all areas of literary study – e.g. research into Renaissance theatrical practice – and that more recently important efforts have been made to ally contemporary literary theory with the traditionally marginal and wholly empiricist redoubt of 'History of the Book'. See e.g. the pioneering work of Moretti 1998 or Joshi's 2002 study of the publication and dissemination of Victorian novels in imperial India.

9 See the essays by Bloch, Lukács, Brecht, Benjamin, and Adorno collected in Taylor et al. 1980.

10 The locus classicus of claims and counter-claims for and about the 'progressive text' is the so-called 'Days of Hope debate' conducted in 1975–6 in the pages of Screen between Colin McArthur and Colin McCabe, collected in Bennett et al. 1981.

11 I am using the term 'audience' here to mean effectively a form of 'implied reader', as a specifically literary construct of the screenplay, to be distinguished both from the spectator constructed (according to classical apparatus theory) by the projected/viewed film, and the actual audience analysed by reception studies and social and economic histories of film.

12 See Langford 2005: 262–7.

13 Steven Zaillian, Schindler's List, final draft, URL: http://www.dailyscript.com/scripts/schindlerslist.html

14 The point is underlined in Spielberg's film by a cut – not indicated in the script – that carries over Schindler's forward momentum out of the office to the next shot of his car speeding away, in true D. W. Griffith style, to avert the seemingly inevitable fate that awaits the women at Auschwitz.

15 For a thorough, theoretically informed discussion of 'Auschwitz' in cinema, see Saxton 2008.

16 See Sereny 1974: 207–8.

17 At Treblinka and the 'Operation Reinhard' exterminations sites in occupied Poland, there were no 'selections' of the kind made infamous by accounts of Auschwitz: bar a few stronger or skilled males held back from every transport to replenish the small group of slave labourers who maintained the camp and facilitated its operation, every single deportee was gassed within hours of arrival.

18 Torte Bluma can be viewed at http://video.google.co.uk/videoplay?docid=42956314 38543012544&ei=G8ZZS-PSB4Wr-AbMs4z0CQ&q=torte+bluma&hl=en#

19 See Langford 2005 and 1999: 21–38.

20 Sereny 1974: 207–8.

References

Bennett, Tony, Boyd-Bowman, Susan, Mercer, Colin and Woollacott, Janet, eds (1981) *Popular Film and Television*, London: BFI.

Boon, Kevin A. (2008) *Script Culture and the American Screenplay*, Detroit, MI: Wayne State University Press.

Bordwell, David, Staiger, Janet and Thompson, Kristin (1985) *The Classical Hollywood Cinema: Film Style and Mode of Production to 1960*, London: Routledge.

Branigan, Edward (1992) *Narrative Comprehension and Film*, London: Routledge.

Fabe, Marilyn (2004) *Closely Watched Films: An Introduction to the Art of Narrative Film Technique*, Berkeley, CA: University of California Press.

Easthope, Anthony (1983) 'The Trajectory of Screen, 1971–79', in Francis Barker, Peter Hulme, Margaret Iverson, and Dianna Loxley. (eds), *The Politics of Theory*, Colchester: University of Essex Press, 121–35.

Jameson, Fredric (1981) *The Political Unconscious: Narrative as a Socially Symbolic Act*, Ithaca, NY: Cornell University Press.

Joshi, Priya (2002) *In Another Country: British Popular Fiction and the Development of the English Novel in India*, New York: Columbia University Press.

Langford, Barry (1999) '"You Cannot Look at This": Thresholds of Unrepresentability in Holocaust Film', *Journal of Holocaust Education* 8: 21–38.

— (2005) *Film Genre: Hollywood and Beyond*, Edinburgh: Edinburgh University Press.

McKee, Robert (1998) *Story: Substance, Structure, Style, and the Principles of Screenwriting*, London: Methuen.

Maras, Steven (2009) *Screenwriting: History, Theory and Practice*, London: Wallflower.

Moretti, Franco (1998) *An Atlas of the European Novel*, London: Verso.

Saxton, Libby (2008) *Haunted Images: Film, Ethics, Testimony and the Holocaust*, London: Wallflower.

Sereny, Gitta (1974) *Into That Darkness: From Mercy Killing to Mass Murder*, London: Jonathan Cape.

Stam, Robert (1999) *Film Theory: An Introduction*, Oxford: Blackwell.

Taylor, Ronald, Jameson, Frederic and Anderson, Perry, eds (1980) *Aesthetics and Politics*, London: Verso.

Thompson, Kristin (1999) *Storytelling in the New Hollywood: Understanding Classical Narrative Technique*, Cambridge, MA: Harvard University Press.

— (2007) *The Frodo Franchise: The Lord of the Rings and Modern Hollywood*, Berkeley, CA: University of California Press.

Wood, Robin (1986) *Hollywood from Vietnam to Reagan*, New York: Columbia University Press.

Index

Titles in italics are for films unless followed by the type of work and/or author's name in brackets, e.g. *The Talented Mr Ripley* (novel) (Highsmith) 239

A Film (Danish Company) 90
Aardman Animation 90
Abel 35
accents 219–20
action-adventure film (1939) 106–20; elements of 108; filmography 122–3; *The Four Feathers* 111–15; genre flexibility 107–9; *Gunga Din* 109–11; *Northwest Passage* 115–16; *Only Angels Have Wings* 117–19, 119–20, 120–1; story form 120–1
Adaptation 251–3, 255–6
adaptations 57, 71, 239–47, *see also Chilean Club*; screenplay; *Talented Mr Ripley*
adolescent adventure narratives 109–15
After Dark 51
Aldrich, Robert 116
Alice In Wonderland 45, 51
All About Eve 40
allegory 233–5
Alleyne, Muriel 48
amateur writers 10, 13, 47, *see also* film writing; professional writers; screenwriters; scripts; silent cinema
American Dog 91
American Playhouse (TV series) 158
American silent cinema *see* silent cinema (America)
Anderson, J. 187
Animal Farm (storyboarding for Halas & Batchelor) *93*
Animated World Faiths: The Story of Guru Nanak (storyboard) *95*

animatics 152–3
animation micro-narrative 89–104; dominant micro-narrative themes 97–103; 'excavation process' 90–1; 'kernel' model 90, 94–5; *Madagascar* problem 91–2; pre-and post-production techniques 95–7; 'script' in animation context 89–90, 92, 95, 146; script as graphic-novel 149–50; storyboards 92–4, *93*, *95*, *96*; storytelling and 'inner logic' 96–7, *see also* cartoons
Anna Karenina 38
antagonists 120
The Apple 180
Archer, William: *Play-making* (textbook) 56
Aristotelian model 177, 194, 209, 212, 251, 253, 256, 259
Armageddon 109
Arnheim, Rudolf 155
Arthur, Jean 117
Asimov, Michael 37
assassination thrillers 72–4, *see also Chilean Club*
Aston, E. and Savona, G. 245
At Five in the Afternoon 180
At the Height of Summer 187, 188
audiences: engagement with story 127–8, 131–2, 140; female, in 1930s 40; response to Production Code Seal of Approval 39, *see also* information design
authorship: and authority in silent film 59–61; and characterization in Mamet's films 210
Azlant, Edward 13, 17

Baby Face 37
The Bachelors Club (screenplay/continuity style script) (Stannard) *54*, 55, *55*

Hepburn, Katharine 40
Hepworth, Cecil 44–5, 50, 51, 52, 58, 60
Hepworth, Margaret 48
hero, universal 194, 206
Herzog, W. 179
Heyman, John 77
Highsmith, Patricia: *The Talented Mr Ripley* (novel) 239
Higson, A. 76
Higson, Andrew 45
Hill, Benny 84
Hill, George 30
Hinson, Hal 209
Hitchcock, Alfred 58
Hodges, Mike 71, 79–80, 80–1, 85
Hollywood Jury 28
holocaust films 257–60
honour, theme of 112–13
House of Games 205, 207–10, 212
human computer interaction 128–31
Hunter, Lew 201

I Come with the Rain 188
The Ice Storm 221–2, 223
Iglesias, Karl 25, 229
I'm No Angel 28, 34
image/imagery: and animation 90; and dialogue 59, 194–5; and digital writing spaces 143–4, 146; and information design 131–2; and visualization 93
imagination 93
improvisation 145
Imrey, Mark 90
In This World 149
Ince, Thomas 238
indie cinema 158, *see also* Raymond, John and Reichardt, Kelly
information design 127–40; and *Groundhog Day* 137–40; and interaction design 128–31; and *Sideways* 132–3; and *To be or Not to Be* 136; and *The White Balloon* 136; and *Witness* 133–4
inter-racial relationships themes 38
inter-titles 58–9
interaction design 128–31
Iran: Makhmalbaf Film House 179–81
Iron Horse 107
iterative design methodologies 147

Jackson, Peter 149–50
Jacobs, Lea 27, 38
Jacobs, Lea and Maltby, Richard 27–8, 40

James, Benedict 49
James, Rian 26, 33
Jameson, Frederic 254–5
Japan Dreaming (drama-documentary) 175
Jarmusch, Jim 158
The Jazz Singer 238
Jenkins, D. 171
The Jewel Thieves Outwitted (shooting script) 52, *53*
J.M.B. 14
John and Karen 101–2
Johnston, T. 186
Jones, Chuck: nine 'rules' of cartoons 97, 103–4
Jones, Grover 33
Jones, K. 161
journals *see* trade journals; *names of journals, e.g. Bioscope*
journey: action-adventure as 120–1
Jumolhari 176, 192–4
Jurgensen, J. 150

Kandahar 180
Kane, Leslie 206
karma 193–4
Kaufman, Charlie 251, 252, 255–6
Kay, Alan 129
Kehr, Dave 165–6
Kelley, Tom 147
Kelly, K. 150
Kember, Joe 58
Kenneally, Thomas 257–8
'kernel' model 90, 94–5
Kharitidi, Alexei 100
Kiarostami, Abbas 179, 181
Killerich, Karsten 90
Kine Weekly (journal) 45, 49, 58
King Solomon's Mine 114
Kitchell, William 15
Klinger, Michael 71, 72, *78*; and Benny Green 75–7; and Collinson 74–5; the Klinger–Green screenplay 76–9, 80–2; Rank and NFFC 82–4, *see also Chilean Club*
Klinger, Tony 83–4
Klinger News (journal) 71, 82
Klosterman, C. 149
Knight, L.C. 202
Koman, R. 142, 148
Korda brothers 111
Kozloff, Sarah 217, 220
Kress, Gunther 144

Povemire, Dan 102
Pre-Code era (1929–34) 24, 28–9; films
    not awarded Seal of Approval 39,
    see also censorship; Production Code;
    women
Presnell, Robert Sr. 32
production *see* film production industry
Production Code (Hays Code) 24,
    26, 28, 31, 37, 38; Mae West and
    34–6; positive effects of 40; Seal of
    Approval *36*, 39, *see also* PCA; Pre-
    Code era; women
professional writers 19, 21; for British
    silent film 46, 47–50, 55, 59–61;
    the Pre-Code era 25–6, 29–36, *see
    also* amateur writers; film writing;
    screenwriters
'proof of concept' videos 150–1
Propp, Vladimir 205
prostitution themes 37
prototypes *see* design prototypes
Pulp 78, 79, 85

Quigley, Martin 28

Rachel's Man 79
Raiders of the Lost Ark 109
Ramis, Harold 138
Rank 78, 82–4, 85
Ranvaud, Donald 176, 191
Raphaelson, Sam 33
Ratatouille 91
Raymond, John and Reichardt, Kelly
    158–71; as collaborators 158–60;
    Old Joy 160–1, 162–6, *162*, 169, 170;
    River of Grass 160, 161–2, 168, 170;
    Wendy and Lucy 166–8, *167*, 169
Raynauld, Isabelle 51
realism, and screenplay dialogue 217–
    36; and believable film world 223–5;
    and dialogue 217–18; and dialogue
    as poetry 232–3; lies, subtext and
    revelation 229–32; metaphor and
    allegory 233–5; and narrative unity
    225–8; real people 220–3
'recipe' analogy 98–9
Red-Headed Woman 31
Reed, Carol 210
Reed, Langford 45–6
Reichardt, Kelly *see* Raymond, John and
    Reichardt, Kelly
Reville, Alma 48–9

Rilla, Wolf 218
Rinzin, Pema 192
Risdon, Elizabeth 49
Rissner, Danton 77–8
River of Grass 160, 161–2, 168, 170
Riza, Riri 176
RKO 109
The Road Warrior 106
'Roadrunner' series 97
Robinson, David 143
Rodriguez, Roberto 150
role models, female: in Post-Code films
    36–41; in Pre-Code films 29, 31–4,
    35, 41
Roosevelt administration 28, 35
Ross, Benjamin 257
Ross, Lillian 151
Rossio, Terry 136
Rubin, Danny 138
rules: design guidelines 135, 137–8;
    Jones's, of cartoons 97, 103–4;
    Wilder's, of screenwriting 127
Runco, Mark and Pritzker, S. 154, 155
Rupert and the Frog Song (storyboard)
    (Dunbar) *96*
Ryan-Carter, Liza 153

Salt, Barry 56, 58
Sargent, Epes Winthrop 7–8, 11, 12, 13,
    14, 15, *16*, 17, 18, 19–20
Satan McAllister's Heir 238
Saving Private Ryan 116
Sawyer, Keith 145
Scarface 107
Scenario Magazine (later *The Photoplay Author*)
    15, *16*
scenarios: in animation micro-narrative
    97; in silent film 45, 51–2, *52*, 238
scene: as micro-narrative theme 101–2
The Scent of Green Papaya 185–7, 188
Schamus, J. *see Ice Storm*
Schindler's List 257–8
Schon, Donald 155
schooling *see* education; rules
Schrader, Paul 145
Schrage, Michael 146, 150
Schwartz, D. 151
Scola, Kathryn 32–3, 37
Scott, Jeffrey 92, 93
Scott, Ridley 115
Screen International (journal) 84
Screen Writer's Guild 39

eBooks